FORD MUSTANG & MERCURY CAPRI

1979-1987 INCLUDES TURBO
SHOP MANUAL

ALAN AHLSTRAND
Editor

CLYMER PUBLICATIONS

World's largest publisher of books
devoted exclusively to automobiles and motorcycles.

A division of INTERTEC PUBLISHING CORPORATION
P.O. Box 12901, Overland Park, Kansas 66212

FIRST EDITION
Revised by Kalton C. Lahue
First Printing October, 1983

SECOND EDITION
Revised by Kalton C. Lahue to include 1984-1985 models
First Printing April, 1985

THIRD EDITION
Revised by Kalton C. Lahue to include 1986 models
First Printing March, 1986

FOURTH EDITION
Revised by Kalton C. Lahue to include 1987 models
First Printing November, 1986
Second Printing May, 1987
Third Printing November, 1987
Fourth Printing April, 1988
Fifth Printing August, 1988
Sixth Printing April, 1989

Printed in U.S.A.

ISBN: 0-89287-378-7

Technical illustrations by Steve Amos.

COVER: Photographed by Michael Brown Photographic Productions, Los Angeles, California. Assisted by Tim Lunde and Larry Rodgers. Mustang courtesy of Ford Motor Company. Capri courtesy of Bill Hopkins Lincoln-Mercury, Torrance, California.

CONTENTS

FORD MUSTANG & MERCURY CAPRI

1979-1987 INCLUDES TURBO
SHOP MANUAL

QUICK REFERENCE DATA

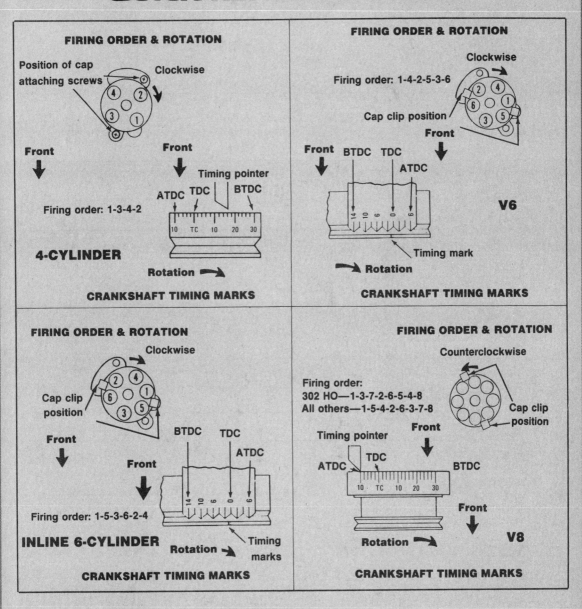

FIRING ORDER & ROTATION

Position of cap attaching screws

Clockwise

4 2

3 1

Front

Firing order: 1-3-4-2

4-CYLINDER

Front

Timing pointer

ATDC TDC BTDC

10 TC 10 20 30

Rotation

CRANKSHAFT TIMING MARKS

FIRING ORDER & ROTATION

Clockwise

Firing order: 1-4-2-5-3-6

Cap clip position

2 4
6 7
3 5

Front

Front BTDC TDC ATDC

14 10 6 0 6

Timing mark

V6

Rotation

CRANKSHAFT TIMING MARKS

FIRING ORDER & ROTATION

Clockwise

2 4
6 1
3 5

Cap clip position

Front

Front

Firing order: 1-5-3-6-2-4

INLINE 6-CYLINDER

BTDC TDC ATDC

14 10 6 0 6

Rotation

Timing marks

CRANKSHAFT TIMING MARKS

FIRING ORDER & ROTATION

Counterclockwise

Firing order:
302 HO—1-3-7-2-6-5-4-8
All others—1-5-4-2-6-3-7-8

Cap clip position

Timing pointer

Front

ATDC TDC BTDC

10 TC 10 20 30

Front

Rotation

V8

CRANKSHAFT TIMING MARKS

RECOMMENDED OIL GRADES

Outside Temperature Range	Oil Viscosity
Single Grade Oils	
– 10 to + 32 degrees F	SAE 10W
+ 10 to + 60 degrees F	SAE 20W-20
+ 32 to + 90 degrees F	SAE 30W
Above + 60 degrees F	SAE 40W
Multigrade Oils	
Below + 32 degrees F	SAE 5W-30*
– 10 to + 90 degrees F	SAE 10W-30
Above + 10 degrees F	SAE 20W-40

*If the vehicle is being operated at sustained highway speeds, the next heavier grade of oil should be used.

TUNE-UP SPECIFICATIONS (1979-1980)[2]

2300 cc	1979	1980
Ignition Timing (BTDC)		
49 state	6(M); 20(A)	(1)
California	6(M); 17(A)	6(M); 12(A)
Turbo (all)	2(M)	6(M)
Curb Idle Speed		
49 state	850(M); 600(A)	(1)
California	850(M); 600(A)	850(M); 750(A)
Turbo (all)	900(M)	850(M)
Fast Idle Speed		
49 state	(1)	(1)
California	1800(all)	2000(all)
Turbo (all)	(1)	1800(M)

2800 cc	1979	
Ignition Timing (BTDC)		
49 state	(1)	
California	6(A)	
Curb Idle Speed		
49 state	850(M); 650 (A)	
California	700(A)	
Fast Idle Speed		
49 state	1300(M); 1600(A)	
California	1750(A)	

200 cid		1980
Ignition Timing (BTDC)		
49 state		(1)
California		10(A)
Curb Idle Speed		
49 state		700(M); 550(A)
California		600(A)
Fast Idle Speed		
49 state		1600(M); 2000(A)
California		2300(A)

255 cid		1980
Ignition Timing (BTDC)		
49 state		6(A)
California		6(A)
Curb Idle Speed		
49 state		500(A)
California		550(A)
Fast Idle Speed		
49 state		2000(A)
California		1800(A)

(continued)

TUNE-UP SPECIFICATIONS (1979-1980)[2] (continued)

302	1979
Ignition Timing	
49 state	12(M); 8 (A)
California	12(A)
Curb Idle Speed	
49 state	800(M); 600(A)
California	600(A)
Fast Idle Speed	
49 state	2300(M); 2100(A)
California	1800(A)

(M) = Manual transmission
(A) = Automatic transmission
(1) = Specifications are given on valve cover decal
(2) For 1981 and later models, see underhood decal for engine specifications.

FUSE RATING

Application	Amperage
Turn signal, back-up lamps	15
Heater (only)	15
Air conditioning/heater	30
Instrument panel lamps	5
Windshield wiper/washer	6
Stop lamps, emergency warnings	15
Courtesy lamps	15
Cigarette lighter, horn	20
Radio	15
Warning lamps	10
Electric choke	25

BULB CHART

Application	SAE Trade Number
Headlight	H-4651
Turn indicator	194
A/C and heater controls	161
Cluster	194
Dome	906
Dual brake warning light	194
Hi beam indicator	194
Backup lights	1156
Side marker	194
Clock	194
Seat belt warning indicator	194
Radio	1893
Stereo tape	37

VALVE ADJUSTMENT, 1979 2800 cc

Intake Valve Just Opening for Cylinder Number	Adjust both Valves For Cylinder Number
5	1
3	4
6	2
1	5
4	3
2	6

ENGINE OIL CAPACITY

Engine	Capacity*
2300 cc	4 qt.
2300 cc turbo	4½ qt.
2800 cc	4½ qt.
200 cid	4 qt.
255 cid	4 qt.
302 cid	4 qt.

*Add 1 qt. with filter change. On 2800 cc engines, add 1/2 qt. on filter change.

SPARK PLUG SPECIFICATIONS

Engine	Type	Gap
2300 cc		
1979-1982	AWSF-42	0.034 in.
1983-on	AWSF-34	0.044 in.
Turbo	AWSF-32	0.034 in.
2800 cc	AWSF-42	0.034 in.
200 cid		
1980	BSF-82	0.050 in.
1981	BRF-82	0.050 in.
1982	BSF-82	0.050 in.
230 cid	AWSF-52	*
255 cid	ASF-52	0.050 in.
302 cid		
49 state	ASF-52	0.050 in.
	ARF-52	0.050 in.
California	ASF-52-6	0.060 in.
	ARF-52-6	0.060 in.
HO	ASF-52	0.044 in.

* See emissions decal.

APPROXIMATE COOLANT CAPACITY*

	1979	1980	1981	1982-on
2300 cc				
Non-AC	8.6	8.6	8.6	8.6
With AC	10.0	9.0	9.0	9.4
2300 cc turbo	8.6	9.2	9.2	9.4
2800 cc				
Non-AC	9.2	—	—	—
With AC	9.4	—	—	—
200 cid				
Non-AC	—	8.1	8.1	8.4
With AC	—	8.1	8.4	8.4
230/255 cid				
Non-AC	—	13.4	14.7	14.7
With AC	—	13.7	15.0	15.0
302 cid				
Non-AC	14.0	—	—	13.1
With AC	14.0	—	—	13.4

* All measurements are specified in quarts. Capacity may vary by ±15 percent. AC = air conditioning.

INTRODUCTION

This detailed, comprehensive manual covers all 1979-1987 Ford Mustangs and 1979-1986 Mercury Capris. The expert text gives complete information on maintenance, repair and overhaul. Hundreds of photos and drawings guide you through every step. The book includes all you need to know to keep your car running right.

Chapters One through Twelve contain general information on all models and specific information on 1979-1980 models. The Supplement at the end of the book contains specific information on 1981 and later models that differs from earlier models.

Where repairs are practical for the owner/mechanic, complete procedures are given. Equally important, difficult jobs are pointed out. Such operations are usually more economically performed by a dealer or independent garage.

A shop manual is a reference. You want to be able to find information fast. As in all Clymer books, this one is designed with this in mind. All chapters are thumb tabbed. Important items are indexed at the rear of the book. All the most frequently used specifications and capacities are summarized on the *Quick Reference Data* pages at the front of the book.

Keep the book handy. Carry it in your glove box. It will help you to better understand your Mustang or Capri, lower repair and maintenance costs and generally improve your satisfaction with your vehicle.

CHAPTER ONE

GENERAL INFORMATION

The troubleshooting, tune-up, maintenance, and step-by-step repair procedures in this book are written for the owner and home mechanic. The text is accompanied by useful photos and diagrams to make the job as clear and correct as possible.

Troubleshooting, tune-up, maintenance, and repair are not difficult if you know what tools and equipment to use and what to do. Anyone not afraid to get their hands dirty, of average intelligence, and with some mechanical ability can perform most of the procedures in this book.

In some cases, a repair job may require tools or skills not reasonably expected of the home mechanic. These procedures are noted in each chapter and it is recommended that you take the job to your dealer, a competent mechanic, or machine shop.

MANUAL ORGANIZATION

This chapter provides general information and safety and service hints. Also included are lists of recommended shop and emergency tools as well as a brief description of troubleshooting and tune-up equipment.

Chapter Two provides methods and suggestions for quick and accurate diagnosis and repair of problems. Troubleshooting procedures discuss typical symptoms and logical methods to pinpoint the trouble.

Chapter Three explains all periodic lubrication and routine maintenance necessary to keep your vehicle running well. Chapter Three also includes recommended tune-up procedures, eliminating the need to constantly consult chapters on the various subassemblies.

Subsequent chapters cover specific systems such as the engine, transmission, and electrical systems. Each of these chapters provides disassembly, repair, and assembly procedures in a simple step-by-step format. If a repair requires special skills or tools, or is otherwise impractical for the home mechanic, it is so indicated. In these cases it is usually faster and less expensive to have the repairs made by a dealer or competent repair shop. Necessary specifications concerning a particular system are included at the end of the appropriate chapter.

When special tools are required to perform a procedure included in this manual, the tool is illustrated either in actual use or alone. It may be possible to rent or borrow these tools. The inventive mechanic may also be able to find a suitable substitute in his tool box, or to fabricate one.

The terms NOTE, CAUTION, and WARNING have specific meanings in this manual. A NOTE provides additional or explanatory information. A CAUTION is used to emphasize areas where equipment damage could result if proper precautions are not taken. A WARNING is used to stress those areas where personal injury or death could result from negligence, in addition to possible mechanical damage.

SERVICE HINTS

Observing the following practices will save time, effort, and frustration, as well as prevent possible injury.

Throughout this manual keep in mind two conventions. "Front" refers to the front of the vehicle. The front of any component, such as the transmission, is that end which faces toward the front of the vehicle. The "left" and "right" sides of the vehicle refer to the orientation of a person sitting in the vehicle facing forward. For example, the steering wheel is on the left side. These rules are simple, but even experienced mechanics occasionally become disoriented.

Most of the service procedures covered are straightforward and can be performed by anyone reasonably handy with tools. It is suggested, however, that you consider your own capabilities carefully before attempting any operation involving major disassembly of the engine.

Some operations, for example, require the use of a press. It would be wiser to have these performed by a shop equipped for such work, rather than to try to do the job yourself with makeshift equipment. Other procedures require precision measurements. Unless you have the skills and equipment required, it would be better to have a qualified repair shop make the measurements for you.

Repairs go much faster and easier if the parts that will be worked on are clean before you begin. There are special cleaners for washing the engine and related parts. Brush or spray on the cleaning solution, let it stand, then rinse it away with a garden hose. Clean all oily or greasy parts with cleaning solvent as you remove them.

WARNING
Never use gasoline as a cleaning agent. It presents an extreme fire hazard. Be sure to work in a well-ventilated area when using cleaning solvent. Keep a fire extinguisher, rated for gasoline fires, handy in any case.

Much of the labor charge for repairs made by dealers is for the removal and disassembly of other parts to reach the defective unit. It is frequently possible to perform the preliminary operations yourself and then take the defective unit in to the dealer for repair, at considerable savings.

Once you have decided to tackle the job yourself, make sure you locate the appropriate section in this manual, and read it entirely. Study the illustrations and text until you have a good idea of what is involved in completing the job satisfactorily. If special tools are required, make arrangements to get them before you start. Also, purchase any known defective parts prior to starting on the procedure. It is frustrating and time-consuming to get partially into a job and then be unable to complete it.

Simple wiring checks can be easily made at home, but knowledge of electronics is almost a necessity for performing tests with complicated electronic testing gear.

During disassembly of parts keep a few general cautions in mind. Force is rarely needed to get things apart. If parts are a tight fit, like a bearing in a case, there is usually a tool designed to separate them. Never use a screwdriver to pry apart parts with machined surfaces such as cylinder head and valve cover. You will mar the surfaces and end up with leaks.

Make diagrams wherever similar-appearing parts are found. You may think you can remember where everything came from — but mistakes are costly. There is also the possibility you may get sidetracked and not return to work for days or even weeks — in which interval, carefully laid out parts may have become disturbed.

Tag all similar internal parts for location, and mark all mating parts for position. Record number and thickness of any shims as they are removed. Small parts such as bolts can be identified by placing them in plastic sandwich bags that are sealed and labeled with masking tape.

Wiring should be tagged with masking tape and marked as each wire is removed. Again, do not rely on memory alone.

When working under the vehicle, do not trust a hydraulic or mechanical jack to hold the vehicle up by itself. Always use jackstands. See **Figure 1**.

Disconnect battery ground cable before working near electrical connections and before disconnecting wires. Never run the engine with the battery disconnected; the alternator could be seriously damaged.

Protect finished surfaces from physical damage or corrosion. Keep gasoline and brake fluid off painted surfaces.

Frozen or very tight bolts and screws can often be loosened by soaking with penetrating oil like Liquid Wrench or WD-40, then sharply striking the bolt head a few times with a hammer and punch (or screwdriver for screws). Avoid heat unless absolutely necessary, since it may melt, warp, or remove the temper from many parts.

Avoid flames or sparks when working near a charging battery or flammable liquids, such as brake fluid or gasoline.

No parts, except those assembled with a press fit, require unusual force during assembly. If a part is hard to remove or install, find out why before proceeding.

Cover all openings after removing parts to keep dirt, small tools, etc., from falling in.

When assembling two parts, start all fasteners, then tighten evenly.

The clutch plate, wiring connections, brake shoes, drums, pads, and discs should be kept clean and free of grease and oil.

When assembling parts, be sure all shims and washers are replaced exactly as they came out.

Whenever a rotating part butts against a stationary part, look for a shim or washer. Use new gaskets if there is any doubt about the condition of old ones. Generally, you should apply gasket cement to one mating surface only, so the parts may be easily disassembled in the future. A thin coat of oil on gaskets helps them seal effectively.

Heavy grease can be used to hold small parts in place if they tend to fall out during assembly. However, keep grease and oil away from electrical, clutch, and brake components.

High spots may be sanded off a piston with sandpaper, but emery cloth and oil do a much more professional job.

Carburetors are best cleaned by disassembling them and soaking the parts in a commercial carburetor cleaner. Never soak gaskets and rubber parts in these cleaners. Never use wire to clean out jets and air passages; they are easily damaged. Use compressed air to blow out the carburetor, but only if the float has been removed first.

Take your time and do the job right. Do not forget that a newly rebuilt engine must be broken in the same as a new one. Refer to your owner's manual for the proper break-in procedures.

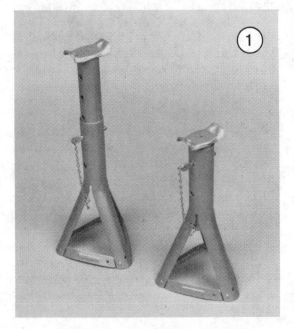

SAFETY FIRST

Professional mechanics can work for years and never sustain a serious injury. If you observe a few rules of common sense and safety, you can enjoy many safe hours servicing your vehicle. You could hurt yourself or damage the vehicle if you ignore these rules.

1. Never use gasoline as a cleaning solvent.

2. Never smoke or use a torch in the vicinity of flammable liquids such as cleaning solvent in open containers.

3. Never smoke or use a torch in an area where batteries are being charged. Highly explosive hydrogen gas is formed during the charging process.

4. Use the proper sized wrenches to avoid damage to nuts and injury to yourself.

5. When loosening a tight or stuck nut, be guided by what would happen if the wrench should slip. Protect yourself accordingly.

6. Keep your work area clean and uncluttered.

7. Wear safety goggles during all operations involving drilling, grinding, or use of a cold chisel.

8. Never use worn tools.

9. Keep a fire extinguisher handy and be sure it is rated for gasoline (Class B) and electrical (Class C) fires.

EXPENDABLE SUPPLIES

Certain expendable supplies are necessary. These include grease, oil, gasket cement, wiping rags, cleaning solvent, and distilled water.

Also, special locking compounds, silicone lubricants, and engine cleaners may be useful. Cleaning solvent is available at most service stations and distilled water for the battery is available at most supermarkets.

SHOP TOOLS

For proper servicing, you will need an assortment of ordinary hand tools (**Figure 2**).

As a minimum, these include:

a. Combination wrenches

b. Sockets

c. Plastic mallet

d. Small hammer

e. Snap ring pliers

f. Gas pliers

g. Phillips screwdrivers

h. Slot (common) screwdrivers

i. Feeler gauges

j. Spark plug gauge

k. Spark plug wrench

Special tools necessary are shown in the chapters covering the particular repair in which they are used.

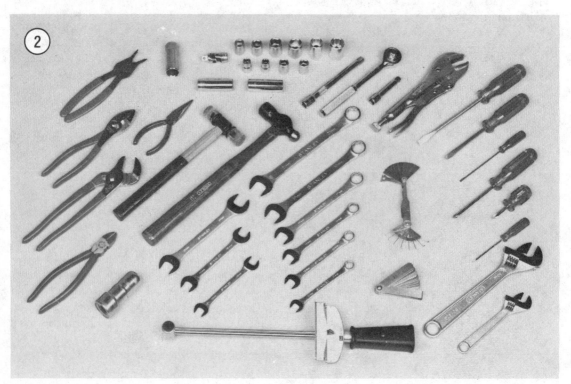

Engine tune-up and troubleshooting procedures require other special tools and equipment. These are described in detail in the following sections.

EMERGENCY TOOL KIT

A small emergency tool kit kept in the trunk is handy for road emergencies which otherwise could leave you stranded. The tools listed below and shown in **Figure 3** will let you handle most roadside repairs.

a. Combination wrenches
b. Crescent (adjustable) wrench
c. Screwdrivers — common and Phillips
d. Pliers — conventional (gas) and needle nose
e. Vise Grips
f. Hammer — plastic and metal
g. Small container of waterless hand cleaner
h. Rags for clean up
i. Silver waterproof sealing tape (duct tape)
j. Flashlight
k. Emergency road flares — at least four
l. Spare drive belts (water pump, alternator, etc.)

TROUBLESHOOTING AND TUNE-UP EQUIPMENT

Voltmeter, Ohmmeter, and Ammeter

For testing the ignition or electrical system, a good voltmeter is required. For automotive use, an instrument covering 0-20 volts is satisfac-

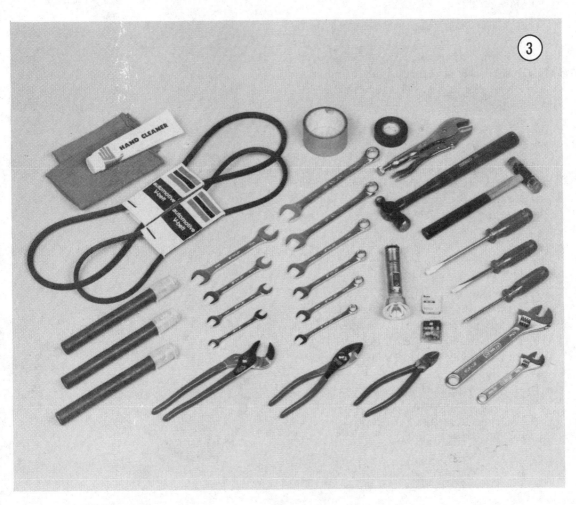

tory. One which also has a 0-2 volt scale is necessary for testing relays, points, or individual contacts where voltage drops are much smaller. Accuracy should be ± ½ volt.

An ohmmeter measures electrical resistance. This instrument is useful for checking continuity (open and short circuits), and testing fuses and lights.

The ammeter measures electrical current. Ammeters for automotive use should cover 0-50 amperes and 0-250 amperes. These are useful for checking battery charging and starting current.

Several inexpensive VOM's (volt-ohm-milli-ammeter) combine all three instruments into one which fits easily in any tool box. See **Figure 4**. However, the ammeter ranges are usually too small for automotive work.

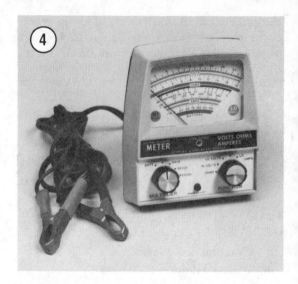

Hydrometer

The hydrometer gives a useful indication of battery condition and charge by measuring the specific gravity of the electrolyte in each cell. See **Figure 5**. Complete details on use and interpretation of readings are provided in the electrical chapter.

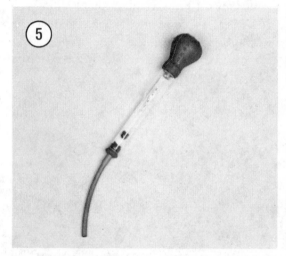

Compression Tester

The compression tester measures the compression pressure built up in each cylinder. The results, when properly interpreted, can indicate general cylinder and valve condition. See **Figure 6**.

Vacuum Gauge

The vacuum gauge (**Figure 7**) is one of the easiest instruments to use, but one of the most difficult for the inexperienced mechanic to interpret. The results, when interpreted with other findings, can provide valuable clues to possible trouble.

To use the vacuum gauge, connect it to a vacuum hose that goes to the intake manifold. Attach it either directly to the hose or to a T-fitting installed into the hose.

NOTE: *Subtract one inch from the reading for every 1,000 ft. elevation.*

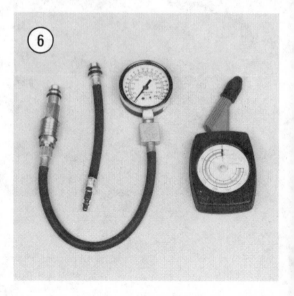

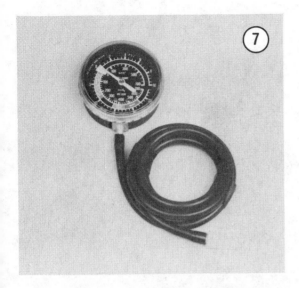

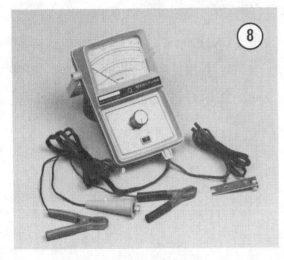

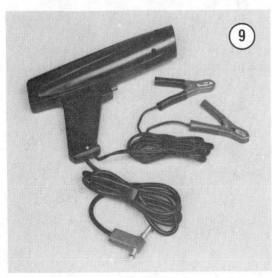

Fuel Pressure Gauge

This instrument is invaluable for evaluating fuel pump performance. Fuel system troubleshooting procedures in this manual use a fuel pressure gauge. Usually a vacuum gauge and fuel pressure gauge are combined.

Dwell Meter (Contact Breaker Point Ignition Only)

A dwell meter measures the distance in degrees of cam rotation that the breaker points remain closed while the engine is running. Since this angle is determined by breaker point gap, dwell angle is an accurate indication of breaker point gap.

Many tachometers intended for tuning and testing incorporate a dwell meter as well. See **Figure 8**. Follow the manufacturer's instructions to measure dwell.

Tachometer

A tachometer is necessary for tuning. See **Figure 8**. Ignition timing and carburetor adjustments must be performed at the specified idle speed. The best instrument for this purpose is one with a low range of 0-1,000 or 0-2,000 rpm for setting idle, and a high range of 0-4,000 or more for setting ignition timing at 3,000 rpm. Extended range (0-6,000 or 0-8,000 rpm) instruments lack accuracy at lower speeds. The instrument should be capable of detecting changes of 25 rpm on the low range.

Strobe Timing Light

This instrument is necessary for tuning, as it permits very accurate ignition timing. The light flashes at precisely the same instant that No. 1 cylinder fires, at which time the timing marks on the engine should align. Refer to Chapter Three for exact location of the timing marks for your engine.

Suitable lights range from inexpensive neon bulb types ($2-3) to powerful xenon strobe lights ($20-40). See **Figure 9**. Neon timing lights are difficult to see and must be used in dimly lit areas. Xenon strobe timing lights can be used outside in bright sunlight. Both types work on this vehicle; use according to the manufacturer's instructions.

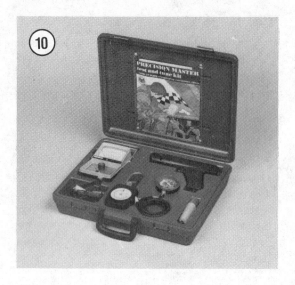

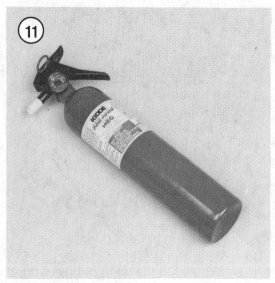

Tune-up Kits

Many manufacturer's offer kits that combine several useful instruments. Some come in a convenient carry case and are usally less expensive than purchasing one instrument at a time. **Figure 10** shows one of the kits that is available. The prices vary with the number of instruments included in the kit.

Fire Extinguisher

A fire extinguisher is a necessity when working on a vehicle. It should be rated for both *Class B* (flammable liquids—gasoline, oil, paint, etc.) and *Class C* (electrical—wiring, etc.) type fires. It should always be kept within reach. See **Figure 11**.

CHAPTER TWO

TROUBLESHOOTING

Troubleshooting can be a relatively simple matter if it is done logically. The first step in any troubleshooting procedure must be defining the symptoms as closely as possible. Subsequent steps involve testing and analyzing areas which could cause the symptoms. A haphazard approach may eventually find the trouble, but in terms of wasted time and unnecessary parts replacement, it can be very costly.

The troubleshooting procedures in this chapter analyze typical symptoms and show logical methods of isolation. These are not the only methods. There may be several approaches to a problem, but all methods must have one thing in common — a logical, systematic approach.

STARTING SYSTEM

The starting system consists of the starter motor and the starter solenoid. The ignition key controls the starter solenoid, which mechanically engages the starter with the engine flywheel, and supplies electrical current to turn the starter motor.

Starting system troubles are relatively easy to find. In most cases, the trouble is a loose or dirty electrical connection. **Figures 1 and 2** provide routines for finding the trouble.

CHARGING SYSTEM

The charging system consists of the alternator (or generator on older vehicles), voltage regulator, and battery. A drive belt driven by the engine crankshaft turns the alternator which produces electrical energy to charge the battery. As engine speed varies, the voltage from the alternator varies. A voltage regulator controls the charging current to the battery and maintains the voltage to the vehicle's electrical system at safe levels. A warning light or gauge on the instrument panel signals the driver when charging is not taking place. Refer to **Figure 3** for a typical charging system.

Complete troubleshooting of the charging system requires test equipment and skills which the average home mechanic does not possess. However, there are a few tests which can be done to pinpoint most troubles.

Charging system trouble may stem from a defective alternator (or generator), voltage regulator, battery, or drive belt. It may also be caused by something as simple as incorrect drive belt tension. The following are symptoms of typical problems you may encounter.

1. *Battery dies frequently, even though the warning lamp indicates no discharge* — This can be caused by a drive belt that is slightly too

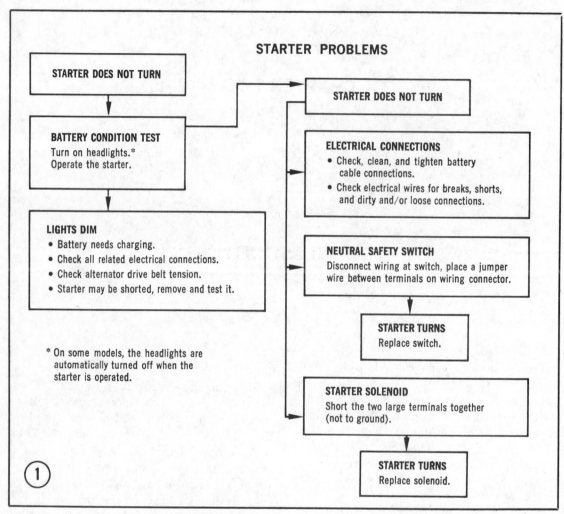

STARTER PROBLEMS

STARTER DOES NOT TURN

BATTERY CONDITION TEST
Turn on headlights.*
Operate the starter.

LIGHTS DIM
• Battery needs charging.
• Check all related electrical connections.
• Check alternator drive belt tension.
• Starter may be shorted, remove and test it.

* On some models, the headlights are
automatically turned off when the
starter is operated.

STARTER DOES NOT TURN

ELECTRICAL CONNECTIONS
• Check, clean, and tighten battery
  cable connections.
• Check electrical wires for breaks, shorts,
  and dirty and/or loose connections.

NEUTRAL SAFETY SWITCH
Disconnect wiring at switch, place a jumper
wire between terminals on wiring connector.

STARTER TURNS
Replace switch.

STARTER SOLENOID
Short the two large terminals together
(not to ground).

STARTER TURNS
Replace solenoid.

①

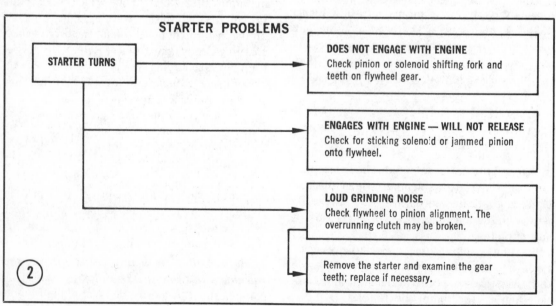

STARTER PROBLEMS

STARTER TURNS

DOES NOT ENGAGE WITH ENGINE
Check pinion or solenoid shifting fork and
teeth on flywheel gear.

ENGAGES WITH ENGINE — WILL NOT RELEASE
Check for sticking solenoid or jammed pinion
onto flywheel.

LOUD GRINDING NOISE
Check flywheel to pinion alignment. The
overrunning clutch may be broken.

Remove the starter and examine the gear
teeth; replace if necessary.

②

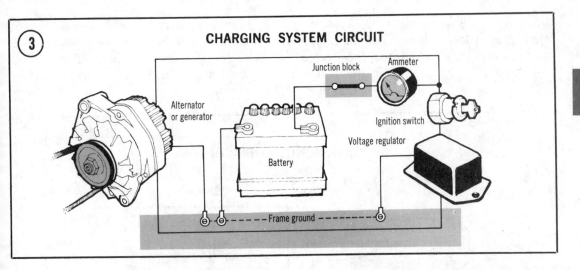

③ **CHARGING SYSTEM CIRCUIT**

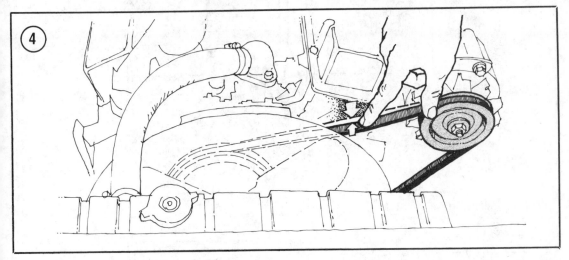

④

2

loose. Grasp the alternator (or generator) pulley and try to turn it. If the pulley can be turned without moving the belt, the drive belt is too loose. As a rule, keep the belt tight enough that it can be deflected about ½ in. under moderate thumb pressure between the pulleys (**Figure 4**). The battery may also be at fault; test the battery condition.

2. *Charging system warning lamp does not come on when ignition switch is turned on* — This may indicate a defective ignition switch, battery, voltage regulator, or lamp. First try to start the vehicle. If it doesn't start, check the ignition switch and battery. If the car starts, remove the warning lamp; test it for continuity with an ohmmeter or substitute a new lamp. If the lamp is good, locate the voltage regulator

and make sure it is properly grounded (try tightening the mounting screws). Also the alternator (or generator) brushes may not be making contact. Test the alternator (or generator) and voltage regulator.

3. *Alternator (or generator) warning lamp comes on and stays on* — This usually indicates that no charging is taking place. First check drive belt tension (**Figure 4**). Then check battery condition, and check all wiring connections in the charging system. If this does not locate the trouble, check the alternator (or generator) and voltage regulator.

4. *Charging system warning lamp flashes on and off intermittently* — This usually indicates the charging system is working intermittently.

Check the drive belt tension (**Figure 4**), and check all electrical connections in the charging system. Check the alternator (or generator). *On generators only*, check the condition of the commutator.

5. *Battery requires frequent additions of water, or lamps require frequent replacement* — The alternator (or generator) is probably overcharging the battery. The voltage regulator is probably at fault.

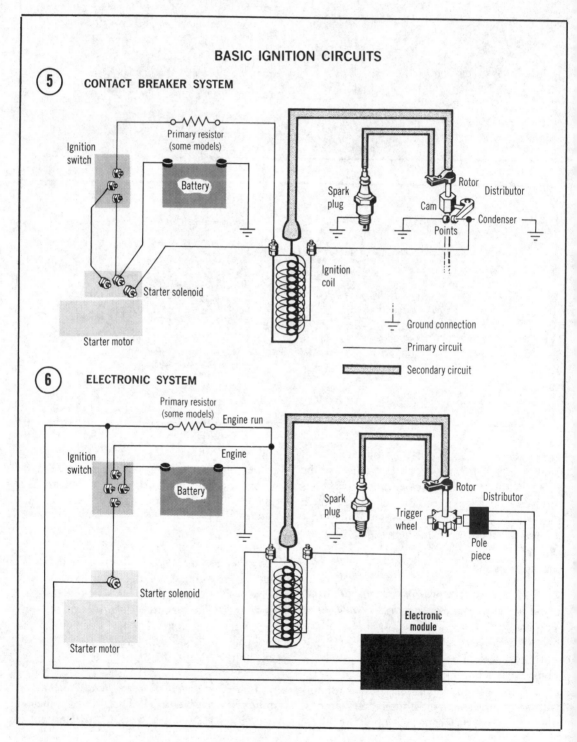

BASIC IGNITION CIRCUITS

⑤ **CONTACT BREAKER SYSTEM**

⑥ **ELECTRONIC SYSTEM**

6. *Excessive noise from the alternator (or generator)* — Check for loose mounting brackets and bolts. The problem may also be worn bearings or the need of lubrication in some cases. If an alternator whines, a shorted diode may be indicated.

IGNITION SYSTEM

The ignition system may be either a conventional contact breaker type or an electronic ignition. See electrical chapter to determine which type you have. **Figures 5 and 6** show simplified diagrams of each type.

Most problems involving failure to start, poor performance, or rough running stem from trouble in the ignition system, particularly in contact breaker systems. Many novice troubleshooters get into trouble when they assume that these symptoms point to the fuel system instead of the ignition system.

Ignition system troubles may be roughly divided between those affecting only one cylinder and those affecting all cylinders. If the trouble affects only one cylinder, it can only be in the spark plug, spark plug wire, or portion of the distributor associated with that cylinder. If the trouble affects all cylinders (weak spark or no spark), then the trouble is in the ignition coil, rotor, distributor, or associated wiring.

The troubleshooting procedures outlined in **Figure 7** (breaker point ignition) or **Figure 8**

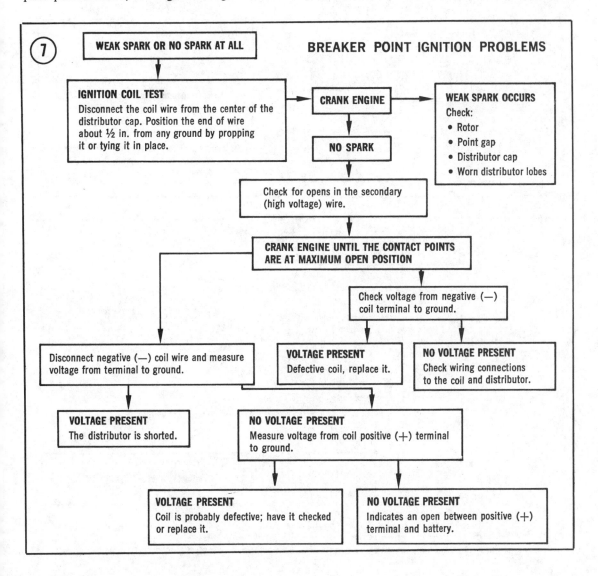

(electronic ignition) will help you isolate ignition problems fast. Of course, they assume that the battery is in good enough condition to crank the engine over at its normal rate.

ENGINE PERFORMANCE

A number of factors can make the engine difficult or impossible to start, or cause rough running, poor performance and so on. The majority of novice troubleshooters immediately suspect the carburetor or fuel injection system. In the majority of cases, though, the trouble exists in the ignition system.

The troubleshooting procedures outlined in **Figures 9 through 14** will help you solve the majority of engine starting troubles in a systematic manner.

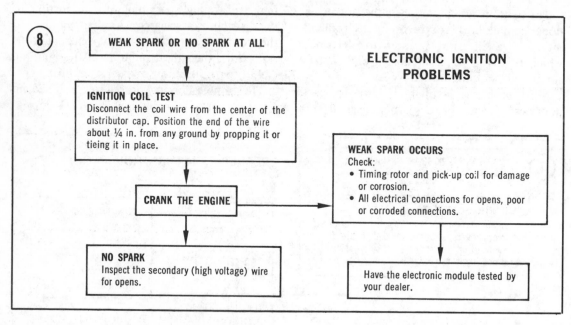

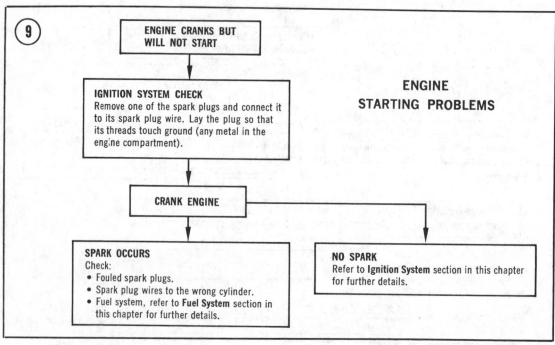

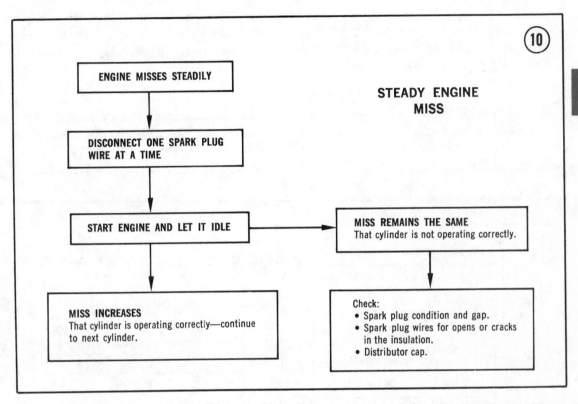

⑩

ENGINE MISSES STEADILY

STEADY ENGINE
MISS

DISCONNECT ONE SPARK PLUG
WIRE AT A TIME

START ENGINE AND LET IT IDLE ➔ MISS REMAINS THE SAME
That cylinder is not operating correctly.

MISS INCREASES
That cylinder is operating correctly—continue
to next cylinder.

Check:
• Spark plug condition and gap.
• Spark plug wires for opens or cracks
  in the insulation.
• Distributor cap.

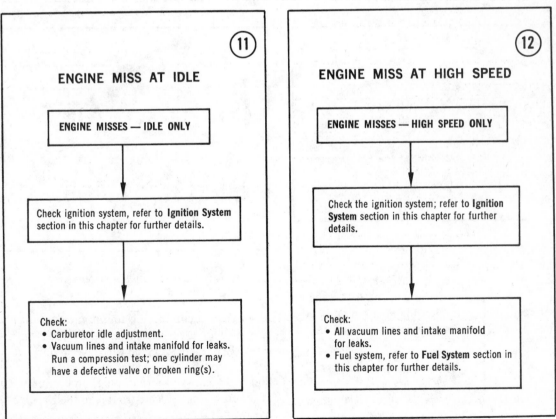

⑪

ENGINE MISS AT IDLE

ENGINE MISSES — IDLE ONLY

Check ignition system, refer to **Ignition System**
section in this chapter for further details.

Check:
• Carburetor idle adjustment.
• Vacuum lines and intake manifold for leaks.
  Run a compression test; one cylinder may
  have a defective valve or broken ring(s).

⑫

ENGINE MISS AT HIGH SPEED

ENGINE MISSES — HIGH SPEED ONLY

Check the ignition system; refer to **Ignition
System** section in this chapter for further
details.

Check:
• All vacuum lines and intake manifold
  for leaks.
• Fuel system, refer to **Fuel System** section in
  this chapter for further details.

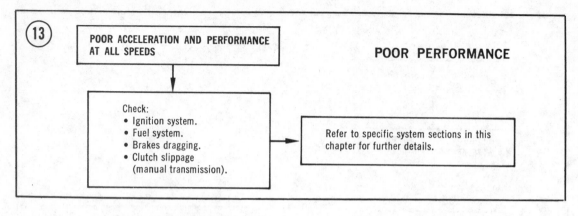

⑬ POOR ACCELERATION AND PERFORMANCE AT ALL SPEEDS

POOR PERFORMANCE

Check:
• Ignition system.
• Fuel system.
• Brakes dragging.
• Clutch slippage (manual transmission).

Refer to specific system sections in this chapter for further details.

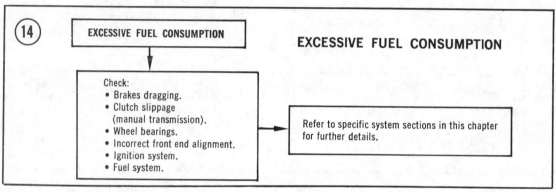

⑭ EXCESSIVE FUEL CONSUMPTION

EXCESSIVE FUEL CONSUMPTION

Check:
• Brakes dragging.
• Clutch slippage (manual transmission).
• Wheel bearings.
• Incorrect front end alignment.
• Ignition system.
• Fuel system.

Refer to specific system sections in this chapter for further details.

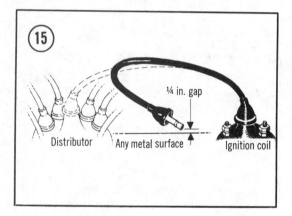

⑮ ¼ in. gap
Distributor   Any metal surface   Ignition coil

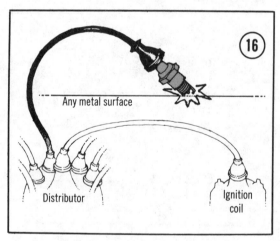

⑯ Any metal surface
Distributor   Ignition coil

Some tests of the ignition system require running the engine with a spark plug or ignition coil wire disconnected. The safest way to do this is to disconnect the wire with the engine stopped, then prop the end of the wire next to a metal surface as shown in **Figures 15 and 16**.

WARNING
Never disconnect a spark plug or ignition coil wire while the engine is running. The high voltage in an ignition system, particularly the newer high-

energy electronic ignition systems could cause serious injury or even death.

Spark plug condition is an important indication of engine performance. Spark plugs in a properly operating engine will have slightly pitted electrodes, and a light tan insulator tip. **Figure 17** shows a normal plug, and a number of others which indicate trouble in their respective cylinders.

- Appearance—Firing tip has deposits of light gray to light tan.
- Can be cleaned, regapped and reused.

- Appearance—Glazed yellow deposits with a slight brownish tint on the insulator tip and ground electrode.
- Replace with new plugs.

- Appearance—Dull, dry black with fluffy carbon deposits on the insulator tip, electrode and exposed shell.
- Caused by—Fuel/air mixture too rich, plug heat range too cold, weak ignition system, dirty air cleaner, faulty automatic choke or excessive idling.
- Can be cleaned, regapped and reused.

- Appearance — Brown colored hardened ash deposits on the insulator tip and ground electrode.
- Caused by—Fuel and/or oil additives.
- Replace with new plugs.

- Appearance — Severely worn or eroded electrodes.
- Caused by—Normal wear or unusual oil and/or fuel additives.
- Replace with new plugs.

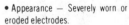

- Appearance—Wet black deposits on insulator and exposed shell.
- Caused by—Excessive oil entering the combustion chamber through worn rings, pistons, valve guides or bearings.
- Replace with new plugs (use a hotter plug if engine is not repaired).

- Appearance — Melted ground electrode.
- Caused by—Overadvanced ignition timing, inoperative ignition advance mechanism, too low of a fuel octane rating, lean fuel/air mixture or carbon deposits in combustion chamber.

- Appearance — Yellow insulator deposits (may sometimes be dark gray, black or tan in color) on the insulator tip.
- Caused by—Highly leaded gasoline.
- Replace with new plugs.

- Appearance—Melted center electrode.
- Caused by—Abnormal combustion due to overadvanced ignition timing or incorrect advance, too low of a fuel octane rating, lean fuel/air mixture, or carbon deposits in combustion chamber.
- Correct engine problem and replace with new plugs.

- Appearance—Yellow glazed deposits indicating melted lead deposits due to hard acceleration.
- Caused by—Highly leaded gasoline.
- Replace with new plugs.

- Appearance—Melted center electrode and white blistered insulator tip.
- Caused by—Incorrect plug heat range selection.
- Replace with new plugs.

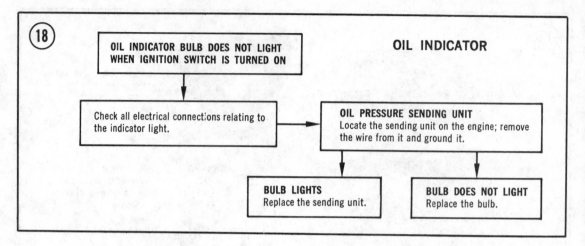

(18) OIL INDICATOR

OIL INDICATOR BULB DOES NOT LIGHT WHEN IGNITION SWITCH IS TURNED ON

Check all electrical connections relating to the indicator light.

OIL PRESSURE SENDING UNIT
Locate the sending unit on the engine; remove the wire from it and ground it.

BULB LIGHTS
Replace the sending unit.

BULB DOES NOT LIGHT
Replace the bulb.

ENGINE OIL PRESSURE LIGHT

Proper oil pressure to the engine is vital. If oil pressure is insufficient, the engine can destroy itself in a comparatively short time.

The oil pressure warning circuit monitors oil pressure constantly. If pressure drops below a predetermined level, the light comes on.

Obviously, it is vital for the warning circuit to be working to signal low oil pressure. Each time you turn on the ignition, but before you start the car, the warning light should come on. If it doesn't, there is trouble in the warning circuit, not the oil pressure system. See **Figure 18** to troubleshoot the warning circuit.

Once the engine is running, the warning light should stay off. If the warning light comes on or acts erratically while the engine is running there is trouble with the engine oil pressure system. *Stop the engine immediately.* Refer to **Figure 19** for possible causes of the problem.

FUEL SYSTEM (CARBURETTED)

Fuel system problems must be isolated to the fuel pump (mechanical or electric), fuel lines, fuel filter, or carburetor. These procedures assume the ignition system is working properly and is correctly adjusted.

1. *Engine will not start* — First make sure that fuel is being delivered to the carburetor. Remove the air cleaner, look into the carburetor throat, and operate the accelerator

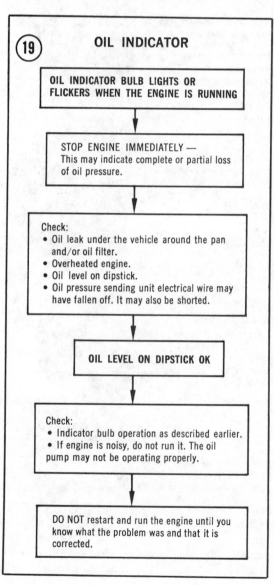

(19) OIL INDICATOR

OIL INDICATOR BULB LIGHTS OR FLICKERS WHEN THE ENGINE IS RUNNING

STOP ENGINE IMMEDIATELY —
This may indicate complete or partial loss of oil pressure.

Check:
• Oil leak under the vehicle around the pan and/or oil filter.
• Overheated engine.
• Oil level on dipstick.
• Oil pressure sending unit electrical wire may have fallen off. It may also be shorted.

OIL LEVEL ON DIPSTICK OK

Check:
• Indicator bulb operation as described earlier.
• If engine is noisy, do not run it. The oil pump may not be operating properly.

DO NOT restart and run the engine until you know what the problem was and that it is corrected.

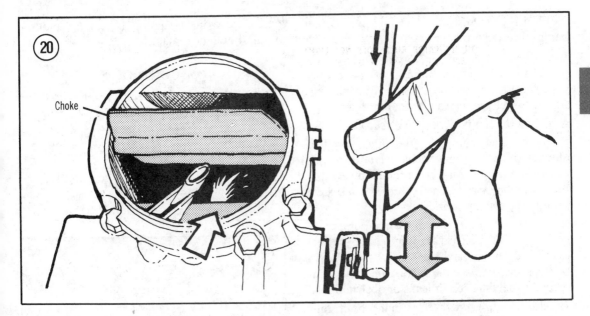

Choke

linkage several times. There should be a stream of fuel from the accelerator pump discharge tube each time the accelerator linkage is depressed (**Figure 20**). If not, check fuel pump delivery (described later), float valve, and float adjustment. If the engine will not start, check the automatic choke parts for sticking or damage. If necessary, rebuild or replace the carburetor.

2. *Engine runs at fast idle* — Check the choke setting. Check the idle speed, idle mixture, and decel valve (if equipped) adjustment.

3. *Rough idle or engine miss with frequent stalling* — Check idle mixture and idle speed adjustments.

4. *Engine "diesels" (continues to run) when ignition is switched off* — Check idle mixture (probably too rich), ignition timing, and idle speed (probably too fast). Check the throttle solenoid (if equipped) for proper operation. Check for overheated engine.

5. *Stumbling when accelerating from idle* — Check the idle speed and mixture adjustments. Check the accelerator pump.

6. *Engine misses at high speed or lacks power* — This indicates possible fuel starvation. Check fuel pump pressure and capacity as described in this chapter. Check float needle valves. Check for a clogged fuel filter or air cleaner.

7. *Black exhaust smoke* — This indicates a badly overrich mixture. Check idle mixture and idle speed adjustment. Check choke setting. Check for excessive fuel pump pressure, leaky floats, or worn needle valves.

8. *Excessive fuel consumption* — Check for overrich mixture. Make sure choke mechanism works properly. Check idle mixture and idle speed. Check for excessive fuel pump pressure, leaky floats, or worn float needle valves.

FUEL SYSTEM
(FUEL INJECTED)

Troubleshooting a fuel injection system requires more thought, experience, and know-how than any other part of the vehicle. A logical approach and proper test equipment are essential in order to successfully find and fix these troubles.

It is best to leave fuel injection troubles to your dealer. In order to isolate a problem to the injection system make sure that the fuel pump is operating properly. Check its performance as described later in this section. Also make sure that fuel filter and air cleaner are not clogged.

FUEL PUMP TEST
(MECHANICAL AND ELECTRIC)

1. Disconnect the fuel inlet line where it enters the carburetor or fuel injection system.

2. Fit a rubber hose over the fuel line so fuel can be directed into a graduated container with about one quart capacity. See **Figure 21**.

3. To avoid accidental starting of the engine, disconnect the secondary coil wire from the coil or disconnect and insulate the coil primary wire.

4. Crank the engine for about 30 seconds.

5. If the fuel pump supplies the specified amount (refer to the fuel chapter later in this book), the trouble may be in the carburetor or fuel injection system. The fuel injection system should be tested by your dealer.

6. If there is no fuel present or the pump cannot supply the specified amount, either the fuel pump is defective or there is an obstruction in the fuel line. Replace the fuel pump and/or inspect the fuel lines for air leaks or obstructions.

7. Also pressure test the fuel pump by installing a T-fitting in the fuel line between the fuel pump and the carburetor. Connect a fuel pressure gauge to the fitting with a short tube **(Figure 22)**.

8. Reconnect the coil wire, start the engine, and record the pressure. Refer to the fuel chapter later in this book for the correct pressure. If the pressure varies from that specified, the pump should be replaced.

9. Stop the engine. The pressure should drop off very slowly. If it drops off rapidly, the outlet valve in the pump is leaking and the pump should be replaced.

EMISSION CONTROL SYSTEMS

Major emission control systems used on nearly all U.S. models include the following:

a. Positive crankcase ventilation (PCV)

b. Thermostatic air cleaner

c. Air injection reaction (AIR)

d. Fuel evaporation control

e. Exhaust gas recirculation (EGR)

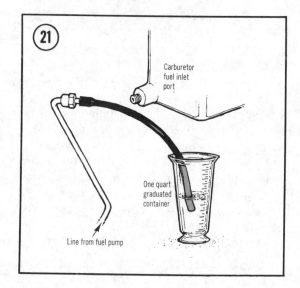

Carburetor fuel inlet port

One quart graduated container

Line from fuel pump

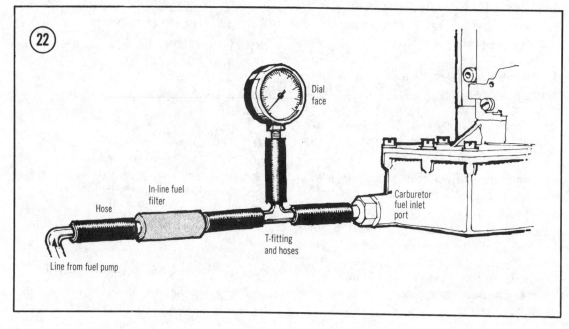

Dial face

In-line fuel filter

Hose

Carburetor fuel inlet port

T-fitting and hoses

Line from fuel pump

Emission control systems vary considerably from model to model. Individual models contain variations of the four systems described here. In addition, they may include other special systems. Use the index to find specific emission control components in other chapters.

Many of the systems and components are factory set and sealed. Without special expensive test equipment, it is impossible to adjust the systems to meet state and federal requirements.

Troubleshooting can also be difficult without special equipment. The procedures described below will help you find emission control parts which have failed, but repairs may have to be entrusted to a dealer or other properly equipped repair shop.

With the proper equipment, you can test the carbon monoxide and hydrocarbon levels.

Figure 23 provides some sources of trouble if the readings are not correct.

Positive Crankcase Ventilation

Fresh air drawn from the air cleaner housing scavenges emissions (e.g., piston blow-by) from the crankcase, then the intake manifold vacuum draws emissions into the intake manifold. They can then be reburned in the normal combustion process. **Figure 24** shows a typical system. **Figure 25** provides a testing procedure.

Thermostatic Air Cleaner

The thermostatically controlled air cleaner maintains incoming air to the engine at a predetermined level, usually about 100°F or higher. It mixes cold air with heated air from the exhaust manifold region. The air cleaner in-

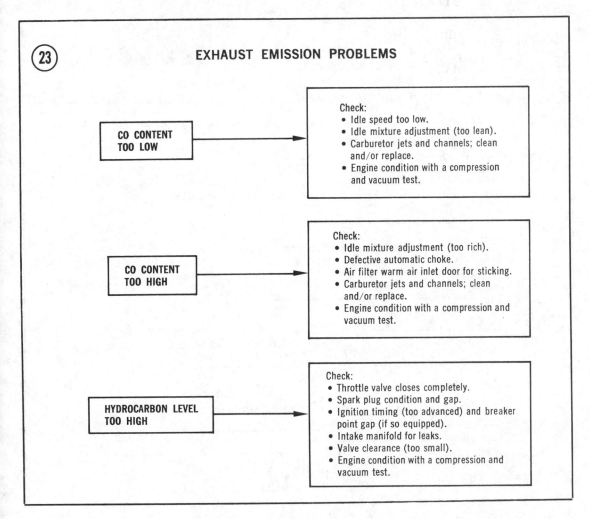

EXHAUST EMISSION PROBLEMS

(23)

CO CONTENT TOO LOW →

Check:
• Idle speed too low.
• Idle mixture adjustment (too lean).
• Carburetor jets and channels; clean and/or replace.
• Engine condition with a compression and vacuum test.

CO CONTENT TOO HIGH →

Check:
• Idle mixture adjustment (too rich).
• Defective automatic choke.
• Air filter warm air inlet door for sticking.
• Carburetor jets and channels; clean and/or replace.
• Engine condition with a compression and vacuum test.

HYDROCARBON LEVEL TOO HIGH →

Check:
• Throttle valve closes completely.
• Spark plug condition and gap.
• Ignition timing (too advanced) and breaker point gap (if so equipped).
• Intake manifold for leaks.
• Valve clearance (too small).
• Engine condition with a compression and vacuum test.

cludes a temperature sensor, vacuum motor, and a hinged door. See **Figure 26**.

The system is comparatively easy to test. See **Figure 27** for the procedure.

Air Injection Reaction System

The air injection reaction system reduces air pollution by oxidizing hydrocarbons and carbon monoxide as they leave the combustion chamber. See **Figure 28**.

The air injection pump, driven by the engine, compresses filtered air and injects it at the exhaust port of each cylinder. The fresh air mixes with the unburned gases in the exhaust and promotes further burning. A check valve prevents exhaust gases from entering and damaging the air pump if the pump becomes inoperative, e.g., from a fan belt failure.

Figure 29 explains the testing procedure for this system.

Fuel Evaporation Control

Fuel vapor from the fuel tank passes through the liquid/vapor separator to the carbon canister. See **Figure 30**. The carbon absorbs and

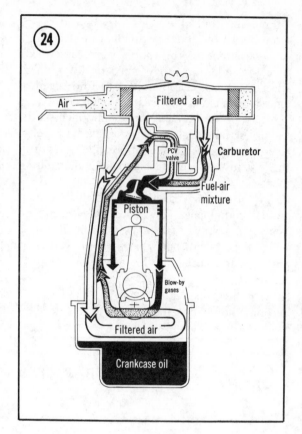

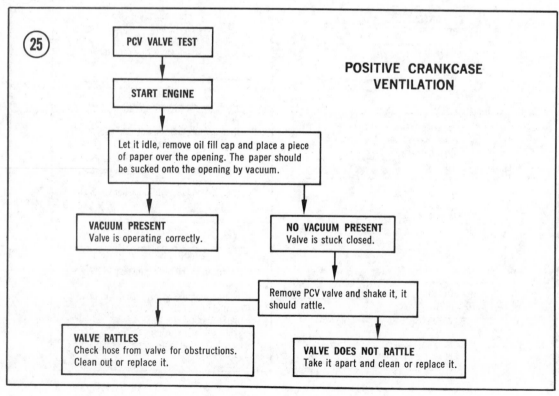

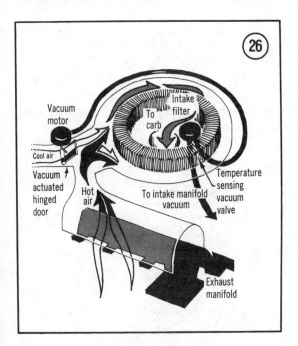

(26)

Vacuum motor

To carb

Intake filter

Cool air

Vacuum actuated hinged door

Hot air

To intake manifold vacuum

Temperature sensing vacuum valve

Exhaust manifold

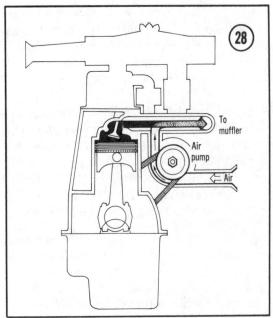

(28)

To muffler

Air pump

Air

2

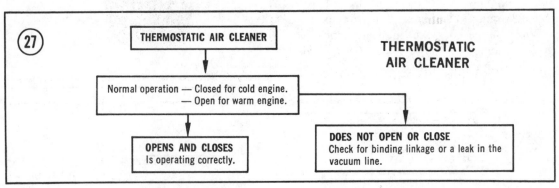

(27)

THERMOSTATIC AIR CLEANER

THERMOSTATIC AIR CLEANER

Normal operation — Closed for cold engine.
— Open for warm engine.

OPENS AND CLOSES
Is operating correctly.

DOES NOT OPEN OR CLOSE
Check for binding linkage or a leak in the vacuum line.

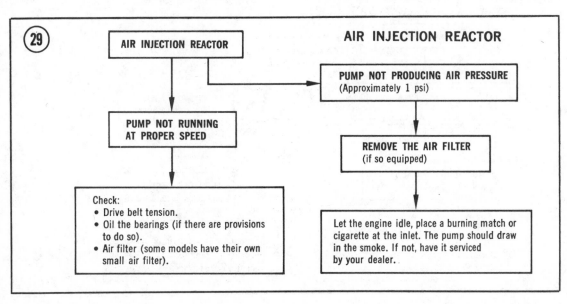

(29)

AIR INJECTION REACTOR

AIR INJECTION REACTOR

PUMP NOT PRODUCING AIR PRESSURE
(Approximately 1 psi)

PUMP NOT RUNNING AT PROPER SPEED

REMOVE THE AIR FILTER
(if so equipped)

Check:
• Drive belt tension.
• Oil the bearings (if there are provisions to do so).
• Air filter (some models have their own small air filter).

Let the engine idle, place a burning match or cigarette at the inlet. The pump should draw in the smoke. If not, have it serviced by your dealer.

stores the vapor when the engine is stopped. When the engine runs, manifold vacuum draws the vapor from the canister. Instead of being released into the atmosphere, the fuel vapor takes part in the normal combustion process.

Exhaust Gas Recirculation

The exhaust gas recirculation (EGR) system is used to reduce the emission of nitrogen oxides (NOx). Relatively inert exhaust gases are introduced into the combustion process to slightly reduce peak temperatures. This reduction in temperature reduces the formation of NOx.

Figure 31 provides a simple test of this system.

ENGINE NOISES

Often the first evidence of an internal engine trouble is a strange noise. That knocking, clicking, or tapping which you never heard before may be warning you of impending trouble.

While engine noises can indicate problems, they are sometimes difficult to interpret correctly; inexperienced mechanics can be seriously misled by them.

Professional mechanics often use a special stethoscope which looks similar to a doctor's stethoscope for isolating engine noises. You can do nearly as well with a "sounding stick" which can be an ordinary piece of doweling or a section of small hose. By placing one end in contact with the area to which you want to listen and the other end near your ear, you can hear

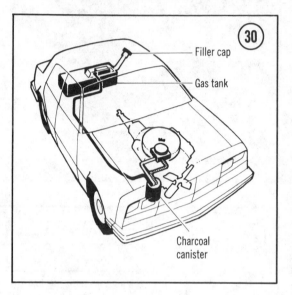

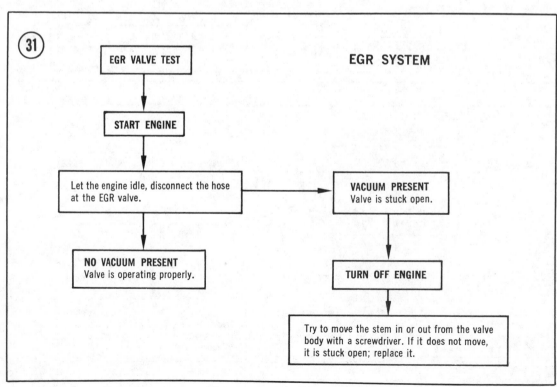

sounds emanating from that area. The first time you do this, you may be horrified at the strange noises coming from even a normal engine. If you can, have an experienced friend or mechanic help you sort the noises out.

Clicking or Tapping Noises

Clicking or tapping noises usually come from the valve train, and indicate excessive valve clearance.

If your vehicle has adjustable valves, the procedure for adjusting the valve clearance is explained in Chapter Three. If your vehicle has hydraulic lifters, the clearance may not be adjustable. The noise may be coming from a collapsed lifter. These may be cleaned or replaced as described in the engine chapter.

A sticking valve may also sound like a valve with excessive clearance. In addition, excessive wear in valve train components can cause similar engine noises.

Knocking Noises

A heavy, dull knocking is usually caused by a worn main bearing. The noise is loudest when the engine is working hard, i.e., accelerating hard at low speed. You may be able to isolate the trouble to a single bearing by disconnecting

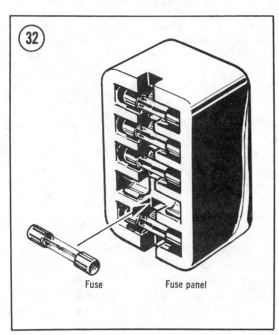

Fuse   Fuse panel

the spark plugs one at a time. When you reach the spark plug nearest the bearing, the knock will be reduced or disappear.

Worn connecting rod bearings may also produce a knock, but the sound is usually more "metallic." As with a main bearing, the noise is worse when accelerating. It may even increase further just as you go from accelerating to coasting. Disconnecting spark plugs will help isolate this knock as well.

A double knock or clicking usually indicates a worn piston pin. Disconnecting spark plugs will isolate this to a particular piston, however, the noise will *increase* when you reach the affected piston.

A loose flywheel and excessive crankshaft end play also produce knocking noises. While similar to main bearing noises, these are usually intermittent, not constant, and they do not change when spark plugs are disconnected.

Some mechanics confuse piston pin noise with piston slap. The double knock will distinguish the piston pin noise. Piston slap is identified by the fact that it is always louder when the engine is cold.

ELECTRICAL ACCESSORIES

Lights and Switches (Interior and Exterior)

1. *Bulb does not light* — Remove the bulb and check for a broken element. Also check the inside of the socket; make sure the contacts are clean and free of corrosion. If the bulb and socket are OK, check to see if a fuse has blown or a circuit breaker has tripped. The fuse panel **(Figure 32)** is usually located under the instrument panel. Replace the blown fuse or reset the circuit breaker. If the fuse blows or the breaker trips again, there is a short in that circuit. Check that circuit all the way to the battery. Look for worn wire insulation or burned wires.

If all the above are all right, check the switch controlling the bulb for continuity with an ohmmeter at the switch terminals. Check the switch contact terminals for loose or dirty electrical connections.

2. *Headlights work but will not switch from either high or low beam* — Check the beam selector switch for continuity with an ohmmeter

at the switch terminals. Check the switch contact terminals for loose or dirty electrical connections.

3. *Brake light switch inoperative* — On mechanically operated switches, usually mounted near the brake pedal arm, adjust the switch to achieve correct mechanical operation. Check the switch for continuity with an ohmmeter at the switch terminals. Check the switch contact terminals for loose or dirty electrical connections.

4. *Back-up lights do not operate* — Check light bulb as described earlier. Locate the switch, normally located near the shift lever. Adjust switch to achieve correct mechanical operation. Check the switch for continuity with an ohmmeter at the switch terminals. Bypass the switch with a jumper wire; if the lights work, replace the switch.

Directional Signals

1. *Directional signals do not operate* — If the indicator light on the instrument panel burns steadily instead of flashing, this usually indicates that one of the exterior lights is burned out. Check all lamps that normally flash. If all are all right, the flasher unit may be defective. Replace it with a good one.

2. *Directional signal indicator light on instrument panel does not light up* — Check the light bulbs as described earlier. Check all electrical connections and check the flasher unit.

3. *Directional signals will not self-cancel* — Check the self-cancelling mechanism located inside the steering column.

4. *Directional signals flash slowly* — Check the condition of the battery and the alternator (or generator) drive belt tension (**Figure 4**). Check the flasher unit and all related electrical connections.

Windshield Wipers

1. *Wipers do not operate* — Check for a blown fuse or circuit breaker that has tripped; replace or reset. Check all related terminals for loose or dirty electrical connections. Check continuity of the control switch with an ohmmeter at the switch terminals. Check the linkage and arms

for loose, broken, or binding parts. Straighten out or replace where necessary.

2. *Wiper motor hums but will not operate* — The motor may be shorted out internally; check and/or replace the motor. Also check for broken or binding linkage and arms.

3. *Wiper arms will not return to the stowed position when turned off* — The motor has a special internal switch for this purpose. Have it inspected by your dealer. Do not attempt this yourself.

Interior Heater

1. *Heater fan does not operate* — Check for a blown fuse or circuit breaker that has tripped. Check the switch for continuity with an ohmmeter at the switch terminals. Check the switch contact terminals for loose or dirty electrical connections.

2. *Heat output is insufficient* — Check the heater hose/engine coolant control valve usually located in the engine compartment; make sure it is in the open position. Ensure that the heater door(s) and cable(s) are operating correctly and are in the open position. Inspect the heat ducts; make sure that they are not crimped or blocked.

COOLING SYSTEM

The temperature gauge or warning light usually signals cooling system troubles before there is any damage. As long as you stop the vehicle at the first indication of trouble, serious damage is unlikely.

In most cases, the trouble will be obvious as soon as you open the hood. If there is coolant or steam leaking, look for a defective radiator, radiator hose, or heater hose. If there is no evidence of leakage, make sure that the fan belt is in good condition. If the trouble is not obvious, refer to **Figures 33 and 34** to help isolate the trouble.

Automotive cooling systems operate under pressure to permit higher operating temperatures without boil-over. The system should be checked periodically to make sure it can withstand normal pressure. **Figure 35** shows the equipment which nearly any service station has for testing the system pressure.

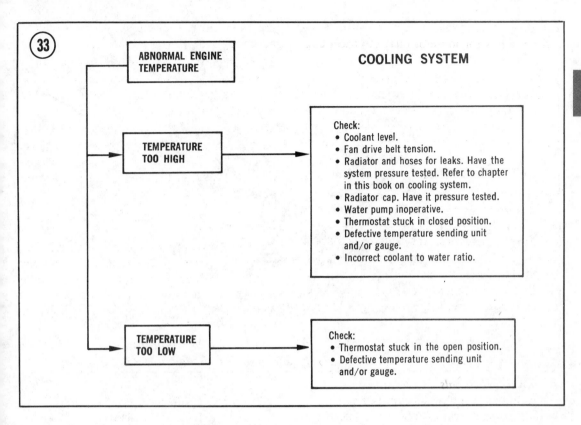

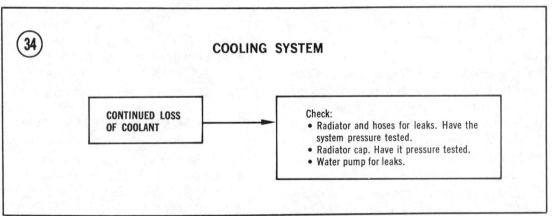

CLUTCH

All clutch troubles except adjustments require transmission removal to identify and cure the problem.

1. *Slippage* — This is most noticeable when accelerating in a high gear at relatively low speed. To check slippage, park the vehicle on a level surface with the handbrake set. Shift to 2nd gear and release the clutch as if driving off. If the clutch is good, the engine will slow and stall. If the clutch slips, continued engine speed will give it away.

Slippage results from insufficient clutch pedal free play, oil or grease on the clutch disc, worn pressure plate, or weak springs.

2. *Drag or failure to release* — This trouble usually causes difficult shifting and gear clash, especially when downshifting. The cause may be excessive clutch pedal free play, warped or bent pressure plate or clutch disc, broken or

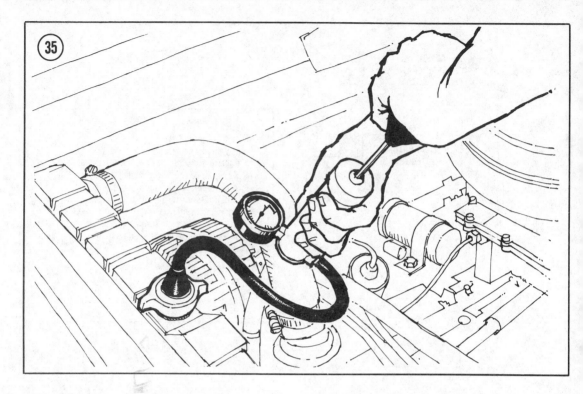

loose linings, or lack of lubrication in pilot bearing. Also check condition of transmission main shaft splines.

3. *Chatter or grabbing* — A number of things can cause this trouble. Check tightness of engine mounts and engine-to-transmission mounting bolts. Check for worn or misaligned pressure plate and misaligned release plate.

4. *Other noises* — Noise usually indicates a dry or defective release or pilot bearing. Check the bearings and replace if necessary. Also check all parts for misalignment and uneven wear.

MANUAL TRANSMISSION/TRANSAXLE

Transmission and transaxle troubles are evident when one or more of the following symptoms appear:

   a. Difficulty changing gears
   b. Gears clash when downshifting
   c. Slipping out of gear
   d. Excessive noise in NEUTRAL
   e. Excessive noise in gear
   f. Oil leaks

Transmission and transaxle repairs are not recommended unless the many special tools required are available.

Transmission and transaxle troubles are sometimes difficult to distinguish from clutch troubles. Eliminate the clutch as a source of trouble before installing a new or rebuilt transmission or transaxle.

AUTOMATIC TRANSMISSION

Most automatic transmission repairs require considerable specialized knowledge and tools. It is impractical for the home mechanic to invest in the tools, since they cost more than a properly rebuilt transmission.

Check fluid level and condition frequently to help prevent future problems. If the fluid is orange or black in color or smells like varnish, it is an indication of some type of damage or failure within the transmission. Have the transmission serviced by your dealer or competent automatic transmission service facility.

BRAKES

Good brakes are vital to the safe operation of the vehicle. Performing the maintenance speci-

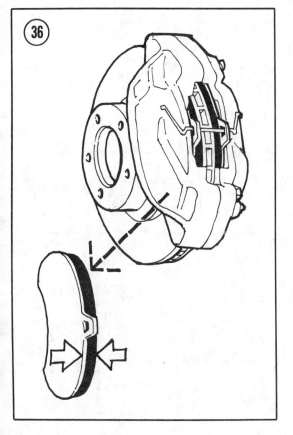

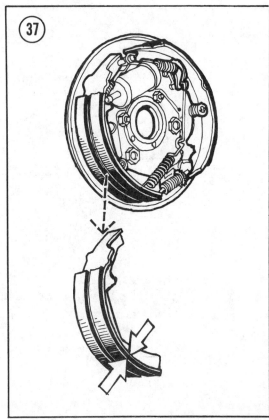

fied in Chapter Three will minimize problems with the brakes. Most importantly, check and maintain the level of fluid in the master cylinder, and check the thickness of the linings on the disc brake pads (**Figure 36**) or drum brake shoes (**Figure 37**).

If trouble develops, **Figures 38 through 40** will help you locate the problem. Refer to the brake chapter for actual repair procedures.

STEERING AND SUSPENSION

Trouble in the suspension or steering is evident when the following occur:

a. Steering is hard
b. Car pulls to one side
c. Car wanders or front wheels wobble
d. Steering has excessive play
e. Tire wear is abnormal

Unusual steering, pulling, or wandering is usually caused by bent or otherwise misaligned suspension parts. This is difficult to check without proper alignment equipment. Refer to the suspension chapter in this book for repairs that you can perform and those that must be left to a dealer or suspension specialist.

If your trouble seems to be excessive play, check wheel bearing adjustment first. This is the most frequent cause. Then check ball-joints (refer to Suspension chapter). Finally, check tie rod end ball-joints by shaking each tie rod. Also check steering gear, or rack-and-pinion assembly to see that it is securely bolted down.

TIRE WEAR ANALYSIS

Abnormal tire wear should be analyzed to determine its causes. The most common causes are the following:

a. Incorrect tire pressure
b. Improper driving
c. Overloading
d. Bad road surfaces
e. Incorrect wheel alignment

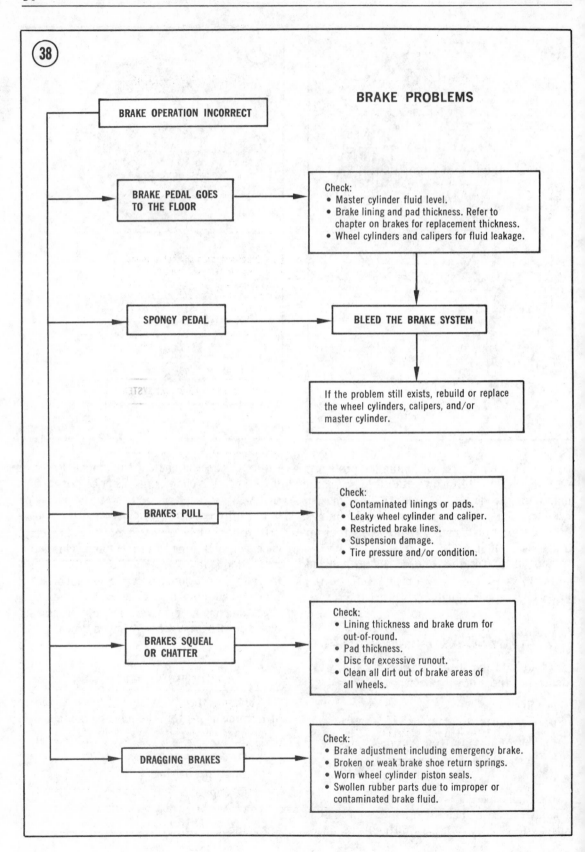

(38)

BRAKE PROBLEMS

BRAKE OPERATION INCORRECT

BRAKE PEDAL GOES TO THE FLOOR →

Check:
- Master cylinder fluid level.
- Brake lining and pad thickness. Refer to chapter on brakes for replacement thickness.
- Wheel cylinders and calipers for fluid leakage.

SPONGY PEDAL →

BLEED THE BRAKE SYSTEM

If the problem still exists, rebuild or replace the wheel cylinders, calipers, and/or master cylinder.

BRAKES PULL →

Check:
- Contaminated linings or pads.
- Leaky wheel cylinder and caliper.
- Restricted brake lines.
- Suspension damage.
- Tire pressure and/or condition.

BRAKES SQUEAL OR CHATTER →

Check:
- Lining thickness and brake drum for out-of-round.
- Pad thickness.
- Disc for excessive runout.
- Clean all dirt out of brake areas of all wheels.

DRAGGING BRAKES →

Check:
- Brake adjustment including emergency brake.
- Broken or weak brake shoe return springs.
- Worn wheel cylinder piston seals.
- Swollen rubber parts due to improper or contaminated brake fluid.

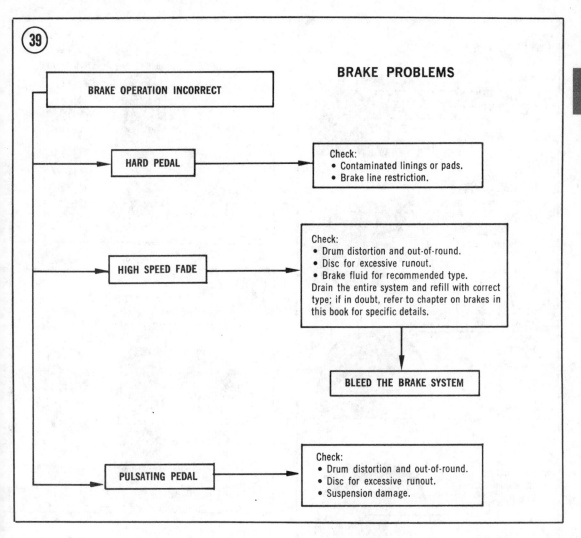

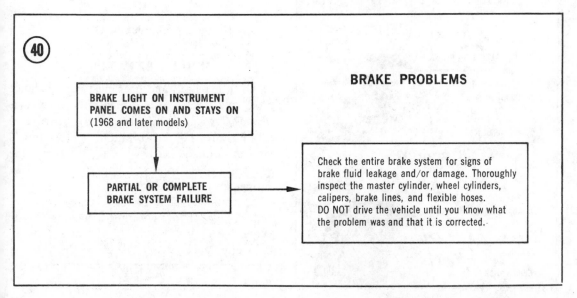

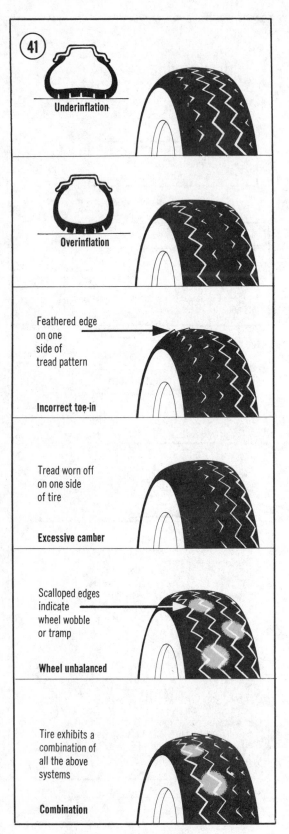

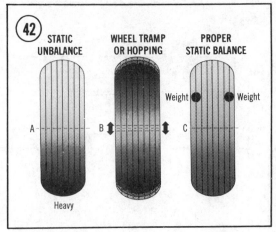

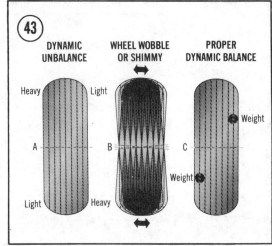

Figure 41 identifies wear patterns and indicates the most probable causes.

WHEEL BALANCING

All four wheels and tires must be in balance along two axes. To be in static balance (**Figure 42**), weight must be evenly distributed around the axis of rotation. (A) shows a statically unbalanced wheel; (B) shows the result — wheel tramp or hopping; (C) shows proper static balance.

To be in dynamic balance (**Figure 43**), the centerline of the weight must coincide with the centerline of the wheel. (A) shows a dynamically unbalanced wheel; (B) shows the result — wheel wobble or shimmy; (C) shows proper dynamic balance.

NOTE: If you own a 1981 or later model, first check the Supplement at the back of the book for any new service information.

CHAPTER THREE

LUBRICATION, MAINTENANCE, AND TUNE-UP

This chapter deals with all the normal maintenance necessary to keep your vehicle running properly. It includes summaries of service intervals in table form (**Tables 1-3**). The last part of the chapter contains a tune-up procedure which simplifies and organizes the process.

Maintenance is scheduled in intervals of months or thousands of miles, whichever comes first. In addition, there are 2 schedules, "A" and "B." The correct schedule is shown on the car's emission decal.

Ford Motor Co. manufactures and recommends its own lubricants for most maintenance procedures. **Table 4** lists recommended oil grades while **Table 5** lists engine oil capacity. **Table 6** lists transmission capacity and viscosities. Recommended lubricants are listed in **Table 7**. Tune-up specifications are listed in **Tables 8-10**.

Tables 1-10 are at the end of the chapter.

FUEL STOP CHECKS

1. Check engine oil level. If necessary, top to the SAFE or MAX mark on the dipstick. See **Figure 1**. See **Table 4** for recommended oil grades.

2. Check coolant level. It should be between the MAX and MIN marks on the plastic bottle.

WARNING
Never remove the radiator cap with the engine hot. The cap may fly off, followed by a fountain of hot coolant.

3. Check level of the windshield washer container. It should be kept full.

CAUTION
Do not use radiator antifreeze in the washer tank. The runoff may damage the car's paint.

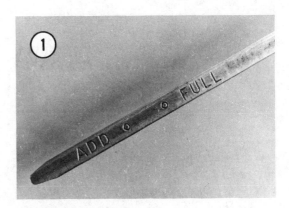

4. On non-maintenance free batteries, check battery electrolyte level. It should be up to the ring inside each filler hole. See **Figure 2**. Fill with distilled water.

5. Check tire pressure. This should be done when the tires are cold (after driving less than one mile). Correct tire pressures for your tire are listed on the right-hand door lock pillar. Maximum pressures are also imprinted on the tires.

6. Check the fluid level in the brake master cylinder. Clean the area around the master cylinder cover. Push the retainer to one side and remove the filler cap from the master cylinders. Lift the cover off and make sure the brake fluid level in both sections is within 1/4 in. of the top of the master cylinder (**Figure 3**). Top up if necessary with DOT 3 or DOT 4 brake fluid.

SCHEDULED MAINTENANCE

All of the following procedures are done at specified intervals of mileage or time. **Table 2** and **Table 3** provide maintenance recommendations and intervals for all vehicles covered in this book.

Engine Oil and Filter Change

Use an oil recommended in **Table 4**.

1. Warm the engine to normal operating temperature. This allows the oil to drain freely.
2. Place a container under the oil pan and remove the drain plug (**Figure 4**). On 255 cid engines, 2 drain plugs are used. Let the oil drain completely (10-15 minutes).
3. Clean the drain plug(s) and check the washers for damage. Install the plug(s) after the oil has been drained.
4. If the filter is being changed (every other oil change typically), position the drain pan beneath it. Then loosen the filter with a filter wrench until oil flows from it. Remove and discard the filter after the oil stops draining. Clean the filter mounting on the engine. Coat the gasket on a new filter with clean oil and screw the filter in until it contacts the engine mounting. Tighten 1/2 turn further by hand. Do not overtighten. Do not tighten with a filter wrench.
5. Remove the oil filler cap on the valve cover

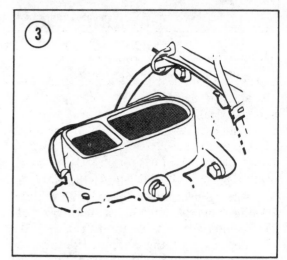

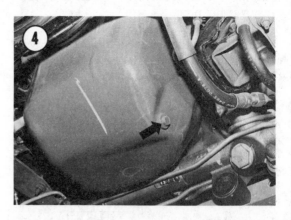

and fill with the recommended oil (**Table 4**). Capacity is listed in **Table 5**.

6. Start the engine. The engine warning light will stay on for approximately 30 seconds. Let the engine run for a few minutes and check for leaks. Check oil level on the dipstick and top up if necessary (**Figure 1**).

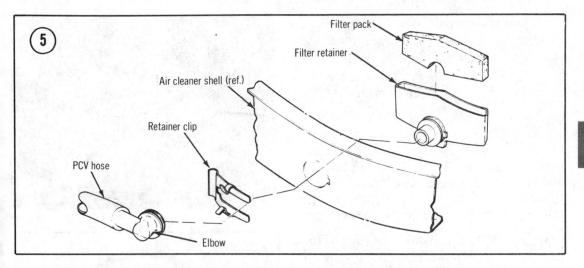

⑤

Filter pack

Filter retainer

Air cleaner shell (ref.)

Retainer clip

PCV hose

Elbow

3

Manual Transmission Oil Level

Park the car on a level surface. Place the transmission in neutral, set the handbrake, and block all 4 wheels. Working beneath the car, clean the area around the filler plug (pipe plug with recessed square head on side of transmission). Remove the plug. The oil should be up to the bottom of the filler hole. If not, top with transmission fluid recommended in **Table 6**.

Automatic Transmission Fluid Level

Park the car on a level surface. Place the transmission in PARK and set the handbrake. Run the engine until warm, then let it idle. Move the shift lever through all gear positions, allowing each gear to engage, then move shift lever back to PARK. Clean the area around the transmission dipstick cap. Remove the dipstick, wipe it clean, and push it all the way back in. Pull the dipstick out and note the fluid level. It should be between the ADD and FULL marks. If the level is below the ADD mark, add fluid through the dipstick tube until the level is between the ADD and FULL marks. Do not add fluid unless the level is at or below the ADD mark. Use only automatic transmission fluid specified in **Table 6**.

> *CAUTION*
> *Do not overfill the transmission, or it may be damaged.*

Rear Axle Oil Level

Park the car on a level surface, set the handbrake, and block the rear wheel. Clean the area around the filler plug. Remove the plug. Oil level should be within 1/4 in. of the bottom of the filler plug hole. Top up with oil recommended in **Table 7**.

Crankcase Emission Filter

To replace the filter, remove the air cleaner cover and filter element. Lift out the old PCV filter pack (**Figure 5**) and install a new one. Reinstall the air cleaner element and cover.

Exhaust Manifold Bolts

The exhaust manifold bolts should be torqued to specifications at the first service interval (**Table 2**). See Chapter Five.

Clutch Pedal Height

Check and adjust as necessary as described in Chapter Eight.

Hinges, Locks, Latches

Lubricate seat track and hood latches with a spray lubricant such as WD-40 or Ford LPS. Operate the latches several times to work in the lubricant. Lubricate door, trunk, and hood latches in the same manner. To lubricate locks, spray a small amount of spray lubricant into the lock cylinder. As an alternative, coat the key with lock oil or graphite. Insert the key and work the lock several times. Remove and clean the key.

Air Cleaner Element

To replace the element remove the air cleaner cover by removing the wing nut(s) securing the cover (**Figure 6**). Remove the cover and lift out the filter element. Install a new element in the reverse order.

Fuel Filter

Two types of fuel filters are used on vehicles discussed. To replace, see Chapter Five.

Fuel Lines

The fuel lines should be inspected periodically for crimps, twists, and signs of gasoline leakage. See Chapter Five.

Intake Manifold Bolts

The intake manifold bolts should be torqued to specifications at the first service interval (**Table 2**). See Chapter Five.

Drive Belts

Inspect the fan belt and all accessory drive belts at each service interval. Replace worn belts. Check and adjust drive belt tension as described in Chapter Six.

Engine Coolant and Cooling Hoses

Remove the radiator cap and check the condition of the coolant. If it looks dirty or rusty, flush the radiator and replace the coolant as described in Chapter Six. Inspect all heater hoses, and the upper and lower radiator hoses. Replace any hoses that are cracked, deteriorated, or extremely soft. Make sure that all hoses are correctly installed (firmly seated on their mating connectors), and all hose clamps are secure. Engine coolant should be drained, and the cooling system flushed and refilled every 24 months regardless of vehicle mileage.

Front Wheel Bearings

At the recommended intervals, remove the front wheel bearings, clean throughly, and repack and install as described in Chapter Nine.

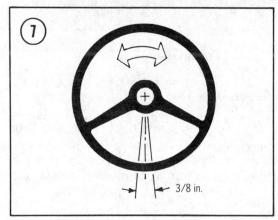

Brake Lines and Linings

On drum brakes, remove the drums and inspect the linings. See Chapter Eleven. Replace brake shoes if linings are worn within 1/32 in. of any rivet, or are contaminated with oil, grease, or brake fluid. Check drums for scoring or uneven wear. Have the drums turned if necessary. Check drums and shoes for blue-tinted areas indicating overheating. Replace any overheated parts. In addition, always replace brake springs if overheated parts are found.

On disc brakes, check the discs for scoring or corrosion. Have the discs turned if necessary. Remove and inspect the pads as described in Chapter Eleven. Replace pads if worn within 1/32 in. of any rivet head, or if the pad linings are contaminated with oil, grease, or brake fluid.

Check wheel cylinders and disc brake calipers for brake fluid leaks. Rebuild or replace leaking cylinders or calipers.

Check all brake lines and hoses for cracks, leaks or wear. If worn, cracked or crimped spots are visible, find the cause of interference and correct it. Replace lines or hoses that are worn or otherwise damaged.

Front Suspension
Ball-joint Lubrication

Securely block the rear wheels so that the car will not roll in either direction. Jack up the front end of the car and place it on jackstands.

> *NOTE*
> *If the car has been parked in temperatures below 20 degrees F, park the vehicle in a heated garage until the ball-joints will accept grease.*

Clean the area around the ball-joint grease plugs. Inject multipurpose grease with a rubber-tipped, hand-operated grease gun. Apply grease until the ball-joint boot swells, then reinstall the grease plug.

> *CAUTION*
> *Do not force so much grease into the ball-joint that it escapes from the ball-joint boot. This will ruin the boot's weather-tight seal.*

PCV System

The PCV (positive crankcase ventilation) system should be cleaned and inspected, and the PCV valve replaced at the interval specified in **Table 2**. See Chapter Five.

Fuel Vapor Emission System
and Evaporative Emission Canister

The fuel vapor emission system includes the fuel tank fill control and venting system, the pressure/vacuum relief fill cap, the fuel tank vapor separator and the evaporative emission canister. The system should be inspected and cleaned at the interval specified in **Table 2**. See Chapter Five for inspection, cleaning, and replacement procedures.

Steering Linkage

The steering linkage should be checked at the intervals specified in **Table 2** for excessive looseness or wear. To do this, turn the steering wheel so that the front wheels are aligned directly ahead. Turn the steering wheel from right to left while having an assistant monitor the movement of the front tires. There should be no more than 3/8 in. free play at the steering wheel rim before the front tires begin to move. See **Figure 7**.

Wheels and Tires

Have wheel alignment and balance checked by a dealer or front-end shop if tire wear becomes unusual or uneven. See **Figure 8** for tire rotation patterns.

> *NOTE*
> *If vehicle is equipped with a temporary spare tire, do not include it in rotation sequence with other 4 tires.*

> *NOTE*
> *Modern radial tires can be switched from side to side, if desired, without affecting vehicle ride quality.*

TUNE-UP

To ensure maximum operating economy and service life, and to comply with regulated exhaust emission standards, a complete tune-up should be performed at the intervals specified in **Table 2**.

The recommended intervals are based on normal use—a combination of highway and city driving. If the vehicle is used extensively for stop-and-go city driving, more frequent tune-ups may be required.

Because different systems in an engine interact, the procedures should be done in the following order:

1. Tighten cylinder head bolts.
2. Adjust valve clearances.
3. Check compression.
4. Perform ignition system work.
5. Adjust carburetor.

Tune-up specifications for all models are found on the Vehicle Emission Control Information Label in the engine compartment (**Figure 9**). If the label is missing, refer to **Table 8** (valve specifications), **Table 9** (spark plug specifications) and **Table 10** (ignition and carburetor specifications).

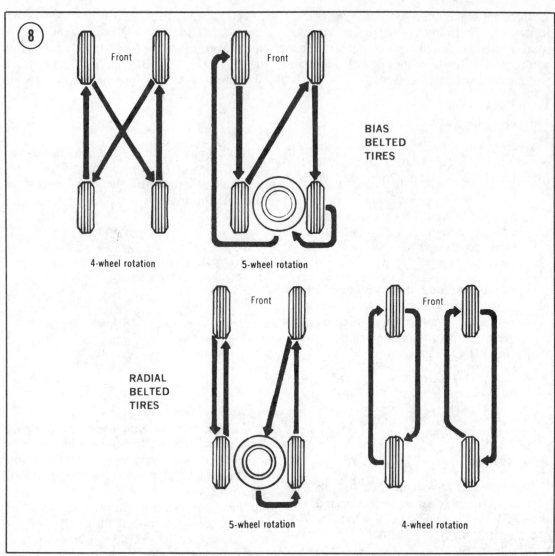

(8)

Front   Front

BIAS
BELTED
TIRES

4-wheel rotation   5-wheel rotation

RADIAL
BELTED
TIRES

Front   Front

5-wheel rotation   4-wheel rotation

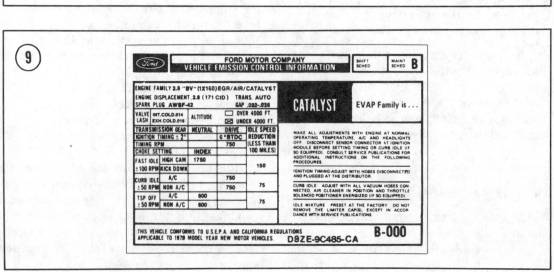

(9)

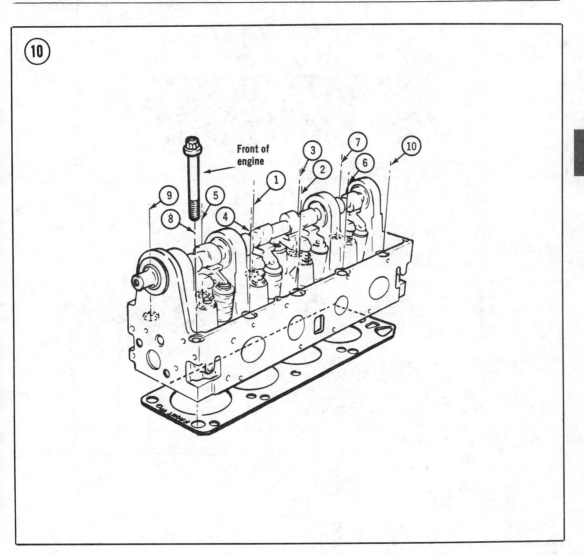

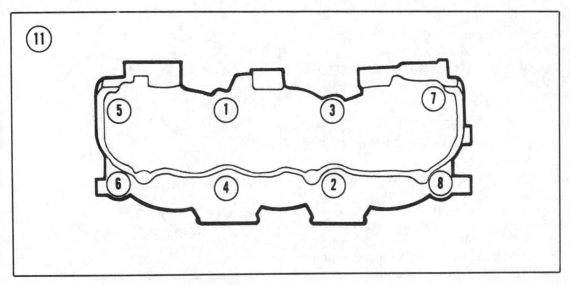

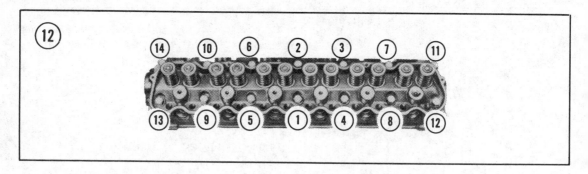

Cylinder Head Bolts

Tighten the cylinder head bolts as follows:
a. On 2300 cc engines, tighten to 60 ft.-lb., then to 80 ft.-lb. in the sequence shown in **Figure 10**.
b. On 2800 cc engines, tighten to 40 ft.-lb., then to 50 ft.-lb. and finally to 65-80 ft.-lb. in the sequence shown in **Figure 11**.
c. On 200 cid engines, tighten to 50 ft.-lb., then to 60 ft.-lb and finally to 75 ft.-lb. in the sequence shown in **Figure 12**.
d. On 255 and 302 cid engines, tighten to 55 ft.-lb., then to 65-72 ft.-lb. in the sequence shown in **Figure 13**.

VALVE ADJUSTMENT
(2300 CC, 200 CID,
255 CID and 302 CID)

The 2300 cc, 200 cid, 255 cid and 302 cid engines do not require periodic valve adjustment. If a problem is suspected in the valve train, the valve spring assembled height, the camshaft dimensions and the valve lash and adjuster clearance should be checked and defective parts replaced. See Chapter Four.

VALVE ADJUSTMENT
(2800 CC)

1. Remove the air cleaner as described in Chapter Five.
2. Remove the rocker arm covers as described in Chapter Four. Torque the rocker arm support bolts to 43-49 ft.-lb.
3. Remove the spark plugs to make it easier to turn the crankshaft.
4. Place a finger on the intake rocker arm for No. 5 cylinder. **Figure 14** identifies cylinders

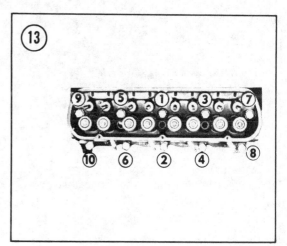

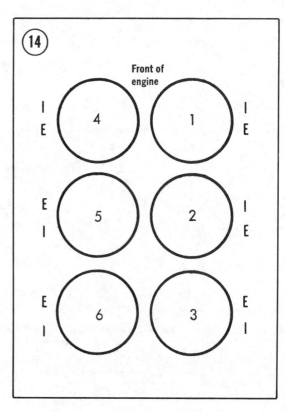

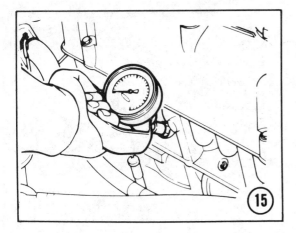

3

and valves. Position your finger so you can feel any rocker arm motion.

5. Turn the engine until No. 5 intake valve just begins to open. This is evident when the valve stem side of the rocker arm starts to go down.

6. Measure clearance in both No. 1 intake valves with a regular feeler gauge (not a step-type). To measure, insert the feeler gauge between the rocker arm and valve stem.

NOTE
The feeler gauge must be inserted in a direction parallel to the rocker arm shaft. Do not insert from the side of the engine toward the center. This will give false readings, and cause excessively tight clearances.

Intake valve clearance is correct when a 0.016 in. feeler gauge has light to moderate drag, and a 0.017 in. gauge is very tight. Exhaust valve clearance is correct when a 0.018 in. has light to moderate drag, and a 0.019 in. gauge is very tight. **Figure 14** identifies intake and exhaust valves.

7. Measure clearance on the remaining valves referring to **Table 8**.

COMPRESSION TEST

An engine with low or uneven compression cannot be properly tuned. Therefore, the engine should be given a compression test before proceeding with the tune-up. Compression testing requires a compression gauge tester of the type discussed in Chapter One.

1. Remove the oil dipstick and check the crankcase oil level. Add oil as required to bring level between MIN and MAX indicator marks on dipstick (**Figure 1**).

2. Remove the spark plugs as described later in this chapter. Remove air cleaner from carburetor and block the throttle and choke wide open.

3. Remove the distributor primary lead from the negative terminal on the coil.

4. Connect a remote starter switch to the starter circuit in accordance with the manufacturer's instructions, or have an assistant operate the starter switch with the ignition key.

5. Firmly insert a compression gauge in each spark plug hole in order, and crank the engine through at least 5 compression strokes to obtain the highest possible reading. Record the reading for each cylinder. See **Figure 15**.

NOTE
If there is more than 20 pounds difference between the high and low reading cylinders, the engine cannot be properly tuned until repairs have been made. The remainder of this procedure may be performed to help determine the kind of repairs that are needed.

6. If low or uneven compression readings were recorded for one or more cylinders, squirt about one tablespoon of motor oil through the spark plug hole of each low-reading cylinder. Repeat the compression test. If compression improves, the problem is probably worn rings. If no improvement is noted, it is likely the valves are burned, sticking, or not seating properly. If 2 adjacent cylinders read low and the oil injection does not increase compression, the problem may be a defective head gasket.

SPARK PLUGS

Removal

1. Remove all dirt and other debris from around spark plugs, using compressed air if available. A tire pump, or a small brush can also be used.

2. Disconnect spark plug wires by grasping the molded boot portion of the wire with Ford tool T74P-6666-A (**Figure 16**). Twist the boot till it loosens, then remove the wire from the plug.

> *CAUTION*
> *Spark plug wires should never be removed by yanking on the wire, as the connection may become damaged.*

> *NOTE*
> *Tag each spark plug wire (masking tape works well) and mark the proper cylinder number. The No. 1 terminal is marked on the spark plug cap. Cylinders are numbered 1-2-3-4 (front to rear) on I-4 engines. I-6 engines are numbered 1-2-3-4-5-6 (front to rear). V-6 engines are numbered (front to rear) starting at right bank 1-2-3, and left bank, 4-5-6. V-8 engines are numbered (front to rear) starting at right bank, 1-2-3-4; left bank, 5-6-7-8.*

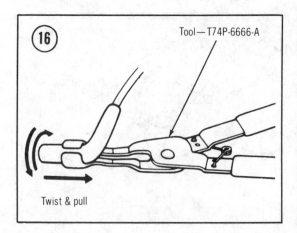
Tool—T74P-6666-A
Twist & pull

3. Using a spark plug wrench remove the spark plugs and lay in order of removal. Compare their condition to the color chart in Chapter Two. Their condition is an indicator of engine condition, and can warn of developing trouble.

Replacement

Spark plugs should be replaced at intervals listed in **Table 2**. If misfiring occurs earlier than the tune-up intervals, spark plugs in good condition can often be cleaned, regapped, and reinstalled with acceptable results. If all new plugs are being installed, skip to Step 3 in the following procedure.

1. Inspect plugs and discard and replace them if they have badly worn electrodes and/or glazed, blistered, or broken porcelain insulators.

2. Clean serviceable plugs with an abrasive cleaner, such as sandblast cleaners found at service stations. File center electrode flat.

3. Verify that all plugs to be installed are of the same make and of the proper heat range number (**Table 9**).

4. Adjust the spark plug gap, using a wire-type feeler gauge (**Figure 17**), to specifications listed in **Table 9**.

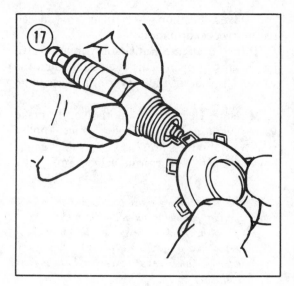

> *CAUTION*
> *Always adjust gap by bending negative or side (never center) electrode. Most spark plug feeler gauges have a slot which can be used for bending the electrode. Never adjust plugs by tapping the electrode on a hard surface. This can cause damage to the plug insulator.*

5. Inspect spark plug hole threads and clean before installing plugs. If required, carbon debris can be removed with a 14 mm x 1.25 SAE spark plug thread chaser (use grease on the chaser to catch chips).

> *CAUTION*
> *Use extreme care when using thread chaser to avoid cross-threading. Also crank the engine several times to blow out any dislodged material from the engine.*

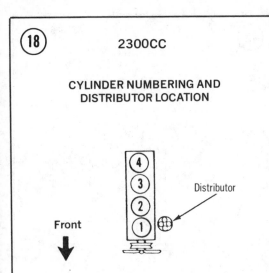

2300CC

CYLINDER NUMBERING AND DISTRIBUTOR LOCATION

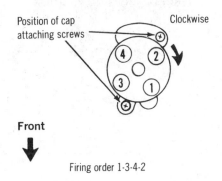

FIRING ORDER AND POSTION

Firing order 1-3-4-2

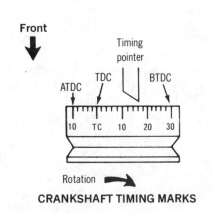

CRANKSHAFT TIMING MARKS

6. Apply a thin film of oil to spark plug threads. Install plug in hole and torque to 10-15 ft.-lb.

NOTE

If torque wrench is not available, tighten spark plugs as tight as possible by hand, then using wrench, tighten another 1/2 turn. Do not overtighten. Excessive torque may change gap setting or squash the gasket so badly it cannot seal.

7. Coat the inside of each spark plug boot with General Electric electrical silicone grease G-627 or equivalent.
8. Reconnect the spark plugs.

IGNITION SYSTEM

All models use the Dura Spark Breakerless Ignition system which does not require point replacement, point gap adjustment, or dwell angle adjustment. If parts fail, they are not repairable and must be replaced. Ignition timing is adjusted initially at the factory and requires no further adjustment or service. However, if the distributor is removed or ignition components replaced, engine timing can be checked by performing the following procedures. Once the car is running, however, have a dealer recheck and adjust ignition timing.

Ignition Timing

Ignition timing requires a stroboscopic timing light of the type discussed in Chapter One. Connect the light according to manufacturer's instructions. Refer to **Figure 18** (2300 cc), **Figure 19** (2800 cc), **Figure 20** (200 cid) or **Figure 21** (255 cid and 302 cid) for engine timing mark identification. Refer to **Table 10** for ignition and carburetion specifications.
1. Clean the crankshaft pulley and timing marks.
2. Using white paint, mark the crankshaft pulley notch and the proper degree mark on the timing scale.
3. Disconnect and plug all distributor vacuum lines.

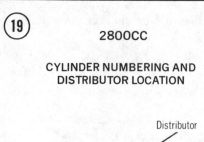

19 2800CC

CYLINDER NUMBERING AND
DISTRIBUTOR LOCATION

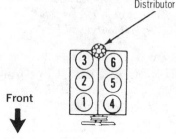

FIRING ORDER AND ROTATION

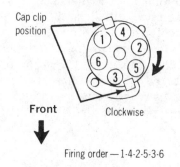

Firing order — 1-4-2-5-3-6

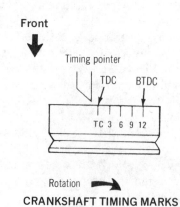

CRANKSHAFT TIMING MARKS

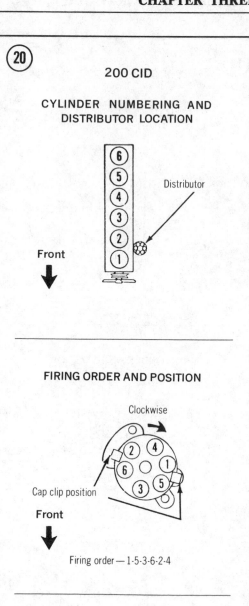

20 200 CID

CYLINDER NUMBERING AND
DISTRIBUTOR LOCATION

FIRING ORDER AND POSITION

Firing order — 1-5-3-6-2-4

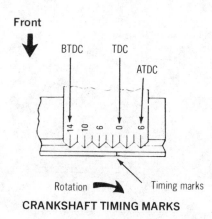

CRANKSHAFT TIMING MARKS

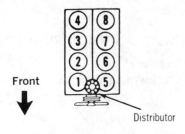

255 CID AND 302 CID

CYLINDER NUMBERING AND DISTRIBUTOR LOCATION

Front

Distributor

FIRING ORDER

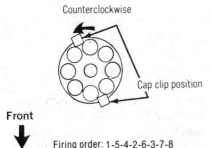

Counterclockwise

Cap clip position

Front

Firing order: 1-5-4-2-6-3-7-8

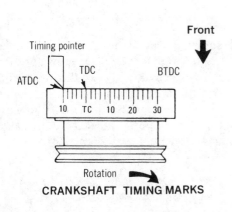

Timing pointer

Front

ATDC

TDC

BTDC

10 TC 10 20 30

Rotation

CRANKSHAFT TIMING MARKS

4. Disconnect the 3-pin switch assembly connector from the dual mode timing ignition module (if so equipped). See **Figure 22**.

5. Connect a timing light and an accurate tachometer following manufacturer's instructions.

NOTE
For the Dura Spark ignition system, only clamp-on inductive timing lights may be used.

CAUTION
For the 302 cid engine, only tachometers calibrated for the Dura Spark 1 ignition systems may be used.

6. Start the engine and check idle speed. If necessary, adjust as described later in this chapter.

7. Point the timing light at the timing marks. If timing is within +/- 2 degrees, do not adjust. If timing is off more than +/- 2 degrees, loosen the distributor lock bolt and turn the distributor to change timing.

3

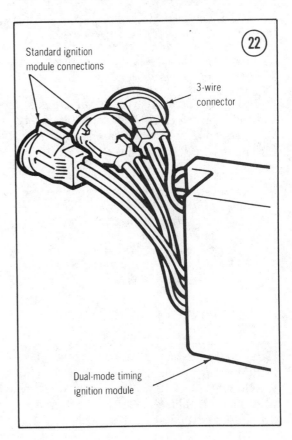

Standard ignition module connections

3-wire connector

Dual-mode timing ignition module

NOTE
To advance timing on 4- or 6-cylinder engines rotate the distributor counterclockwise. To advance timing on V8 engines, rotate the distributor clockwise.

8. Tighten the lock bolt and recheck the adjustment.

WARNING
Do not touch the spark plug or coil wires with the engine running. This can cause a painful shock, even if the insulation is in perfect condition.

9. Unplug and reconnect the vacuum line hoses to the distributor. Remove all test equipment and reconnect the 3-pin switch assembly (if so equipped). See **Figure 22**.

CARBURETOR

Carburetor adjustments include idle mixture, idle speed, and fast (choke on) idle speed adjustments.

NOTE
Before attempting to adjust carburetor settings, the ignition system should be tuned and timed, using the procedures given earlier in this chapter.

During the period covered, vehicles used 2-barrel carburetors on 2300 cc, 2800 cc, 255 cid, and 302 cid engines, and 1-barrel carburetors on 200 cid engines.

NOTE
In making carburetor adjustments, always refer to the Vehicle Emission Control Information decal (Figure 9) located in the engine compartment for correct idle speeds for your vehicle. The speeds listed in Table 10 should be used only if the decal is missing or cannot be read.

IDLE MIXTURE ADJUSTMENT

Idle fuel mixture adjustments on all 1979-1980 models require special test equipment, special tools, and a special enrichment substance. Idle mixture adjustment should, therefore, be referred to your dealer or a competent garage.

MODEL 5200 2-V AND 6500 FEEDBACK CARBURETORS

Curb and Fast Idle Speed Adjustment

Curb and fast idle speed adjustments on 1979-1980 models require special test equipment and special tools. Curb and idle mixture adjustments should, therefore, be referred to your dealer or a competent garage.

MODEL 2150 2-V CARBURETOR

Fast Idle and Curb Idle Speed Adjustments

1. Set the parking brake and block the wheels so that the car cannot move.
2. Remove the air cleaner and set aside on top of engine as discussed in Chapter Five.

NOTE
Leave all vacuum hoses attached to the air cleaner. The air cleaner must be in position when measuring engine speeds.

3. Check the throttle and choke linkages for freedom of movement and lubricate or repair, as required.
4. Start engine and warm to normal operating temperature.
5. Connect a tachometer to the engine.
6. Disconnect the fuel evaporative purge valve signal vacuum hose at the vacuum hose T-connection. Close off the open port, and plug the vacuum hose.

CAUTION
To prevent damaging the purge valve, do not disconnect the vacuum hose at the purge valve (Figure 23).

7. If so equipped, remove the spark delay valve and route the distributor primary vacuum advance directly to the distributor primary diaphragm (advance side).
8. If so equipped, remove the EGR/PVS valve located in the vacuum line at the EGR valve, and plug the vacuum line (**Figure 24**).

NOTE
If an EGR/PVS valve is not used in the vacuum line, do not disconnect the EGR vacuum hose.

9. Connect the thermactor dump valve vacuum hose to the manifold vacuum hose. Plug the original vacuum source line.

10. If the vehicle is equipped with air conditioning, turn the air conditioner off.

11. Ensure that the engine is at normal operating temperature, and that the choke plate is fully opened.

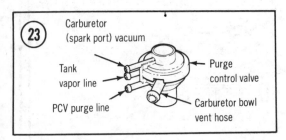

Carburetor
(spark port) vacuum

Tank
vapor line

PCV purge line

Purge
control valve

Carburetor bowl
vent hose

12. Run engine at 2,500 rpm for 15 seconds, then set the throttle linkage so that the fast idle adjustment screw rests on the high step of the fast idle cam as shown in **Figure 25** and allow engine to run for approximately 45 seconds. After allowing the rpm to stabilize, adjust the fast idle speed to 1,800 rpm. Recheck fast idle speed and adjust as necessary to bring it to specification.

13. Refer to information on vehicle emission control information decal and place the transmission selector lever in specified gear.

14. On vehicles equipped with an anti-dieseling solenoid, adjust the curb idle speed to the specifications shown on the vehicle emission control information decal by rotating the long screw until the specified curb

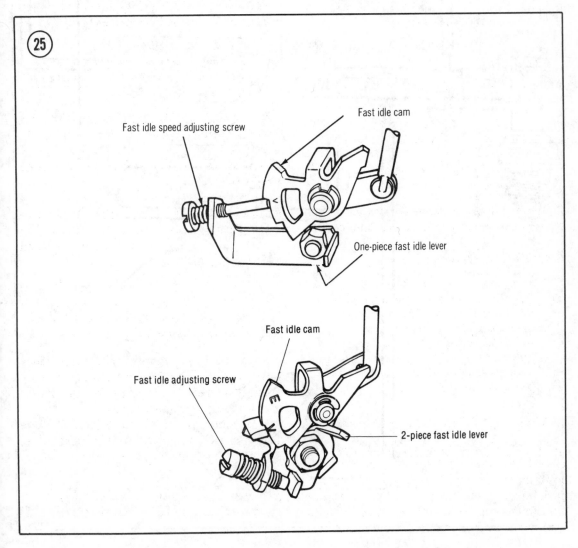

Fast idle speed adjusting screw

Fast idle cam

One-piece fast idle lever

Fast idle cam

Fast idle adjusting screw

2-piece fast idle lever

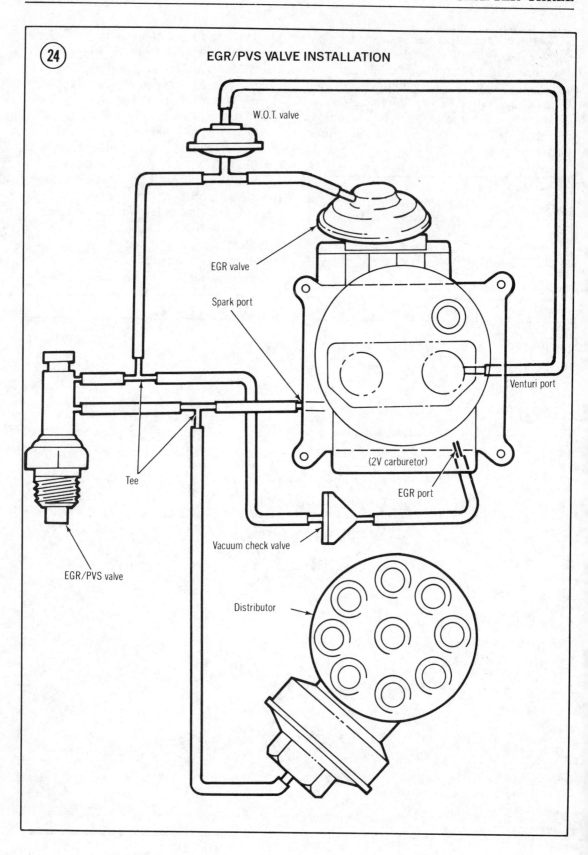

(24) EGR/PVS VALVE INSTALLATION

W.O.T. valve

EGR valve

Spark port

Venturi port

Tee

(2V carburetor)

EGR port

EGR/PVS valve

Vacuum check valve

Distributor

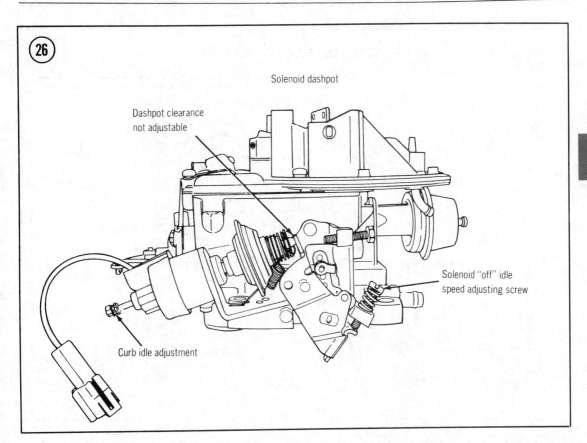

(26)

Solenoid dashpot

Dashpot clearance
not adjustable

Solenoid "off" idle
speed adjusting screw

Curb idle adjustment

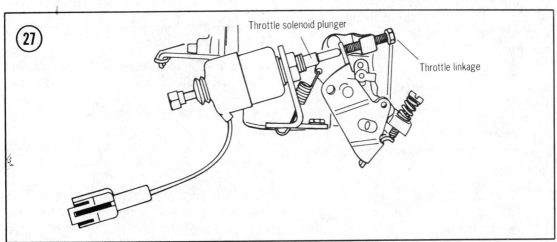

(27)

Throttle solenoid plunger

Throttle linkage

idle rpm is obtained. Adjustment is obtained by turning the long screw at end of anti-dieseling solenoid (**Figure 26**). For vehicles not equipped with the anti-dieseling solenoid, adjust the conventional curb idle speed screw in or out to obtain the idle speed specified on the vehicle emission control information decal.

15. After adjusting curb idle speed on vehicles equipped with the anti-diesling solenoid, unplug the solenoid electrical connector, and collapse the solenoid plunger by forcing the throttle linkage against the plunger (**Figure 27**). Ensure that the solenoid assembly does not move in its mounting bracket while collapsing the solenoid plunger.

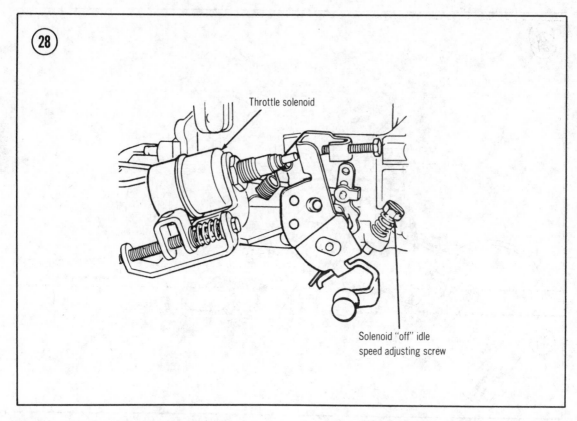

Throttle solenoid

Solenoid "off" idle
speed adjusting screw

16. Adjust the solenoid-off idle speed adjusting screw (**Figure 28**) to obtain the lower (TSP-off) rpm specified on the vehicle emission control information decal.

17. On vehicles not equipped with the anti-dieseling solenoid, collapse the dashpot plunger and measure clearance between plunger and throttle lever pad, if so equipped. See **Figure 29**. Adjust to obtain correct clearance specified on vehicle emission control information decal.

> *NOTE*
> *On vehicles equipped with dashpot solenoid, dashpot clearance must be adjusted each time curb idle speed is adjusted.*

18. Reconnect the solenoid electrical connector.
19. Repeat Steps 14-18 to ensure curb idle speeds are correct.
20. Stop engine and reinstall all equipment removed to perform idle speed adjustments.

MODEL 2700 2-V CARBURETOR

Fast Idle and Curb
Idle Speed Adjustments

1. Remove the air cleaner, disconnect the fuel evaporative purge valve signal vacuum hose, as detailed in the *Model 2150 2-V Carburetor Fast Idle and Curb Idle Speed Adjustment* procedures.
2. Bring the engine up to operating temperature and check the throttle and choke linkage for freedom of operation.
3. Remove the EGR vacuum line at the EGR valve, and plug the vacuum line (**Figure 24**).
4. Disconnect and plug the advance side vacuum line to the distributor.
5. Ensure that the engine is at normal operating temperature, and that the cold enrichment is fully seated.
6. Set the throttle linkage so that the fast idle adjusting screw is on the high step of the choke cam and allow the engine to run until the rpm has stabilized. Adjust the fast idle to specifications shown on the vehicle emission control information decal. See **Figure 30**.

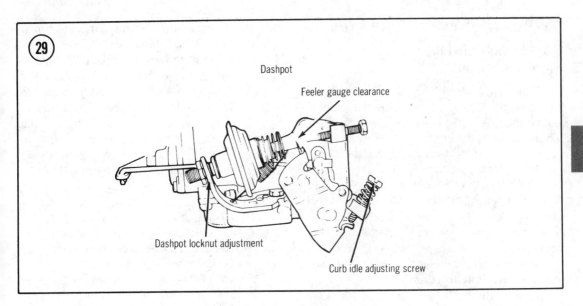

Dashpot

Feeler gauge clearance

Dashpot locknut adjustment

Curb idle adjusting screw

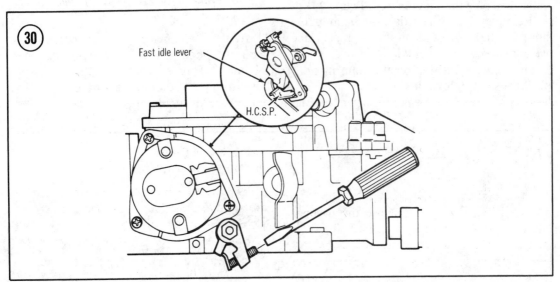

Fast idle lever

H.C.S.P.

7. On vehicles equipped with vacuum operated throttle modulators with solenoid device, adjust the throttle stop screw to specification listed on the vehicle emission control information decal with the air conditioner off and gear selector in DRIVE. On vehicles equippd with vacuum operated throttle modulator but no solenoid device, adjust throttle stop screw in same manner.

NOTE

If curb idle speed operates in an erratic manner with air conditioner on, refer vehicle to Ford dealer for adjustment requiring special tools and procedures.

8. After adjusting curb idle, the accelerator pump lever lash must be adjusted. Push down on top of the nylon nut, located on the accelerator pump, to remove linkage clearance.

9. Measure between the top of the accelerator pump stem and the accelerator pump lever. Adjust to specifications shown on the vehicle emission control information decal.

10. Reinstall all equipment and hoses previously disconnected to perform this adjustment.

MODEL 7200VV CARBURETOR

Fast Idle and Curb Idle Speed Adjustments

1. Remove the air cleaner and lay it aside on top of engine. Leave vacuum hoses attached to air cleaner. When measuring engine speeds, air cleaner must be installed to carburetor.

2. Set the parking brake and block the wheels so the car cannot roll.

3. Check the throttle and choke linkages for freedom of movement and lubricate or repair as required.

4. Start engine and warm to normal operating temperature.

5. Connect a tachometer to engine following manufacturer's instructions.

6. Remove the EGR vacuum line at the EGR valve, and plug the vacuum line (**Figure 24**).

7. Remove the evaporative emission purge hose at the intake manifold, and plug the vacuum hose at the manifold.

8. On vehicles with automatic transmission, place the selector lever in PARK.

9. Ensure that the engine is at normal operating temperature. Start engine and run at 2,000 rpm for 10 seconds.

10. Stop engine and set the throttle linkage so that the fast idle adjustment screw rests on the high step of the choke cam and allow engine to run for 15 seconds to stabilize. Check engine speed. If rpm drops off after running one minute after start, adjust fast idle screw to specification shown on the vehicle emission control information decal. See **Figure 31**.

NOTE
A secondary fast idle vacuum operated throttle modulator (VOTM) or a VOTM with dashpot is provided to ensure intermediate fast idle speeds during cold engine operation. If engine operates roughly during cold engine operation, perform Steps 11-15. If engine runs correctly during cold engine operation, proceed to Step 16.

11. With the engine off, disconnect the vacuum hose at the vacuum operated modulator. Then connect a length of accessory hose from the manifold vacuum to the VOTM or the VOTM with dashpot.

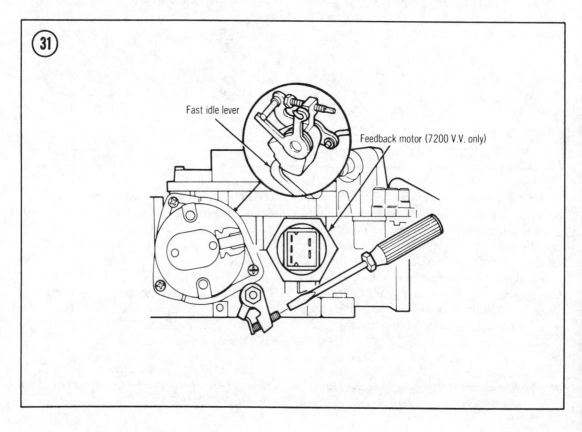

Fast idle lever

Feedback motor (7200 V.V. only)

12. If the vehicle is equipped with air conditioning, turn the air conditioner off.

13. Start engine and ensure it is operating at normal operating temperature and check rpm.

14. If rpm is higher than specified on vehicle emission control decal, loosen the locknut (VOTM carburetors) securing the VOTM to its mounting bracket and adjust VOTM to correct specification. On vehicles equipped with VOTM with dashpot, turn the long VOTM/dashpot mounting bracket adjusting screw to obtain correct specification.

15. If rpm is lower than specified, turn engine off. On VOTM carburetors, loosen the locknut securing the VOTM to its mounting bracket and turn 3 full turns, and tighten locknut. On vehicles equipped with VOTM with dashpot, turn the long VOTM/dashpot mounting bracket adjusting screw 3 full turns. When correct idle is obtained, remove the accessory vacuum lines.

16. On engine equipped with VOTM with dashpot, adjust the curb idle speed to the specifications shown on the vehicle emission decal. This adjustment is made by turning the throttle stop adjusting screw to obtain the specified curb idle rpm. When curb idle is correct, collapse the dashpot plunger by forcing the throttle linkage against the plunger and measure distance between plunger and throttle lever pad. Adjust to specifications.

17. On engines equipped with VOTM only, adjust the curb idle speed to the specifications shown on the vehicle emission decal. This adjustment is made by turning the throttle stop adjusting screw to obtain the specified curb idle rpm.

NOTE
*After the curb idle speed is adjusted, the accelerator pump lever lash preload must be adjusted. Refer to **Figure 32** for Steps 18-20.*

18. Push down nylon nut on top of the accelerator pump rod to decrease linkage clearance.

19. Turn nylon nut clockwise to obtain a 0.010-0.030 in. clearance between top of accelerator pump stem and accelerator pump lever.

20. Turn the accelerator pump rod counterclockwise one full turn to set accelerator lever lash preload.

21. Reinstall all equipment, and reconnect all hoses previously disconnected to perform this adjustment.

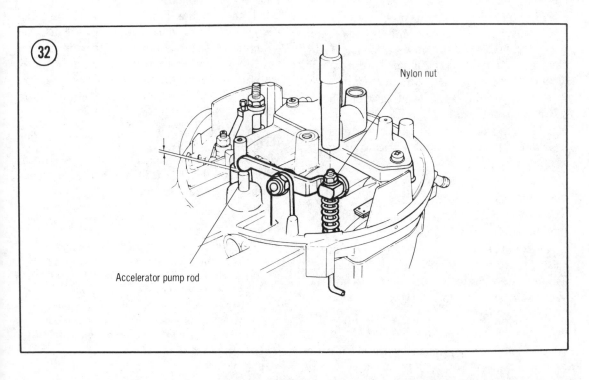

Figure 32 — Accelerator pump rod, Nylon nut

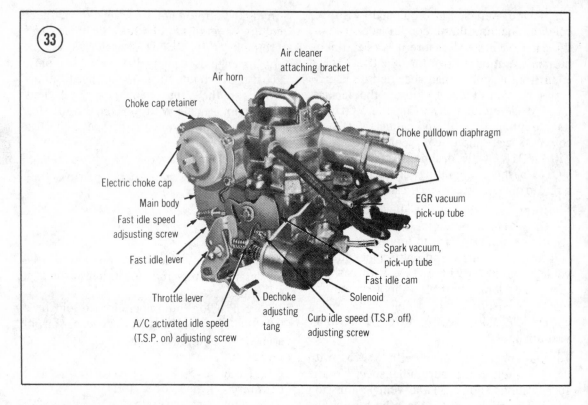

(33)

Air cleaner
attaching bracket

Air horn

Choke cap retainer

Choke pulldown diaphragm

Electric choke cap

EGR vacuum
pick-up tube

Main body

Fast idle speed
adjsusting screw

Spark vacuum,
pick-up tube

Fast idle lever

Fast idle cam

Throttle lever

Dechoke
adjusting
tang

Solenoid

A/C activated idle speed
(T.S.P. on) adjusting screw

Curb idle speed (T.S.P. off)
adjusting screw

MODEL 1946-C CARBURETOR

Fast Idle and Curb Idle
Speed Adjustments

Refer to **Figure 33** for this procedure.

1. Remove the air cleaner and lay it aside on engine. Leave vacuum hoses attached to air cleaner. When checking engine speeds, air cleaner must be installed to carburetor.

2. Set the parking brake and block the wheels so the car cannot roll.

3. Check the throttle and choke linkages for freedom of movement and lubricate or repair as required.

4. Start the engine and warm to normal operating temperature.

5. Connect a tachometer to engine following manufacturer's instructions.

6. Disconnect the fuel evaporative purge valve vacuum hose at the vacuum T-connection. Plug both the open port and the vacuum hose.

7. Remove the EGR vacuum line at the EGR valve, and plug the vacuum line (**Figure 24**).

8. On vehicles equipped with automatic transmission, place the selector in PARK.

9. Ensure that the engine is at normal operating temperature, and that the choke plate is fully opened.

10. Run engine at 2,500 rpm for 15 seconds, then set the throttle linkage so that the fast idle adjustment screw is on the high step of cam and allow engine to run until the rpm has stabilized. Adjust the fast idle to specification on the vehicle emission control information decal.

11. Remove plug from EGR vacuum line, and reconnect vacuum line to EGR valve.

12. Referring to vehicle emission control information decal, place the gear selector lever in specified gear, and measure each required engine speed.

NOTE
Before each engine speed measurement, run engine at 2,500 rpm for 15 seconds in PARK, then allow engine to return to curb idle. Measure curb idle within 2 minutes after engine returns to idle. If engine does not reach specified rpm shown on vehicle emission control information decal, perform Steps 13 and 14.

13. On vehicles equipped with anti-dieseling solenoid with blue plastic connector cap, adjust the curb idle speed to specifications. This adjustment is made by turning the TSP-on adjusting screw until curb idle rpm is reached.

14. On vehicles not equipped with anti-dieseling solenoid, turn the throttle adjusting screw until the specified curb idle rpm is reached. If equipped with dashpot solenoid, collapse the solenoid plunger by forcing the throttle linkage against the plunger. Measure clearance between the plunger and the throttle lever pad with a feeler gauge. Adjust to specification shown on the vehicle emission control information decal.

NOTE
On carburetors equipped with a dashpot solenoid, the plunger to throttle lever pad clearace must be adjusted each time the curb idle speed is adjusted.

15. Reinstall all equipment and reconnect all hoses previously disconnected to perform this adjustment.

Table 1   FUEL STOP CHECKS

Item	Procedure
Engine oil	Check level
Engine coolant	Check level
Windshield washers	Check container level
Battery electrolyte	Check level
Brake fluid	Check level

Table 2   SCHEDULED MAINTENANCE — 1979-1980

Every 5,000 miles or 5 months, whichever comes first

- Change engine oil (1)
- Replace oil filter
- Check ignition timing
- Check carburetor adjustments (A models only)
- Check valve clearance (2800cc A models engines)
- Check and adjust automatic transmission intermediate band and reverse band (if so equipped during severe service only)
- Check air cleaner element and replace if necessary (A models only)
- Check coolant condition and protection (2)
- Check cooling hoses and clamps
- Check brake master cylinder fluid level
- Check power steering pump fluid level

Every 10,000 miles or 10 months, whichever comes first

- Change engine oil (1)
- Replace oil filter
- Check drive belt condition and tension (B schedule)
- Check valve clearance (2800 cc B schedule engines)
- Check carburetor adjustments (B schedule)
- Check clutch pedal free play
- Adjust automatic transmission bands (severe service only)
- Inspect spark plug wires and connections
- Check coolant condition and protection (2)
- Check cooling hoses and clamps

Every 20,000 miles or 20 months, whichever comes first

- Change engine oil (1)
- Replace oil filter
- Check drive belt condition and tension (A schedule)
- Replace spark plugs (A schedule) (3)
- Replace PCV valve (A schedule)
- Check idle fuel mixture (A schedule)
- Check thermactor delay valve (A schedule)
- Check choke system (A schedule)
- Check valve clearance (2800 cc A schedule engines)
- Check clutch pedal free play
- Drain and refill automatic transmission (severe service only)
- Check coolant condition and protection (2)
- Check cooling hoses and clamps

(continued)

Table 2   SCHEDULED MAINTENANCE — 1979-1980 (continued)

Every 30,000 miles or 30 months, whichever comes first
- Change engine oil (1)
- Replace oil filter
- Check drive belt condition and tension (B schedule)
- Replace carburetor air cleaner
- Replace crankcase emission filter
- Replace spark plugs (B schedule) (3)
- Replace PCV valve (B schedule)
- Check idle fuel mixture (B schedule)
- Check choke system (B schedule)
- Check valve clearance (2800 cc B schedule engines)
- Check clutch pedal free play
- Drain and refill automatic transmission (severe service only)
- Inspect exhaust system (including heat shields)
- Inspect brake linings, line, and hoses
- Lubricate front wheel bearings
- Lubricate front suspension
- Lubricate steering linkage
- Check master cylinder reservoir fluid level
- Check coolant condition and protection (2)
- Check cooling hoses and clamps

Every 40,000 miles or 40 months, whichever comes first
- Change engine oil (1)
- Replace oil filter
- Check drive belt tension and adjustment (A schedule)
- Replace spark plugs (A schedule (3))
- Check thermactor delay valve
- Check choke system (A schedule)
- Check valve clearance (2800 cc A schedule engines)
- Check clutch pedal free play
- Drain and refill automatic transmission (severe service only)
- Check coolant condition and protection (2)
- Check cooling hoses and clamps

Every 50,000 miles or 50 months, whichever comes first
- Change engine oil (1)
- Replace oil filter
- Check clutch pedal free play
- Check cooling hoses and clamps
- Replace coolant

1. Turbocharged 2300 cc engines require oil and filter change at 3,000 mile intervals.
2. Change coolant if dirty, or if vehicle is used under severe service conditions.
3. Replace 200 cid California equipped vehicle spark plugs every 50,000 miles or 30 months, whichever comes first.

3

Table 3   NON-SCHEDULED MAINTENANCE — ALL YEARS

The following maintenance operations are not required at definite mileage or time intervals, but should be performed when needed. These services are not covered by the warranty.

Maintenance Operation	Frequency Observation
Check headlamp alignment.	Light beam appears too high or too low while driving with a normal load.
Adjust parking brake	Parking brake does not hold the vehicle on a reasonable grade.
Adjust automatic transmission neutral switch.	Starter will not engage with the shift selector in N (neutral) or P (park): or back-up light does operate.
Lubricate door and hinges.	Doors or hinges bind during opening or closing, or noisy operation.
Check tires, wheel balance and front wheel toe. (Caster and camber are preset at the factory and are not adjustable.)	Poor handling characteristics and/or abnormal tire wear are experienced.
Check windshield washer fluid level — add fluid if required.	If washers do not spray fluid when operated.
Check alternator and regulator output.	Slow engine cranking, hard starting, headlights dim at engine idle speed, early or repeat electrical component failures.
Check operation of lights, horn, turn signals, windshield wipers and washers, instruments, vent system, heater and accessories.	As required.
Check brake warning light operation.	At engine start-up.
Check operation of the clutch.	As required.
Check engine oil level.	As required — at each fuel stop.
Lubricate door locks, door latches, and hood latch.	Difficult to operate or noisy.
Adjust steering gear, steering linkage or front wheel bearings. Check suspension and frame for loose attachments.	Excessive steering wheel play, loose steering system or front wheel shimmy.
Check wheel torque nuts.	Within 500 miles after new vehicle delivery or wheel removal.
Lubricate automatic transmission kickdown linkage.	Abnormal accelerator pressure needed for forced downshift.
Replace windshield wiper blades.	Wiper blades do not clean windshield after windshield and blades have been properly cleaned.
Inspect and rotate tires and check tire pressures.	Poor handling characteristics and/or abnormal tire wear are experienced.
Check and adjust transmission controls and shift operations.	When hard shifting is encountered.

(continued)

Table 3   NON-SCHEDULED MAINTENANCE — ALL YEARS (continued)

Maintenance Operation	Frequency Observation
Check for fuel, coolant, oil or other fluid leaks.	At frequent intervals.
Check seat and should belt buckles, release mechanisms and belt webbing.	As required.
Inspect the exhaust system for broken, damaged, or missing parts.	Excessive noise or smell of fumes

Table 4   RECOMMENDED OIL GRADES

Outside Temperature Range	Oil Viscosity
Single Grade Oils	
− 10 to + 32 degrees F	SAE 10W
+ 10 to + 60 degrees F	SAE 20W-20
+ 32 to + 90 degrees F	SAE 30W
Above + 60 degrees F	SAE 40W
Multigrade Oils	
Below + 32 degrees F	SAE 5W-30*
− 10 to + 90 degrees F	SAE 10W-30
Above + 10 degrees F	SAE 20W-40

*If the vehicle is being operated at sustained highway speeds, the next heavier grade of oil should be used.

Table 5   ENGINE OIL CAPACITY

Engine	Capacity*
2300 cc	4 qt.
2300 cc turbo	4½ qt.
2800 cc	4½ qt.
200 cid	4 qt.
255 cid	4 qt.
302 cid	4 qt.

*Add 1 qt. with filter change. On 2800 cc engines, add ½ qt. on filter change.

Table 6   TRANSMISSION OIL

Transmission*	Oil Grade	Capacity
C3 automatic		
1979	ATF Type F	8 qt.
C4 automatic		
1979	ATF Type F	6 ¾ qt.
1980	Dexron II	8 ½ qt.
Manual transmissions	Standard transmission lubricant	to bottom of filler hole

*Refer to vehicle identification label for transmission type.

Table 7   RECOMMENDED LUBRICANTS

Engine oil	API Service SE or SF
Brake fluid	DOT 3, DOT 4
Latches, body hinges	Polyethylene grease
Lock cylinders	Lock lubricant
Ball-joints	Ball-joint lube
Steering gear	Steering gear lubricant
Rear axle	Ford hypoid gear lube
Non-power steering	Ford hypoid gear lube
Manual transmission	Ford standard transmission fluid
Automatic transmission	Dexron II (1980 C4); Type F (all others)
Front and rear wheel bearings	Long life lubricant
Speedometer cable	Speedometer cable lube
Engine coolant	Ethylene glycol type
Parking brake cable	Polyethylene grease
Drive shaft, universal joints	Multi-purpose grease

Table 8   Valve Adjustment, 1979 2800 cc

Intake Valve Just Opening for Cylinder Number	Adjust both Valves For Cylinder Number
5 3 6 1 4 2	1 4 2 5 3 6

Table 9   SPARK PLUG SPECIFICATIONS

Application	Type	Gap
2300 cc	AWSF-42	0.034 in.
2300 cc turbo	AWSF-32	0.034 in.
2800 cc	AWSF-42	0.034 in.
200 cid	BSF-82	0.050 in
255 cid	ASF-52	0.050 in.
302 cid 49-state	ASF-52 ARF-52	0.50 in. 0.50 in.
California	ASF-52-6 ARF-52-6	0.60 in. 0.60 in.

Table 10   TUNE-UP SPECIFICATIONS

2300 cc	1979	1980
Ignition Timing (BTDC)		
49 state	6(M); 20(A)	(1)
California	6(M); 17(A)	6(M); 12(A)
Turbo (all)	2(M)	6(M)
Curb Idle Speed		
49 state	850(M); 600(A)	(1)
California	850(M); 600(A)	850(M); 750(A)
Turbo (all)	900(M)	850(M)
Fast Idle Speed		
49 state	(1)	(1)
California	1800(all)	2000(all)
Turbo (all)	(1)	1800(M)
2800 cc	**1979**	
Ignition Timing (BTDC)		
49 state	(1)	
California	6(A)	
Curb Idle Speed		
49 state	850(M); 650 (A)	
California	700(A)	
Fast Idle Speed		
49 state	1300(M); 1600(A)	
California	1750(A)	
200 cid		**1980**
Ignition Timing (BTDC)		
49 state		(1)
California		10(A)
Curb Idle Speed		
49 state		700(M); 550(A)
California		600(A)
Fast Idle Speed		
49 state		1600(M); 2000(A)
California		2300(A)

(continued)

3

Table 10   TUNE-UP SPECIFICATIONS (continued)

302 cid	1979	
Ignition Timing (BTDC) 49 state California	12(M); 8 (A) 12(A)	
Curb Idle Speed 49 state California	800(M); 600(A) 600(A)	
Fast Idle Speed 49 state California	2300(M); 2100(A) 1800(A)	
255 cid		**1980**
Ignition Timing (BTDC) 49 state California		6(A) 6(A)
Curb Idle Speed 49 state California		500(A) 550(A)
Fast Idle Speed 49 state California		2000(A) 1800(A)
(M) = Manual transmission (A) = Automatic transmission (1) = Specifications are given on valve cover decal		

NOTE: If you own a 1981 or later model, first check the Supplement at the back of the book for any new service information.

CHAPTER FOUR

ENGINE

A 2300 cc 4-cylinder OHC engine is standard on all vehicles (**Figure 1**). Optional engines are a 2800 cc 60 degree OHV 6-cylinder, available on 1979 models (**Figure 2**); a 200 cid OHV inline 6-cylinder, available on 1980 models (**Figure 3**); a 255 cid OHV V8, available on 1980 models (**Figure 4**); and the 302 cid OHV V8, available on 1979 models (**Figure 5**).

The 2300 cc, 2800 cc, and 200 cid engines use lightweight cast iron cylinder blocks. The crankshaft in the 2300 cc, 255 cid and 302 cid engines is supported on 5 main bearings. The 2800 cc engine uses 4 bearings; the 200 cid engine uses 7 bearings. The 255 cid and 302 cid engines share the same basic design.

An optional turbocharged engine is available for both 1979 and 1980 2300 cc engines. Service procedures for the optional turbocharger will be found in Chapter Twelve. Before servicing a turbocharged engine, refer to Chapter Twelve and review all procedures. Procedures not covered in Chapter Twelve are the same for non-turbocharged 2300 cc engines.

Specifications for the 2300 cc engine are given in **Table 1**, for the 2800 cc engine in **Table 2**, for the 200 cid engine in **Table 3**, for the 255 cid engine **Table 4**, and for the 302 cid engine in **Table 5**.

Tables 1-5 are at the end of the chapter.

ENGINE REMOVAL

To remove any of the engines from the vehicle, perform the following steps.

1. Scribe alignment marks directly onto the underside of the hood around the hood hinges then remove the hood.
2. Disconnect negative cable from battery.
3. Drain the engine coolant and engine oil.
4. Disconnect the upper and lower radiator hoses at the radiator and the engine, then remove the hoses.

> NOTE
> *On vehicles equipped with automatic transmissions, disconnect the transmission oil cooler inlet and outlet lines from the bottom of the radiator. Plug all lines and fittings to prevent loss of transmission fluid, and contamination of lines.*

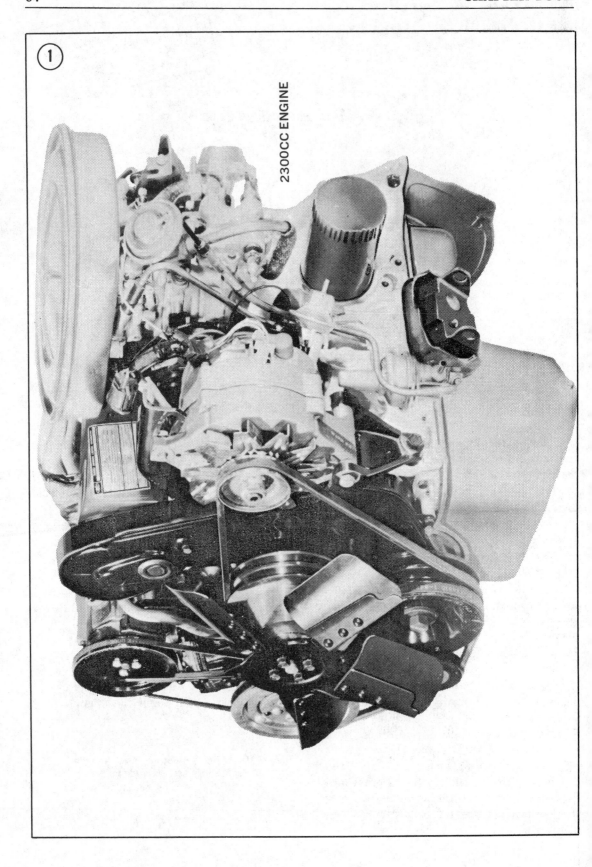

① 2300CC ENGINE

2800CC ENGINE

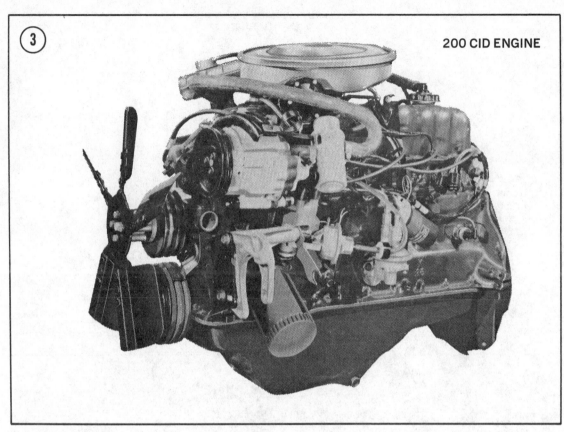

③ 200 CID ENGINE

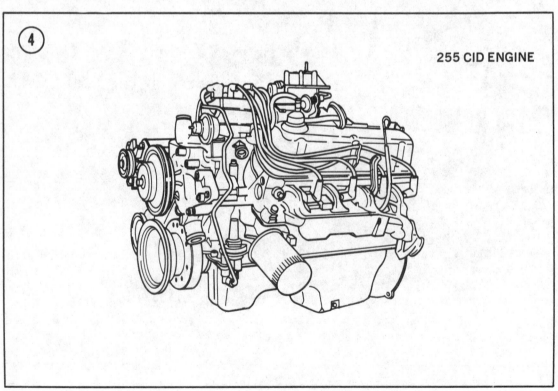

④ 255 CID ENGINE

⑤ 302 CID ENGINE

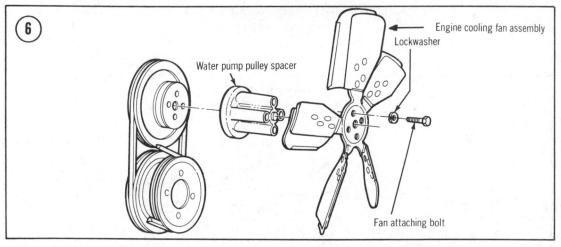

⑥

Water pump pulley spacer

Engine cooling fan assembly

Lockwasher

Fan attaching bolt

5. Remove the radiator shroud as described in Chapter Six. If necessary to gain clearance at the front of the engine, remove the 4 bolts attaching the fan, then remove the fan and spacer-pulley as required (**Figure 6**). On turbocharged engines equipped with electric fan, remove the U-shaped retainer clip from end of motor shaft and remove fan (**Figure 7**).

WARNING
Before working under the hood on 2300 cc turbocharged vehicles, disconnect the electric cooling fan motor. The electric fan is mounted behind the radiator and can be started at any time by an increase in underhood temperature, even with the ignition switch turned off.

6. Remove the air cleaner and intake duct assembly as described in Chapter Five. For 2300 cc vehicles with turbocharger, refer to Chapter Twelve and remove the turbocharger unit.
7. Remove the exhaust manifold shroud from the right side of the engine (2300 cc engines).
8. Disconnect the heater hose.
9. Disconnect the throttle cable from the carburetor (Chapter Five).

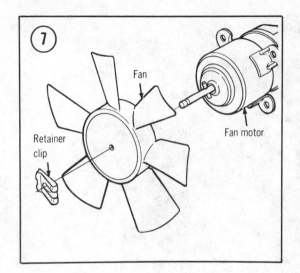

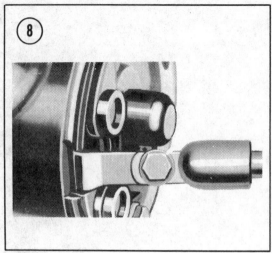

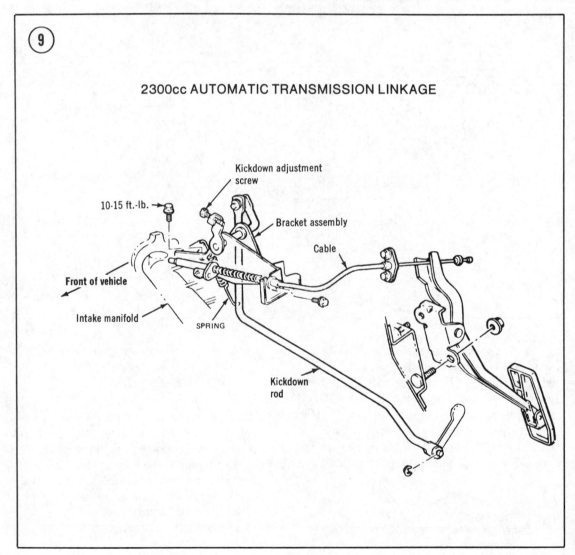

2300cc AUTOMATIC TRANSMISSION LINKAGE

Kickdown adjustment screw

10-15 ft.-lb.

Bracket assembly

Cable

Front of vehicle

Intake manifold

SPRING

Kickdown rod

10. Label and detach the wires and connectors attached to the alternator, then remove the alternator (Chapter Seven).

11. Disconnect the starter cable at the starter terminal and note the position for reinstallation (**Figure 8**).

12. On automatic transmission models, detach the downshift rod at the accelerator cable mounting bracket near the carburetor (**Figure 9** or **Figure 10**).

13. Disconnect all ground wires from the engine block.

14. On models equipped with air conditioning, remove the compressor from its mounting bracket. See **Figures 11-14**.

> *WARNING*
> *Never disconnect refrigerant lines. The refrigerant creates freezing temperatures when it evaporates, and poisonous gases if discharged near an open flame. If disconnecting the refrigerant lines becomes necessary, refer the job to a dealer or an air conditioning specialist.*

4

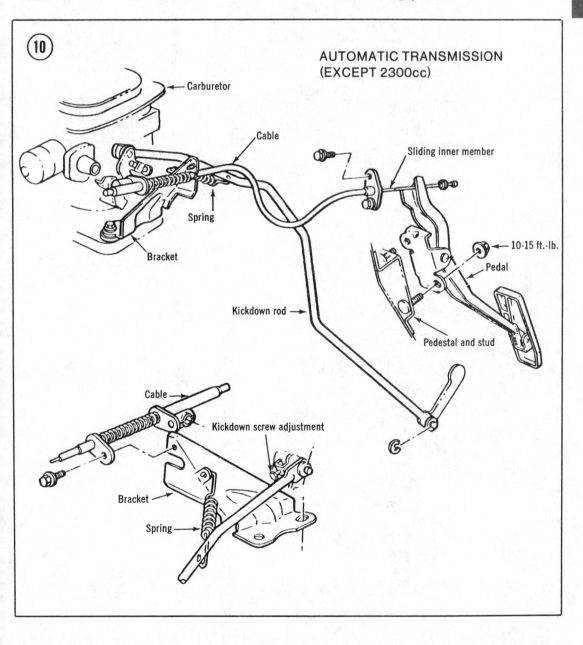

(10)

AUTOMATIC TRANSMISSION
(EXCEPT 2300cc)

Carburetor

Cable

Sliding inner member

Spring

Bracket

10-15 ft.-lb.

Pedal

Kickdown rod

Pedestal and stud

Cable

Kickdown screw adjustment

Bracket

Spring

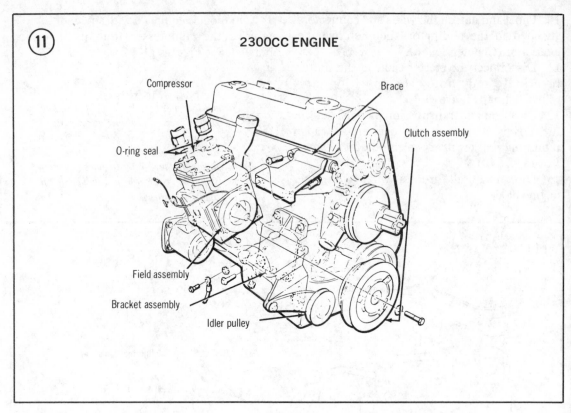

(11) **2300CC ENGINE**

Compressor
Brace
O-ring seal
Clutch assembly
Field assembly
Bracket assembly
Idler pulley

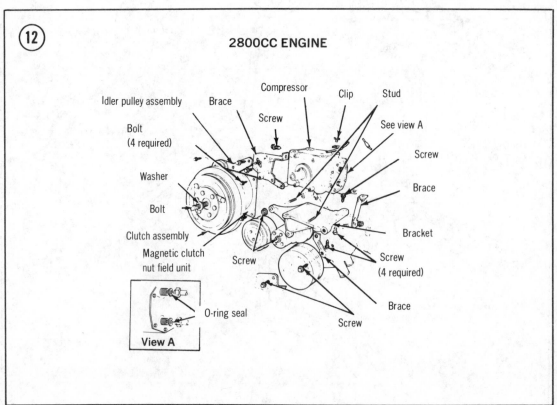

(12) **2800CC ENGINE**

Idler pulley assembly
Brace
Compressor
Clip
Stud
Screw
See view A
Bolt
(4 required)
Screw
Washer
Brace
Bolt
Bracket
Clutch assembly
Magnetic clutch
nut field unit
Screw
Screw
(4 required)
O-ring seal
Brace
View A
Screw

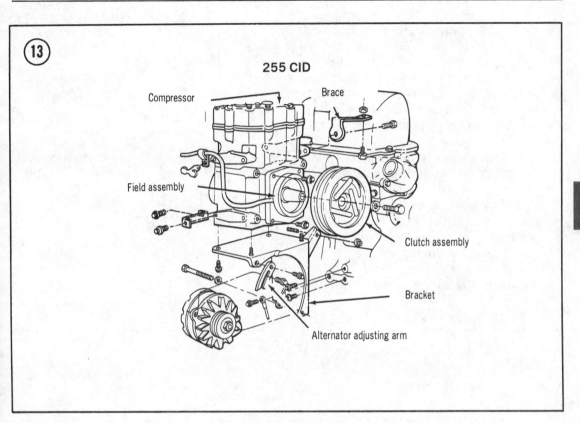

⑬

255 CID

Compressor

Brace

Field assembly

Clutch assembly

Bracket

Alternator adjusting arm

4

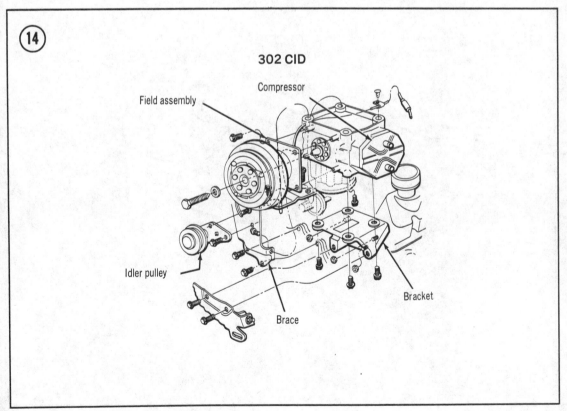

⑭

302 CID

Field assembly

Compressor

Idler pulley

Bracket

Brace

15. On models equipped with power steering, detach the power steering pump bracket from the engine, remove the drive belt from the pump, then position the power steering pump out of the way.

16. On models equipped with power brakes, disconnect the brake vacuum line at the intake manifold (**Figure 15**).

17. Detach the inlet line from the fuel pump then plug the line to prevent siphoning gas from the fuel tank. The fuel pump on the 2800 cc engines is mounted to the engine on the lower left side of the cylinder block. The fuel pump on all other engines is mounted to the left side of the engine front cover.

18. Disconnect the primary (thin) wires and the secondary (thick) wire from the ignition coil.

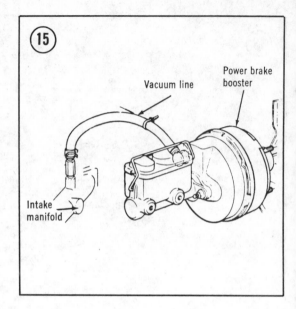

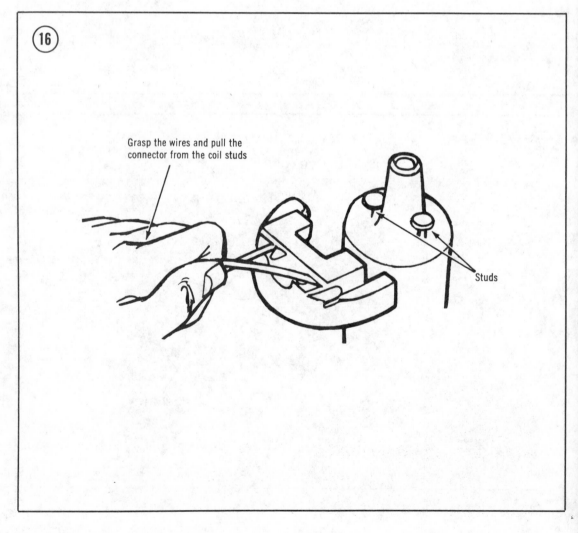

NOTE

*The primary leads are connected to the ignition coil through a special connector. See **Figure 16** for proper removal of this connector.*

19. Disconnect the wires from the oil pressure and water temperature senders.

20. Remove the wiring harness from the engine wire looms and position out of the way of engine removal. Check to ensure that no other external wiring is connected to the engine block.

21. Jack up the front end of the car and place it on jackstands.

22. On manual transmission models, detach the clutch cable from the release lever (Chapter Eight).

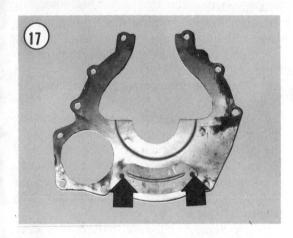

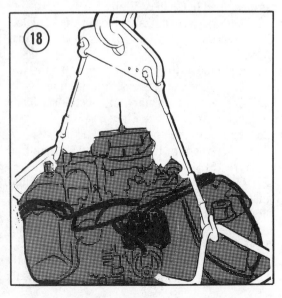

23. On automatic transmission models, disconnect the downshift rod from the downshift control lever (Chapter Eight).

24. Detach the muffler inlet pipe at the exhaust manifold (Chapter Five).

25. Disconnect the transmission oil cooler lines from the retaining clip at the cylinder block, and position them out of the way.

26. Detach the automatic transmission filler tube from the cylinder block and move slightly out of the way.

27. Remove the starter, and position the ground strap (if installed) out of the way.

28. On automatic transmission models, remove the 2 torque converter drain plug access cover bolts and the access cover (**Figure 17**). Detach the torque converter from the flywheel as described in Chapter Eight.

29. Remove the flywheel housing (manual transmissions) or torque converter housing (automatic transmissions) upper attaching bolts.

30. Remove the through bolts from the right and left front engine mounts.

31. Remove the remaining flywheel housing (manual transmission) or torque converter (automatic transmission) bolts.

32. Remove the jackstands and carefully lower the vehicle.

33. Support the front of the transmission and flywheel housing (manual transmissions) or converter housing (automatic transmissions), with a jack to prevent damage to the transmission.

34. Using a hoist, attach a lifting sling or chain to the engine. Lifting hooks are available from dealers to attach to existing lifting brackets on engines to ease engine removal (**Figure 18**).

NOTE

Recheck at this point to be sure nothing will hamper engine removal, and that all accessories, tubes, hoses and wires are positioned out of the way.

35. Raise the engine slightly, then carefully disengage it from the transmission. Carefully remove the engine from the engine compartment, tilting if necessary, to be sure the rear cover plate or other engine components are not damaged.

36. Once the engine is clear of the car, lower it to a suitable support or stand. Secure the engine in the support or stand.

37. Engine removal is now complete. Inspect rubber motor mount insulators for wear or damage, and replace before reinstalling engine if these conditions exist.

ENGINE INSTALLATION

Engine installation is basically the reverse of the removal procedure. Torque specifications are listed at the end of this chapter.

1. Attach an engine lifting sling or chain to the lifting bracket.

2. Lift the engine from the workstand or support, and position above the engine compartment.

3. On manual transmission models, align the clutch disc with the flywheel using an aligning tool as shown in **Figure 19**. These can be bought at many auto parts stores.

4. Lower the engine into the engine compartment, making sure the exhaust manifolds are aligned with the muffler inlet pipes (Chapter Five). On 200 cid engines, make sure the guide pins in the block engage the holes in the flywheel housing.

5. On vehicles with automatic transmissions, start the converter pilot shaft into the crankshaft pilot bearing.

6. On vehicles with manual transmissions, start the transmission mainshaft into the clutch disc. It may be necessary to roll the car in gear, or rotate the crankshaft to properly align the transmission shaft splines and the clutch disc splines. However, *the crankshaft should always be rotated in the clockwise direction as viewed from the front of the engine.* If the transmission shaft will not enter the flywheel splines after having been installed into the clutch disc, rotate the crankshaft further (clockwise) until the transmission shaft is fully seated.

7. Install the flywheel housing (or coverter housing) upper attaching bolts, making sure the rear cover plate pilot studs engage the housing, then remove the jack from under the transmission.

8. Install the through bolts in the right-front and left-front motor mounts and torque to specification.

9. Remove the hoist and lifting sling or chain.

10. Raise the front end of the car and place it on jackstands.

11. Install the remaining flywheel housing (or converter housing) attaching bolts, then torque all attaching bolts to specifications.

12. On 200 cid engines with manual transmissions, install the clutch equalizer shaft and arm bracket. Connect the clutch retracting spring.

13. On 200 cid engines, install the engine left and right mount to the underbody bracket.

14. Connect muffler inlet pipes to the exhaust manifold(s), and torque nuts to specifications.

15. On vehicles with automatic transmissions, attach the converter to the flywheel, and tighten the bolts to specifications (Chapter Eight). Install the converter access cover and attaching bolts.

16. Install the starter and attaching bolts, and tighten to specification.

17. Connect the plugged fuel line from the gas tank to the inlet of the fuel pump.

18. Connect the transmission filler tube to the cylinder block.

19. Install the transmission oil cooler lines in the cylinder block retaining clips.

20. Connect the automatic transmission downshift rod to the downshift control lever at the transmission. Position the top end of the rod for connection at the carburetor. See **Figure 9** or **Figure 10**.

21. Attach the clutch cable to the release lever as described in Chapter Eight.

22. Remove jackstands and lower the vehicle.

23. Replace the wiring harness in its original position.

24. Reconnect the wires to the oil pressure sender and the water temperature sender.

25. Connect the primary and secondary leads to the ignition coil. See **Figure 16**.

26. Connect the power brake booster (if installed) vacuum line to the intake manifold (**Figure 15**).

27. On vehicles equipped with power steering, install the drive belt, power steering pump, bracket, and bracket attaching bolts. Adjust drive belt tension as described in Chapter Seven.

28. On vehicles equipped with air conditioning, install the compressor in its

mounting bracket, being careful not to crimp or unnecessarily bend the refrigerant lines. Install the drive belt and adjust for proper tension as described in Chapter Seven. See **Figures 11-14** for compressor installation.

29. On vehicles equipped with automatic transmissions, connect the top end of the downshift rod to the carburetor throttle linkage as shown in **Figure 9** or **Figure 10**.

30. Connect the throttle cable to the throttle linkage at the carburetor after the downshift rod is installed.

31. Connect heater hoses in their original position.

32. Install the alternator and attaching bolts to the alternator bracket. Referring to the wire labeling attached during engine removal, reconnect the alternator, then install the drive belt and adjust as described in Chapter Seven.

33. On 2300 cc engines, install the exhaust manifold shroud.

34. Install the air cleaner and intake duct assembly.

35. Install the spacer, fan, radiator, and shrouding.

36. Connect the upper and lower radiator hoses. If the vehicle is equipped with

automatic transmission, connect the 2 transmission oil cooler lines to the oil cooler at the bottom of the radiator.

37. Refill and bleed the cooling system as described in Chapter Six.

38. Fill the engine crankcase with the proper grade and quality of oil (Chapter Three).

39. If the vehicle is equipped with automatic transmission, perform *Transmission Downshift Linkage Adjustment* (Chapter Eight). If the vehicle is equipped with manual transmission, perform *Clutch Adjustment* (Chapter Eight).

40. Make sure that no hoses, ground straps, or wiring have been inadvertently left disconnected. On turbocharged vehicles, connect the electric cooling fan wiring if so equipped.

41. Connect the negative cable to the battery. Operate the engine at fast idle while checking gaskets and hose connections for leaks. Continue to operate the engine at this speed until normal operating temperature is obtained.

NOTE
Check oil level in the automatic transmission while the engine is idling. Top up as necessary to prevent damage to the engine.

42. Check ignition timing and carburetor adjustment. Refer to Chapter Three.

43. Install the hood in accordance with the scribe marks made during removal procedure.

44. Road test the vehicle for proper operation.

OVERHAUL SEQUENCE

The following sequences are basic outlines that tell how much of the engine needs to be removed and disassembled to perform specific types of service. The sequences are designed to keep engine disassembly to a minimum, thus avoiding unnecessary work. The major assemblies mentioned in these sequences are covered in detail under their own individual headings within this chapter, unless otherwise noted.

To use these sequences, first determine what type of engine service you plan to do (a valve job, for example), then turn to the sequence that covers that type of service.

Perform a specific step within a sequence, turn to the heading covering the major assembly or component mentioned in that step, and perform the removal and inspection procedures contained under that heading. To reassemble or install, reverse the sequences, performing the installation or assembly procedures contained under that major heading.

Decarbonizing or Valve Service

1. Remove the exhaust and intake manifolds (Chapter Five).
2. On 2800 cc, 255 cid, and 302 cid engines, remove the valve rocker assembly. On 2300 cc and 200 cid engines, remove the rocker arms.
3. Remove the cylinder head.
4. Remove and inspect the valves. Inspect valve seats, grinding when necessary. Inspect valve guides and ream as needed.
5. Assemble by reversing Steps 1-4.

Ring and Connecting Rod Service

1. Perform Steps 1-3 for valve service.
2. Remove the oil pan.
3. Remove the oil pump.
4. Remove the pistons together with the connecting rods.
5. Remove the piston rings, then remove the pistons from the connecting rods.
6. Inspect the pistons, piston pins, and connecting rods. Replace as needed.
7. Assemble by reversing Steps 1-6.

General Overhaul

1. Remove the engine from the car as described previously.
2. Remove the motor mounts (front and rear).
3. Remove the fuel pump, carburetor, and intake and exhaust manifolds (Chapter Five).
4. Remove the fan, spacer (if installed), pulley, water pump, and thermostat (Chapter Six).
5. Remove the distributor (Chapter Seven).
6. Remove the oil pressure and water temperature senders.
7. On 2300 cc engines, remove auxiliary shaft.
8. Remove the PCV valve (Chapter Three).
9. Remove the oil filter.

10. On 2800 cc, 255 cid, and 302 cid engines, remove the valve rocker assembly. On 2300 cc and 200 cid engines, remove the rocker arms.
11. Remove the cylinder head.
12. Remove the camshaft.
13. Remove the oil pan.
14. Remove the oil pump.
15. Remove the pistons together with the connecting rods.
16. Remove the flywheel.
17. Remove the crankshaft and main bearings.
18. Assemble by reversing Steps 1-17.

ROCKER ASSEMBLY

Rocker Arm Cover Removal/Installation

1. Remove the air cleaner and intake duct assembly (Chapter Five).
2. Disconnect the spark plug wires from the spark plugs and the wire looms (Chapter Three).

NOTE
Steps 3-5 apply to 2300 cc and 200 cid engines only.

3. Disconnect or move the choke heater hose out of the way (2300 cc). Remove the accelerator control cable bracket (200 cid).
4. Disconnect, or move out of the way, any other hoses preventing removal of the rocker arm cover.
5. Remove the rocker arm cover attaching bolts, then remove the rocker arm cover and gasket. **Figure 20** shows removal of 2300 cc engine rocker arm cover and gasket. The 200 cid engine is similar.

NOTE
Steps 6-9 apply to 2800 cc, 255 cid, and 302 cid engines only.

6. Remove emission control equipment and hoses, as necessary, to remove rocker arm cover.
7. Disconnect the spark plug wires from the plugs by twisting and pulling the molded cap only. Remove the spark plug wires from the retainers on top of the rocker arm covers, then position the wires out of the way (Chapter Three).

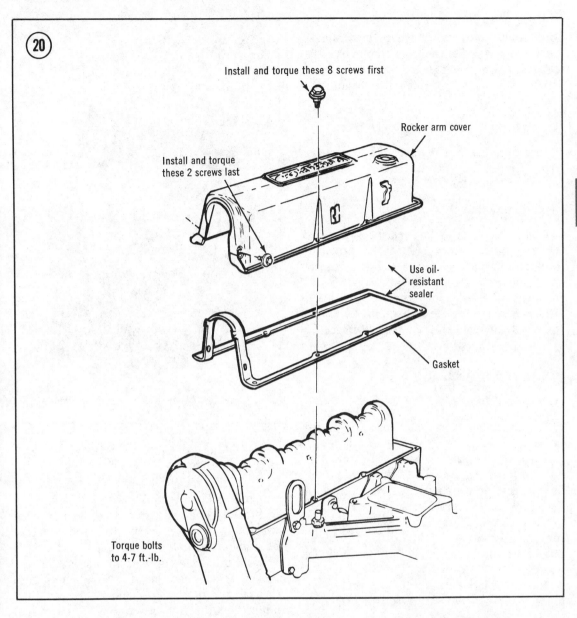

Install and torque these 8 screws first

Rocker arm cover

Install and torque these 2 screws last

Use oil-resistant sealer

Gasket

Torque bolts to 4-7 ft.-lb.

4

8. If the carburetor throttle linkage interferes with removal, disconnect the throttle cable from the linkage, then disconnect the linkage mounting bracket (Chapter Five).

9. Remove the rocker arm cover attaching screws, then remove the cover and gasket.

10. Installation is the reverse of these steps. Use a new gasket, coated on the rocker arm cover side with oil-resistant gasket sealer. On 2300 cc engines, tighten rocker arm cover attaching bolts to specifications as shown in **Figure 20**. On 200 cid engines, tighten rocker arm cover attaching bolts to specifications. On

2800 cc, 255 cid, and 302 cid engines, tighten rocker arm cover attaching screws to specifications. Before installing spark plug caps onto spark plugs, coat inside of cap with silicone grease.

Rocker Arm
Removal/Installation (2300 cc)

1. Remove the rocker arm cover as described earlier.

2. Turn the engine by hand until the low side of the camshaft contacts the rocker arm being removed.

3. Using a valve spring compressor such as Ford tool T74P-6565-B (**Figure 21**) compress the valve spring just enough to remove the rocker arm over the valve lash adjuster.

NOTE
A pry bar may be used for rocker arm removal if a special tool is not available.

4. Installation is the reverse of these steps. Apply Lubriplate to all friction surfaces (including valve stem tips).

Inspection (2300 cc)

1. Check rocker arms for wear or scuffing at the valve stem end. Also check camshaft contact surface and pivot (valve lash adjuster) end. Replace rocker arm if visibly worn.
2. Check valve lash adjusters for wear or other visible damage as described in *Camshaft Inspection* later in this chapter. Replace as required.

Rocker Assembly and
Pushrod Removal/Installation
(2800 cc and 200 cid)

1. Remove the rocker arm cover as described earlier.
2. Remove the rocker arm shaft retaining bolts by loosening each bolt 2 turns at a time, in sequence, until all bolts are free of the cylinder heads. See **Figure 22** for 2800 cc engines or **Figure 23** for 200 cid engines. Then lift the rocker assembly and oil baffle (mounted below the rocker assembly) off the cylinder head.
3. Lift the pushrods out of their bores. Make a holder to keep the pushrods in order. The pushrods must be reinstalled in the same bores from which they were removed.
4. Installation is the reverse of these steps. Apply white grease such as Lubriplate to both ends of the pushrods, the valve stem tips, and the rocker arm ends (contact points). Tighten rocker arm shaft retaining bolts to specifications, then adjust valve clearance (2800 cc). See Chapter Three.

Disassembly (2800 cc and 200 cid)

1. Referring to **Figure 24** for 2800 cc engines and **Figure 25** for 200 cid engines, remove the

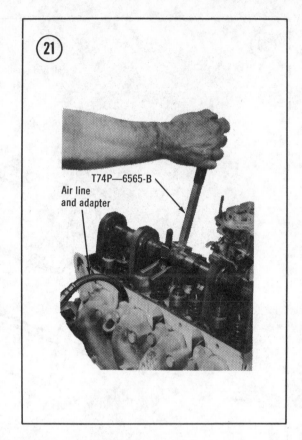

spring washer and pin from one end of the rocker arm shaft.
2. Slide the rocker arms, rocker arm shaft supports, and spring off the shaft. Be sure to mark the individual parts in the sequence in which they were removed, so that the parts can be reassembled in their original positions.
3. Drill a hole in the plug in one end of the rocker arm shaft. Insert a long steel rod through the drilled hole and knock the plug out of the other end of the shaft. Remove the drilled plug from the shaft by using the steel rod from the opposite end of the shaft.

Inspection (2800 cc and 200 cid)

1. Clean all parts in solvent and make sure all oil passages in the rocker arms, supports and shaft are clear.
2. Check the pushrods for wear or damage, particularly at the ends. Check the pushrods for straightness by rolling on a piece of glass. A clicking sound will be heard if the pushrod is bent even slightly. Replace as required.

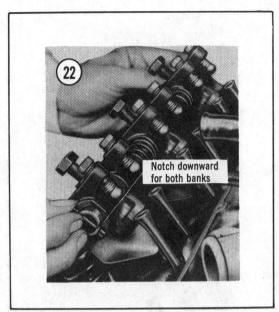

Notch downward for both banks

NOTE
If you have a dial gauge, rotate the pushrods between accurate centers (V-blocks) with the dial gauge contacting the center of the pushrod. Replace the pushrod if runout (eccentricity) is greater than 0.020 in.

3. Check the rocker arm shafts and rocker arms for signs of seizure or excessive wear. Clearance between rocker arms and rocker arm shafts should be 0.001-0.0035 in. Maximum permissible clearance is 0.006 in. This measurement should be made with a feeler gauge.

4. Check the valve stem contact surface on the rocker arm for wear. Replace worn rocker arms. Do not attempt to smooth rocker arms bores or contact surfaces.

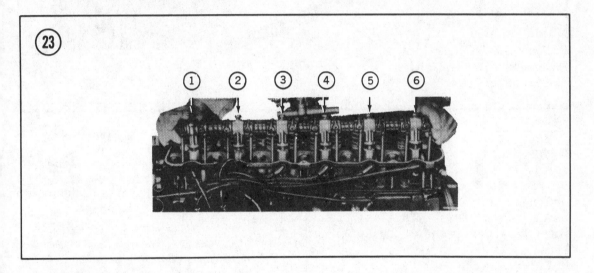

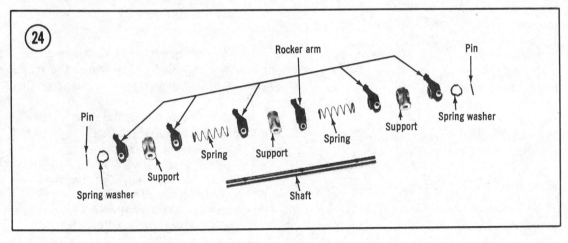

Rocker arm — Pin — Spring washer — Support — Spring — Support — Shaft — Support — Spring — Support — Spring — Pin — Spring washer

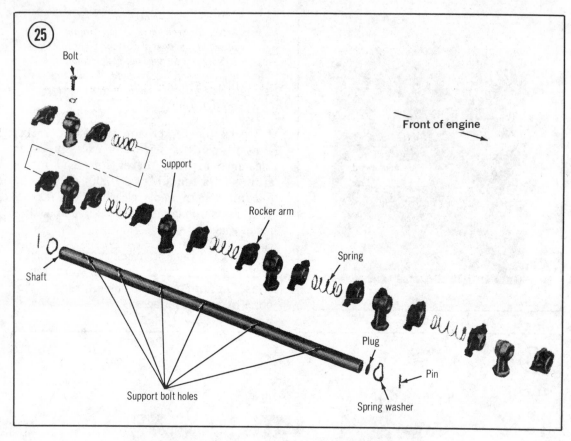

Bolt

Front of engine

Support

Rocker arm

Spring

Shaft

Plug

Pin

Support bolt holes

Spring washer

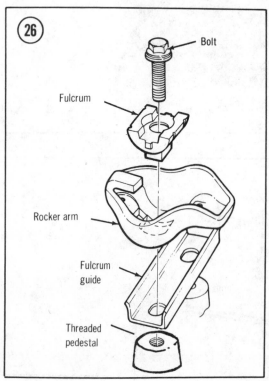

Bolt

Fulcrum

Rocker arm

Fulcrum guide

Threaded pedestal

Assembly (2800 cc and 200 cid)

Refer to **Figure 24** (2800 cc) or **Figure 25** (200 cid) for the following procedure.

1. Tap new plugs into the ends of the rocker arm shaft.

NOTE
Apply Lubriplate or equivalent to the rocker arm shaft and friction surfaces of all other components of the rocker assembly, before assembly, to provide initial lubrication.

2. Install a spring washer and pin in one end of the rocker arm shaft, then install the rocker arms, supports, and springs in their original location.

3. Install the pin and spring washer in the other end of the rocker arm shaft.

CAUTION
*On 2800 cc engines, the notch in the front face of the rocker arm shaft must point downward when the rocker assembly is in a normal position (**Figure 22**) to ensure that the rocker arm shaft oil holes are*

properly oriented. On 200 cid engines, the oil holes in the shaft must be installed facing downward. If the rocker arm shafts are not properly oriented, lubrication will be cut off from the rocker assembly, resulting in rocker assembly failure.

Rocker Arm Removal/Installation (255 cid and 302 cid)

1. Remove the valve rocker arm cover as described earlier.
2. Turn the engine by hand until the low side of the camshaft contacts the rocker arm being removed.
3. Loosen and remove the rocker arm bolt, fulcrum seat, rocker arm, and fulcrum guide (**Figure 26**).

4. Installation is the reverse of these steps. Apply Lubriplate to all rocker arm and fulcrum seat friction surfaces before installation.

Inspection (255 cid and 302 cid)

Check the pad at the valve end of the rocker arm for scuffing or abnormal wear. If the pad is grooved, replace the rocker arm.

Valve Lash Adjuster Removal/Installation (2300 cc)

1. Remove rocker arms as discussed earlier in this chapter.
2. Lift out the valve lash adjuster from its bore (**Figure 27**).

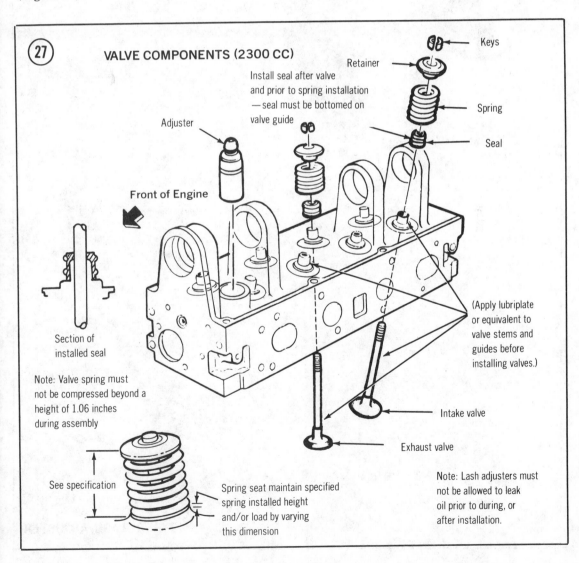

(27) **VALVE COMPONENTS (2300 CC)**

Keys

Retainer

Install seal after valve and prior to spring installation —seal must be bottomed on valve guide

Spring

Adjuster

Seal

Front of Engine

(Apply lubriplate or equivalent to valve stems and guides before installing valves.)

Section of installed seal

Note: Valve spring must not be compressed beyond a height of 1.06 inches during assembly

Intake valve

Exhaust valve

See specification

Spring seat maintain specified spring installed height and/or load by varying this dimension

Note: Lash adjusters must not be allowed to leak oil prior to during, or after installation.

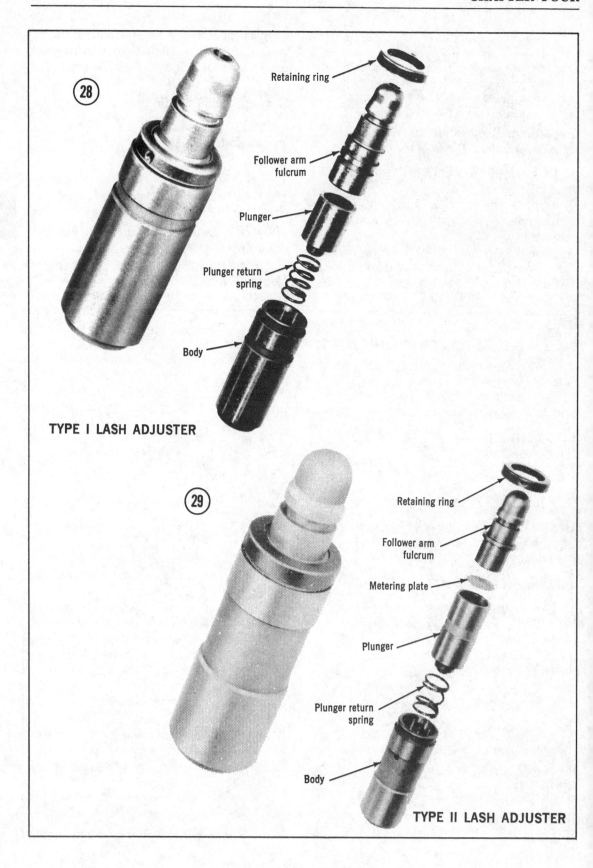

TYPE I LASH ADJUSTER

TYPE II LASH ADJUSTER

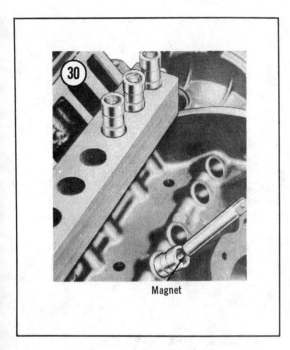

Magnet

3. Installation is the reverse of these steps. Apply Lubriplate to all friction surfaces (including valve stem tips).

Valve Lash Adjuster Inspection (2300 cc)

On 1979 models, 2 types of hydraulic valve adjusters are used (**Figure 28** and **Figure 29**). On 1980 models, only the Type 1 lash adjuster (**Figure 28**) is used. Testing of the valve lash adjusters requires a special test fixture and should be referred to a dealer.

Valve Tappet Removal/Inspection

1. *2800 cc and 200 cid engines only:* Remove the cylinder head as discussed later in this chapter.
2. *255 cid and 302 cid engines only:* Remove the rocker arms as discussed earlier in this chapter. Remove the pushrods and install in order in a holder so that pushrods may be installed in the same bores from which they were removed.
3. Using a magnet, as shown in **Figure 30**, remove the valve tappets from their bores and place them in a rack so that they may be reinstalled in their original locations.
4. Installation is the reverse of these steps. Apply Lubriplate to tappets and tappet bores, pushrod ends, valve stem tips, fulcrum seat,

and rocker arms before installation. Adjust valve clearances (2800 cc) after installation. See Chapter Three.

Valve Tappet Inspection

1. Throughly clean tappets in solvent.
2. Check the tappets for wear or scores. Replace any tappets that show these conditions.
3. Check the bottom surface of each tappet to make sure it is slightly convex. If the bottom (camshaft contact) surface is worn flat, the tappet may be reused in its original location and with the original camshaft.

CYLINDER HEAD

Some of the following procedures must be performed by a dealer or competent machine shop, since they require special knowledge and expensive machine tools. Others, while possible for the home mechanic, are difficult or time-consuming. A general practice among those who do their own service is to remove the cylinder head, perform disassembly except valve removal, and take the head to a machine shop for inspection and service. Since the cost is relatively low in proportion to the required effort and equipment, this may be the best approach even for more experienced owners.

Removal (2300 cc and 200 cid)

1. Drain the cooling system.
2. Remove the air cleaner and intake duct assembly (Chapter Five).
3. On 2300 cc engines, remove the exhaust manifold (Chapter Five). On 200 cid engines, detach the muffler inlet pipe at the exhaust manifold. Pull the inlet pipe down and position out of the way.
4. *2300 cc engines only:* Remove the intake manifold, together with the carburetor and EGR valve (if so equipped). See Chapter Five.
5. *200 cid engines only:* Disconnect the fuel inlet line at the fuel filter hose (Chapter Five).
6. Remove the rocker arm cover as described earlier in this chapter.
7. Remove the front cover and timing belt (2300 cc) or timing cover and chain (200 cid) as discussed later in this chapter.

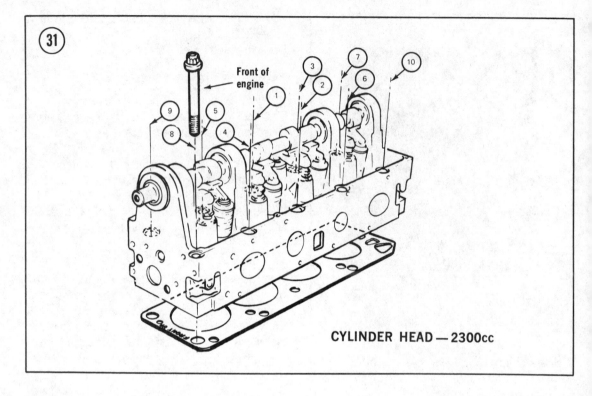

Front of
engine

CYLINDER HEAD — 2300cc

8. Loosen the cylinder head bolts in the sequence given in **Figure 31** (2300 cc) or **Figure 32** (200 cid). The bolts should be loosened in 2 progressive stages to prevent warping of the cylinder head.

9. Lift the cylinder head away from the block, remove the cylinder head gasket, then place the cylinder head on a soft surface to prevent scratching or otherwise damaging the cylinder head-to-engine block mating surface. Do not lay the cylinder head on its mating surface.

Installation (2300 cc and 200 cid)

1. Be sure the cylinder head and engine block mating surfaces, and the cylinder bores are clean and free of deposits, sealant, or other debris. Check all visible oil passages in the cylinder head and engine block for cleanliness.

2. Install a new cylinder head gasket. Never reuse an old head gasket. Do not use gasket sealer on the gasket.

3. Place the cylinder head on the block and align with the head gasket. Put the head bolts into their mounting holes and insert through the head gasket into the engine block.

NOTE
If the cylinder head and head gasket are difficult to align, make guide pins by cutting the heads off 2 cylinder head mounting bolts. Install the guide pins in 2 diagonally opposite mounting holes in the engine block.

4. Tighten the cylinder head mounting bolts in the sequence given in **Figure 31** (2300 cc) or **Figure 32** (200 cid). Tighten the head bolts in 2 steps. First, each bolt should be tightened in the sequences indicated to 60 ft.-lb. (2300 cc) or 55 ft.-lb. (200 cid). Second and final torques should be 80-90 ft.-lb (2300 cc) or 70-75 ft.-lb. (200 cid).

5. Perform Steps 1-7 of the *Removal* procedure in reverse order to complete installation.

Removal
(2800 cc, 255 cid, and 302 cid)

1. Remove the air cleaner and intake duct assembly (Chapter Five).

2. Remove the intake manifold and carburetor as an assembly (Chapter Five).

3. Remove the rocker arm covers as described earlier in this chapter.

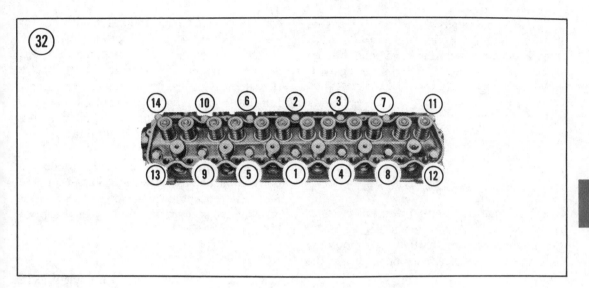

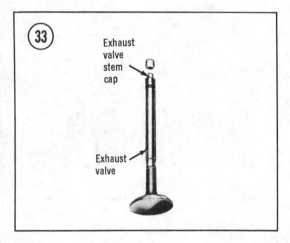

4. *255 cid and 302 cid only:* If the left cylinder head is to be removed on a vehicle equipped with air conditioning or power steering, refer to *Engine Removal* procedures described earlier in this chapter for disconnection, repositioning, or removal of the accessories. If the right-hand cylinder head is to be removed, remove the alternator mounting bracket bolt and spacer, and the ignition coil.

5. Remove the exhaust manifold (Chapter Five).

6. *2800 cid only:* Remove the rocker assembly and pushrods as described earlier in this chapter.

7. Loosen the rocker arm stud nuts so that the rocker arms can be rotated to the side (away from the pushrods). Remove the pushrods, and install in order in a holder (as described earlier in this chapter). Remove the exhaust valve stem caps (**Figure 33**).

8. Remove the cylinder head attaching bolts in 2 stages to prevent warping of the cylinder head. Discard the cylinder head gasket.

> *NOTE*
> *If the cylinder head is difficult to remove, try turning the engine over by hand with the spark plugs installed. The compression in the cylinders should force the cylinder head loose.*

9. Once the cylinder head is removed from the engine, lay it on a soft surface so as not to damage the cylinder head-to-engine block mating surface.

Installation
(2800 cc, 255 cid, and 302 cid)

1. Clean the cylinder head mating surfaces and the engine block, intake manifold, and valve rocker arm cover surfaces to which the cylinder head mounts. Be sure that the cylinder bores are clean, and check all visible oil and water passages for cleanliness.

2. Install a new cylinder head gasket(s). Never reuse an old head gasket. Do not use gasket sealer on head gaskets. Left and right cylinder head gasket are different on 2800 cc engines. Ensure that gaskets are installed with the marked words "FRONT" and "TOP" toward the front of the car and the top of the cylinder block.

3. *2800 cc only:* Install cylinder head on engine block by sliding carefully over guide studs (**Figure 34**), then inserting head bolts through their mounting hole, the cylinder head gasket, and into the engine block.

NOTE
If the head(s) and gasket are difficult to align, make guide pins by cutting the heads off 2 cylinder head mounting bolts. Install the guide pins in 2 diagonally opposite mounting holes in the engine block.

4. *255 cid and 302 cid only:* Install cylinder head over the dowel pins in the engine block, then insert head bolts through their mounting hole, the cylinder head gasket, and into the engine block.

5. Tighten the head bolts in the sequence given in **Figure 35** (2800 cc) or **Figure 36** (255 cid and 302 cid). Cylinder head bolts should be tightened in 3 steps. First, each bolt should be tightened in the sequences indicated to 40 ft.-lb. (2800 cc) or 50 ft.-lb. (255 cid and 302 cid). Second, each bolt should be tightened to 51 ft.-lb. (2800 cc), or 65 ft.-lb. (255 cid and 302 cid). Third, and final torques, should be 65-80 ft.-lb. (2800 cc) or 65-72 ft.-lb. (255 cid and 302 cid).

6. Clean the pushrods in solvent and blow out the oil passages in the pushrods with compressed air. Check end of the pushrods for nicks, grooves, roughness, or excessive wear. Check all pushrods for straightness, as described under *Rocker Assembly* or *Rocker Arm* description earlier in this chapter. Apply Lubriplate or equivalent to both ends of each pushrod before installing in original position. On 255 cid and 302 engines, install the exhaust valve stem caps (**Figure 33**).

7. The remainder of the installation procedure is accomplished by performing Steps 1-7 of the *Removal* procedure in reverse order. After installation, perform the tune-up as described in Chapter Three.

Inspection

1. Check the cylinder head for coolant leaks before attempting cleaning.

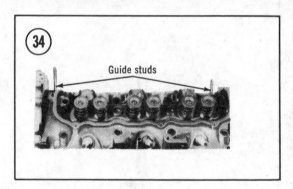

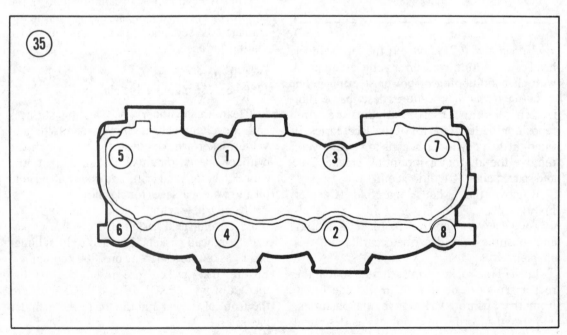

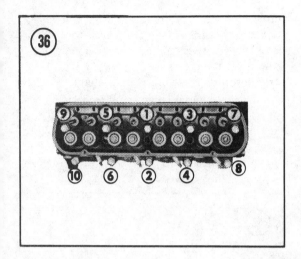

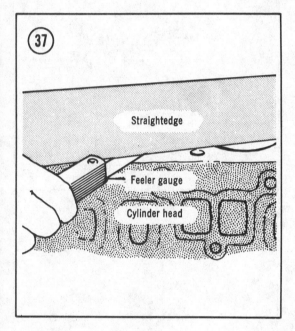

Straightedge

Feeler gauge

Cylinder head

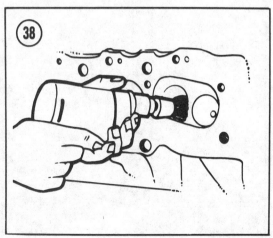

2. Clean the cylinder head throughly in solvent. While cleaning, check for cracks or other visible damage. Look for corrosion or foreign material in oil or water passages. Clean the passages with a stiff spiral wire brush, then blow them out with compressed air.

3. **Check the cylinder head-to-block mating surface for flatness. Place an accurate straightedge along the surface. If there is any gap (cylinder head warp) between the straightedge and the cylinder head, measure the gap with a feeler gauge (Figure 37). Measure lengthwise and diagonally across the head. Maximum permissible head warp is 0.003 in. for any 6 in. surface of the cylinder head length, or 0.006 in. overall. Have the head milled by a dealer or competent machine shop if cylinder head warp is excessive. Maximum of 0.010 in. may be removed from the head.**

4. Check the condition of cylinder head guide studs (if installed) and replace damaged or excessively worn studs.

Decarbonizing

1. Without removing the valves, remove all deposits from the combustion chambers, intake ports, and exhaust ports. This operation should be done with a wire brush dipped in solvent (**Figure 38**).

2. After carbon is removed from the combustion chamber and ports, clean the entire cylinder head in solvent.

3. Using the same method, clean away all carbon on the piston tops.

> *CAUTION*
> *Do not attempt to remove the carbon ridge on the cylinder wall at the top of the cylinder bore.*

VALVES AND VALVE SEATS

Valve Removal

1. On 2800 cc and 200 cid engines, remove the rocker assembly. On 2300 cc, 255 cid, and 302 cid engines, remove the individual rocker arms. See procedures earlier in this chapter.

2. Remove cylinder head as described earlier.

3. On 255 cid and 302 cid engines, remove the exhaust valve step caps.

4. Compress each valve spring with a valve spring compressor (**Figure 39**). Remove the retainer locks (valve keepers), then release tension on the valve spring. Remove the valve spring retainers, spring, and valve. **Figure 40** shows valve components for 2800 cc engines; other engine valve components are similar.

5. Label all parts for reassembly.

> *CAUTION*
> *To prevent valve guide damage, remove any burrs from valve stem grooves before removing the valves through the combustion chamber.*

Valve and Valve Guide Inspection

1. Clean the valves with a wire brush and solvent. Discard cracked, warped, or burned valves.

2. Measure valve stem diameter at top, center, and bottom for wear. Use a micrometer or have the measurements done by a dealer or competent machine shop. Also measure the length of each valve, and the maximum diameter of each valve head. See **Figure 41** and **Tables 1-5** for the valve measurements.

3. If valve stem ends are grooved or nicked only slightly, have them ground smooth by a dealer or competent machine shop. No more than 0.010 in. may be ground from the valve stem ends.

4. If valve faces are only slightly pitted, they may be refaced by a dealer or competent machine shop. The edge of the valve head

must not be less than 1/32 in. thick after refacing (**Figure 41**).

5. Remove all carbon and varnish from valve guides with a stiff spiral wire brush.

> *NOTE*
> *The next step assumes that all valves have been measured and are within specifications. For valves with worn stems, proceed to Step 7.*

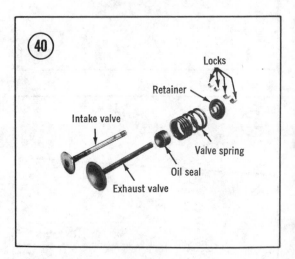

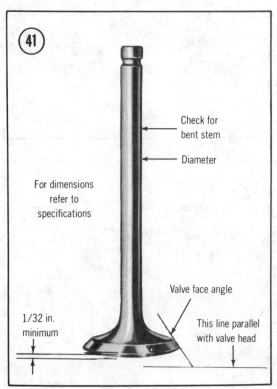

6. Insert each valve into the guide from which it was removed. Hold valve slightly off its seat and rock it back and forth in a direction parallel with the rocker arms. This is the direction in which the greatest wear normally occurs. If the valve rocks more than slightly, the valve guide is worn and should be reamed for an oversize valve stem as described later in this chapter.

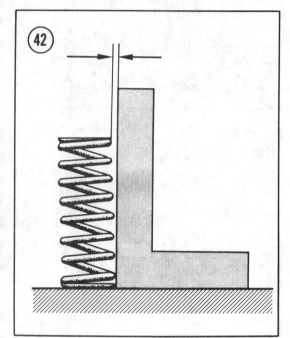

7. If there is any doubt about valve guide condition after performing Step 6, measure the valve guide at top, center, and bottom with a small bore gauge. Compare the valve guide measurements with the specifications listed at the end of this chapter, to determine stem-to-guide clearance. If clearance is excessive, have valve guides reamed for oversized valve stems.

8. Check the valve springs for deformation with a square (**Figure 42**). Replace any spring more than 5/64 in. out-of-square.

9. Test the valve springs under load with a spring tester (**Figure 43**). Compare with specifications at end of chapter. Replace any springs that do not meet specifications.

10. Inspect valve seats. If worn or burned, they must be reconditioned. Valve seat reconditioning should be done by a dealer or competent machine shop, although the procedure is described later in this section.

Valve Guide Reaming

Valve guides on all engines are integral with the cylinder head. When guides are worn, they must be reamed to accept a valve with an oversize stem. This is a precise job that should be left to a dealer or competent machine shop. **Figure 44** shows a valve guide being reamed.

Valve Seat Reconditioning

This job is best left to a dealer or competent machine shop. The following procedure is provided in the event you are not near a dealer. Refer to **Figure 45**.

1. Grind all valve seats to 45 degree angle. Remove only enough stock to clean up the seat or eliminate runout.

2. Measure the width of the refaced seat. Compare refaced seat width with specifications at the end of this chapter. If seat width is above the maximum, remove stock from the top or bottom of the seat as necessary. Use a 30 degree stone for the top of the valve seat, and a 60 degree stone for the bottom.

3. Grind all valves to a 44 degree angle. Do not lap out the interference fit of valves and seats after grinding.

4. Check the fit of each valve to its seat. To do this, coat the valve face with Prussian blue marking fluid. Insert the valve in the guide, then rotate the valve under light pressure against its seat. If the valve seats properly, the blue will transfer evenly to the valve face.

Valve Installation

1. Coat the valve stems with oil and install them in the cylinder head.

2. Install the valve stem seals, springs, and spring retainers. Compress the valve springs and install the keepers. Ford tool T73-P-6571-A can be used to install the valve stem seals on all engines (**Figure 46**). If Ford tool is not available, a screwdriver may be used to carefully push the seal down over the valve stem until the seal contacts the top of the valve guide. **Figure 47** shows the valve guide installation procedure for 2300 cc engines.

Valve Spring, Retainer, Seal, and Lock Replacement (Cylinder Head Installed)

A defective valve spring, retainer, seal, or lock can be replaced without removing the cylinder head, as long as the valve is undamaged. An air compressor capable of at least 140 psi is required, as well as a spark plug hole adapter for the compressor (**Figure 21**).

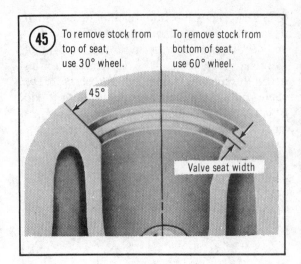

To remove stock from top of seat, use 30° wheel.

To remove stock from bottom of seat, use 60° wheel.

45°

Valve seat width

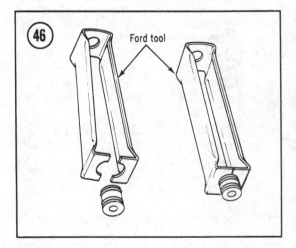

Ford tool

The compressor can be rented from an equipment rental dealer if you do not have one.

1. On 2800 cc and 200 cid engines, remove the rocker assembly. On 2300 cc, 255 cid, and 302 cid engines, remove both rocker arms (intake and exhaust) from the cylinder being worked on.

2. Attach spark plug hole adapter and the air compressor to the spark plug hole (**Figure 21**). Apply a minimum of 140 psi air pressure to the cylinder.

3. Compress the valve spring and remove the retainer locks, spring retainer and valve spring as described under *Valve Removal*. Discard the valve stem seal. Wrap tape or a rubber band around the end of the valve stem so the valve will not fall through the guide into the cylinder.

4. Slide the valve up and down to make sure it does not bind in the valve guide. If the valve does bind, the cylinder head will have to be removed for repairs.

5. If a defective valve stem seal is to be replaced, press on the new seal as described under *Valve Installation.*

6. Install the valve spring retainer, and retainer locks as described under *Valve Installation.* Install the rocker assembly (2800 cc and 200 cid) or intake and exhaust rocker arms (2300 cc, 255 cid, and 302 cid).

FRONT COVER, CAMSHAFT BELT, DRIVE SPROCKETS, FRONT SEALS, AND AUXILIARY SHAFT (2300 CC)

Front Cover and Camshaft Belt Removal/Installation

1. Remove the fan shroud, fan, spacer and fan pulley (Chapter Six).

2. Remove the 4 front cover attaching bolts (**Figure 48**), then remove the front cover. With chalk, draw an arrow on the camshaft belt, in the normal direction of rotation (clockwise). If the belt is to be reinstalled, it must move in the same direction.

3. Turn the engine over in a clockwise direction by using a wrench on the crankshaft pulley bolt, until the number one piston is at top dead center on the compression stroke.

> *CAUTION*
> *Turn the engine over only in its normal direction of rotation (clockwise as viewed from the front of the car). Reversing the direction of rotation may cause the camshaft belt to slip on the sprockets, disturbing the engine timing.*

When the crankshaft is correctly positioned, the 0 degree (TDC) mark on the vibration damper will align with the timing pointer on the front of the engine (**Figure 49**), the distributor rotor (or armature) will point as described in Chapter Seven, and the camshaft timing pointer will align with the timing mark on the camshaft drive sprocket.

4. Loosen the camshaft belt tensioner adjustment bolt (**Figure 50**), then position the tension adjusting tool, as shown in **Figure 51**, on the tension spring roll pin, and release the belt tensioner as far as possible. Tighten the adjustment bolt to hold the belt tensioner in the fully released position.

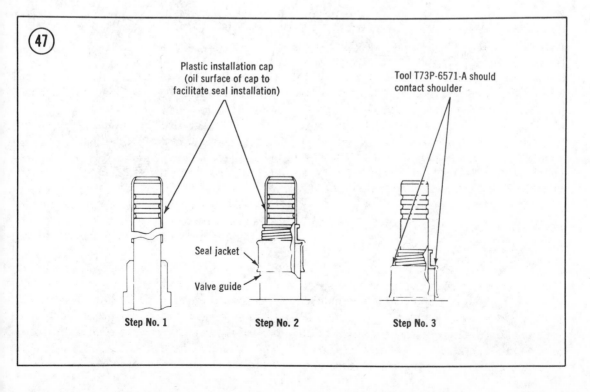

(47)

Plastic installation cap
(oil surface of cap to
facilitate seal installation)

Tool T73P-6571-A should
contact shoulder

Seal jacket

Valve guide

Step No. 1   Step No. 2   Step No. 3

5. Remove the crankshaft pulley attaching bolt, the crankshaft pulley and damper, and the camshaft timing belt guide (**Figure 48**).

6. Remove the camshaft belt and inspect it for wear, missing teeth or other damage. Replace the belt if any of these conditions exist.

CAUTION
Do not bend or twist the belt or use sharp instruments on it when removing it. Also keep grease and oil out of contact with it; they will cause it to deteriorate and render it unserviceable. Also do not rotate any of the camshaft belt sprockets while the belt is removed. Rotating any of the sprockets will upset engine timing.

7. Make sure the timing marks on the vibration damper and front of the engine, the camshaft sprocket and timing pointer, and the distributor rotor (armature) and body are properly aligned, as described in Step 3. See **Figure 49**.

8. Install the camshaft belt on the 3 drive sprockets (camshaft sprocket, auxiliary shaft sprocket and camshaft sprocket) and the camshaft belt tensioner. Align the belt fore and aft on the sprockets.

9. Loosen the camshaft belt tensioner adjustment bolt (**Figure 50**) to allow the tensioner to move against the belts.

10. Remove the spark plugs, then rotate the crankshaft 2 complete revolutions in the normal direction of rotation to remove slack from the camshaft belt.

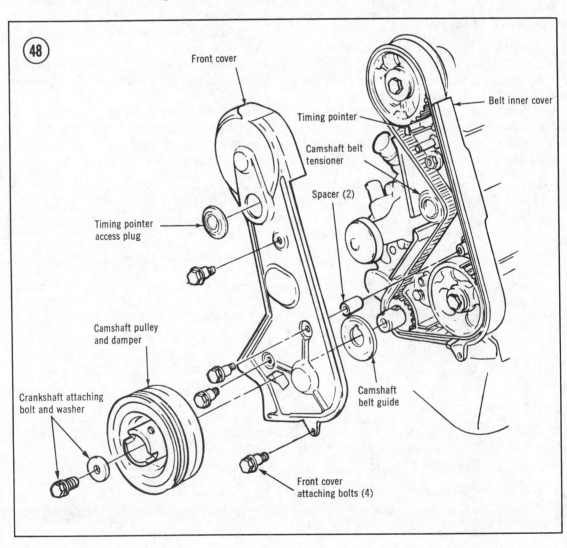

48

Front cover
Timing pointer
Belt inner cover
Camshaft belt tensioner
Timing pointer access plug
Spacer (2)
Camshaft pulley and damper
Crankshaft attaching bolt and washer
Camshaft belt guide
Front cover attaching bolts (4)

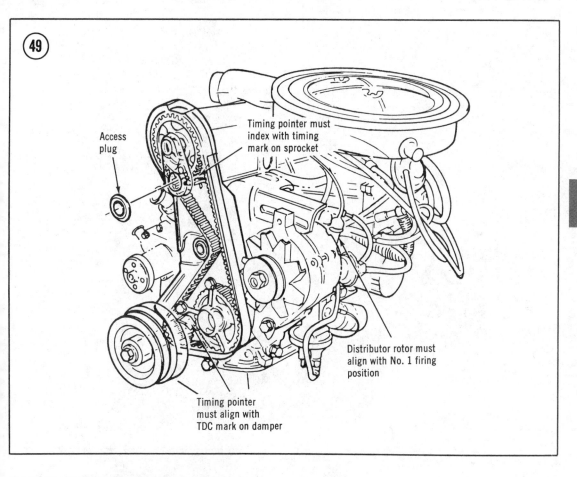

Access plug

Timing pointer must index with timing mark on sprocket

Distributor rotor must align with No. 1 firing position

Timing pointer must align with TDC mark on damper

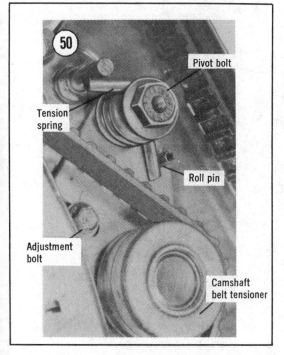

Pivot bolt

Tension spring

Roll pin

Adjustment bolt

Camshaft belt tensioner

CAUTION
The spark plugs must be removed prior to rotating the engine to prevent the camshaft belt from jumping sprocketed teeth during engine rotation.

11. Tighten the camshaft belt tensioner adjustment and pivot bolts (**Figure 50**) to specifications (end of chapter).

12. Recheck alignment of timing marks as described earlier.

13. Install the camshaft belt guide, the crankshaft pulley and damper, and the crankshaft pulley bolt (**Figure 48**). Tighten the crankshaft pulley bolt to specifications (end of chapter).

14. Install the front cover and tighten the 4 front cover attaching bolts to specification (end of chapter).

15. Check the ignition timing as described in Chapter Three, and adjust as needed.

Belt tensioner
adjusting tool
T74P-6254-A

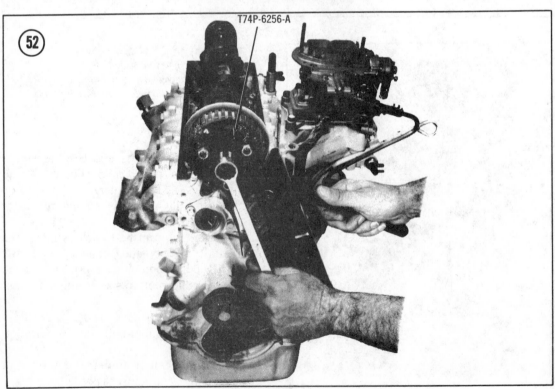

T74P-6256-A

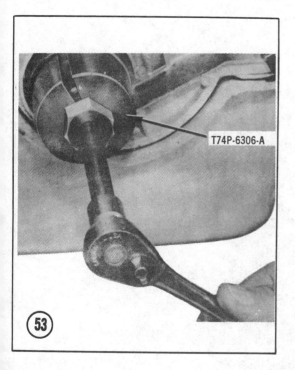

T74P-6306-A

(53)

Sprocket and Front Seal Replacement

Replacement procedures for the camshaft drive sprocket, the auxiliary shaft drive sprocket, the crankshaft sprocket, and the camshaft, auxiliary shaft, and cylinder front cover seals are provided in the following steps.

1. Remove the front cover and camshaft belt as described earlier.

2. If the camshaft, auxiliary shaft or crankshaft drive sprockets are to be removed, special, multipurpose tools are required to remove the sprockets from the shafts. **Figure 52** shows removal of the camshaft sprocket. The same tool and method are used to remove the auxiliary shaft sprocket. **Figure 53** shows removal of the crankshaft sprocket.

Installation of the sprocket is basically the reverse of this procedure. However, the threaded insert in the sprocket puller must be removed during camshaft sprocket or auxiliary shaft sprocket installation (**Figure 54**), to

4

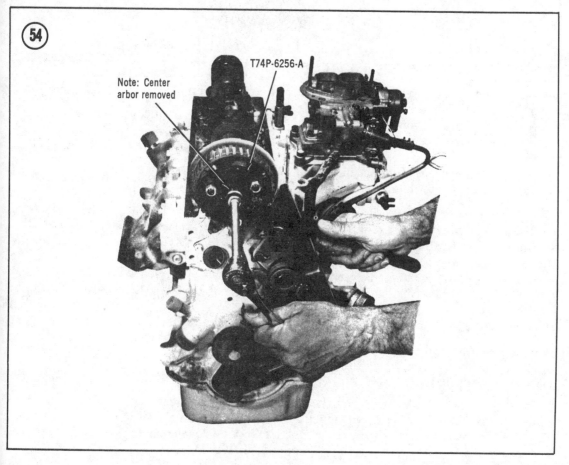

(54)

Note: Center arbor removed

T74P-6256-A

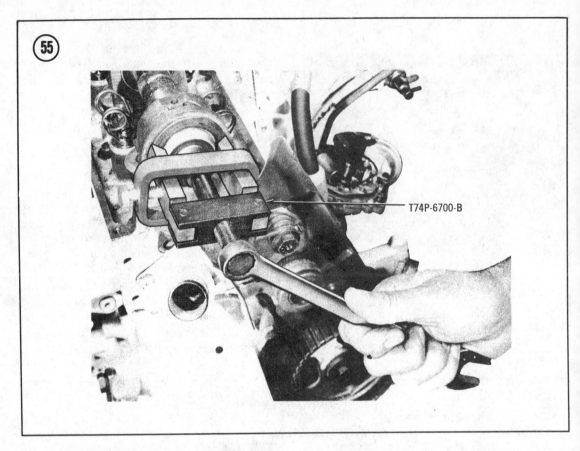

T74P-6700-B

allow the center attaching bolt to be installed and tightened. (See the specifications at the end of this chapter for proper torque values.) No special tool is required to install crankshaft sprocket. Always use a new attaching bolt when replacing the camshaft sprocket, or wrap the old bolt threads with Teflon tape.

3. To replace the camshaft seal or auxiliary shaft seal, use a common seal removal tool as shown in **Figure 55**. Be sure that the jaws of the tool are gripping the thin edges of the seal very tightly before operating the jack-screw portion of the tool. If a seal removal tool is not available, insert a screwdriver into the seal as shown in **Figure 56**, then pry out the seal.

4. Install new camshaft or auxiliary shaft seals by tapping in gently with a hollow drift having the same outer diameter as the seal.

5. To remove the cylinder front cover seal, install the seal removal tool as shown in **Figure 57**, then remove and install the seal as described earlier.

Auxiliary Shaft Removal/Installation

1. Remove the front cover and camshaft belt as described earlier.
2. Remove the auxiliary shaft sprocket as described earlier.
3. Remove the distributor (Chapter Seven) and fuel pump (Chapter Five).
4. Remove the 3 attaching bolts securing the auxiliary shaft cover to the block (**Figure 58**).
5. Remove the 2 attaching screws securing the auxiliary shaft retaining (thrust) plate to the engine block then remove the retaining plate.
6. Carefully withdraw the auxiliary shaft from the engine block, being careful that the fuel pump eccentric and distributor drive gear are not allowed to touch the auxiliary shaft bearing surfaces.
7. Examine the auxiliary shaft bearings for obvious wear or damage. If the bearing is visibly worn or defective, remove it with an internal puller such as Ford tool T58L-101-A and a slide hammer such as Ford tool T59L-100-B (**Figure 59**).

NOTE
If the engine is out of the car and you do not have the necessary tools, take the engine block to a dealer or competent machine shop for auxiliary shaft bearing replacement.

8. Installation is the reverse of these steps. If the auxiliary shaft bearings were removed, install the new bearings using a hollow drift of suitable size or Ford tool T57T-7003-A.

Tighten all attaching hardware to specifications (end of chapter).

FRONT COVER, TIMING GEARS, AND FRONT OIL SEAL (2800 CC)

1. Remove the oil pan as described later under *Oil Pan Removal.*

2. Drain the cooling system. Remove the radiator, shrouding, fan and water pump (Chapter Six).

3. Remove the air conditioner compressor and bracket as described under *Engine Removal* (if vehicle is so equipped).

4. Remove the alternator and drive belt as described under *Engine Removal.*

5. Remove the crankshaft pulley using a suitable puller (**Figure 60**).

6. Remove the front cover retaining bolts, and remove the cover.

7. Examine the front cover plate gasket for leaks or other obvious damage. If the front cover plate gasket needs replacement, remove the 2 attaching bolts (**Figure 61**), then the front cover plate.

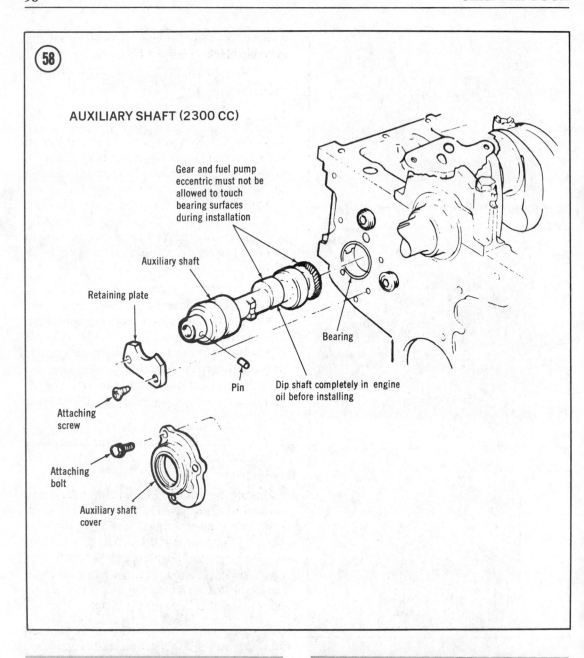

58

AUXILIARY SHAFT (2300 CC)

Gear and fuel pump
eccentric must not be
allowed to touch
bearing surfaces
during installation

Auxiliary shaft

Retaining plate

Bearing

Pin

Dip shaft completely in engine
oil before installing

Attaching
screw

Attaching
bolt

Auxiliary shaft
cover

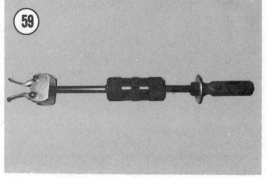

59

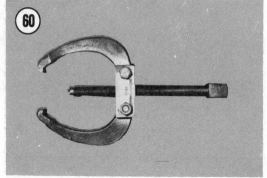

60

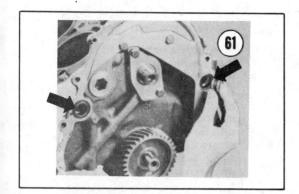

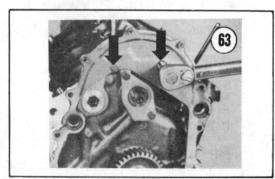

Tool T74P-6019-A

8. Remove the 2 guide sleeves from the cylinder block (**Figure 61**), and examine the seal rings on each guide sleeve for leakage or other damage. Replace if necessary.

Front Cover Installation

1. Clean all mating surfaces of gasket material. If the front cover plate gasket is to be replaced, apply sealing compound to the gasket surfaces on the cylinder block and the back side of the front cover plate. Position the gasket and front cover plate on the cylinder block (**Figure 62**), and temporarily install 4 front cover screws to position and hold the gasket and cover plate in place.

2. Install and tighten the 2 cover plate attaching bolts (**Figure 63**), then remove the 4 front cover attaching screws that were temporarily installed.

3. Install the guide sleeves in the cylinder block with the chamfered side of the sleeve toward the front cover (**Figure 61**). Do not use gasket sealer on the guide sleeves or their seal rings.

4. Apply sealing compound to the front cover gasket surface, then position the gasket on the front cover.

5. Install the front cover on the engine and start all retaining screws 2-3 turns. Center the front cover by inserting Ford tool shown in **Figure 64** into the crankshaft pulley opening in the front cover, or by inserting a hollow drift of approximate size to center the front cover on the crankshaft. Tighten front cover attaching bolts to specifications (end of chapter).

6. Install crankshaft pulley and tighten attaching bolt to specification (end of chapter).

7. Install the oil pan as described in *Oil Pan Installation* later in this chapter.

8. Install the air conditioning compressor (if so equipped), the alternator and drive belts, the water pump, fan, shroud and radiator, and any other parts previously removed to provide clearance. Adjust drive belt tension (Chapter Six).

9. Ensure that all cooling system hoses are properly installed, then fill the cooling system with coolant (Chapter Six).

4

Timing Gear Removal

1. Remove the front cover as described previously.

2. Check the camshaft end play as described later in this chapter, and replace the thrust plate and spacer rings, as required, to achieve the proper end play. See specifications (end of chapter).

3. Remove the camshaft sprocket retaining bolt and washer (**Figure 65**), then slide the sprocket off the camshaft. Make sure not to lose the camshaft key.

4. Using a gear puller (**Figure 66**), remove the crankshaft timing sprocket, then remove the key from the crankshaft (**Figure 65**).

Timing Gear Installation

1. Install the key in the camshaft (if removed previously), then align the keyway in the camshaft sprocket with the key in the camshaft and slide the sprocket onto the camshaft. Make sure that the sprocket seats tightly against the camshaft spacer (**Figure 67**).

2. Position the key in the crankshaft (**Figure 65**) then align the crankshaft sprocket keyway and install the sprocket as shown in **Figure 68**.

3. Install the front cover and accessory equipment as described in *Front Cover Installation.*

Front Oil Seal Replacement (In Chassis)

1. Remove the radiator, shroud, fan, crankshaft pulley and water pump drive belt, as described in *Front Cover Removal.*

NOTE
It is not necessary to remove the front cover to replace the front oil seal.

2. Using the Ford tool shown in **Figure 69**, remove the front cover oil seal.

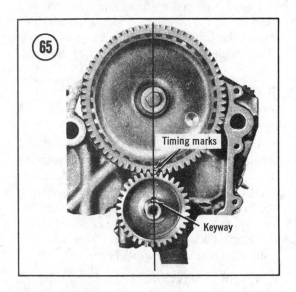

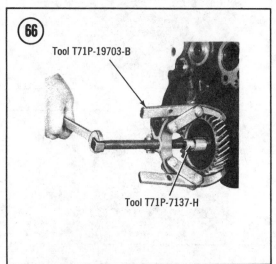

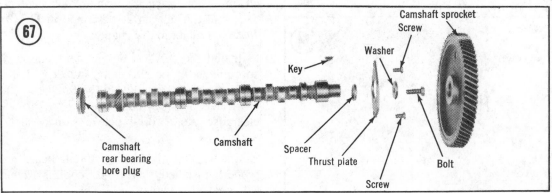

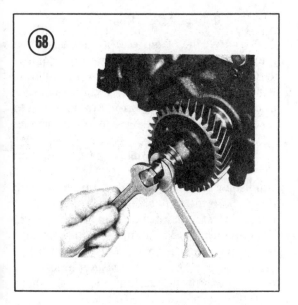

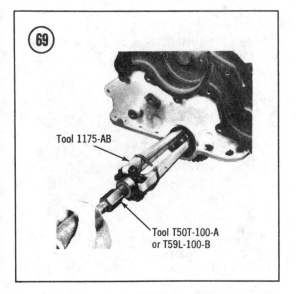

3. Before installing, coat the new front cover oil seal with Lubriplate or equivalent. Using the Ford tool shown in **Figure 70**, or a hollow drift of the same diameter as the seal, slide the new oil seal onto the crankshaft. Drive the oil seal onto the crankshaft, using the drift or special tool, until the seal butts against the front cover.

4. The remainder of the installation is the reverse of removal.

Front Oil Seal Removal/Installation (Front Cover Removed)

1. Support the front cover, as shown in **Figure 71**, to prevent damage to the cover while driving out the front seal.

2. Drive the seal out of the front cover using the Ford tool shown in **Figure 71**, or a hollow drift of the same diameter as the seal.

3. Before installing, coat the new oil seal with Lubriplate or equivalent. Carefully drive the new oil seal into the front cover using the Ford tool shown in **Figure 72**, or a hollow drift of the same diameter as the oil seal.

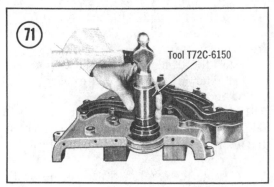

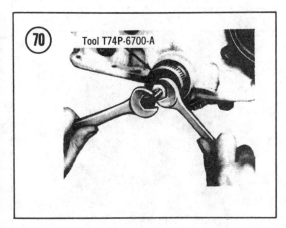

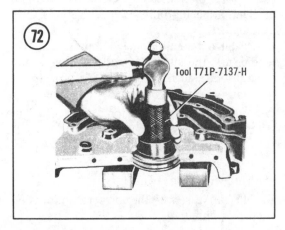

FRONT COVER, TIMING CHAIN, AND FRONT OIL SEAL (200 CID)

Front Cover Removal

1. Drain the crankcase.
2. Drain the cooling system. Remove the radiator, shrouding, fan, and pulley (Chapter Six).
3. Remove the air conditioner compressor and bracket as described under *Engine Removal* (if vehicle is so equipped).
4. Remove the alternator and drive belt as described under *Engine Removal*.
5. Remove the crankshaft damper using a suitable puller (**Figure 60**).
6. Remove the front cover retaining bolts from the front cover and oil pan, then pry the top front cover away from engine block using a thin bladed knife to cut gasket flush with the cylinder block front face.

Front Cover Installation

1. Clean all mating surfaces of gasket material. Apply sealing compound to the gasket surfaces on the cylinder block and the back side of the front cover plate.
2. Install the front cover on the engine and start all retaining screws 2-3 turns. Center the front cover by inserting Ford tool T61K-6019-A (**Figure 73**) into the crankshaft damper opening in the front cover. Tighten the front cover attaching bolts to specifications (end of chapter).
3. Lubricate the crankshaft damper hub with Lubriplate, then install the crankshaft damper. Tighten attaching bolts to specifications (end of chapter).
4. Install air conditioning compressor (if so equipped), the alternator and drive belts, the fan, shroud and radiator, and any other parts previously removed to provide clearance.
5. Adjust drive belt tension as described in Chapter Six.
6. Ensure that all cooling system hoses are properly installed, then fill the cooling system with proper coolant (Chapter Six).
7. Fill crankcase with the correct amount of oil (Chapter Three).

Timing Chain and Gear Removal

1. Remove the front cover as described previously to gain access to the timing gears.
2. Check timing chain deflection as follows. Rotate the crankshaft in a counterclockwise direction (viewed from front of vehicle) to take up slack on the left side of the timing chain.
3. Measure distance from a reference point on the cylinder block (**Figure 74**). Rotate the crankshaft in the opposite direction to take up the slack in the right side of the timing chain. Force the left side of the timing chain toward the reference mark, and measure the distance to the reference mark once again. The difference between the 2 measurements is the timing chain deflection. Timing chain deflection must not exceed 0.500 in.

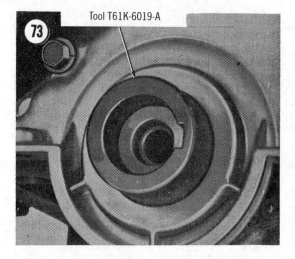

Tool T61K-6019-A
73

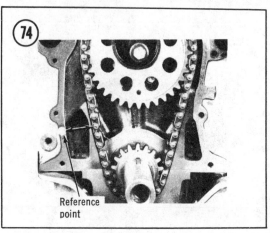

74

Reference point

(75)

4. Turn the engine by hand until the timing marks on the camshaft sprocket and crankshaft sprocket are aligned as shown in **Figure 75**.

5. Remove the camshaft sprocket attaching bolt and washer.

6. Slide both sprockets and the timing chain forward and remove as an assembly.

7. Installation is the reverse of these steps. Be sure that the timing marks on the camshaft and crankshaft sprockets are aligned as shown in **Figure 75**. Oil the timing chain after installing on the camshaft and crankshaft sprockets with SAE motor oil. Tighten the camshaft sprocket attaching bolts to specifications (end of chapter).

Front Oil Seal Removal/Installation

1. Remove the front cover as described earlier.

2. Support the front cover around the area of the oil seal. Drive the seal out of the front cover with the Ford tool shown in **Figure 76**, or a suitable drift.

3. Coat the new front oil seal with grease, turn the front cover over, and drive in the new seal using the Ford tool shown in **Figure 76** or a suitable drift.

4. Install the front cover as described earlier.

FRONT COVER, TIMING CHAIN AND DRIVE SPROCKETS, AND FRONT OIL SEAL (255 CID AND 302 CID)

Front Cover Removal

1. Drain the cooling system, then remove the radiator, shroud, fan, spacer, and radiator hoses (Chapter Six).

2. Remove the air conditioner drive belt and idler pulley bracket (if so equipped), alternator drive belt, power steering drive belt and power steering pump (if so equipped), and all accessory brackets which attach the water pump.

3. Remove the water pump pulley attaching bolts, then remove the water pump pulley.

4. Disconnect the heater hose and water pump hose at the water pump.

5. Drain the crankcase and remove the oil level dipstick.

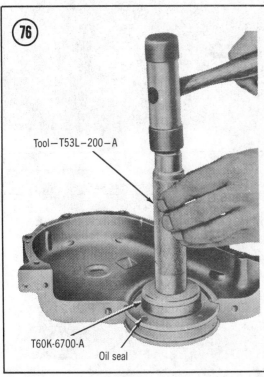

(76)

Tool—T53L—200—A

T60K-6700-A

Oil seal

6. Remove the crankshaft pulley attaching bolts (**Figure 77**). Remove the pulley from the vibration damper.

7. Remove the vibration damper attaching bolt and washer (**Figure 77**). Install a puller on the vibration damper as shown in **Figure 78** and remove the vibration damper.

8. Remove the oil pan-to-front cover attaching bolts, then use a thin bladed knife to cut the oil pan-to-front cover gasket flush with the cylinder block front face.

9. Remove the front cover-to-cylinder block attaching bolts, and remove the front cover and water pump as an assembly.

10. If a new cylinder front cover is to be installed, detach the water pump, gasket, and dipstick tube from the old front cover, and install on the new front cover, using a new water pump-to-front cover gasket.

CAUTION
Mating surfaces must be cleaned of all old gasket sealing material before installing the new gasket.

Front Cover Installation

Installation is the reverse of the removal procedure with the following additional steps.

1. Discard the front cover gasket, then clean the front cover, oil pan and cylinder block gasket mating surfaces of all gasket and sealer material.

NOTE
*A new front oil seal should be installed in the front cover each time the front cover is removed. Refer to the **Front Cover Removal/Installation** procedure described later in this chapter.*

2. Coat the gasket surface of the oil pan-to-front cover attaching area with gasket sealer. Cut and position that portion of a new gasket on the oil pan and apply gasket sealer to the cut ends of the new gasket.

3. Coat the gasket surfaces of the front cover and cylinder block with gasket sealer. Install new gasket.

4. Install the front cover on the cylinder block, being careful to avoid damage to the mating gaskets and front cover seal.

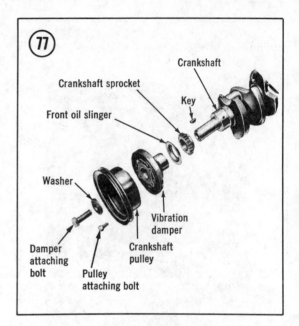

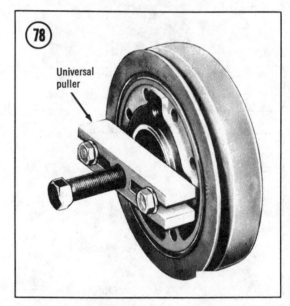

5. Coat the threads of the front cover attaching bolts with oil-resistant sealer. Install all attaching bolts using the Ford tool shown in **Figure 79**, or a drift of suitable size to align front cover. Tighten the oil pan-to-front cover attaching bolts to specifications (end of chapter). Tighten the front cover-to-cylinder block attaching bolts to specifications and remove the alignment tool or drift.

6. Apply Lubriplate or equivalent to the surface area of the vibration damper inner hub that contacts the front oil seal, then apply white grease to the front of the crankshaft and install the vibration damper.

7. Install the vibration damper using the Ford tool shown in **Figure 80**, or an equivalent device and tighten vibration damper attaching bolt to specification (end of chapter).

8. Start the engine and operate at a fast idle to check for oil or coolant leaks.

Timing Chain and Sprocket Removal/Installation

1. Remove the cylinder front cover as described earlier.

2. Disconnect the outlet line from the fuel pump. Remove the fuel pump attaching bolts and lay the pump to one side with the flexible fuel line still attached.

3. Remove the front oil slinger from the crankshaft (**Figure 77**).

4. Check timing chain deflection as follows. Rotate the crankshaft in a counterclockwise direction (viewed from front of vehicle) to take up slack on the left side of the timing chain.

5. Measure distance from a reference point on the cylinder block (**Figure 74**). Rotate the crankshaft in the opposite direction to take up the slack in the right side of the timing chain. Force the left side of the timing chain toward the reference mark, and measure the distance to the reference mark once again. The difference between the 2 measurements is the timing chain deflection. Timing chain deflection must not exceed 0.500 in.

6. Turn the engine by hand until the timing marks on the camshaft sprocket and crankshaft sprocket are aligned as shown in **Figure 81**.

7. Remove the camshaft sprocket attaching bolt, washer and 2 piece fuel pump eccentric (**Figure 82**).

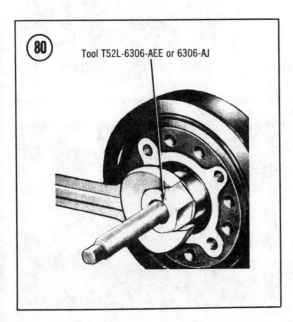
Tool T52L-6306-AEE or 6306-AJ

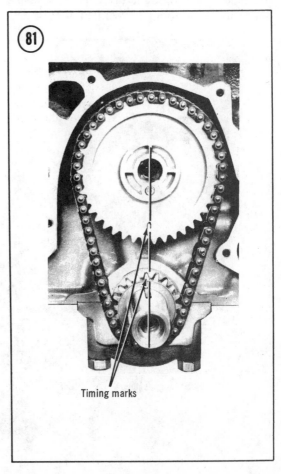
Timing marks

8. Slide both sprockets and the timing chain forward and remove as an assembly (**Figure 83**).

9. Installation is the reverse of these steps. Be sure that the timing marks on the camshaft and crankshaft sprockets are aligned as shown in **Figure 81** before installing the assembled sprockets and timing chain. Install the 2-piece fuel pump eccentric and crankshaft front oil slinger as shown in **Figure 82**, then tighten the camshaft sprocket attaching bolt to specification (end of chapter).

Front Oil Seal Removal/Installation

1. Remove the cylinder front cover as described earlier.

2. Support the front cover around the area of the oil seal. Drive the seal out of the front cover with the Ford tool shown in **Figure 84**, or a suitable drift.

3. Coat the new front oil seal with grease, turn the front cover over, and drive in the new seal using the Ford tool shown in **Figure 84** or a

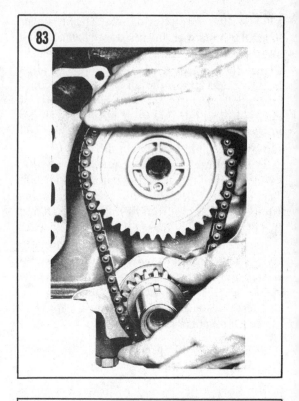

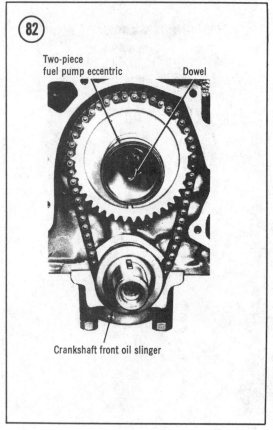

Two-piece
fuel pump eccentric   Dowel

Crankshaft front oil slinger

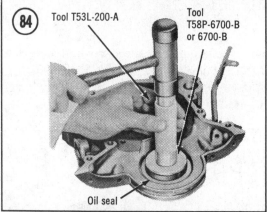

Tool T53L-200-A   Tool
                         T58P-6700-B
                         or 6700-B

Oil seal

suitable drift. The oil seal must be fully seated in the front cover recess.

4. Install the front cover as described earlier.

CAMSHAFT

On engines covered in this manual, it is possible to replace the camshaft with the engine in the vehicle. The following procedures detail in-vehicle removal. To remove the camshaft from the engine with the engine out of the vehicle, refer to *Engine Removal* procedure, then continue with that portion of the following procedure to remove and install the camshaft in the engine block.

Removal/Installation (2300 cc)

1. Remove the camshaft front cover and timing belt as described earlier in this chapter.

2. Check camshaft end play before removal. To do this, push the camshaft as far toward the rear of the engine as it will go. Install a dial gauge on the front of the engine with the pointer touching the front of the camshaft sprocket (**Figure 85**). Set the dial gauge at zero, then pry the camshaft forward as far as it will go with a large screwdriver. If the dial gauge reading exceeds 0.009 in., replace the camshaft thrust (retaining) plate (**Figure 86**).

4

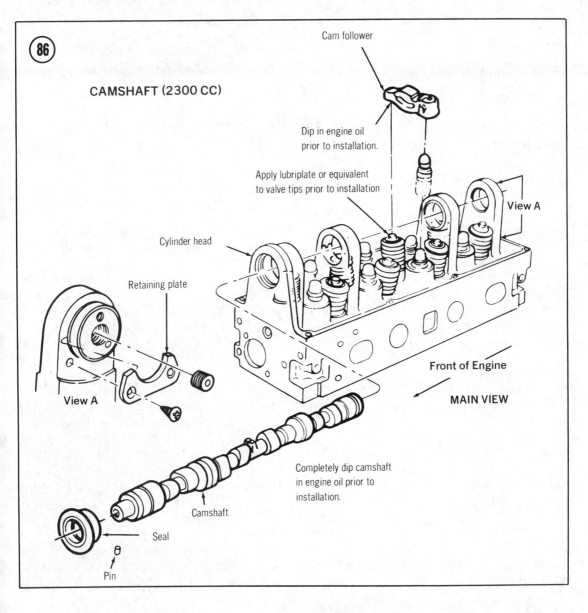

86

CAMSHAFT (2300 CC)

Cam follower

Dip in engine oil prior to installation.

Apply lubriplate or equivalent to valve tips prior to installation

View A

Cylinder head

Retaining plate

View A

Front of Engine

MAIN VIEW

Completely dip camshaft in engine oil prior to installation.

Camshaft

Seal

Pin

3. Remove the rocker arm cover and rocker arms as described earlier in this chapter.

4. Remove the camshaft sprocket and seal as described earlier in this chapter.

5. Remove the thrust (retaining) plate from the rear camshaft support stand on the cylinder head (**Figure 86**).

6. Carefully remove the camshaft from the bearings. Do not let the cam lobes touch or nick the bearings.

7. Installation is the reverse of these steps. Dip the camshaft completely in engine oil before installation. Carefully install the camshaft so as not to touch or nick the bearings. Tighten the thrust (retaining) plate attaching screws to 6-9 ft.-lb. Align all timing marks as described for timing belt installation.

Removal/Installation (200 cid)

1. Remove the cylinder head as discussed earlier in this chapter.

2. Remove the cylinder front cover as discussed earlier in this chapter.

3. Remove the oil dipstick.

4. Remove the oil pump and inlet tube as discussed later in this chapter.

5. Check camshaft end play. To do this, push the camshaft as far forward toward the rear of the engine as it will go. Install a dial gauge on the front of the engine with the pointer touching the camshaft sprocket retaining bolt or washer (**Figure 87**). Set the dial gauge at zero, then pry the camshaft forward as far as it will go with a large screwdriver. If the dial gauge reading exceeds 0.009 in., replace the camshaft thrust (retaining) plate, to reduce camshaft end play to within specifications (end of chapter). Replacement of the thrust plate is accomplished during camshaft installation procedures.

6. Remove the timing gears.

7. Remove the camshaft thrust plate from the front of the camshaft, then carefully remove the camshaft from its bearings. Do not let the cam lobes touch or nick the bearing surfaces. See **Figure 88**.

8. Installation is the reverse of these steps. Dip the camshaft completely in engine oil before installation. Carefully install the camshaft so as not to touch or nick the bearing

surfaces. Install the thrust plate with the oil groove toward the rear of the engine. Tighten the thrust plate attaching bolts to 12-18 ft.-lb. Align all timing marks as described for timing chain and drive sprocket installation.

Removal/Installation
(2800 cc, 255 cid, and 302 cid)

1. Drain the cooling system, then remove the radiator, shrouding, fan, and water pump (Chapter Six).

2. Remove the oil pan as described under *Oil Pan Removal.*

3. Remove the camshaft front cover as described earlier in this chapter.

4. Check camshaft end play. To do this, push the camshaft as far toward the rear of the engine as it will go. Install a dial gauge on the front of the engine with the pointer touching the camshaft sprocket retaining bolt or washer (**Figure 89** for 2800 cc engines or **Figure 90** for 255 cid and 302 cid engines). Set the dial gauge at zero, then pry the camshaft forward as far as it will go with a large screwdriver. If the dial gauge reading exceeds 0.009 in., replace the camshaft thrust (retaining) plate, and spacer (2800 cc engines only), to reduce camshaft end play to within specifications (end of chapter). Replacement of the thrust plate is accomplished during camshaft installation procedures.

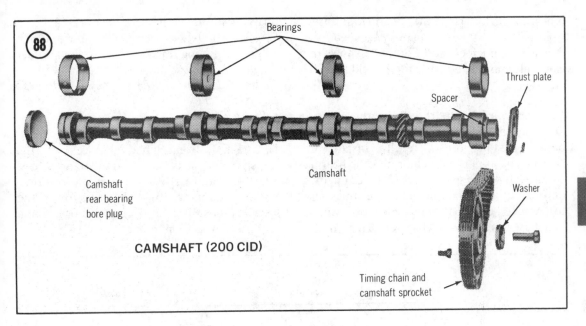

Bearings

Thrust plate

Spacer

Camshaft

Camshaft rear bearing bore plug

Washer

CAMSHAFT (200 CID)

Timing chain and camshaft sprocket

4

Tool 4201-C

5. Remove the timing gears (2800 cc engines), or timing chain and drive sprockets (255 cid and 302 cid engines).

6. Remove the oil pump as described later in this chapter.

7. Remove the fuel pump (Chapter Five).

8. Remove the distributor (Chapter Seven).

9. Perform all steps under the *Cylinder Head Removal* procedure described earlier in this chapter, except removal of the cylinder head attaching bolts, the cylinder head gasket, and the cylinder head.

NOTE
Under normal circumstances, it is a good idea to remove the cylinder head for inspection of the head, valves, and cylinder at this time because of the level to which the engine has been disassembled. Replacement of a camshaft should normally be accompanied by inspection, cleaning and service (as required) of the rest of the valve train.

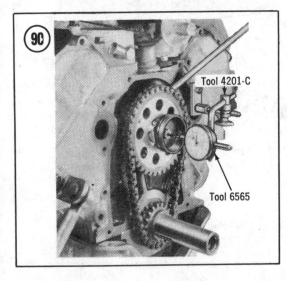

Tool 4201-C

Tool 6565

10. Remove the valve lifters as discussed under the *Valve Tappet Removal/Installation* procedure described earlier in this chapter.

11. Remove the thrust (retaining) plate and spacer (2800 cc engines only) from the front of the camshaft, then carefully remove the camshaft from its bearings. Rotate the camshaft while removing. Do not let the cam

lobes touch or nick the bearing surfaces. **Figure 91** shows the camshaft and related parts for 2800 cc engines, and **Figure 92** shows the camshaft and related parts for 255 cid and 302 cid engines.

12. Installation is the reverse of these steps. Dip the camshaft completely in engine oil before installation. Carefully install the camshaft so as not to touch or nick the bearing surfaces. Install a spacer ring (2800 cc engines only) and thrust plate of the proper thickness to reduce camshaft end play to within specifications (end of chapter). Tighten the

thrust plate attaching screws to 12-15 ft.-lb. (2800 cc) or 9-12 ft.-lb. (255 cid and 302 cid). Align all timing marks as described under *Timing Gear Installation (2800 cc)* or *Timing Chain and Sprocket Removal/Installation, 255 cid and 302 cid.*

Camshaft Inspection

1. Check all machined surfaces of the camshaft for nicks or grooves. Minor defects may be removed with a smooth oilstone. Severe damage or wear beyond the specifications, listed at the end of this chapter, requires replacement of the camshaft.

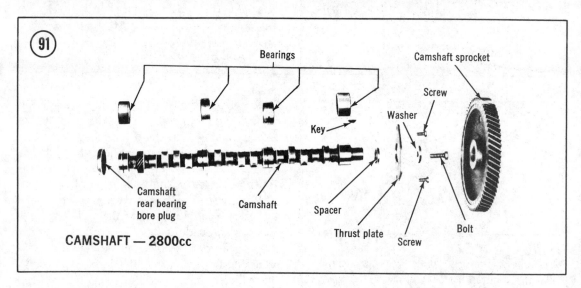

CAMSHAFT — 2800cc

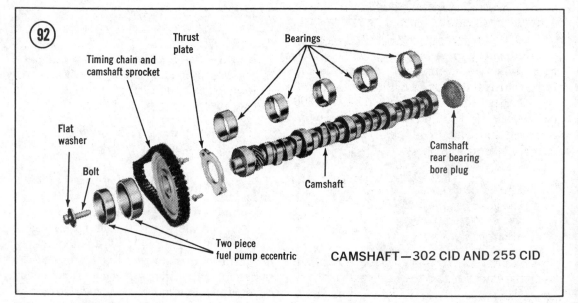

CAMSHAFT—302 CID AND 255 CID

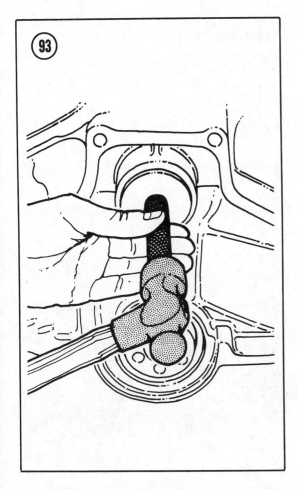

2. Measure the inner diameter of the camshaft bearings, being careful not to damage the bearing material. Compare this measurement with the specifications listed at the end of this chapter. If the bearings are excessively worn, grooved, pitted, or scored, have them replaced by a dealer or competent machine shop. If the camshaft bearings are to be replaced, the cylinder head (2300 cc) or engine block (2800 cc, 200 cid, 255 cid, and 302 cid) must be removed and taken to a dealer or machine shop for bearing installation.

> *CAUTION*
> *All camshaft bearings should be replaced, even if only one bearing is worn. Otherwise the camshaft may be out of alignment when reinstalled.*

3. Measure the outer diameter of the camshaft journals. Compare this measurement with the specifications listed at the end of this chapter.

Replace the camshaft if the journals exceed the wear or out-of-round specification listed at the end of this chapter.

4. Subtract the journal diameter measurement from the bearing diameter measurement to determine the bearing-to-journal clearance. If this clearance exceeds the specifications listed at the end of this chapter, either the camshaft bearings or the camshaft (or both) is worn and must be replaced. Compare both the journal and bearing measurements with the nominal values to determine which must be replaced.

5. On 200 cid, 2800 cc, 255 cid, and 302 cid engines, inspect the camshaft rear bearing bore plug (**Figure 88**, **Figure 91**, or **Figure 92**) for oil leakage. If oil leakage is evident, replace the plug as described in *Camshaft Rear Bore Plug Removal/Installation*, or refer the job to a dealer or competent garage.

Camshaft Rear Bearing Bore Plug Removal/Installation

If the engine is removed from the vehicle, replacement of the camshaft rear bearing bore plug is accomplished by drilling a small hole in the plug, inserting a screwdriver, or other covenient device, and prying the plug out of the engine block. If the engine is installed in the vehicle, the following procedure should be followed.

1. Remove the transmission (Chapter Eight).
2. Remove the clutch components (manual transmission) or torque converter (automatic transmission) and housing as described in Chapter Eight.
3. Remove the flywheel attaching bolts and the flywheel as described later in this chapter.
4. Remove the engine rear cover plate, then remove the bore plug as described earlier.
5. Installation is the reverse of these steps. Install the bore plug using a hollow drift of suitable diameter (**Figure 93**).

PISTON/CONNECTING ROD ASSEMBLIES

Piston/Connecting Rod Removal

1. Remove the cylinder head as discussed earlier.
2. Remove the oil pan as discussed later.

3. Remove the carbon ridge at the top of the cylinder bores with a ridge reamer. See **Figure 94**.

> *CAUTION*
> *Do not remove more than 1/32 in. into the ring travel area when using the ridge reamer.*

4. Rotate the crankshaft until the piston is at bottom dead center, and the connecting rod is centered in the cylinder bore.

5. Unbolt the connecting rod cap (**Figure 95**), and remove the rod cap and bearing from the crankshaft.

6. Free the connecting rod and piston assembly from the crankshaft by tapping gently with a wooden hammer. Remove the connecting rod bearing, then push the piston and connecting rod assembly out of the cylinder bore using a wooden hammer handle as shown in **Figure 96**.

> *NOTE*
> *Check the connecting rods, caps, and pistons for cylinder number marking.*

> *Make your own marks if there are none (**Figure 97**). These marks are extremely important during reassembly to ensure that the same parts are installed in the cylinders from which they were removed.*

7. Remove the rings using a ring remover. See **Figure 98**.

Piston Pin Removal/Installation

Pistons on all engines are press-fitted on the connecting rods, and slip fit into the pistons. Removal requires an arbor press, or similar

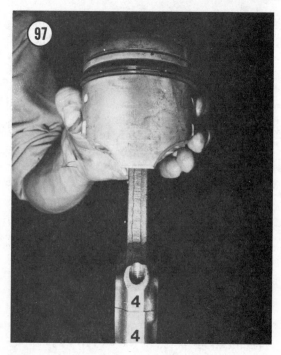

device, and a suitable support tool. This is a job for a dealer or machine shop, equipped to fit the pistons and pin, as well as align the pistons with the connecting rods.

Piston Clearance Check

This procedure should be performed at room temperature (70 degrees F).

1. Measure the cylinder bore as described under *Cylinder Bore Inspection.*

2. Measure the piston diameter at the piston pin centerline height, and 90 degrees to the piston pin axis.

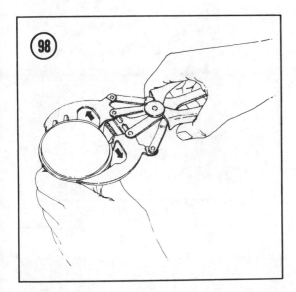

3. Determine the difference between the cylinder bore and piston diameter. This gives the piston clearance. Compare this figure with the specification listed at the end of the chapter.

4. Repeat the procedure for all cylinders and pistons.

Piston Ring Fitting/Installation

1. Check the ring gap of each piston ring. To do this, first press the ring about one inch down the cylinder bore and square it by tapping gently with an inverted piston.

> *NOTE*
> *If the cylinders have not been rebored, check the ring gap at the bottom of the ring travel, where the cylinder is least worn.*

2. Measure the ring gap with a feeler gauge as shown in **Figure 99**. Compare the ring gap with the specifications at the end of this chapter. If the ring gap is not within specifications, use another set of rings.

3. Check side clearance of the rings as shown in **Figure 100**. Place the feeler gauge beneath the ring and insert all the way into the ring groove. The feeler gauge should slide all the way around the piston without binding. Any wear that occurs will form a step at the inner

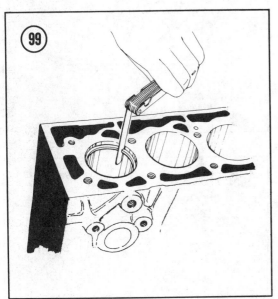

portion of the ring groove's lower edge. If large steps are detected (**Figure 101**), the pistons should be replaced. Compare the inserted feeler gauge with the specifications at the end of this chapter.

4. Using a ring expander tool, carefully install the oil control ring assembly, then the compression rings. The top side of the compression rings are marked and must be installed toward the top of the piston.

5. When installing the oil ring assembly, position the gaps in the assembly rings as shown in **Figure 102**.

Connecting Rod Inspection

1. Check the pistons for shiny, scuffed areas above the piston pins on one side and below

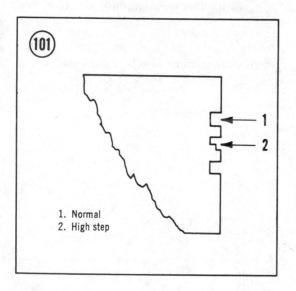

1. Normal
2. High step

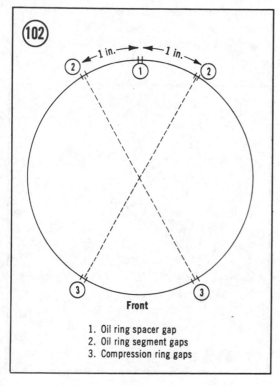

Front

1. Oil ring spacer gap
2. Oil ring segment gaps
3. Compression ring gaps

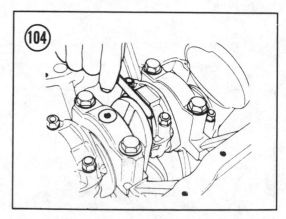

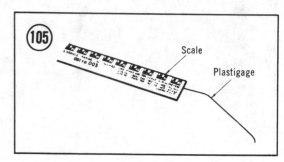

Scale

Plastigage

the piston pin on the other. This indicates a bent connecting rod.

2. Have the connecting rods checked by your dealer or a competent machine shop for twisting, bends, and overall straightness and alignment. **Figure 103** shows a typical connecting rod aligner. If necessary, have connecting rods realigned to meet specifications listed at the end of this chapter.

3. Install the connecting rods and bearings on the crankshaft. Insert a feeler gauge between the side of the connecting rod big end and the crankshaft (**Figure 104**) and measure side clearance. Normal clearance is 0.0035-0.0105 in. for 2300 cc engines, 0.004-0.011 in. for 2800 cc engines, 0.0035-0.0105 in. for 200 cid engines, and 0.010-0.020 in. for 255 cid and 302 cid engines. Maximum is 0.014 in. for 2300 cc, 2800 cc, and 200 cid engines, and 0.023 in. for 255 cid and 302 cid engines.

Measuring Bearing Clearance

1. Assemble connecting rods with bearings on the proper crankshaft journal. Do not tighten.

2. Cut a piece of Plastigage (**Figure 105**) the width of the bearing. Insert the Plastigage between the crankshaft journal and connecting rod bearing.

NOTE
Do not place the Plastigage over a crankshaft journal oil hole.

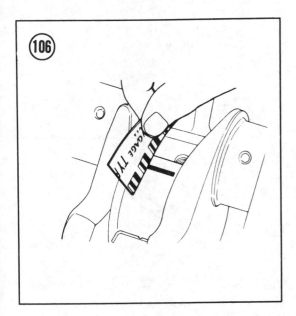

3. Install connecting rod cap and torque to 30-36 ft.-lb. for 2300 cc engines, 21-25 ft.-lb. for 2800 cc and 200 cid engines, and 19-24 ft.-lb. for 255 cid and 302 cid engines. Do not rotate the crankshaft while Plastigage is in place.

4. Remove the connecting rod cap. Bearing clearance is determined by comparing width of flattened Plastigage with scale markings on the Plastigage envelope (**Figure 106**). Compare Plastigage measurement with the specifications listed at end of this chapter.

Piston/Connecting Rod Installation

1. Remove cylinder wall glaze with a hone if new piston rings are to be installed. Follow hone manufacturer's recommendations.

2. Oil piston rings, pistons, and cylinder walls with light engine oil. Be sure to install pistons in same cylinders from which they were removed or to which they were fitted.

3. Install piston rings on piston. Be sure ring gaps are properly spaced around the piston as shown in **Figure 107**.

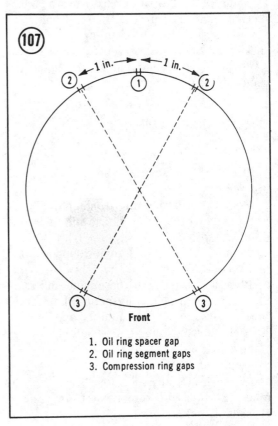

Front

1. Oil ring spacer gap
2. Oil ring segment gaps
3. Compression ring gaps

4. Install piston ring compressor on piston. Push piston into the cylinder with a hammer handle until it is slightly below top of cylinder. Be sure to guide connecting rods to avoid damage to crankshaft journals. See **Figure 108**.

NOTE
Install piston with notch in the piston head facing toward the front of the engine.

5. Check bearing clearance. See *Measuring Bearing Clearance*, this chapter. Apply a light coat of engine oil to the journals and bearings after the bearings have been fitted.
6. Turn crankshaft throw to bottom of its stroke. Push piston down until connecting rod bearings seat on crankshaft journal.
7. Install connecting rod cap. Tighten nuts to specifications.
8. Check side clearance between connecting rods on each crankshaft journal after piston and connecting rod assemblies are installed.
9. Disassemble, clean, and assemble oil pump. Clean oil pump inlet tube screen and oil pan and block gasket surfaces. Prime oil pump by filling either inlet or outlet port with engine oil and rotating pump shaft to distribute oil within housing. Install oil pump and oil pan. Install cylinder heads. See *Oil Pump* and *Cylinder Head* sections in this chapter for removal/installation procedures.

OIL PAN
(2300 CC)

Removal

1. Drain the engine oil and remove the dipstick.
2. Remove the fan shroud (Chapter Six).
3. Raise the front of the vehicle and support it on jackstands.
4. Remove right and left engine support bolts and nuts.
5. Place a jack beneath the engine and raise engine in engine compartment. Place wood blocks between engine mounts and chassis brackets. Lower engine onto wood blocks and remove jack.
6. Remove bolts securing sway bar to vehicle and remove sway bar. Remove steering gear retaining bolts and lower gear from vehicle (Chapter Nine).

7. Remove the oil pan attaching bolts. Remove the oil pan and gasket. See **Figure 109**.

NOTE
Before removing oil pan, position No. 4 piston at top dead center in cylinder to allow rear portion of oil pan to clear crankshaft throw.

Installation

1. Clean the oil pump pickup screen and filler tube. See **Figure 110**.

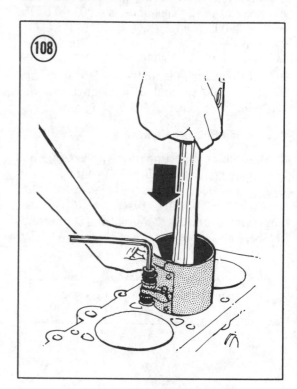

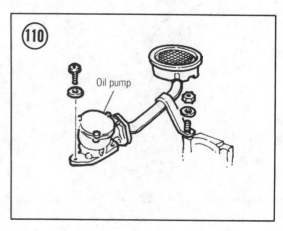

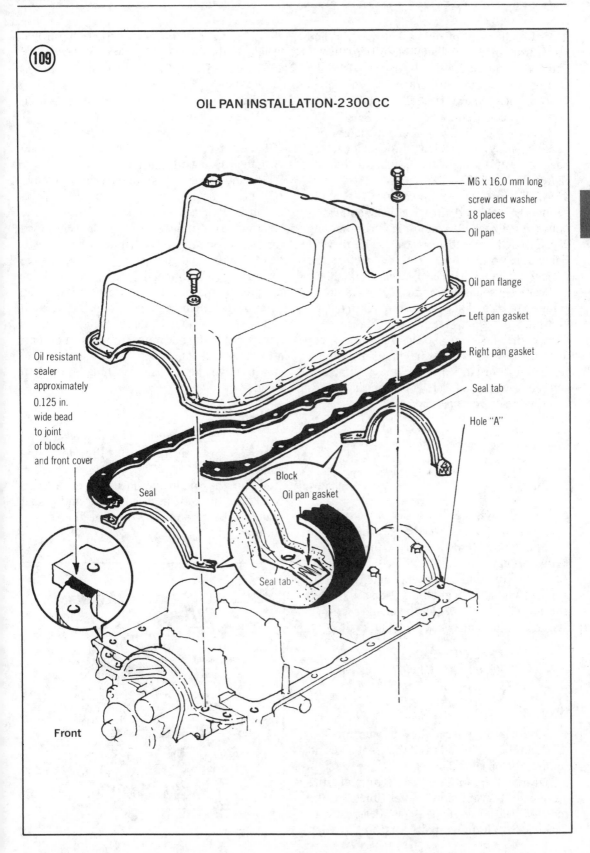

OIL PAN INSTALLATION-2300 CC

M6 x 16.0 mm long screw and washer 18 places

Oil pan

Oil pan flange

Left pan gasket

Right pan gasket

Seal tab

Hole "A"

Oil resistant sealer approximately 0.125 in. wide bead to joint of block and front cover

Seal

Block

Oil pan gasket

Seal tab

Front

2. Clean all traces of old gasket material and sealer from oil pan, cylinder block, front cover and rear main bearing cap. Be sure to clean the seal groove in the front cover and rear main bearing cap (**Figure 109**). Be careful not to gouge the sealing surfaces.

3. Coat the oil pan flange and pan side of pan gaskets with gasket sealer. Allow sealer to dry past the wet stage. Install gaskets to oil pan flange (**Figure 109**).

4. Apply gasket sealer to joint between the cylinder block and front cover, and joint between cylinder block and rear main bearing cap. Install front and rear seals (**Figure 109**) being sure to install the rear seal before the sealer on the rear main bearing cap is cured.

5. Position the oil pan and gasket against the cylinder block and install the four 8 mm oil pan attaching screws as shown in **Figure 109**. Check the oil pan and gasket for proper alignment with the remaining attachment holes, and install the remaining attaching screws. Tighten all screws to specifications listed at the end of this chapter.

NOTE
Tightening sequence for the oil pan attaching screws should begin at hole "A," and proceed clockwise around the oil pan (Figure 109).

6. Reinstall the steering gear and sway bar (Chapter Nine). Place jack beneath engine and raise engine. Remove wood blocks from between engine mounts and chassis brackets. Lower engine and install left and right side engine support bolts and nuts. Replace the fan shroud (Chapter Six). Fill the crankcase, then start the engine and check for oil leaks.

OIL PAN
(2800 CC, 200 CID,
355 CID, and 302 CID)

Removal

1. Disconnect the negative battery terminal.
2. Drain the engine oil from the crankcase and remove the oil level dipstick.
3. Drain the radiator. Disconnect the automatic transmission cooler lines at the radiator (if so equipped) as described in Chapter Six. Remove bolts attaching the fan

shroud to the radiator, and position the shroud back over the fan.

4. Raise the front of the vehicle and support it on jackstands.
5. Disconnect the cable from the starter. Remove starter (Chapter Seven).
6. Disconnect the sway bar at the end links (Chapter Nine). Rotate the bar to provide clearance during oil pan removal.
7. Remove rack and pinion steering assembly (Chapter Nine).
8. On 200 cid and 302 engines, position the steering gear out of the way to allow clearance for the oil pan removal (Chapter Nine).
9. On 2800 cc and 200 cid engines, remove the through bolts connecting the front motor mounts to the attaching brackets. Raise the front of the engine sufficiently to allow the oil pan to be removed. Place wooden blocks between the front motor mounts and their attaching brackets.
10. Remove the oil pan attaching bolts, then remove the oil pan.

Installation

Installation is basically the reverse of the removal procedure, with the following additional steps.

1. Clean the mating surfaces of the engine block and the oil pan of all sealer and gasket material. Be careful not to gouge the sealing surfaces.

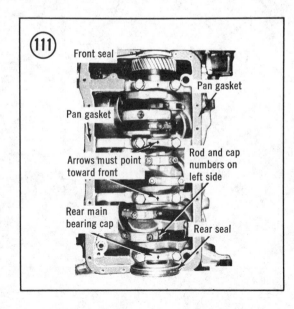

Front seal

Pan gasket

Pan gasket

Arrows must point toward front

Rod and cap numbers on left side

Rear main bearing cap

Rear seal

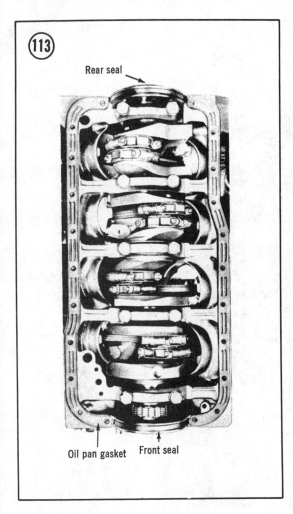

(113)

Rear seal

Oil pan gasket   Front seal

2. Coat the engine block mating surfaces of the oil pan gaskets with oil-resistant sealer. Once tacky, position the oil pan gaskets on the cylinder block, and align with the oil pan mounting holes in the engine block. See **Figure 111** for 2800 cc engines, **Figure 112** for 200 cid engines, or **Figure 113** for 255 cid and 302 cid engines.

3. Install the oil pan-to-engine block seals as shown in **Figure 111** (2800 cc), **Figure 112** (200 cid) or **Figure 113** (255 cid and 302 cid), secured in place with contact cement, or a suitable sealant material.

4. Position the oil pan on the cylinder block. On 2800 cc engines, install 4 attaching bolts as shown in **Figure 114** to secure the front and rear of the oil pan, then install the remaining bolts and tighten in the sequence shown in **Figure 114** to the specifications listed at the end of this chapter. For 200 cid, 255 cid, and 302 cid engines, install an attaching bolt, finger-tight, on each side of the oil pan, then install the remaining oil pan attaching bolts. Tighten the oil pan bolts from the center outward in each direction to the specifications listed at the end of this chapter.

5. Perform the steps of the removal procedure in reverse order to complete installation.

6. Start the engine and check for oil or coolant leaks.

4

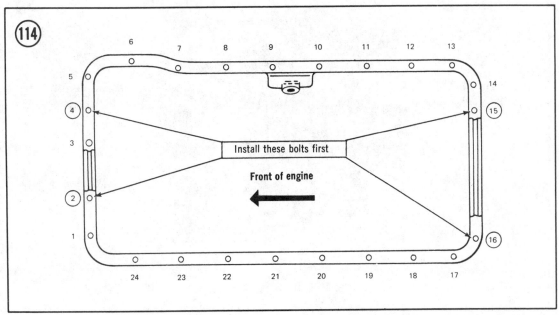

(114)

Install these bolts first

Front of engine

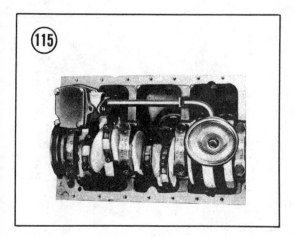

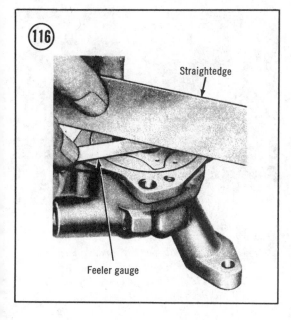

Straightedge

Feeler gauge

OIL PUMP

Removal/Installation

All oil pumps are located inside the oil pan.

1. Remove the oil pan as described earlier.
2. On 2300 cc, 2800 cc, 255 cid, and 302 cid engines, remove the bolt that attaches the inlet tube assembly and oil pickup screen to the block. **Figure 115** shows a typical inlet tube assembly.
3. Remove the bolts securing the inlet tube assembly to the oil pump body. Remove the inlet tube assembly and gasket.
4. Remove the bolts attaching the oil pump body to the engine block, then remove the oil pump.

NOTE
Be sure that the oil pump drive (intermediate) shaft is removed from the engine block when the oil pump is removed.

5. After disassembly, repair and reassembly, or replacement, prime the pump by filling it with engine oil and rotating the oil pump drive shaft to distribute oil throughout the pump.
6. Install the oil pump drive shaft in the engine block until the shaft is firmly seated. Install the oil pump to the engine block and secure with the oil pump attaching bolts.

NOTE
Do not force the oil pump into position if it will not seal readily; the drive shaft may be misaligned. Rotate drive shaft until oil pump seats easily.

7. Install the inlet tube assembly to the oil pump body, then tighten all bolts to specifications listed at the end of this chapter. On 2300 cc, 2800 cc, 255 cid and 302 cid engines, secure the inlet tube assembly to the engine block, and tighten attaching nuts to specification listed at the end of this chapter. Install the oil pan as described earlier.

Disassembly, Inspection, and Assembly

NOTE
The oil pump on 2800 cc engines is not repairable. If defective, it must be replaced.

1. Separate the pickup tube and screen from the pump body.
2. Remove the cover attaching screws and cover.
3. Lift the inner and outer rotors from the pump body.
4. Thoroughly clean all parts in solvent.
5. Measure rotor end clearance by placing a straightedge over the pump body and rotor assembly, then inserting a feeler gauge between the rotor and the straightedge (**Figure 116**). Rotor end play should be 0.001-0.004 in.

NOTE
The 2-piece inner rotor shaft and outer rotor are replaced only as an assembly. The individual parts are not replaceable.

6. Measure between the outer rotor (outer race) and the pump body with a feeler gauge. See **Figure 117**. This clearance should be 0.001-0.013 in.

7. If the pump rotors are worn, replace them as a set. If any other parts are worn or damaged, replace the entire oil pump.

8. Assembly is the reversal of the disassembly procedure. Be sure the identification marks on inner and outer rotors face downward when the pump and engine are installed. Use a new gasket between pickup tube and pump body.

CRANKSHAFT, MAIN BEARINGS, AND SEALS

1. Remove the engine from the vehicle as described under *Engine Removal* earlier in this chapter.

2. On 2300 cc engines, remove the front cover, camshaft belt, crankshaft sprocket, and front cover oil seal as described earlier in this chapter.

3. On 2800 cc engines, remove the front cover, timing gears, and front oil seal as described earlier in this chapter.

4. On 200 cid, 255 cid, and 302 cid engines, remove the front cover, timing chain and drive sprockets as discussed earlier in this chapter.

5. Disconnect the spark plug wires from the spark plugs, then remove the spark plugs from the cylinders.

6. Remove the flywheel (manual or automatic) from the rear of the crankshaft as described under *Flywheel Removal* later in this chapter, then remove the engine rear cover plate.

7. Remove the oil pan as described under *Oil Pan Removal* earlier in this chapter.

8. Remove the oil pump as described under *Oil Pump Removal* earlier in this chapter.

9. Before removing the crankshaft, check crankshaft end play. Use a large screwdriver or pry bar to force the crankshaft as far toward the front of the engine as it will go, then measure the clearance between the front of the thrust bearing and the crankshaft using a feeler gauge (**Figure 118**). In all engines, the thrust bearing is the third main bearing from the front of the engine. Replace the thrust bearing if the crankshaft end play exceeds the specification listed at the end of this chapter.

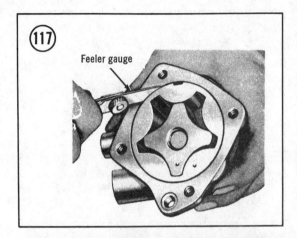
Feeler gauge

NOTE
Crankshaft, main bearing, and crankshaft rear oil seal arrangements are shown in **Figure 119** *(2300 cc),* **Figure 120** *(2800 cc),* **Figure 121** *(200 cid), and* **Figure 122** *(255 cid and 302 cid). Refer to these illustrations as required, during removal, inspection, and installation procedures.*

10. Check the rod and main bearing caps for match marks or numbers. Make your own marks if there are none.

11. Remove the connecting rod bolts and lift off the rod caps with bearing inserts in place. Place the rod caps in order of removal for easy installation.

12. Remove the main bearing cap bolts, then remove the main bearing caps with bearing inserts.

13. Push the connecting rod/piston assemblies toward the top of each cylinder to provide a clearance for crankshaft removal and installation.

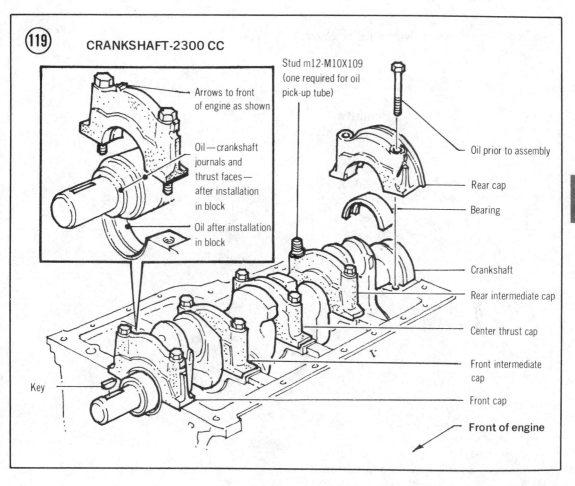

(119) **CRANKSHAFT-2300 CC**

Arrows to front of engine as shown

Oil—crankshaft journals and thrust faces— after installation in block

Oil after installation in block

Stud m12-M10X109 (one required for oil pick-up tube)

Oil prior to assembly

Rear cap

Bearing

Crankshaft

Rear intermediate cap

Center thrust cap

Front intermediate cap

Front cap

Key

Front of engine

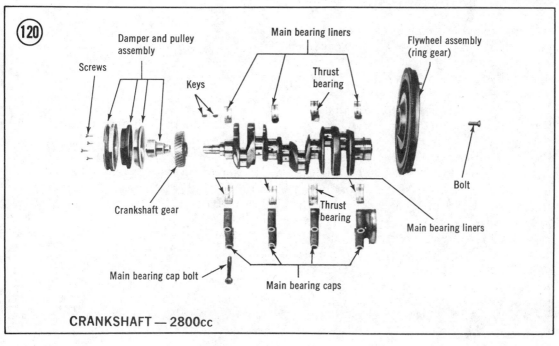

(120)

Damper and pulley assembly

Main bearing liners

Flywheel assembly (ring gear)

Screws

Keys

Thrust bearing

Crankshaft gear

Bolt

Thrust bearing

Main bearing liners

Main bearing cap bolt

Main bearing caps

CRANKSHAFT — 2800cc

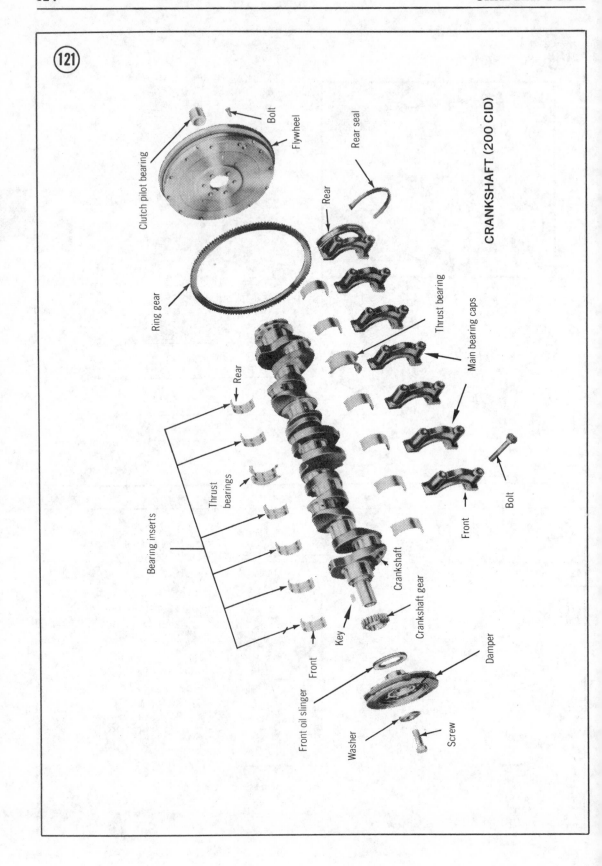

CRANKSHAFT (200 CID)

(121)

Bolt

Flywheel

Clutch pilot bearing

Rear seal

Rear

Ring gear

Thrust bearing

Main bearing caps

Rear

Bearing inserts

Thrust bearings

Bolt

Crankshaft

Crankshaft gear

Front

Front

Key

Front oil slinger

Damper

Washer

Screw

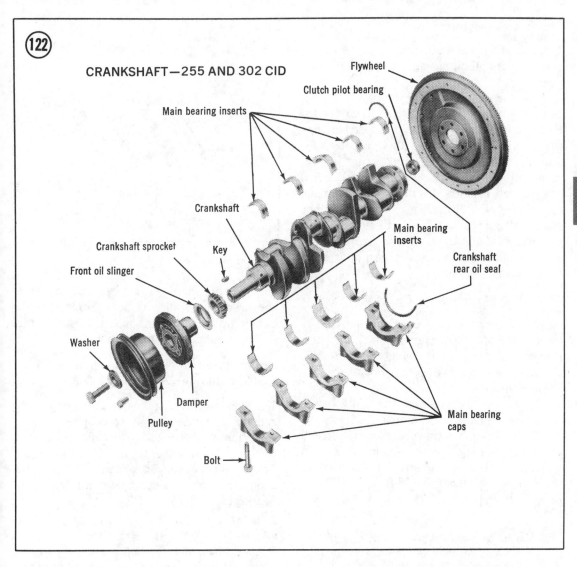

(122) CRANKSHAFT—255 AND 302 CID

Flywheel
Clutch pilot bearing
Main bearing inserts
Crankshaft
Crankshaft sprocket
Key
Main bearing inserts
Crankshaft rear oil seal
Front oil slinger
Washer
Damper
Pulley
Bolt
Main bearing caps

4

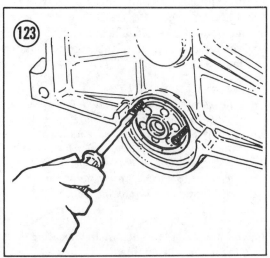

(123)

14. Carefully remove the crankshaft from the main bearing journals in the block so that the thrust bearing surfaces are not damaged. Handle the crankshaft with care to avoid damage to the crankshaft finished surfaces.

15. Remove the main bearings from the journals in the cylinder block, then place them to the side in the order of removal.

16. On all engines (except 2800 cc), remove the 2 halves of the crankshaft rear oil seal from the cylinder block and the rear main bearing cap, then discard. On 2800 cc engines, insert a sheet metal screw on each side of the rear oil seal (**Figure 123**), then remove the rear oil seal by pulling on both sheet metals screws with pliers.

Crankshaft Inspection

1. Clean the crankshaft throughly in solvent, and blow out all oil passages with compressed air.

2. Examine connecting rod journals and main bearing journals for wear, scoring, or cracks. Check all journals against the specifications listed at the end of this chapter for out-of-roundness, taper, and wear. Inspect crankshaft oil seal mating surfaces for nicks, sharp edges, or burrs that might cause damage to the rear oil seal during installation. Minor crankshaft journal scores can be dressed with an oilstone. However, if the journals are severely marred or exceed the wear limit, have the crankshaft refinished.

Measuring Main Bearing Clearance

1. Install the main bearings previously removed from the cylinder block in their original positions, then install the crankshaft on these bearings taking care not to damage the sides of the thrust bearing.

2. Cut a piece of Plastigage the width of the main bearing journal to be measured. Lay the Plastigage on the main bearing journal. Install the main bearing cap, complete with main bearing insert and tighten to 60 ft.-lb., then to 80-90 ft.-lb. (2300 cc), 65-75 ft.-lb. (2800 cc), or 60-70 ft.-lb. (200 cid, 255 cid and 302 cid).

> *NOTE*
> *Do not place Plastigage across crankshaft oil holes. Do not rotate the crankshaft while the Plastigage is in place.*

3. Remove the main bearing cap and bearing insert. Compare the width of the flattened Plastigage to the markings on the envelope to determine main bearing clearance (**Figure 124**). Compare the narrowest point on the Plastigage with the widest point to determine journal taper.

4. If wear is greater than the specifications listed at the end of this chapter, a 0.001 or 0.002 in. undersize bearing may be used on 1/2 of the journal in combination with the standard bearing on the other half. If the undersize bearings are used on more than one journal, the undersize bearing should be installed in the cylinder block, not in the

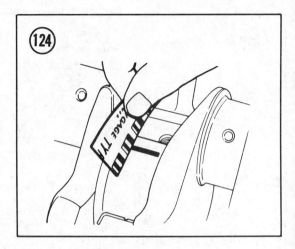

main bearing cap. If this does not produce the correct crankshaft-to-main bearing clearance, the crankshaft should be refinished by a dealer or a competent machine shop, and undersize main bearings installed.

Crankshaft Rear Oil Seal Installation (2300 cc, 200 cid, 255 cid, and 302 cid)

1. Clean the rear oil seal grooves in the cylinder block and rear main bearing cap with abrush and solvent such as lacquer thinner or non-petroleum solvent. Also clean the areas where silicone rubber sealer is to be later applied to the cylinder block and rear main bearing cap. See **Figure 125**.

2. Dip the halves of the seal in clean engine oil.

3. Carefully install 1/2 of the seal in its groove in the cylinder block and the other 1/2 of the seal in its groove in the rear main bearing cap as shown in **Figure 126**. The lip of the installed seal must face the front of the engine as shown in **Figure 126**.

> *CAUTION*
> *Be sure no rubber is shaved from the outside of the seals by the groove edges in the cylinder block or rear main bearing cap during installation. Do not allow any engine oil to drip on the area of the cylinder block or rear main bearing cap to which silicone rubber sealer will later be applied.*

On 2300 cc engines, ensure that the rear seal halves are installed so that the locating tabs face the rear of the engine.

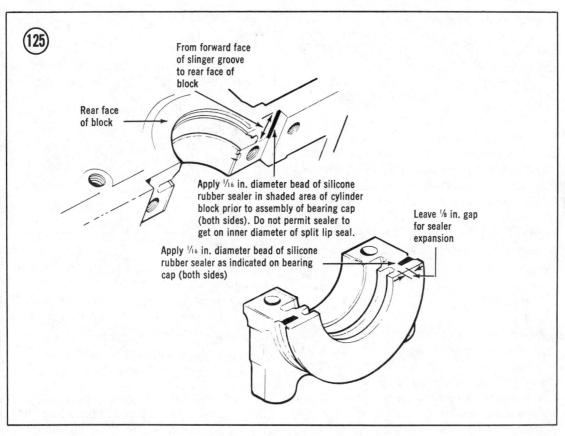

(125)

From forward face of slinger groove to rear face of block

Rear face of block →

Apply ¹⁄₁₆ in. diameter bead of silicone rubber sealer in shaded area of cylinder block prior to assembly of bearing cap (both sides). Do not permit sealer to get on inner diameter of split lip seal.

Apply ¹⁄₁₆ in. diameter bead of silicone rubber sealer as indicated on bearing cap (both sides)

Leave ⅛ in. gap for sealer expansion

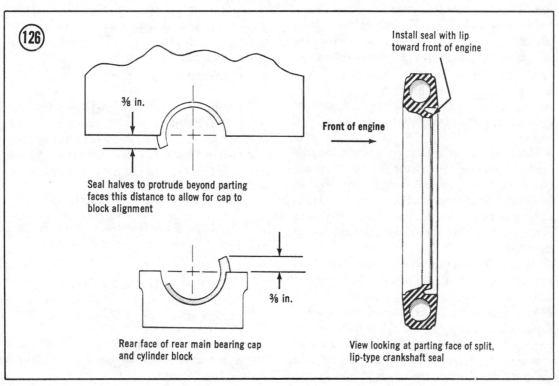

(126)

Install seal with lip toward front of engine

⅜ in.

Seal halves to protrude beyond parting faces this distance to allow for cap to block alignment

Front of engine →

⅜ in.

Rear face of rear main bearing cap and cylinder block

View looking at parting face of split, lip-type crankshaft seal

4. The remainder of the rear oil seal installation procedures are covered under *Crankshaft and Main Bearing Installation* covered later in this chapter.

Crankshaft Rear Oil Seal Installation (2800 cc)

Installation procedures for the 2800 cc engine, crankshaft rear oil seal are covered under the *Crankshaft and Main Bearing Installation* procedure provided later in this chapter.

Crankshaft Main Bearing Installation

1. On 2300 cc, 200 cid, 255 cid, and 302 cid engines, make sure the *Rear Oil Seal Installation* procedures contained earlier in this chapter have been performed before proceeding.
2. With the main bearings removed from the bearing caps and the cylinder block, clean the main bearing bores in the cylinder block, the main bearing caps, and the main bearing inserts with lacquer thinner to remove all foreign material.
3. If the old main bearings are being reinstalled, be sure that they are reinstalled in the main bearing caps and cylinder bores from which they were removed. If new bearings (or undersize bearings) are being installed, be sure that they are installed in the proper location. The tangs on the backside of all main bearings should match with the grooves in the cylinder block bores and the main bearing caps.
4. Coat the main bearing surfaces and the crankshaft journals with clean, heavy engine oil.
5. Carefully lay the crankshaft in the main bearings installed in the cylinder block, being careful not to damage the sides of the thrust bearings.
6. Install all main bearing caps, except the rear main bearing cap and the center thrust bearing cap.
7. Apply an even 1/16 in. of silicone rubber sealer to the areas of the cylinder block and rear main bearing cap shown in **Figure 125**. Install all the rear main bearing caps and tighten cap bolts to specifications listed at the

end of this chapter (2300 cc, 200 cid, 255 cid, and 302 cid engines only).
8. Install the remaining bearing cap bolts (except the center thrust bearing) and tighten to specifications listed at the end of this chapter.
9. Install the main bearing cap over the thrust bearing, and tighten cap bolts finger-tight.
10. Using large screwdrivers or pry bars, force the crankshaft as far forward as possible, and the thrust bearing cap as far rearward as possible. This aligns the 2 halves of the thrust bearing. Holding the crankshaft and thrust bearing in this position, tighten the thrust bearing cap nuts to specifications listed at the end of this chapter. See **Figure 127**.
11. Reinstall the connecting rods and caps on the crankshaft.
12. On the 2800 cc engines, install the crankshaft rear oil seal by coating the inside of the seal with Lubriplate and the outer surface of the seal with clean engine oil. Position the seal in the recess between the cylinder block and the rear end of the crankshaft. Drive the seal into position using a hollow drift of appropriate diameter (**Figure 128**). Be sure the seal is firmly seated.
13. The remainder of the installation procedure is accomplished by performing Steps 1-8 of the removal procedure in reverse order.

FLYWHEEL (MANUAL TRANSMISSION)

Removal/Installation

1. Remove the transmission as described in Chapter Eight.
2. Remove the clutch from the flywheel as described in Chapter Eight.
3. Remove the 6 bolts attaching the flywheel to the crankshaft (**Figure 129**) and remove the flywheel.
4. Installation is the reverse of these steps. Tighten the flywheel bolts gradually in a diagonal pattern. Metric bolts are used the 2300 cc engine (10 mm). Tighten these bolts to 56-64 ft.-lb. Tighten the bolts on the 2800 cc engine to 47-51 ft.-lb. On 200 cid, 255 cid, and 302 cid engines, tighten the bolts to 75-85 ft.-lb.

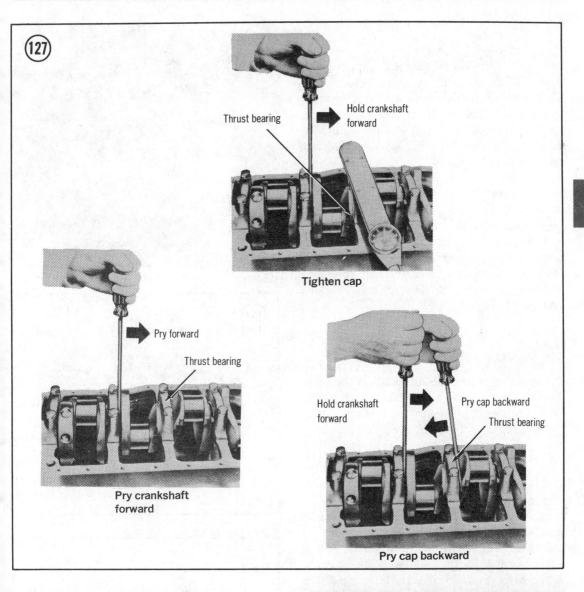

Thrust bearing

Hold crankshaft forward

Tighten cap

Pry forward

Thrust bearing

Pry crankshaft forward

Hold crankshaft forward

Pry cap backward

Thrust bearing

Pry cap backward

4

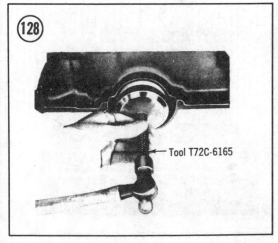

Tool T72C-6165

Inspection

1. Check the flywheel for cracks or heat damage (blue-tinted area). Replace the flywheel if these conditions are detected.

2. Check the friction surface of the flywheel for wear or scoring. If necessary, have the flywheel turned to smooth it. This should be done by a competent machine shop. Do not remove more than 0.045 in. from the flywheel friction surface.

3. Check the ring gear for worn or damaged teeth. If wear or damage is evident, have a new ring gear shrunk onto the flywheel.

4. Check the flywheel face for runout. Connect a dial gauge as shown in **Figure 130** to the flywheel. Maximum permissible runout is 0.005 in. (2300 cc and 2800 cc) and 0.010 in. (200 cid, 255 cid, and 302 cid).

FLYWHEEL (AUTOMATIC TRANSMISSION)

Inspection procedures are basically the same as for the manual transmission flywheel. However, the automatic transmission ring gear must be replaced if the ring gear is defective.

CYLINDER BLOCK INSPECTION

1. Clean the cylinder block thoroughly with solvent and check all freeze plugs for leaks. Replace any plugs that are suspect. It is a good idea, at this level of disassembly, to replace all the freeze plugs. While cleaning, check oil and water passages for dirt, sludge, and corrosion. If the passages are very dirty or clogged, the block should be boiled out by a dealer or competent automotive shop.

2. Examine the cylinder block for cracks. It is a good idea to take the block to a dealer or competent automotive shop for magnafluxing, to locate any hairline cracks that might escape visual examination.

3. Check all machined gasket surfaces for nicks or burrs. If necessary, smooth the surfaces with an oilstone.

4. Check the cylinder head mating surface(s) of the block for flatness. Use an accurate straightedge and feeler gauge as shown in **Figure 131**. Maximum cylinder head warp is 0.003 in. or less over any 6 inches, in any

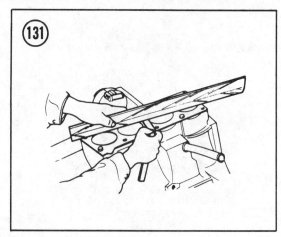

direction, and 0.006 in. over the full length of the cylinder block. Have the block resurfaced by a machine shop if warp is in excess of specification. Do not remove more than 0.010 in. from the block/cylinder head mating surface.

5. Measure the cylinder bores for out-of-roundness, or excessive wear, with a bore gauge (**Figure 132**). Measure the cylinder bores at top and bottom, in both the front-to-rear and side-to-side directions.

Compare the measurements to specifications at the end of this chapter. If the cylinders exceed maximum tolerances, they must be rebored. Cylinder reboring is a job for a dealer or competent machine shop.

NOTE
When reboring cylinders, the main bearing caps must be installed and torqued to specifications to prevent distortion of main bearing bores.

4

Tables are on the following pages.

Table 1   2300 cc ENGINE SPECIFICATIONS

General Specifications
   Piston displacement   2300 cc (140 cu. in.)
   Bore   3.780 in.
   Stroke   3.126 in.
   Oil Pressure (hot at   40-60 psi
     2,000 rpm)
   Compression pressure   Lowest cylinder within 75%
     (cranking speed)   of highest
   Firing order   1-3-4-2

Cylinder Head
   Valve guide bore diameter   0.3433-0.3443 in.
     (standard intake and exhaust)
   Valve seat width, intake   0.060-0.080 in.
   Valve seat width, exhaust   0.070-0.090 in.
   Valve seat angle   45°
   Valve seat runout (maximum)   0.0016 in.
   Valve arrangement (front to rear)   E-I-E-I-E-I-E-I

Rocker Arm
   Rocker arm to cam clearance
     Intake   0.008 in. (cold)
     Exhaust   0.010 in. (cold)
   Rocker arm ratio   1.64:1

Valve Lash Adjusters
   Diameter   0.8422-0.8427 in.
   Clearance to bore   0.0007-0.0027 in.
   Gap at cam (collapsed)
     Nominal   0.040-0.050 in.
     Maximum   0.035-0.055 in.

Valve Springs
   Approximate free length   1.89 in.
   Assembled height   1 17/32-1 19/32 in.
   Pressure at length
     Intake   71-79 @ 1.56 in.
     Exhaust   159-175 @ 1.16 in.
   Maximum out of square   0.078 in.

Valves
   Stem-to-guide clearance
     Intake   0.0010-0.0027 in.
     Exhaust   0.0015-0.0032 in.
     Wear limit   0.0055 in.
   Face angle   44°
   Valve face runout   0.0020 in.
   Head diameter
     Intake   1.73-1.74 in.
     Exhaust   1.49-1.50 in.
   Stem diameter, standard
     Intake   0.3416-0.3423 in.
     Exhaust   0.3411-0.3418 in.

(continued)

Table 1   2300 cc ENGINE SPECIFICATIONS (continued)

Camshaft	
Lobe lift	
Intake	0.2437 in.
Exhaust	0.2437 in.
Maximum lift loss	0.005 in.
Journal-to-bearing clearance	
Standard	0.001-0.003 in.
Maximum	0.006 in.
Journal diameter	1.7713-1.7720 in.
Journal runout	0.005 in. (maximum)
Journal out-of-round	0.0005 in. (maximum)
End play	
Nominal	0.001-0.007 in.
Maximum	0.009 in.
Auxiliary Shaft	
Bearing clearance	0.0006-0.0026 in.
End play	0.001-0.007 in.
Cylinder Block	
Bore diameter	3.7795-3.7831 in.
Bore diameter wear limit	+0.005 in.
Out-of-round (maximum)	0.001 in.
Taper (maximum)	0.010 in.
Main bearing bore diameter	2.5902-2.5910 in.
Crankshaft	
Main bearing journal diameter	2.3982-2.3990 in.
Main bearing journal wear limit	+0.005 in.
Main bearing journal runout (maximum)	0.002 in.
Main bearing journal out-of-round (maximum)	0.0006 in.
Main bearing journal taper (maximum)	0.0006 in per in.
Connecting rod journal diameter	2.0462-2.0472 in.
Connecting rod journal taper (maximum)	0.0006 in.
Journal out-of-round (maximum)	0.0006 in.
Crankshaft free end play	0.004-0.008 in.
Crankshaft free end play wear limit	0.012 in.
Main Bearings	
Clearance to crankshaft	
Standard	0.0008-0.0015 in.
Permissible	0.0008-0.0026 in.
Connecting Rod Bearings	
Clearance to crankshaft	
Standard	0.0035-0.0105 in.
Permissible	0.014 in.
Connecting Rods	
Piston pin bore diameter	
Non-turbo	0.9123-0.9126 in.
Turbo	0.9124-0.9127 in.
Bearing bore	2.1720-2.1728 in.
Bearing bore out-of-round and taper (max.)	0.0004 in.
Alignment*	
Twist	0.024 in.
Bend	0.012 in.
Side clearance	0.0035-0.0105 in.

(continued)

Table 1   2300 cc ENGINE SPECIFICATIONS (continued)

Pistons	
Diameter, standard (non-turbo engine)	
Coded red	3.7780-3.7786 in.
Coded blue	3.7792-3.7798 in.
Diameter, standard (turbo engine)	
Coded red	3.7760-3.7766 in.
Coded blue	3.7772-3.7778 in.
Clearance to cylinder bore	
Non-turbo	0.0014-0.0022 in.
Turbo	0.0034-0.0042 in.
Pin bore diameter	
Non-turbo	0.9123-0.9126 in.
Turbo	0.9124-0.9127 in.
Ring groove width	
Compression	0.080-0.081 in.
Oil	0.188-0.189 in.
Piston pins	
Length	3.010-3.040 in.
Diameter	0.9119-0.9124 in.
Clearance to piston	0.0002-0.0004 in.
Clearance to connecting rod	Interference fit
Piston Rings	
Compression ring width	0.077-0.078 in.
Compression ring side clearance	
Normal	0.002-0.004 in.
Wear limit	0.006 in.
Oil ring side clearance	Snug
Ring end gap	
Compression	0.010-0.020 in.
Oil	0.015-0.055 in.
Flywheel	
Clutch face runout	0.005 in.
Oil Pump	
Rotor end clearance	0.0015-0.0030 in.
Outer race to housing clearance	0.001-0.013 in.

*Bearing bore and pin bushing must be parallel and in same vertical plane within 0.004 in. at ends of 8 in. long bar measured at 4 in. from either side of connecting rod.

Table 2   2800 cc ENGINE SPECIFICATIONS

General Specifications	
Piston displacement	1200 cc (170.9 cu. in.)
Bore	3.66 in.
Stroke	2.70 in.
Oil pressure (hot at 2,000 rpm)	40-60 psi
Compression pressure (cranking speed)	Lowest cylinder within 75% of highest
Cylinder Head	
Valve guide bore diameter	0.3174-0.3184 in.
Valve seat width	0.060-0.079 in.
Valve seat angle	45°
Valve seat runout (maximum)	0.0015 in.
Valve arrangement (front to rear)	I-E-E-I-E-I (L.H.) I-E-I-E-E-I (R.H.)
Rocker Assembly	
Rocker arm shaft diameter	0.7799-0.7811 in.
Rocker arm bore diameter	0.7380-0.7842 in.
Rocker arm ratio	1.46:1
Tappets	
Diameter	0.8736-0.8741 in.
Clearance to bore	0.0009-0.0024 in.
Valve stem to rocker arm clearance (valve clearance)	
Intake	0.016 in. (cold)
Exhaust	0.018 in. (cold)
Valve Springs	
Approximate free length	1.91 in.
Assembled height	$1^{37}/_{64}$-$1^{39}/_{64}$ in.
Pressure at length	60-68 @ 1.585 in. 138-149 @ 1.222 in.
Maximum out-of-square	0.078 in.
Valves	
Stem-to-guide clearance	
Intake	0.0008-0.0025 in.
Exhaust	0.0018-0.0035 in.
Wear limit (both)	0.0055 in.
Face angle	44°
Head diameter	
Intake	1.562-1.577 in.
Exhaust	1.261-1.276 in.
Stem diameter, standard	
Intake	0.3159-0.3167 in.
Exhaust	0.3149-0.3156 in.
Camshaft	
Lobe lift	0.2555 in.
Journal-to-bearing clearance	0.0010-0.0026 in.
Wear limit	0.006 in.
Journal diameter	
No. 1	1.6497-1.6505 in.
No. 2	1.6347-1.6355 in.
No. 3	1.6197-1.6205 in.
No. 4	1.6047-1.6055 in.
Bearing diameter	
No. 1	1.6515-1.6523 in.
No. 2	1.6365-1.6373 in.
No. 3	1.6215-1.6223 in.
No. 4	1.6065-1.6073 in.

(continued)

4

Table 2   2800 cc ENGINE SPECIFICATIONS (continued)

Camshaft (continued)	
Journal runout (maximum)	0.005 in.
Journal out-of-round (max.)	0.0003 in.
End play	
Nominal	0.0008-0.0040 in.
Maximum	0.0090 in.
Cylinder Block	
Bore diameter	3.6614-3.6630 in.
Out-of-round (maximum)	0.0015 in.
Taper (maximum)	0.010 in.
Main bearing bore diameter	2.3866-2.3874 in.
Bore diameter wear limit	+0.005 in.
Crankshaft	
Main bearing journal diameter	2.2433-2.2441 in.
Main bearing journal wear limit	0.005 in.
Main bearing journal runout (maximum)	0.002 in.
Main bearing journal out-of-round	
(maximum)	0.0006 in.
Main bearing journal taper (maximum)	0.0006 in. per in.
Connecting rod journal diameter	2.1252-2.1260 in.
Connecting rod journal taper (maximum)	0.0006 in. per in.
Journal out-of-round (maximum)	0.0006 in.
Crankshaft free end play	0.004-0.008 in.
Crankshaft free end play wear limit	0.012 in.
Main Bearings	
Clearance to crankshaft	
Standard	0.0008-0.0015 in.
Permissible	0.0005-0.0019 in.
Connecting Rod Bearings	
Clearance to crankshaft	
Standard	0.0006-0.0016 in.
Permissible	0.0005-0.0022 in.
Connecting Rods	
Piston pin bore diameter	0.9450-0.9452 in.
Bearing bore	2.2370-2.2378 in.
Bearing bore out-of-round (maximum)	0.0004 in.
Alignment*	
Twist	0.006 in.
Bend	0.002 in.
Side clearance	0.004-0.011 in.
Pistons	
Diameter, standard	3.6605-3.6614-5 in.
Clearance to cylinder bore	0.001-0.002 in.
Pin bore diameter	0.9450-0.9452 in.
Ring groove width	
Upper compression	0.0803-0.0811 in.
Lower compression	0.1197-0.1205 in.
Oil	0.1579-0.1587 in.

(continued)

Table 2   2800 cc ENGINE SPECIFICATIONS (continued)

Piston Pins	
Length	2.835-2.866 in.
Diameter	0.9446-0.9450 in.
Clearance to piston	0.0003-0.0006 in.
Clearance to connecting rod	Interference fit
Piston Rings	
Compression ring width	0.0778-0.0783 in. (top)
	0.1172-0.1177 in. (bottom)
Compression ring side clearance	
Normal	0.0020-0.0033 in.
Wear limit	0.006 in.
Oil ring side clearance	snug
Ring gap	
Compression	0.015-0.023 in.
Oil	0.015-0.055 in.
Flywheel	
Clutch face runout	0.005 in.
Oil Pump	
Rotor end clearance	0.004 in. maximum
Outer race to housing clearance	0.001-0.013 in.

*Bearing bore and pin bushing must be parallel and in same vertical plane within 0.004 in. at ends of 8 in. long bar measured at 4 in. from either side of connecting rod.

4

Table 3   200 cid   ENGINE SPECIFICATIONS

General specifications	
Piston displacement	3273 cc (200 cu. in.)
Bore	3.68 in.
Stroke	3.13 in.
Oil pressure (hot at 2,000 rpm)	30-50 psi
Firing order	1-5-3-6-2-4
Compression pressure	Lowest cylinder within 75% of
(cranking speed)	highest
Cylinder Head	
Valve guide bore diameter	0.3115-0.3125 in.
Valve seat width	
Intake	0.060-0.080 in.
Exhaust	0.070-0.090 in.
Valve seat angle	45°
Valve seat runout (maximum)	0.002 in.
Valve arrangement (front to rear)	E-I-I-E-I-E-E-I-E-I-I-E
Valve Springs	
Approximate free length	1.79 in.
Assembled height	$1\frac{9}{16}$-$1\frac{19}{32}$ in.
Pressure at length	
Intake	51-57 @ 1.59
Exhaust	142-158 @ 1.222
Maximum out-of-square	0.078 in.
Valves	
Stem-to-guide clearance	
Intake	0.0008-0.0025 in.
Exhaust	0.0010-0.0027 in.
Face angle	44°
Head diameter	
Intake	1.739-1.763 in.
Exhaust	1.378-1.402 in.
Stem diameter, standard	
Intake	0.3100-0.3107 in.
Exhaust	0.3098-0.3105 in.
Camshaft	
Lobe lift	0.245 in.
Maximum lift loss	0.005 in.
Journal-to-bearing clearance	0.001-0.003 in.
Journal-to-bearing wear limit	0.006 in.
Journal diameter	1.8095-1.8105 in.
Bearing inside diameter	1.8115-1.8125 in.
Journal runout (maximum)	0.005 in.
End play	
Nominal	0.001-0.007 in.
Maximum	0.009 in.
Cylinder Block	
Bore diameter	3.6800-3.6848 in.
Out-of-round (maximum)	0.0015 in.
Taper (maximum)	0.010 in.
Main bearing bore diameter	2.4012-2.4020 in.
Crankshaft	
Main bearing journal diameter	2.2482-2.2490 in.
Main bearing journal wear limit	0.0006 in.
Main bearing journal runout	
(maximum)	0.002 in.
Main bearing journal out-of-round	
(maximum)	0.0006 in.
Main bearing journal taper	
(maximum)	0.0006 in. per in.
Connecting rod journal diameter	2.2132-2.21240 in.

(continued)

Table 3   200 cid   ENGINE SPECIFICATIONS (continued)

Crankshaft (continued)	
Connecting rod journal taper (maximum)	0.0006 in. per in.
Journal out-of-round (maximum)	0.0006 in.
Crankshaft free end play	0.004-0.008 in.
Crankshaft free end play wear	
limit	0.012 in.
Main Bearings	
Clearance to crankshaft	
Standard	0.0008-0.0015 in.
Permissible	0.0008-0.0024 in.
Connecting Rod Bearings	
Clearance to crankshaft	
Standard	0.0008-0.0015 in.
Permissible	0.0008-0.0024 in.
Connecting Rods	
Piston pin bore diameter	0.9104-0.9112 in.
Bearing bore	2.2390-2.2398 in.
Bearing bore out-of-round	
and taper (maximum)	0.0004 in.
Alignment*	
Twist	0.024 in.
Bend	0.012 in.
Side clearance	
Standard	0.0035-0.0105 in.
Wear limit	0.014 in.
Pistons	
Diameter, standard	
Coded red	3.6784-3.6790 in.
Coded blue	3.6796-3.67802 in.
Clearance to cylinder bore	0.0013-0.0021 in.
Pin bore diameter	0.9124-0.9127 in.
Ring groove width	
Compression	0.080-0.081 in.
Oil	0.188-0.189 in.
Piston Pins	
Length	3.010-3.040 in.
Diameter	0.9119-0.9124 in.
Clearance to piston	0.0003-0.0005 in.
Clearance to connecting rod	Interference fit
Piston Rings	
Compression ring width	0.077-0.078 in.
Compression ring side clearance	
Normal	0.002-0.004 in.
Wear limit	0.006 in.
Oil ring side clearance	Snug
Compression ring gap	0.008-0.016 in.
Oil ring steer rail gap	0.015-0.055 in.
Flywheel	
Clutch race runout	0.010 in.
Oil Pump	
Rotor end clearance	0.004 in.
Outer race to housing	0.001-0.013 in.

*Bearing bore and pin bushing must be parallel and in same vertical plane within 0.004 in. at ends of 8 in. long bar measured at 4 in. from either side of connecting rod.

Table 4   255 cid ENGINE SPECIFICATIONS

General Specifications	
Piston displacement	4184 cc (255 cu. in.)
Bore	3.68 in.
Stroke	3.00 in.
Oil pressure (hot at 2,000 rpm)	40-60 psi
Firing order	1-5-4-2-6-3-7-8
Compression pressure (cranking speed)	Lowest cylinder within 75% of highest
Cylinder Head	
Valve guide bore diameter	0.3433-0.3443 in.
Valve seat width	0.060-0.80 in.
Valve seat angle	45°
Valve seat runout (maximum)	0.002 in.
Valve arrangement (front to rear)	E-I-E-I-E-I-E-I (L.H.) I-E-I-E-I-E-I-E (R.H.)
Valve Springs	
Approximate free length	
Intake	2.04 in.
Exhaust	1.85 in.
Assembled height	
Intake	$1\frac{43}{64}-1\frac{45}{64}$ in.
Exhaust	$1\frac{37}{64}-1\frac{39}{64}$ in.
Pressure at length	
Intake	74-82 lb. @ 1.78 in. 190-212 lb. @ 1.36 in.
Exhaust	76-84 lb. @ 1.60 in. 190-210 lb. @ 1.20 in.
Maximum out-of-square	0.078 in.
Valves	
Stem-to-guide clearance	
Intake	0.0010 in.
Exhaust	0.0015 in.
Face angle	44°
Head diameter	
Intake	1.770 in.
Exhaust	1.439 in.
Stem diameter, standard	
Intake	0.3416-0.3423 in.
Exhaust	0.3411-0.3418 in.
Camshaft	
Lobe lift	0.2375 in.
Maximum lift loss	0.005 in.
Journal-to-bearing clearance	0.001-0.003 in.
Journal-to-bearing wear limit	0.006 in.
Journal diameter	
No. 1	2.0805-2.0815 in.
No. 2	2.0655-2.0665 in.
No. 3	2.0505-2.0515 in.
No. 4	2.0355-2.0365 in.
No. 5	2.0205-2.0215 in.

(continued)

Table 4   255 cid   ENGINE SPECIFICATIONS (continued)

Camshaft (continued)	
Bearing diameter	
No. 1	2.0825-2.0835 in.
No. 2	2.0675-2.0685 in.
No. 3	2.0525-2.0535 in.
No. 4	2.0375-2.0385 in.
No. 5	2.0225-2.0235 in.
Journal runout (maximum)	0.005 in.
Journal out-of-round (maximum)	0.005 in.
End play	
Nominal	0.001-0.007 in.
Maximum	0.009 in.
Cylinder Block	
Bore diameter	3.6800-3.6835 in.
Out-of-round (maximum)	0.0015 in.
Taper (maximum)	0.010 in.
Main bearing bore diameter	2.4412-2.4420 in.
Crankshaft	
Main bearing journal diameter	2.2490-2.2482 in.
Main bearing journal wear	
limit	0.005 in.
Main bearing journal runout	
(maximum)	0.002 in.
Main bearing journal out-of-round	
(maximum)	0.0006 in.
Main bearing journal taper	
(maximum)	0.0006 in. per in.
Connecting rod journal	
diameter	2.1328-2.1236 in.
Connecting rod journal taper	
(maximum	0.0006 in per in.
Journal out-of-round	
(maximum)	0.0006 in.
Crankshaft free end play	0.004-0.008 in.
Crankshaft free end play	
wear limit	0.012 in.
Main Bearings	
Clearance to crankshaft	
Standard	
No. 1	0.0001-0.0015 in.
All others	0.0004-0.0015 in.
Permissible	
No. 1	0.0001-0.0007 in.
All others	0.0004-0.0021 in.
Connecting Rod Bearings	
Clearance to crankshaft	
Standard	0.0008-0.0015 in.
Permissible	0.0008-0.0024 in.
Connecting Rods	
Piston pin bore diameter	0.9124-0.9127 in.
Bearing bore	2.2390-2.2398 in.
Bearing bore out-of-round and	
taper (maximum)	0.0004 in.
Alignment*	
Twist	0.024 in.
Bend	0.012 in.
Side clearance	0.010-0.020 in.
(continued)	

Table 4   255 cid ENGINE SPECIFICATIONS (continued)

Pistons	
Diameter, standard	
Coded red	3.6784-3.6790 in.
Coded blue	3.6798-3.6804 in.
Clearance to bore	0.0018-0.0026 in.
Ring groove width	
Upper compression	0.080-0.081 in.
Lower compression	0.080-0.081 in.
Oil	0.188-0.189 in.
Piston Pins	
Length	3.010-3.040 in.
Diameter	0.9119-0.0124 in.
Clearance to piston	0.0002-0.0004 in.
Clearance to connecting rod	Interference fit
Piston Rings	
Compression ring width	0.077-0.078 in.
Compression side clearance	
Normal	0.002-0.004 in.
Wear limit	0.006 in.
Oil ring side clearance	Snug
Compression ring gap	0.010-0.020 in.
Oil ring steel rail gap	0.015-0.055 in.
Flywheel	
Clutch race runout	0.010 in.
Oil Pump	
Rotor end clearance	0.001-0.004 in.
Outer race top housing	0.001-0.013 in.
Timing Chain	
Maximum deflection	0.005 in.

*Bearing bore and pin bushing must be parallel and in same vertical plane within 0.004 in. at ends of 8 in. long bar measured at 4 in. from either side of connecting rod.

Table 5   302 cid ENGINE SPECIFICATIONS

General Specifications	
Piston displacement	4950cc (302 cu. in.)
Bore	4.00 in.
Stroke	3.00 in.
Oil pressure (hot at 2,000 rpm)	40-65 psi
Firing order	1-5-4-2-6-3-7-8
Compression pressure (cranking speed)	Lowest cylinder within 75% of highest
Cylinder Head	
Valve guide bore diameter	0.34433-0.3443 in.
Valve seat width	0.060-0.080 in.
Valve seat angle	45°
Valve seat runout (maximum)	0.002 in.
Valve arrangement (front to rear)	E-I-E-I-E-I-E-I (L.H.)
	I-E-I-E-I-E-I-E (R.H.)
Valve Springs	
Approximate free length	
Intake	2.04 in.
Exhaust	1.85 in.
Assembled height	
Intake	$1\frac{43}{64}$-$1\frac{45}{64}$ in.
Exhaust	$1\frac{37}{64}$-$1\frac{39}{64}$ in.

(continued)

Table 5   302 cid **ENGINE SPECIFICATIONS** (continued)

Pressure at length	
Intake	74-82 lb. @ 1.78 in.
	190-212 lb. @ 1.36 in.
Exhaust	76-84 lb. @ 1.60 in.
	190-210 lb. @ 1.20 in.
Maximum out-of-square	0.078 in.
Valves	
Stem-to-guide clearance	
Intake	0.0010-0.0027 in.
Exhaust	0.0015-0.0032 in.
Face angle	44°
Head diameter	
Intake	1.770-1.794 in.
Exhaust	1.439-1.463 in.
Stem diameter, standard	
Intake	0.3416-0.3423 in.
Exhaust	0.3411-0.3418 in.
Camshaft	
Lobe lift	
Intake	0.2375 in.
Exhaust	0.2474 in.
Maximum lift loss	0.005 in.
Journal-to-bearing clearance	0.001-0.003 in.
Journal-to-bearing wear limit	0.006 in.
Journal diameter	
No. 1	2.0805-2.0815 in.
No. 2	2.0655-2.0665 in.
No. 3	2.0505-2.0515 in.
No. 4	2.0355-2.0365 in.
No. 5	2.0205-2.0215 in.
Bearing diameter	
No. 1	2.0825-2.0835 in.
No. 2	2.0675-2.0685 in.
No. 3	2.525-2.0535 in.
No. 4	2.0375-2.0385 in.
No. 5	2.0225-2.0235 in.
Journal runout (maximum)	0.0005 in.
Journal out-of-round (maximum)	0.0005 in.
End play	
Nominal	0.001-0.007 in.
Maximum	0.009 in.
Cylinder Block	
Bore diameter	4.004-4.0052 in.
Out-of-round (maximum)	0.0015 in.
Taper (maximum)	0.010 in.
Main bearing bore diameter	2.4412-2.4420 in.
Crankshaft	
Main bearing journal diameter	2.2482-2.2490 in.
Main bearing journal wear limit	0.005 in.
Main bearing journal runout (maximum)	0.002 in.
Main bearing journal out-of-round (maximum)	0.0006 in.
Main bearing journal taper (maximum)	0.0006 in. per in.
Connecting rod journal diameter	2.1228-2.1236 in.
Connecting rod journal taper (maximum)	0.0006 in.
Journal out-of-round (maximum)	0.0006 in.
Crankshaft free end play	0.004-0.008 in.
Crankshaft free and play wear limit	0.012 in.

(continued)

4

Table 5   302 cid ENGINE SPECIFICATIONS

Main Bearings	
Clearance to crankshaft	
Standard	
No. 1	0.0001-0.0005 in.
All others	0.0004-0.0015 in.
Permissible	
No. 1	0.0001-0.0017 in.
All others	0.0004-0.0021 in.
Connecting Rod Bearings	
Clearance to crankshaft	
Standard	0.008-0.0015 in.
Permissible	0.0007-0.0024 in.
Connecting Rods	
Piston pin bore diameter	0.9104-0.9112 in.
Bearing bore	2.2390-2.2398 in.
Bearing bore out-of-round	
and taper (maximum)	0.0004 in.
Alignment*	
Twist	0.024 in.
Bend	0.012 in.
Side clearance	0.010-0.020 in.
Pistons	
Diameter, standard	
Coded red	3.9984-3.9990 in.
Coded blue	3.9996-4.0002 in.
Clearance to cylinder bore	0.0018-0.0026 in.
Pin bore diameter	0.9124-0.9127 in.
Ring groove width	
Upper compression	0.080-0.081 in.
Lower compression	0.080-0.081 in.
Oil	0.1880-0.1890 in.
Piston Pins	
Length	3.010-3.040 in.
Diameter	0.9119-0.9124 in.
Clearance to piston	0.0002-0.0004 in.
Clearance to connecting rod	Interference fit
Piston Rings	
Compression ring width	0.077-0.078 in.
Compression ring side clearance	
Normal	0.002-0.004 in.
Wear limit	0.006 in.
Oil ring side clearance	Snug
Compression ring gap	0.010-0.020 in.
Oil ring steel rail gap	0.015-0.055 in.
Flywheel	
Clutch face runout	0.010 in.
Oil Pump	
Rotor end clearance	0.001-0.004 in.
Outer race to housing	0.001-0.013 in.
Timing Chain	
Maximum deflection	0.005 in.

*Bearing bore and pin bushing must be parallel and in same vertical plane within 0.004 in. at ends of 8 in. long bar measured at 4 in. from either side of connecting rod.

Table 6   TIGHTENING TORQUES, 2300 cc ENGINE

Item	Torque (ft.-lb.)	Metric Sizes
Auxiliary shaft cover bolt	6-9	M6
Auxiliary shaft gear bolt	28-40	M10
Auxiliary shaft thrust plate bolt	6-9	M6
Belt tensioner timing pivot bolt	28-40	M10
Belt tensioner timing bolt	14-21	M8
Camshaft gear bolt	50-71	M12
Camshaft thrust plate bolts	6-9	M6
Carburetor to spacer stud	7.5-15	M8
Carburetor to spacer nut	10-14	M8
Carburetor spacer to manifold bolt	14-21	M8
Connecting rod cap nuts	Step 1 25-30	M9
	Step 2 30-36	—
Crankshaft damper bolt	100-120	M14
Cylinder front cover bolt	6-9	M6
Cylinder head bolt	Step 1 50-60	M12
	Step 2 80-90	—
Distributor clamp bolt	14-21	M10
Distributor vacuum tube to intake manifold adapter	5-8	—
EGR valve spacer bolt	14-21	M8
EGR tube to exhaust manifold connection	9-11	—
EGR tube nut	9-11	—
Exhaust manifold to cylinder head bolt, stud, or nut	Step 1 5-7	M10
	Step 2 16-23	—
Flywheel to crankshaft bolt	56-64	M10
Fuel pump to cylinder block	14-21	M8
Intake manifold to cylinder head bolt/nut (non-turbo)	Step 1 5-7	M8
	Step 2 13-18	—
Intake manifold to cylinder head bolt/nut (turbo)	Step 1 5-7	M8
	Step 2 18-24	—
Main bearing cap bolts	Step 1 50-60	M12
	Step 2 80-90	—
Oil pressure sending unit to cylinder block	8-18	—
Oil pump pickup tube to pump	14-21	M8
Oil pump to cylinder block	14-21	M8
Oil pan drain plug	15-25	M14
Oil pan to cylinder block bolts	6-8	M6
	8-10	M8
Oil filter insert to block	20-25	—
Rocker arm cover bolts	6-8	M6
Spark plugs to cylinder head	5-10	M14
Temperature sending unit to cylinder block	8-18	—
Thermactor check valve to exhaust manifold	17-20	—
Water jacket drain plug	23-28	—
Water pump cylinder block bolt	14-21	M8
*General tightening torques	6-9	M6
	14-21	M8
	28-40	M10
	50-71	M12
	80-114	M14
	12-18	1/4-18 pipe
	23-33	3/8-18 pipe

*If not otherwise specified.

4

Table 7   TIGHTENING TORQUES, 2800 cc ENGINE

Item	Torque (ft.-lb.)	Metric Size
Alternator adjusting arm to alternator	24-40	—
Alternator bracket to cylinder block	28-40	M10
Alternator bracket to cylinder head	18-25	M8
Alternator adjusting arm to front cover	50-71	M12
Alternator pivot bolt	45-60	—
Camshaft gear bolt	30-36	M10
Camshaft thrust plate bolt	12-15	M8
Carburetor spacer (stud)	3-5	—
Carburetor adapter to manifold stud	3-5	—
Carburetor to spacer nut	4-18	M8
Connecting rod cap nuts	21-25	M8
Crankshaft damper bolt	92-103	M12
Crankcase vent valve	11-14	—
Cylinder head bolts	Step 1 29-40	M12
	Step 2 40-51	—
	Step 3 65-80	—
Distributor clamp bolt	12-15	M8
EGR tube fittings	15-20	—
EGR valve to spacer bolt	12-15	M8
Exhaust manifold to EGR pipe (connector)	25-35	—
Exhaust manifold to cylinder head bolt or stud	20-30	M8
Flywheel to crankshaft bolt	47-51	M10
Front cover to cylinder block bolt	12-15	M8
Front plate to cylinder block bolt	12-15	M8
Fuel pump to cylinder block bolt	17-21	M8
Intake manifold to cylinder block bolt or nut	Step 1 3-6	M8
	Step 2 6-11	—
	Step 3 11-15	—
	Step 4 15-18	—
Intake manifold to cylinder block stud	10-12	M8
Main bearing cap bolt	65-75	M12
Monolithic timing pointer to front cover bolt	7-9	M6
Oil pump pick-up tube to pump bolt	7-9	M6
Oil pump pick-up tube to main bearing cap bolt	12-15	M8
Oil pan drain plug	21-38	M14
Oil pan to cylinder block bolt	7-10	M6
Oil filter to cylinder block insert	10-15	—
Oil filter	See text	—
Rocker arm cover bolt	3-5	M6

(continued)

Table 7   TIGHTENING TORQUES, 2800 cc ENGINE (continued)

Item	Torque (ft.-lb.)	Metric Size
Rocker arms shaft support bolt	43-49	M10
Thermactor pump bracket to cylinder block	28-40	M10
Thermactor pump bracket to cylinder head bolt	18-25	M8
Thermactor pump adjusting arm to pump bolt	22-32	—
Thermactor pump pivot bolt	30-45	—
Water jacket drain plug to cylinder block	14-18	—
Water outlet connection bolt	12-15	M8
Water pump to cylinder block bolt	7-9	M6
Water temperature sending unit	7-11	—
*General tightening torques	6-9	M6
	14-21	M8
	28-40	M10
	50-71	M12
	80-114	M14
	5-8	1/8 pipe
	12-18	1/4 pipe
	22-33	3/8 pipe
	25-35	1/2 pipe
*If not otherwise specified		

Table 8   TIGHTENING TORQUES, 200 cid ENGINE

Item	Torque (ft.-lb.)
Alternator bracket to cylinder block bolt	35-50
Alternator adjusting arm to cylinder block	15-20
Alternator adjusting arm to alternator	24-34
Camshaft sprocket to camshaft	35-45
Camshaft thrust plate to cylinder block	12-18
Carburetor mounting nuts	12-15
Carburetor mounting stud	15 maximum
Connecting rod cap nuts	21-26
Cylinder front cover bolts	6-9
Cylinder head bolts	Step 1 50-55
	Step 2 60-65
	Step 3 70-75
Damper or pulley to crankshaft	85-100
Distributor clamp hold down bolt	17-25
Exhaust manifold to cylinder head	18-24
Fan to water pump hub bolt	12-18
Fuel pump to cylinder block or front cover	12-18
Flywheel to crankshaft	75-85
Main bearing cap bolts	60-70
Oil filter insert to cylinder block	10-15
Oil filter	See text
Oil inlet tube to oil pump	10-15
Oil pan drain plug	15-25
Oil pan to cylinder block	7-9
Oil pump to cylinder block	10-15
Pulley to damper bolt	35-50
Rocker arm support shaft to cylinder head	30-35
Spark plug to cylinder head	10-15
Thermactor pump bracket to cylinder block	12-18
Thermactor pump pivot bolt	22-32
Thermactor pump adjusting arm to pump	24-34
Thermactor pump adjusting arm to cylinder block	12-18
Thermactor pump pulley to pump hub	130-180 in.-lb.
Valve rocker arm cover	3-5
*General tightening torques	
$\frac{1}{4}$-20	6-9
$\frac{5}{16}$-18	12-18
$\frac{3}{8}$-16	22-32
$\frac{7}{16}$-14	40-55
$\frac{1}{2}$-13	55-80
$\frac{9}{16}$-18	85-120

*If not otherwise specified.

Table 9   TIGHTENING TORQUES, 255 CID AND 302 CID ENGINES

Item	Torque (ft.-lb)
Alternator bracket to cylinder block bolt	12-18
Alternator adjustment arm to cylinder block bolt	12-18
Alternator adjustment arm to alternator bolt	24-40
Carburetor attaching nut	12-15
Camshaft sprocket gear to camshaft bolt	40-45
Camshaft thrust plate to cylinder block bolt	9-12
Carburetor mounting stud	15 maximum
Connecting rod nuts	19-24
Cylinder front cover bolt	12-18
Cylinder head bolts	Step 1 55-65
	Step 2 65-72
Damper to crankshaft bolt	70-90
Distributor hold-down bolt	18-26
Exhaust manifold to cylinder head bolt	18-24
Fan to water pump hub bolt	12-18
Flywheel to crankshaft bolt	75-85
Fuel pump to cylinder block front cover bolt	19-27
Intake manifold to cylinder head bolt	23-25
Main bearing cap bolts	60-70
Oil filter insert to cylinder block adapter bolt	20-30
Oil filter	See text
Oil inlet tube to oil pump bolt	10-15
Oil pan drain plug	15-25
Oil pan to cylinder block bolt	9-11
Oil pump to cylinder block bolt	22-32
Oil inlet tube to main bearing cap nuts	22-32
Pulley to damper bolt	35-50
Rocker arm stud bolt to cylinder head	18-35
Spark plug to cylinder head	10-15
Thermactor pump bracket to cylinder block bolt	30-45
Thermactor pump pivot bolt	22-32
Thermactor pump adjustment arm to pump	22-32
Thermactor pump pulley to pump hub	130-180 in.-lb.
Valve to rocker arm cover bolt	3-5
Water outlet housing bolt	9-12
Water pump to cylinder block front cover bolt	12-18
*General tightening torques:	
$\frac{1}{4}$-20	6-9
$\frac{5}{16}$-18	12-18
$\frac{3}{8}$-16	22-32
$\frac{7}{16}$-14	40-55
$\frac{1}{2}$-13	55-80
$\frac{9}{16}$-18	85-120
*If not otherwise specified	

4

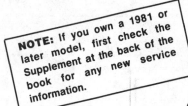
NOTE: If you own a 1981 or later model, first check the Supplement at the back of the book for any new service information.

CHAPTER FIVE

FUEL, EXHAUST, AND EMISSION CONTROL SYSTEMS

— The fuel system consists of a rear mounted fuel tank connected through a fuel line to a mechanical fuel pump. The pump delivers fuel through a fuel filter to either a 1-barrel or 2-barrel carburetor.

Both single and dual exhaust systems are available on all models. The exact parts included in each exhaust system are described later in this chapter.

Basic emission control devices used are also covered in this chapter. These devices include the fuel vapor emission control system, the PCV system, the EGR system and spark delay valve, and the Thermactor system.

When servicing your vehicle's fuel, exhaust, or emission systems, refer to the vehicle emission control information label which can usually be found in the engine compartment (**Figure 1**). Most emission system work is best left to your dealer, since expensive and specialized equipment is often needed. However, those systems which can be serviced will be discussed in this chapter.

Specifications (**Table 1**) are at the end of the chapter.

AIR CLEANER

Refer to **Figure 2** for this procedure. Shown is a typical air cleaner and duct assembly for V8 engines; 4- and 6-cylinder engines are similar.

1. Disconnect the crankcase ventilation system closure hose at the air cleaner body by removing the clip securing the elbow to the air cleaner shell (**Figure 3**).

2. Disconnect the fresh air pickup tube from the duct and valve assembly.

3. On 2300 cc engines, disconnect the line from the vacuum source to the bimetal switch inside the air cleaner, at the air cleaner.

4. Disconnect the temperature vacuum switch at the vacuum harness. On 2800 cc engines, also disconnect the vacuum vent valve harness at the air cleaner body.

5. Loosen the heat shroud riser tube pipe clamp (**Figure 2**), then disconnect the heat shroud riser tube from the duct and valve assembly.

6. Remove the wing nut attaching air cleaner cover to carburetor air horn.

7. Ensure that all vacuum lines and hoses are disconnected from the air cleaner body, and duct and valve assembly, then lift the air cleaner from the engine. If the air cleaner element is to be replaced, remove the air cleaner cover from the air cleaner body, then lift the filter element from the air cleaner body.

8. Inspect the carburetor-to-air cleaner body gasket and replace if necessary.

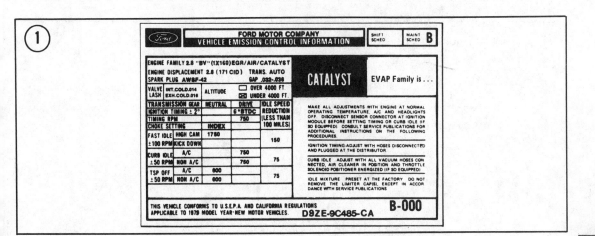

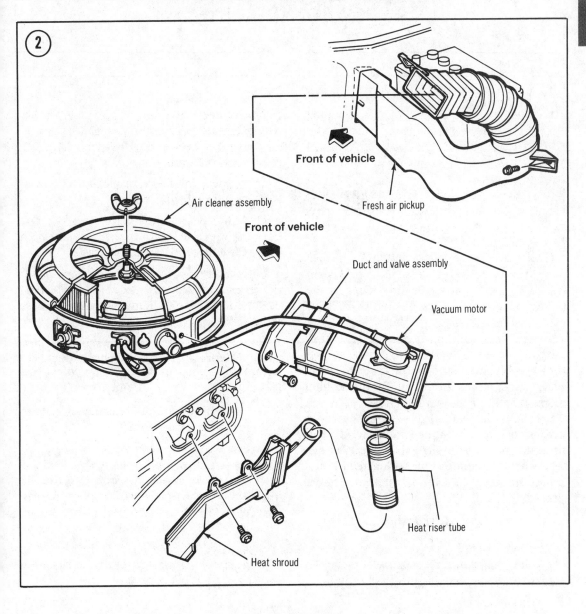

Front of vehicle

Fresh air pickup

Air cleaner assembly

Front of vehicle

Duct and valve assembly

Vacuum motor

Heat riser tube

Heat shroud

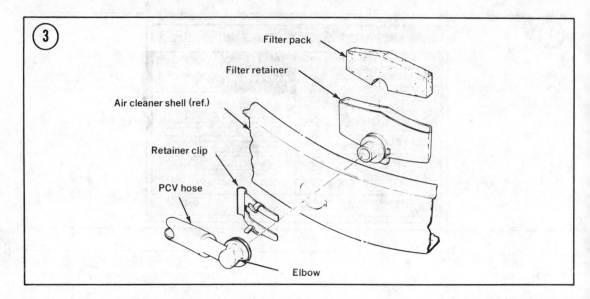

③ Filter pack

Filter retainer

Air cleaner shell (ref.)

Retainer clip

PCV hose

Elbow

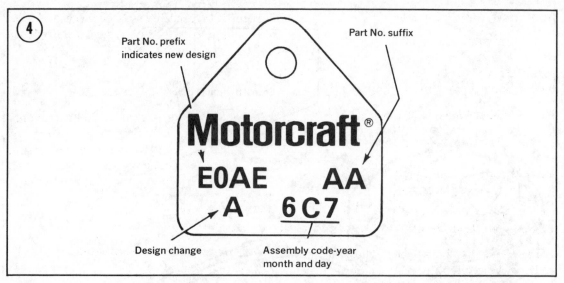

④ Part No. prefix
indicates new design

Part No. suffix

Motorcraft®

EOAE   AA

A   6 C 7

Design change   Assembly code-year
month and day

9. Wipe all inside surfaces of the air cleaner body with a clean cloth, then install the filter element in the air cleaner body.

10. Install the air cleaner body on the carburetor, making sure the duct and valve assembly are properly aligned.

11. The remainder of the installation procedure is the reverse of the removal procedure.

CARBURETORS

Carburetor Types

Six different carburetors were used for 1979 and 1980 models. Many are similar, however,

with minor changes made for Federal and California emission requirements. Following is a brief description of each.

NOTE
An identification tag is attached to each non-variable venturi carburetor (Figure 4). On variable venturi carburetors, identification codes are stamped directly into the upper body casting over the float bowl (Figure 5). Refer to the tag or code to determine your vehicle's carburetor type before performing the following service procedures.

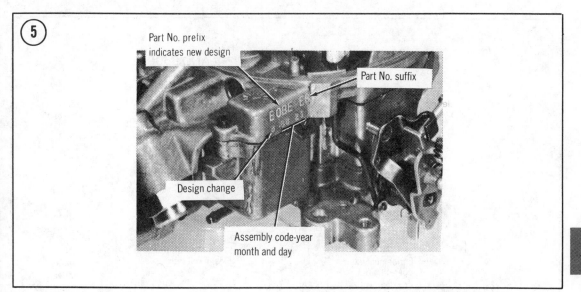

⑤

Part No. prefix indicates new design

Part No. suffix

Design change

Assembly code-year month and day

5

Motorcraft Model 5200 2-V

This model is a 2-stage, 2-venturi carburetor. A fully electrically heated automatic choke is used to provide choke pull-off soon after engine starting.

Holley/Weber Model 6500 Feedback

This carburetor is similar to the Model 5200 except it is used only on vehicles manufactured for sale in California which use a Feedback Electronic Control System.

Motorcraft Model 2150 2-V

This model has 2 main assemblies: the main body and the air horn. The air horn, which covers the main body, contains the choke plate and the fuel bowl vent valve. Each barrel contains both a main and booster venturi.

Motorcraft Model 2700 VV

This carburetor uses a dual-element venturi valve which moves in and out of the air flowing into the carburetor throats, thus varying the area of the venturi according to engine speed and load. The venturi valve is controlled by engine vacuum and throttle position.

Motorcraft Model 7200 Feedback

This carburetor is similar to Model 2700 VV

except it is used only on vehicles manufactured for sale in California which use Feedback Electronic Control System.

Holley Model 1946-C

This carburetor is used on 200 cid engines equipped with automatic transmissions. A multitude of systems are used to provide appropriate air/fuel mixture ratios for fuel economy, driveability and emission requirements.

Carburetor Removal/Installation

1. Remove the air cleaner and duct assembly as described earlier in this chapter.
2. Label and disconnect the fuel and vacuum lines. Plug the fuel lines so they won't drip.
3. Disconnect the electrical lead to the electric choke heater.
4. On Model 5200 carburetors, remove the hex head screw and washer attaching the water cover to the choke housing.
5. Disconnect throttle linkage at carburetor.
6. Remove the nuts attaching the carburetor to the intake manifold and remove.
7. Install in the reverse order using a new gasket. After installing carburetor on vehicle, refer to Chapter Three for carburetor adjustments.

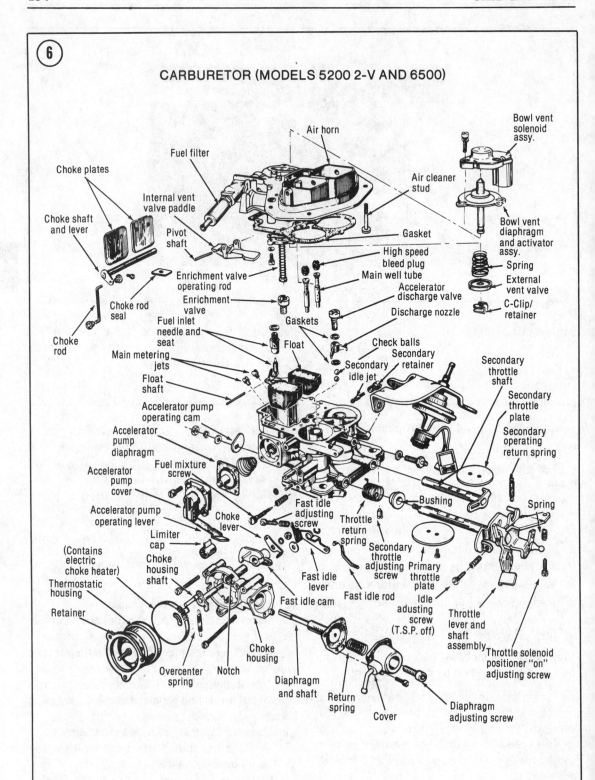

⑥

CARBURETOR (MODELS 5200 2-V AND 6500)

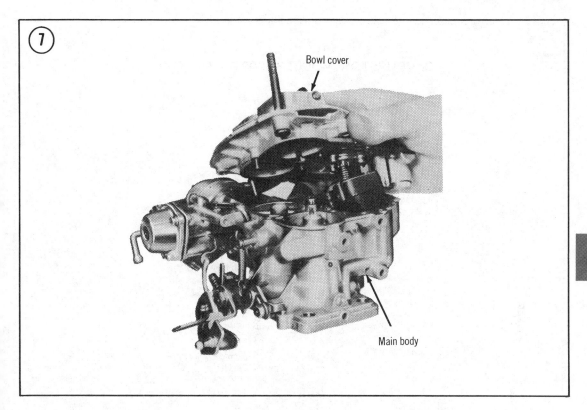

Bowl cover

Main body

Disassembly (Model 5200 2-V and 6500 Feedback)

Refer to **Figure 6**.

1. Remove the air horn bowl screws and plastic bushings from the choke rod. Lift air horn bowl cover up and remove. See **Figure 7**.

2. Remove float pin, float and inlet needle from air horn bowl cover.

3. Remove the inlet needle seat and gasket.

4. Remove vent cover screws attaching solenoid to cover and remove cover.

5. Remove screws securing the thermostatic housing to main body and remove housing, index plate and retaining ring as one unit.

6. Remove 4 screws securing accelerator pump cover and remove pump cover, diaphragm and return spring.

7. From inside main body, remove primary and secondary high speed bleed and main well tube. Note size of main well tubes for installation purposes.

8. Turn idle limiter cap to stop and remove idle limiter cap.

NOTE
When removing adjustment needles, count turns required to lightly seat needle, and record turns for installation.

9. Remove secondary throttle return spring from arm on throttle lever assembly.

10. Remove nut securing primary throttle shaft and remove accelerator pump.

Disassembly (Model 2150 2-V)

Refer to **Figure 8**.

1. Remove the air cleaner as described in this chapter.

2. Remove choke control rod retainer clip from choke rod plate.

3. Remove screws attaching air horn to main body, lift up air horn and remove.

4. Loosen screw securing choke control rod to choke shaft lever. Remove rod from air horn.

5. Remove retaining clip securing fast idle cam and remove cam.

6. Remove screws securing thermostatic choke housing to side of main body. Pull housing, clamp and gasket away from main body.

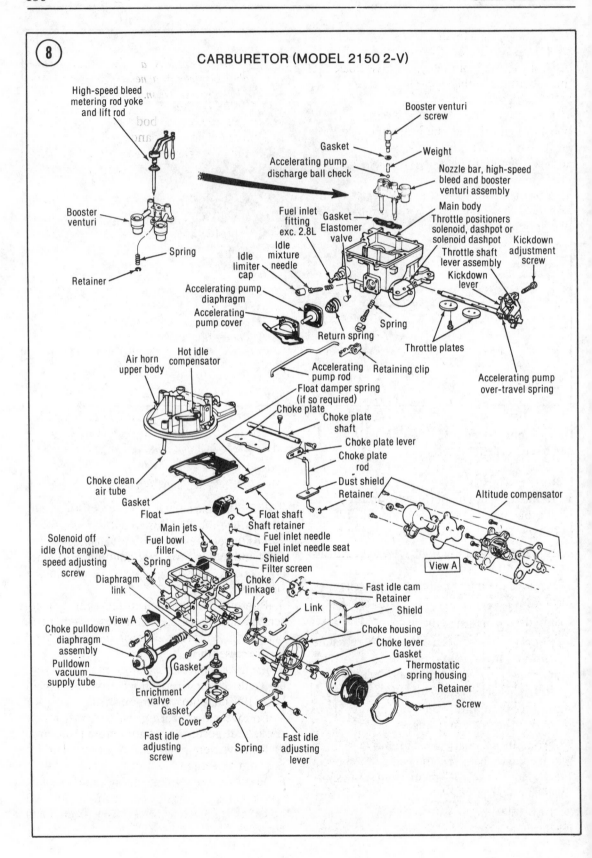

⑧ CARBURETOR (MODEL 2150 2-V)

High-speed bleed metering rod yoke and lift rod

Booster venturi screw

Gasket

Weight

Accelerating pump discharge ball check

Nozzle bar, high-speed bleed and booster venturi assembly

Booster venturi

Spring

Retainer

Fuel inlet fitting exc. 2.8L

Gasket

Elastomer valve

Main body

Throttle positioners solenoid, dashpot or solenoid dashpot

Idle limiter cap

Idle mixture needle

Throttle shaft lever assembly

Kickdown adjustment screw

Accelerating pump diaphragm

Accelerating pump cover

Kickdown lever

Spring

Return spring

Throttle plates

Air horn upper body

Hot idle compensator

Accelerating pump rod

Retaining clip

Accelerating pump over-travel spring

Float damper spring (if so required)

Choke plate

Choke plate shaft

Choke plate lever

Choke plate rod

Choke clean air tube

Gasket

Float

Dust shield

Retainer

Altitude compensator

Float shaft

Shaft retainer

Fuel inlet needle

Fuel inlet needle seat

Shield

Filter screen

View A

Main jets

Fuel bowl filler

Spring

Solenoid off idle (hot engine) speed adjusting screw

Diaphragm link

Choke linkage

Fast idle cam

Retainer

Link

Shield

View A

Choke housing

Choke lever

Gasket

Thermostatic spring housing

Retainer

Screw

Choke pulldown diaphragm assembly

Pulldown vacuum supply tube

Gasket

Enrichment valve

Gasket

Cover

Fast idle adjusting screw

Spring

Fast idle adjusting lever

7. Pry float shaft retainer clip from fuel inlet seat with screwdriver (**Figure 9**).

8. From inside main body, remove float, fuel inlet needle assembly and float shaft.

9. Remove main jets.

10. Remove the booster venturi screw, booster venturi and metering rod assembly and gasket. Turn main body over to allow accelerating pump discharge weight and ball to fall.

11. Remove screws securing accelerator pump and remove accelerator pump cover, diaphragm assembly and spring.

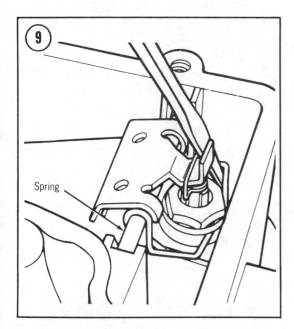

Spring

NOTE
*Located directly behind the accelerator pump diaphragm is a small elastomer valve. If removed, a new valve must be used during installation. See **Figure 8**.*

12. Invert the main body and remove the enrichment valve cover and gasket.

13. Remove screws securing altitude compensator to main body and remove (if so equipped).

14. Remove screws securing the throttle plates and lift out the plates. Remove any burrs on the throttle shaft, then slide it out of the carburetor.

NOTE
*Before removing throttle plates, lightly mark each throttle plate and its corresponding bore for proper installation (**Figure 10**).*

Disassembly (Model 2700 VV and 7200 Feedback)

If Model 2700 VV and 7200 Feedback carburetors become unserviceable, it is advisable to install a reconditioned carburetor.

Disassembly (Model 1946-C)

Refer to **Figure 11**.

1. Remove the air cleaner and duct assembly as mentioned previously in this chapter.

2. Remove 3 screws securing choke retainer and remove retainer, gasket, and bimetal spring cover.

3. Remove 2 pulldown diaphragm bracket screws, disconnect vacuum hose from main body and remove pulldown diaphragm and linkage assembly.

4. Remove 3 screws securing fuel bowl vent cover to top of air horn. Lift fuel bowl vent cover up and remove from air horn.

Remove cover, spring and gasket from air horn. Note position of spring before removing.

5. Remove vent bowl retaining screw and lift vent bowl assembly from seat.

6. Remove the fast idle cam retainer and fast idle cam.

7. Remove choke control lever screw from choke shaft.

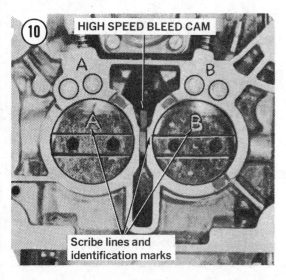

HIGH SPEED BLEED CAM

A   B

A   B

Scribe lines and identification marks

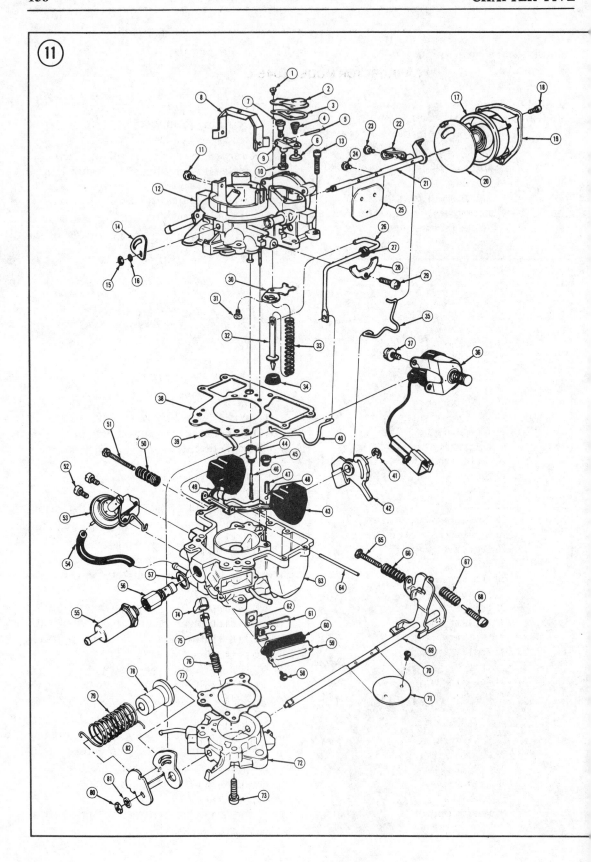

CARBURETOR MODEL 1946-C

1. Screw
2. Bowl vent cover
3. Vent cover gasket
4. Vent valve spring
5. Vent valve hinge pin
6. Vent valve
7. Vent valve hinge
   attaching screw
8. Air cleaner bracket
9. Vent valve arm
10. Vent valve adjusting screw
11. Air cleaner bracket screw
12. Air horn
13. Screw
14. Choke pulldown lever
15. Choke shaft nut
16. Lockwasher
17. Choke bimetal
   spring cover
18. Screw
19. Choke cover retainer
20. Choke housing gasket
21. Choke shaft and
   lever assembly
22. Choke control lever
23. Screw
24. Screw
25. Choke plate
26. Accelerator pump operating rod
27. Accelerator pump rod grommet
28. Rod retaining clamp
29. Screw
30. Accelerator pump spring
   retaining spring
31. Screw
32. Accelerator pump
   piston stem
33. Accelerator pump
   spring
34. Accelerator pump
   piston cup
35. Fast idle cam link
36. Anti-diesel solenoid
37. Screw
38. Air horn gasket
39. Float hinge retainer
40. Accelerator pump
   operating link
41. Retaining clip

42. Fast idle cam
43. Float assembly
44. Power body valve
45. Main metering jet
46. Power valve pin
47. Accelerator pump weight
48. Accelerator pump check ball
49. Power valve spring
50. Spring
51. Low idle (solenoid off)
   adjusting screw
52. Screw
53. Choke pulldown diaphragm
   assembly
54. Choke diaphragm
   vacuum hose
55. Fuel filter
56. Fuel inlet needle and
   seat assembly
57. Gasket
58. Screw
59. Hot idle compensator cover
60. Cover gasket
61. Hot idle compensator
62. Gasket
63. Main body assembly
64. Float hinge pin
65. Curb idle adjusting screw
66. Spring
67. Spring
68. Fast idle adjusting screw
69. Throttle shaft lever
   and assembly
70. Screw
71. Throttle plate
72. Throttle body assembly
73. Throttle body screw
74. Limiter cap
75. Idle fuel mixture
   adusting screw
76. Spring
77. Throttle body gasket
78. Throttle return
   spring bushing
80. Nut
81. Lockwasher
82. Throttle return
   spring bracket

5

8. Remove nut and lockwasher from end of throttle return spring bracket. Detach return spring from throttle body and remove spring and bracket.

9. Remove the accelerator pump link from pump operating rod.

10. Remove 7 screws attaching air horn to main body and remove air horn.

> *NOTE*
> *Do not pry air horn to remove. Use a plastic hammer and gently tap side of air horn to loosen.*

11. Remove the accelerator pump operating rod screw and retainer clamp. Rotate the pump operating rod and detach the pump drive spring and accelerator pump assembly.

12. Remove the pump operating rod and grommet from the bowl cover.

> *NOTE*
> *The main tube well cannot be removed from the main body. To clean, direct compressed air from both inside and outside cover into tube.*

13. Remove 3 thermostat housing screws and remove retainer, housing and gasket.

14. Turn main body over to allow accelerator pump discharge weight and ball to fall from body housing.

15. Remove the fuel filter, needle and seat assembly and gasket from side of main body.

16. Remove the float shaft clip and remove float shaft and float.

17. Remove main jet.

18. Remove 2 screws securing hot idle compensator cover and remove cover, HIC valve, and gaskets from main body.

19. Remove 3 screws attaching main body to throttle body. Tap both body assemblies and remove.

20. Remove solenoid.

> *NOTE*
> *Do not remove the throttle plate or shaft from throttle body. If wear is evident, the complete throttle body assembly must be replaced.*

Inspection (All Models)

1. Throughly clean all parts (except diaphragm, vent bowl assemblies and pump plunger and cup) in solvent or dip-in carburetor cleaner following manufacturer's instructions. O-rings, gaskets, and diaphragms should be replaced if they are included in the repair kit. If not, clean them with a lint-free cloth.

> *CAUTION*
> *Do not insert objects such as drill bits or pieces of wire into jets and passages while cleaning them. These openings are carefully calibrated, and scratching them may seriously affect carburetor and engine performance.*

2. To prevent damage to gasket surfaces, do not use metal scrapers to remove gasket residue. Instead, use a nylon scraper or similar hard plastic material.

3. Check the needle valve and seat for wear. Replace as needed.

4. Check all castings for cracks or damage.

5. Check all mixture screws for wear at the tip. Replace screw if wear is detected.

6. Adjust the float level as discussed later in this chapter.

Assembly

Assembly is the reverse of disassembly, plus the following.

1. Use new gaskets and seals.

2. Be sure the main jets and air bleed are installed in the correct holes. Refer to the correct figure number as required.

3. Adjust curb idle speed, fast idle speed, and idle mixture as discussed in Chapter Three.

Float Adjustment

After disassembling carburetor, adjust the float height as discussed in the following procedures.

Float Adjustment
(Model 5200 2-V
and 6500 Feedback)

Hold the bowl upside down so the float rests lightly on the needle valve (**Figure 12**).

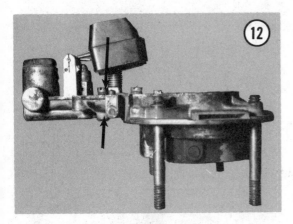

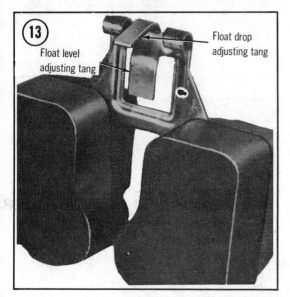

Float level adjusting tang

Float drop adjusting tang

Measure the clearance indicated in the figure. This should be 0.45 in. If necessary, bend adjusting tang shown in **Figure 13** to change setting.

Float Adjustment (Model 2150 2-V Dry)

This is a preliminary adjustment to be done with the fuel bowl empty. The wet adjustment procedure must be done with the carburetor on the engine.

1. Press down on the float hinge to raise the float as far as it will go.
2. Measure the distance from the gasket surface of the carburetor body to the top of the float. If using the cardboard gauge included in Ford rebuild kits, position the gauge as shown in **Figure 14**. If using a ruler, position it in the center of the float, and 1/8 in. from the non-hinged end.
3. Correct depth is 7/16 in. If necessary, bend the tab on the float hinge end to change depth.

Float Adjustment (Model 2150 2-V Wet)

This procedure is done with the carburetor installed on the vehicle.

1. Warm the engine to normal operating temperature. Park the car on a level surface and turn off the engine.
2. Remove the air cleaner.

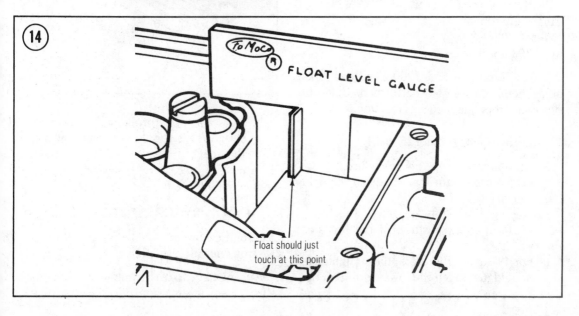

FLOAT LEVEL GAUGE

Float should just touch at this point

5

3. Remove the air horn attaching screws and carburetor tag. Don't remove the air horn or jet.

4. Let the engine idle for a few minutes with the air horn loose.

5. With the engine idling, remove the air horn. Measure depth from the carburetor body gasket surface to the top of the gasoline in the fuel bowl. See **Figure 15**.

> *NOTE*
> *This measurement must be taken at least 1/4 in. from the fuel bowl walls, because the fuel level is higher at the edges than in the center.*

6. Specified depth is 13/16 in. Adjust if necessary by bending the tab on the hinged end of the float. Bending the tab up raises fuel level; bending it down lowers fuel level.

> *WARNING*
> *Turn off the engine before making adjustments. Otherwise splashed gasoline may catch fire. This could destroy the car and seriously injure anyone nearby.*

7. Check the adjustment by putting the air horn on, holding it down, and letting the engine idle for a few minutes. Then remove the air horn and measure fuel depth again. Repeat this process until fuel level is correct.

8. Once fuel level is correct, install the air horn, using a new gasket. Be sure the choke plate rod moves freely in its dust shield.

Float Adjustment (Model 2700 VV and 7200 Feedback)

Model 2700 VV and 7200 Feedback float adjustment should be performed by your dealer or other qualified service shop.

Float Adjustment (Model 1946-C)

Refer to **Figure 16** for this procedure.

1. Hold the carburetor main body so the float hangs down.

2. By laying a straightedge across the lower body surface, check position of the floats as follows:

   a. For 49-state carburetors, the straightedge should just touch the lowest point on the float.

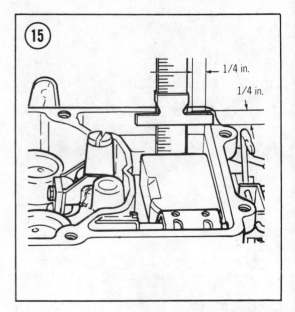

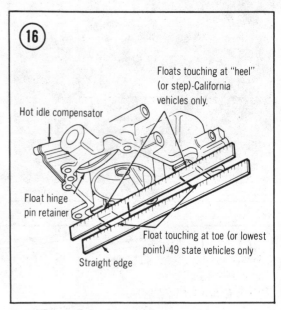

   b. For the California carburetors, the straightedge should just touch the step of the float.

3. Adjust if necessary by bending the tab contacting the needle seat.

CARBURETOR ADJUSTMENTS

Automatic Choke Testing and Adjustment

Automatic choke testing and adjustment affects vehicle emission output, and requires

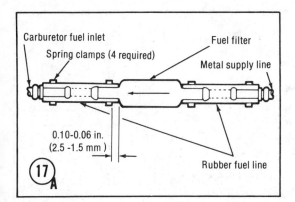

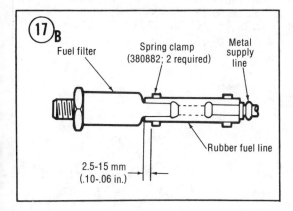

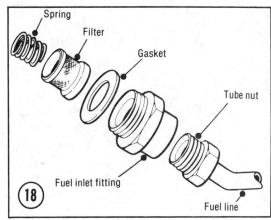

special test equipment. As such, all choke testing and adjustment should be referred to a Ford dealer or a competent garage.

Accelerator Pump Stroke Adjustment

Accelerator pump stroke is factory set for a particular engine application and should not be readjusted.

**Idle Mixture,
Curb and Fast
Idle Adjustments**

Idle mixture, curb, and fast idle adjustments are discussed in Chapter Three.

FUEL FILTER

**Replacement
(Except 2700/7200 VV Carburetors)**

The screw-in and inline fuel filters shown in **Figure 17A** and **Figure 17B** are used on all engines except those which use the 2700 and 7200 VV carburetors. These filters cannot be cleaned. If dirty or clogged they must be replaced.

1. Remove the air cleaner assembly.
2. Remove the inlet hose to fuel filter line spring-type clamp. On inline fuel filters, remove the outlet hose clamp also and then remove the filter. On screw-in filters, unscrew the filter from the carburetor.
3. Discard the fuel filter, hose and clamps.
4. Installation is the reverse of these steps. Screw-in filter tightening torque is 90-125 in.-lb. Start engine and check for leaks.

**Replacement
(2700/7200 VV Carburetors)**

Refer to **Figure 18** for this procedure.
1. Remove the air cleaner assembly.
2. Hold the fuel inlet fitting with a wrench. Then unscrew the fuel line tube nut from the fuel inlet fitting.
3. Discard the gasket and filter.
4. Installation is the reverse of these steps. Apply oil to the fuel tube nut threads and tube flare before installation. Start engine and check for leaks.

ACCELERATOR CABLE

Removal/Installation

The following removal/installation procedure covers all vehicles. Refer to **Figure 19** and **Figure 20** for details on specific throttle cable installations for different engines and transmission configurations.

1. Working below the dash, push the nylon bushing securing the accelerator cable to the accelerator pedal arm out of its slot, then remove the retaining clip attached to the accelerator cable at the dash panel.

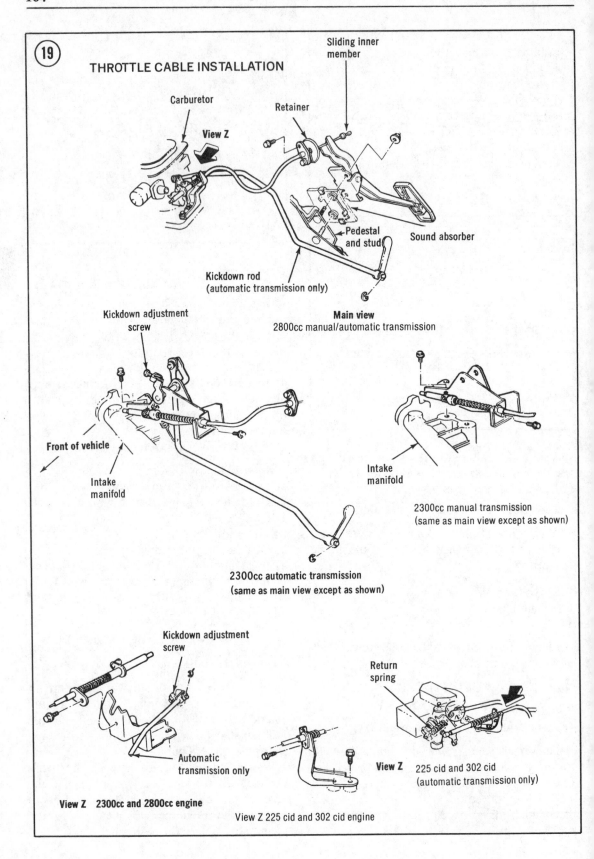

(19)

THROTTLE CABLE INSTALLATION

Sliding inner member

Carburetor

View Z

Retainer

Pedestal and stud

Sound absorber

Kickdown rod
(automatic transmission only)

Kickdown adjustment screw

Main view
2800cc manual/automatic transmission

Front of vehicle

Intake manifold

Intake manifold

2300cc manual transmission
(same as main view except as shown)

2300cc automatic transmission
(same as main view except as shown)

Kickdown adjustment screw

Return spring

Automatic transmission only

View Z 225 cid and 302 cid
(automatic transmission only)

View Z   2300cc and 2800cc engine

View Z 225 cid and 302 cid engine

2. Working under the hood, disconnect the accelerator cable at the carburetor throttle lever, being sure not to pull on the accelerator during disconnection.

3. Disconnect the accelerator cable attaching screws from the engine mounting bracket.

4. Remove the screws attaching the accelerator cable to firewall.

5. Remove the accelerator cable from the vehicle.

6. Installation is the reverse of these steps.

FUEL PUMP

Non-repairable fuel pumps are used on all engines. If troubleshooting procedures in Chapter Two indicate a defective fuel pump, it must be replaced. Refer to **Table 1** for fuel pump flow specifications.

Fuel Pump Replacement

On 2800 cc engines, the fuel pump is mounted on the lower left side of the cylinder

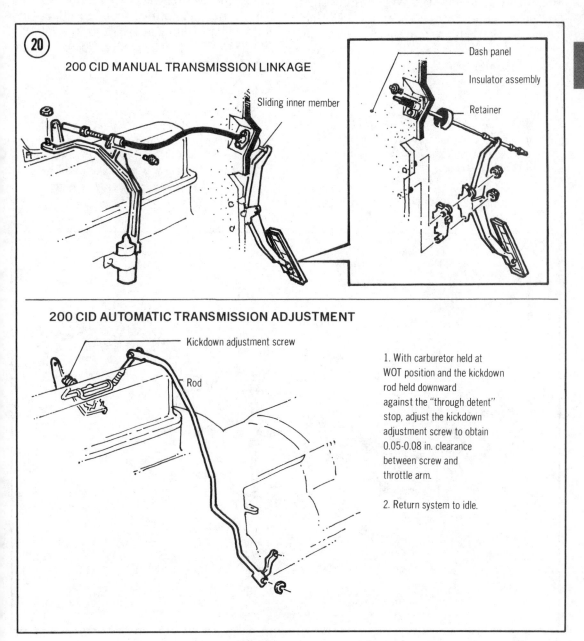

(20)

200 CID MANUAL TRANSMISSION LINKAGE

Sliding inner member

Dash panel

Insulator assembly

Retainer

5

200 CID AUTOMATIC TRANSMISSION ADJUSTMENT

Kickdown adjustment screw

Rod

1. With carburetor held at WOT position and the kickdown rod held downward against the "through detent" stop, adjust the kickdown adjustment screw to obtain 0.05-0.08 in. clearance between screw and throttle arm.

2. Return system to idle.

block; on all other engines, the pump is mounted on the left side of the cylinder front cover.

1. Disconnect both fuel lines from the pump.

2. Remove 2 bolts securing the fuel pump to the engine block or front cover, then lift the pump away from the engine.

3. Installation is the reverse of these steps. Remove all gasket material from the fuel pump and mounting pad. Apply oil-resistant gasket sealer to both sides of the new fuel pump gasket, then position the new gasket on the pump flange and install pump and gasket on the mounting pad.

NOTE
Make sure the fuel pump rocker arm is riding on the camshaft eccentric before attaching bolts. Tighten attaching bolts to specifications (end of chapter).

4. Operate engine and check for leaks.

FUEL TANK AND LINES

The fuel tank and lines incorporate a fuel vapor emission control system. The only regular maintenance required for the fuel tanks, line, and the fuel vapor emission control system, is replacement of the carbon-filled evaporative emission canister. Replacement of this canister is described in the emission control system part of this chapter. Problems may be caused in the system by leaks, kinked or pinched fuel line, or restricted fuel flow or a deformed fuel tank. Fuel tank and fuel line routing positions for the 2300 cc, 200/255 cid, and 2800 cc/302 cid engines are shown in **Figures 21-23**.

Repairing Leaks

WARNING
Soldering or welding procedures on the fuel tank are best left to an expert because of the extremely volatile nature of gasoline fumes. A fuel tank is capable of exploding and killing or seriously burning anyone nearby.

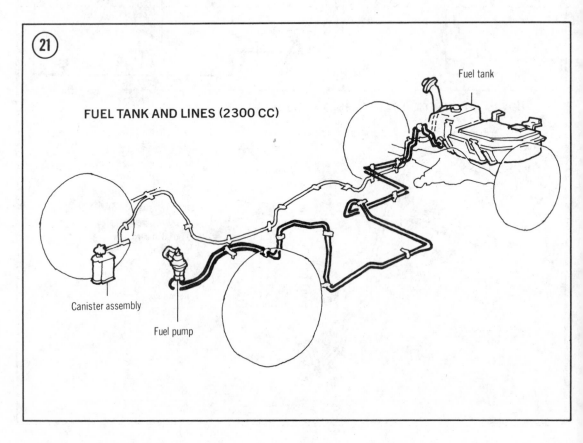

(21)

FUEL TANK AND LINES (2300 CC)

Fuel tank

Canister assembly

Fuel pump

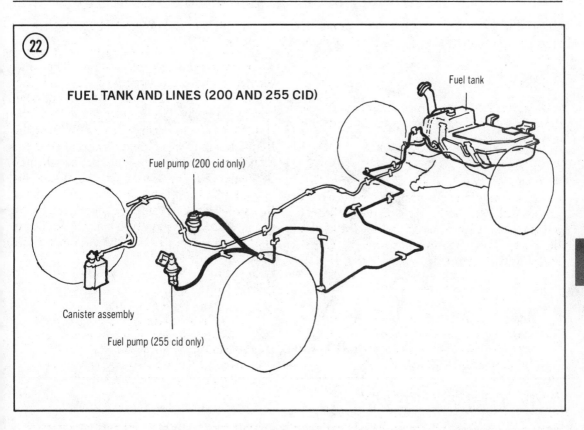

FUEL TANK AND LINES (200 AND 255 CID)

Fuel tank

Fuel pump (200 cid only)

Canister assembly

Fuel pump (255 cid only)

5

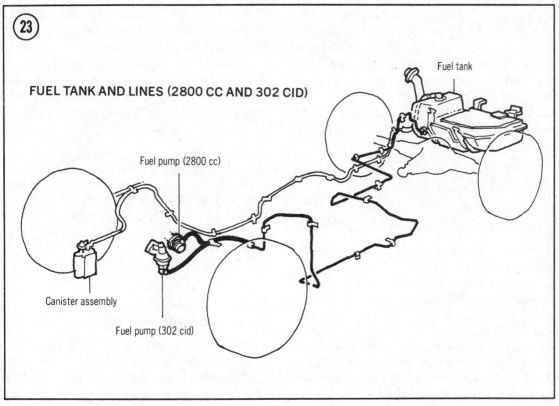

FUEL TANK AND LINES (2800 CC AND 302 CID)

Fuel tank

Fuel pump (2800 cc)

Canister assembly

Fuel pump (302 cid)

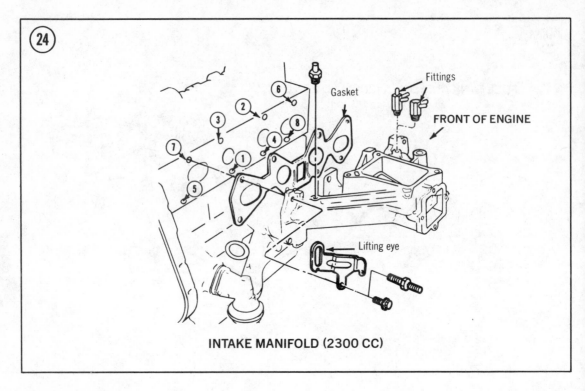

INTAKE MANIFOLD (2300 CC)

Fuel Line Repairs

Damaged sections of fuel lines less than one foot long can be cut out and replaced with a section of rubber fuel hose. Damaged sections longer than a foot can be replaced by a piece of metal fuel line spliced into the fuel line with 2 short sections of rubber fuel hose. All metal fuel line ends must be cut with a tube cutter, reamed, and flared. Motor oil may be used on metal line ends to make installation easier. Do not use any other lubricant.

INTAKE MANIFOLDS

Intake Manifold
Removal/Installation (2300 cc)

1. Drain the radiator below the level of the intake manifold.
2. Remove the air cleaner and duct assembly as described earlier in this chapter.
3. Remove the carburetor as described earlier in this chapter.
4. Disconnect the PCV valve from the hose connecting it to the carburetor spacer.
5. Disconnect all vacuum lines and emission hoses from the intake manifold.

6. Remove dipstick.
7. Remove 2 distributor cap screws.
8. Remove bolts attaching the intake manifold to the cylinder head (**Figure 24**), and remove intake manifold from the engine.
9. Remove all gasket material from the manifold and cylinder head mating surfaces. Check manifold for cracks or damaged gasket surfaces. Replace intake manifold-to-cylinder head gasket if necessary.

10. Installation is the reverse of these steps. Apply gasket sealer compound to the mating surfaces of the intake manifold and the cylinder head. Place the intake manifold gasket in position, then install the intake manifold and tighten the attaching bolts finger-tight. Tighten the intake manifold attaching bolts to 14-21 ft.-lb. in sequence shown in **Figure 24**.

Intake Manifold
Removal/Installation (2800 cc)

1. Drain the radiator below the level of the intake manifold.
2. Remove the air cleaner and duct assembly as described earlier in this chapter.

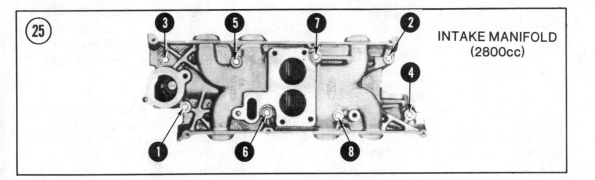

(25) INTAKE MANIFOLD (2800cc)

5

3. Remove the carburetor as described earlier in this chapter.

4. Remove the top radiator hose from the intake manifold, and remove the bypass hose from the thermostat to the intake manifold, at the intake manifold.

5. Remove the distributor cap and spark plug wires as an assembly, then disconnect the primary lead to the distributor and the distributor vacuum lines.

6. Remove the distributor as described in Chapter Seven.

7. Disconnect and mark all vacuum lines and emission hoses obstructing removal of the intake manifold and rocker arm covers.

8. Remove the rocker arm covers as described under *Rocker Arm Cover Removal* in Chapter Four.

9. Remove intake manifold attaching bolts and nuts (**Figure 25**). Tap manifold lightly with a plastic or rubber hammer to break gasket seal, then lift the intake manifold off of the engine.

10. Clean the intake manifold and cylinder head mating surfaces of all old gasket material and sealing compound.

11. Installation is the reverse of these steps. Apply sealing compound to the mating surfaces of the intake manifold and the cylinder heads. Place the intake manifold in position on the cylinder head, making sure that the tab on the right cylinder head fits into the cutout of the manifold gasket. Apply sealing compound to the intake manifold retaining bolt bosses, then install the intake manifold. Tighten the intake manifold retaining bolts in the sequence shown in **Figure 25**. Tighten intake manifold bolts in 4 steps as follows:

a. 3-6 ft.-lb.
b. 6-11 ft.-lb.
c. 11-16 ft.-lb.
d. 15-18 ft.-lb.

After engine has been operated, retighten all bolts/nuts to 15-18 ft.-lb.

**Intake Manifold
Removal/Installation (200 cid)**

Intake manifold removal/installation for the 200 cid engine is accomplished under *Exhaust Manifold Removal/Installation (200 cid)* discussed later in this chapter.

**Intake Manifold
Removal/Installation (255/302 cid)**

1. Drain the radiator below the level of the intake manifold.

2. Disconnect the automatic choke heat tube at the inlet near the right rocker arm cover. Disconnect the upper radiator hose at the coolant outlet housing (**Figure 26**), and the water pump bypass hose at the coolant outlet housing.

3. Remove the air cleaner and duct assembly as described earlier in this chapter.

4. Disconnect the automatic transmission and power brake booster vacuum lines at the intake manifold, if so equipped.

5. Disconnect all electrical leads from the ignition coil.

6. Disconnect the accelerator cable and speed control cable from the carburetor if the vehicle is so equipped.

7. Disconnect the spark plug wires from the spark plugs, remove the wires from the looms on the rocker arm covers, then remove the distributor cap and the spark plug wires as an

assembly. Refer to Chapter Three for correct spark plug cap removal procedure.

8. Remove the carburetor as described earlier in this chapter.

9. Remove the distributor as described in Chapter Seven.

10. Disconnect the crankcase ventilation hose PCV valve and oil filler cap at the left rocker arm cover.

11. If the vehicle is equipped with air conditioning, remove the air conditioning compressor-to-intake manifold brackets.

12. Remove the intake manifold from the engine.

NOTE
It may be necessary to pry the intake manifold away from the cyinder heads. Use caution when removing the intake manifold to avoid possible damage to the gasket sealing surfaces.

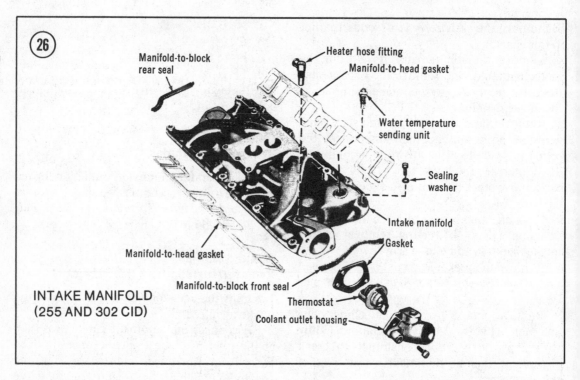

(26)

Manifold-to-block rear seal

Heater hose fitting

Manifold-to-head gasket

Water temperature sending unit

Sealing washer

Intake manifold

Gasket

Manifold-to-head gasket

Manifold-to-block front seal

Thermostat

Coolant outlet housing

INTAKE MANIFOLD (255 AND 302 CID)

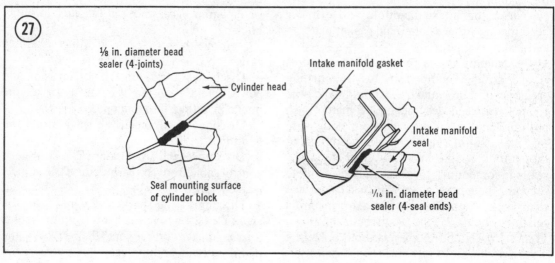

(27)

⅛ in. diameter bead sealer (4-joints)

Cylinder head

Seal mounting surface of cylinder block

Intake manifold gasket

Intake manifold seal

1/16 in. diameter bead sealer (4-seal ends)

13. Disconnect the lead from the water temperature sending unit (**Figure 26**) then remove the heater hose from the intake manifold and check to see that all hoses, vacuum lines, and electrical connections are disconnected from the intake manifold.

14. Remove the intake manifold gasket and seal material and clean the intake manifold-to-cylinder head mating surfaces. Discard the sealing washers around the intake

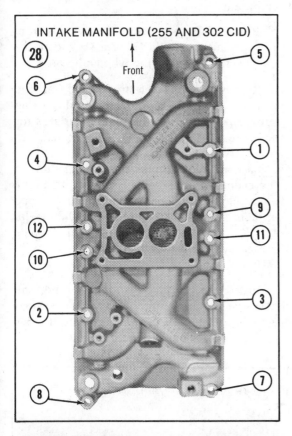

INTAKE MANIFOLD (255 AND 302 CID)

Front

manifold attaching bolts.

15. Installation is the reverse of these steps. Ensure that the intake manifold-to-cylinder head mating surfaces are clean of all gasket material. Ensure that the cylinder block surfaces are clean in the area where the front and rear intake manifold-to-cylinder block seals were removed. Cleaning the mating surfaces is accomplished by using a solvent such as lacquer thinner. Apply a 1/8 in. bead of silicone rubber sealer to the mating surface points shown in **Figure 27**.

16. Position the front and rear intake manifold-to-cylinder block seals on the cylinder block then place the intake manifold gaskets on the cylinder heads with the gaskets interlocked with the front and rear seal tabs as shown in **Figure 27**. Be sure the intake manifold gaskets are properly aligned with the intake ports in the cylinder heads. Apply a 1/16 in. bead of silicone rubber sealer to each end of the intake manifold front and rear seal as shown in **Figure 27**.

NOTE
The silicone rubber sealer sets up in approximately 15 minutes, making it important to complete the manifold installation quickly.

17. Install the intake manifold using new sealing washers around the intake manifold attaching bolts, then tighten the intake manifold bolts to 23-25 ft.-lb. in the sequence shown in **Figure 28**.

18. Reinstall all equipment previously removed. Reconnect all hoses, lines, wires, and emission control devices previously removed. Fill the cooling system, then start the engine and check for oil, fuel, or water leaks. Installation is now complete.

EXHAUST MANIFOLD

Exhaust Manifold
Removal/Installation (2300 cc)

1. Unbolt the exhaust manifold heat shroud from the exhaust manifold and remove. Disconnect the heat riser tube from the air cleaner duct assembly.

2. Disconnect the down pipe from the exhaust manifold (**Figure 29**).

3. Disconnect the Thermactor check valve (**Figure 30**) at the exhaust manifold, then disconnect any remaining lines, ground straps, etc., connected to the exhaust manifold.

4. Remove the 8 manifold attaching bolts/studs, then remove the engine lifting eye (**Figure 30**). Lift the exhaust manifold off the engine.

5. Clean all gasket material from the exhaust manifold-to-cylinder head mating surfaces, and from the exhaust manifold-to-down pipe mating surfaces. Inspect the manifold for cracks or damage to the mating surfaces and replace if necessary.

6. Installation is the reverse of these steps. Lightly coat the exhaust manifold-to-cylinder head mating surfaces with graphite grease. Install a new gasket between the exhaust manifold and the down pipe. Install the exhaust manifold, then tighten the exhaust manifold-to-cylinder head attaching bolts to 8 ft.-lb. In a second step, tighten all manifold attaching bolts to 16-23 ft.-lb. Tighten the exhaust manifold attaching bolts in the sequence shown in **Figure 30**. Tighten the exhaust manifold-to-down pipe attaching nuts to 17-25 ft.-lb.

Exhaust Manifold
Removal/Installation (2800 cc)

1. Remove the air cleaner and duct assembly as described earlier in this chapter.

2. Remove the exhaust manifold shroud attaching bolts (right side only) and the manifold shroud-to-duct assembly heat riser tube.

3. Disconnect the exhaust manifold-to-down pipe attaching nuts, then remove Thermactor system components, as necessary, to allow removal of exhaust manifolds.

4. Disconnect the choke heat tube at the carburetor.

5. Remove the 6 attaching bolts/studs from each exhaust manifold (**Figure 31**) and lift the exhaust manifolds off the cylinder heads.

6. Remove all gasket material from the exhaust manifold-to-cylinder head mating surfaces, and inspect the mating surfaces for scratches or other damage. Repair as necessary. Install new exhaust gaskets and the exhaust manifold on the positioning studs in the cylinder head, then install the remaining attaching bolts/studs and tighten in the sequence shown in **Figure 31** to 20-30 ft.-lb. Install a new exhaust manifold-to-down pipe gasket, and tighten the attaching bolts to 25-35 ft.-lb.

7. Install the exhaust manifold shroud, the heat rising tube, the Thermactor system components removed previously, and the air cleaner duct assembly.

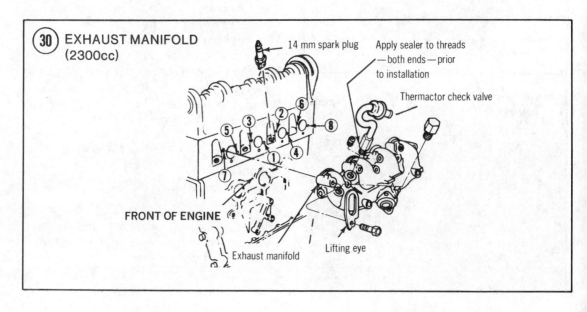

30 EXHAUST MANIFOLD (2300cc)

14 mm spark plug

Apply sealer to threads —both ends—prior to installation

Thermactor check valve

FRONT OF ENGINE

Exhaust manifold

Lifting eye

Exhaust Manifold
Removal/Installation (200 cid)

1. Remove the air cleaner and duct assembly as described earlier in this chapter.

2. Disconnect the exhaust manifold-to-down pipe attaching nuts, then remove EGR tube and emission components, as necessary, to allow removal of exhaust manifold.

3. Remove the 11 attaching bolts from the exhaust manifold (**Figure 32**), and lift the exhaust manifold off the cylinder head.

4. Remove all gasket material from the exhaust manifold-to-cylinder head mating surfaces, and inspect the mating surfaces for scratches or other damage. Repair as necessary. Install new exhaust gaskets and the exhaust manifold on the positioning studs in the cylinder head, then install the remaining attaching bolts and tighten in the sequence shown in **Figure 32** to 18-24 ft.-lb. Install new exhaust manifold-to-down pipe gasket, and tighten attaching nuts to 17-25 ft.-lb.

5. Install the EGR tube and emission components removed previously, and the air cleaner duct assembly.

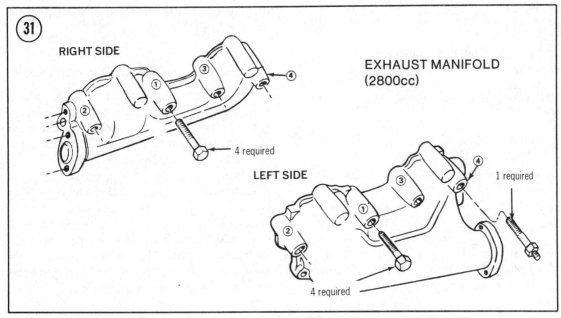

(31)

RIGHT SIDE

EXHAUST MANIFOLD
(2800cc)

4 required

LEFT SIDE

1 required

4 required

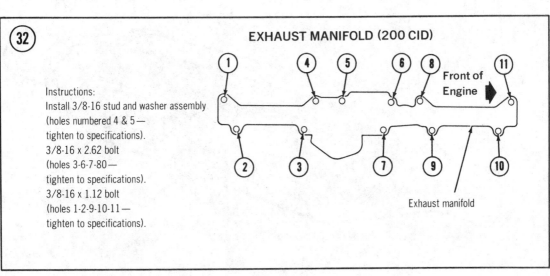

(32) EXHAUST MANIFOLD (200 CID)

Instructions:
Install 3/8-16 stud and washer assembly
(holes numbered 4 & 5 —
tighten to specifications).
3/8-16 x 2.62 bolt
(holes 3-6-7-80 —
tighten to specifications).
3/8-16 x 1.12 bolt
(holes 1-2-9-10-11 —
tighten to specifications).

Front of
Engine

Exhaust manifold

Exhaust Manifold
Removal/Installation (255 and 302 cid)

1. Remove the air cleaner duct assembly.
2. Disconnect the automatic choke heat chamber air inlet hose from the inlet tube near the right rocker arm cover.
3. Remove the heat stove/exhaust manifold shroud and the heat riser tube to the air cleaner duct assembly.
4. Disconnect the nuts attaching the exhaust manifold to the down pipe, then disconnect the spark plug wires and remove the spark plugs.
5. Remove the exhaust manifold heat shields, then remove the exhaust manifold-to-cylinder head attaching bolts and washers, and lift the exhaust manifold from the engine.
6. Clean the exhaust manifold-to-cylinder head and the down pipe mating surfaces of all gasket material and check for cracks or other damage.

NOTE
On the right exhaust manifold, ensure that the automatic choke air inlet and outlet hoses are completely open and the cover does not leak.

7. Install the exhaust manifold with a new gasket, and tighten exhaust manifold-to-cylinder head attaching bolts to 18-24 ft.-lb.

8. Install components by reversing the above steps.

EMISSION CONTROL SYSTEMS

Various emission control systems are used on vehicles covered in this manual. The type of system installed on a specific vehicle depends upon the model year, the state in which the vehicle was purchased, the type of engine installed in the vehicle, and the optional equipment installed in the vehicle. Where emission control system service is possible, procedures have been included. In other systems, the service should be referred to your local dealer.

CATALYTIC CONVERTER SYSTEMS

Catalytic converters reduce air pollutants by prompting further burning of the exhaust gases. Vehicles covered in this book use from 1-4 converters; all are located in the exhaust line ahead of the muffler (**Figure 33**). While the converter does not require periodic maintenance, it should be checked (see *Exhaust System Removal* later in this chapter). However, if it becomes necessary to replace the converter, it is more economical to have a dealership or other competent garage perform the service because of special tools and installation requirements.

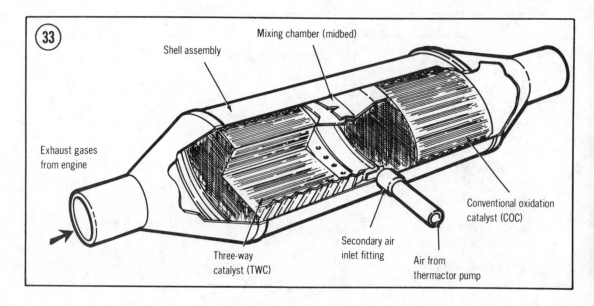

(33)

Shell assembly

Mixing chamber (midbed)

Exhaust gases from engine

Three-way catalyst (TWC)

Secondary air inlet fitting

Air from thermactor pump

Conventional oxidation catalyst (COC)

EXHAUST GAS RECIRCULATION SYSTEM

This system recirculates a small amount of exhaust gas into the incoming air/fuel mixture, lowering combustion temperatures and reducing nitrogen oxide emissions (NOX). The amount of exhaust gas reintroduced into the cycle and the timing of the cycle are controlled by engine vacuum, temperature, and other factors. The delay valve (spark delay valve) delays vacuum advance signals from the carburetor to the distributor, thereby retarding distributor advance during acceleration. **Figure 34** shows a typical EGR system.

EGR (Exhaust Gas Recirculation) Valve

The EGR valve shown in **Figure 35** is operated by vacuum, and is attached to a

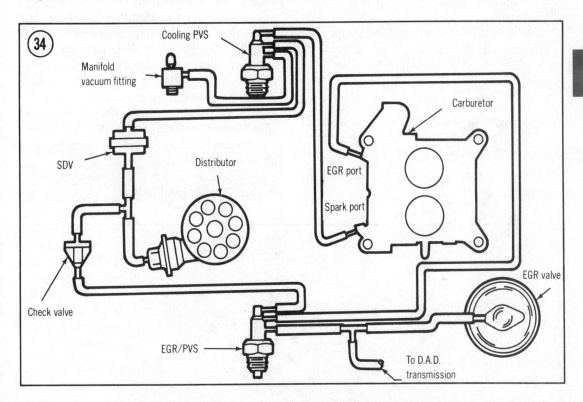

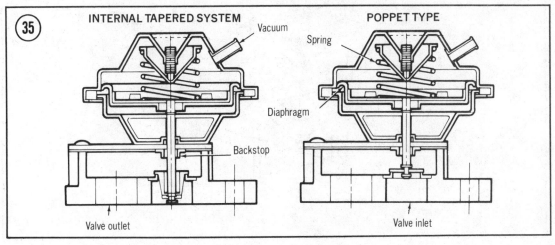

spacer mounted between the carburetor and intake manifold (**Figure 36**). When the valve opens, exhaust gas enters the intake manifold. When the valve closes it prevents the exhaust gases from entering the intake passages.

Cleaning and Inspection

1. Remove the EGR valve from the engine (**Figure 36**).
2. Check the valve and spacer passages for carbon buildup. Clean with a wire brush if it is necessary.
3. Check EGR valve gasket for damage. The gasket should be replaced, but if the engine was idling roughly, this may have been the cause.

> *NOTE*
> *Remove the carburetor spacer from the engine before cleaning, or carbon will fall into the intake manifold.*

4. Check vacuum hoses for damage. Replace as needed.

5. If the problem has not been located, have the EGR system tested by a dealer or other competent garage.

THERMACTOR SYSTEM

A "Thermactor" air injection system is installed on certain engines to reduce carbon monoxide and hydrogen content of combustion by-produce gases by injecting fresh air into the hot exhaust gas stream as it leaves the combustion chamber. A pump supplies air under pressure to the exhaust port near the exhaust valve by either an external air manifold or internal drilled passages in the cylinder head or exhaust manifold. The oxygen in the fresh air, plus the heat of the burning gases, causes further oxidation (burning) which converts the exhaust gases into carbon dioxide and water. The major components of a typical thermactor system are shown in **Figure 37**.

Service to the Thermactor system should be referred to your local dealer.

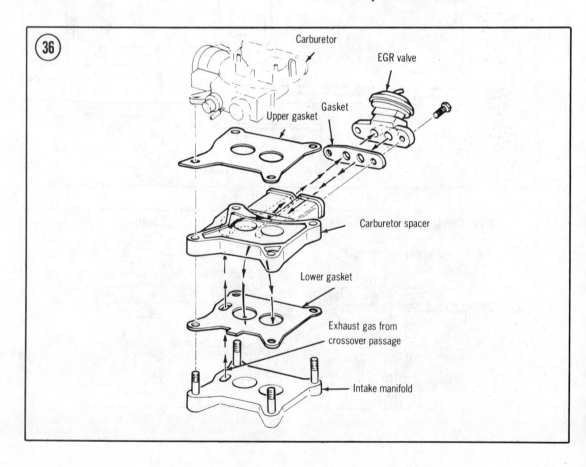

(36) Carburetor
EGR valve
Gasket
Upper gasket
Carburetor spacer
Lower gasket
Exhaust gas from crossover passage
Intake manifold

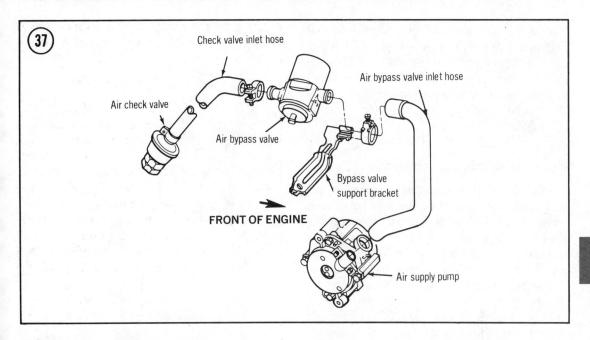

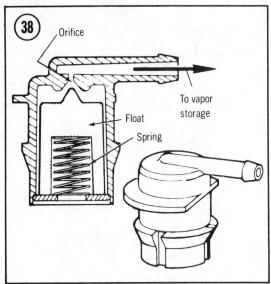

FUEL VAPOR EMISSION CONTROL SYSTEMS

As a part of the standard fuel system, all passenger cars are equipped with a fuel vapor emission control system. This system includes a fill control and venting system, a pressure/vacuum gas tank filler cap, and a vapor storage system. The fill control and venting system limits gasoline tank filling to allow approximately 10 to 12 percent air space when the fuel tank is filled to capacity. This air space provides adequate breathing volume for the fuel tank vapor separator to operate properly under all normal conditions. The vapor storage system consists of a fuel tank vapor separator and a carbon-filled evaporative emisson canister, used to separate and store vapors from the fuel tank for later purging into the air filter. The pressure/vacuum fuel tank filler cap operates as a check valve, preventing fuel vapors from escaping from the tank through the cap under normal circumstances, while allowing air to enter the fuel tank as gasoline is used.

Pressure/Vacuum Fuel Tank Filler Cap

To test the fuel tank filler cap for proper operation, take it to a service station and have the cap tested for proper relief valve operation. Vacuum relief should occur at 0 to 1/4 psi negative, while pressure relief should occur at 3/4 to 1-1/4 psi positive. If the valve relief points are out of specification, replace the filler cap.

Fuel Tank Vapor Separator

The fuel tank vapor separator (**Figure 38**) makes use of a small orifice to allow vapor from the fuel tank to pass into a line running forward to the evaporative emission canister for storage. The separator mounts directly on the top of the fuel tank and is removed or installed in the same manner as a PCV valve by pushing the separator into or pulling it out of a grommet type seal. To check the vapor separator for proper operation, remove it from the fuel tank and check the orifice for freedom of air flow.

Evaporative Emission Canister

The evaporative emission canister stores fuel tank vapor passed by the fuel tank vapor separator. Fuel stored in a canister is purged to the engine by means of a hose connected from the canister to the air cleaner. The canister is mounted on the frame rail in the engine compartment and is connected as shown in **Figure 39** for 2300 cc, 2800 cc, and 200 cid vehicles. **Figure 40** represents 255 cid and 302 cid vehicles. The canister should be inspected at the intervals specified in Chapter Three. To do this, remove the bolt securing the canister

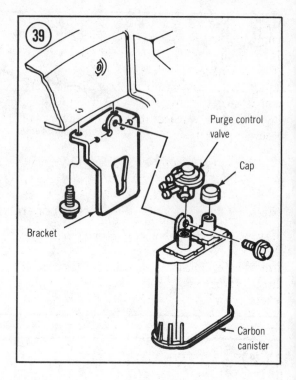

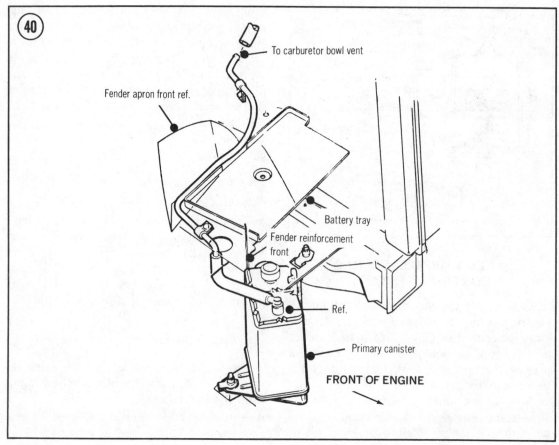

to the frame rail then disconnect the hoses connected to the top of the canister. Loosen the attaching bolt and straps securing the top of the canister to the canister body, then remove the top of the canister. Inspect the canister for contamination by water, oil, or gasoline, and replace it if contaminated or otherwise damaged.

PCV (POSITIVE CRANKCASE VENTILATION) VALVE AND CRANKCASE VENT CAP

The closed ventilation system is designed to prevent fumes or gases from escaping through the engine oil filler or breather cap to the atmosphere. These vapors are controlled by directing them back into the intake manifold where they are consumed in the normal combustion process. **Figure 41** shows a PCV system for the 2300 cc engine. Other systems are similar.

The carburetor air cleaner provides the air source for this system. Air passes through a filter located in the air cleaner, then through a hose connecting the air cleaner to the oil filler cap. The air filler cap is sealed at the filler opening to prevent the entrance of atmospheric air. The air flows from the oil filler cap and into the lower crankcase. The air/crankcase gas mixture flows from the crankcase through a flow-regulating valve (PCV valve) into the intake manifold through the crankcase vent hose, tube, and fittings. This process goes on constantly while the engine is running. Refer to Chapter Three for PCV valve service.

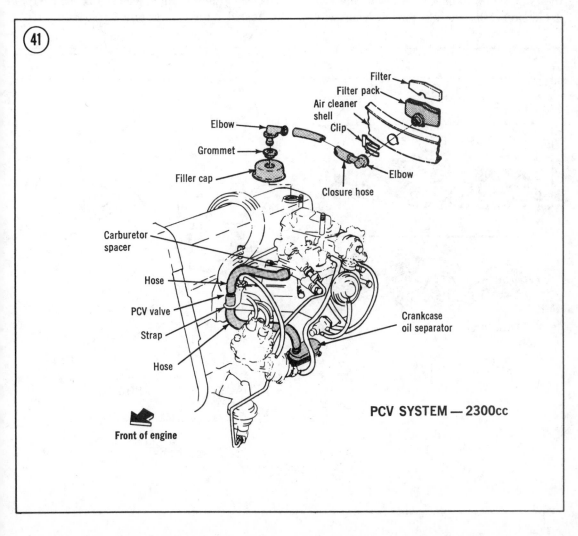

PCV SYSTEM — 2300cc

EXHAUST SYSTEMS

Different factory installed exhaust systems are used on vehicles covered in this manual. In addition, service replacement exhaust systems may be installed on your vehicle. As such, you should inspect the exhaust system on your vehicle, compare the installed system to the factory-installed systems shown in **Figure 42** (2300 cc), **Figure 43** (2800 cc), **Figure 44** (200 cid), **Figure 45** (255 cid), or **Figure 46** (302 cid), then use the following removal/installation procedures as a guide in performing exhaust system services.

Resonator Inlet Pipe
(Down Pipe) Removal/Installation

1. Raise the vehicle to provide working space, then support the vehicle with jackstands.
2. Support resonator inlet pipe with soft wire.

3. On 2300 and 2800 cc engines, remove screws attaching front hanger insulator to the inlet pipe bracket, remove bolts attaching converter inlet flange to inlet pipe, and remove nuts attaching the inlet pipe flange to the exhaust manifold and remove the inlet pipe.
4. On 200 cid engines, remove bolts attaching converter inlet flange to the inlet pipe, remove nuts securing the inlet pipe flange to the exhaust manifold, and remove the inlet pipe.
5. On 255 and 302 cid engines remove bolts attaching converter inlet flange to the Y-pipe and remove nuts attaching the Y-pipe flange to the exhaust manifold and remove the Y-pipe.
6. Check removed parts for excessive rust, and for damage caused by bottoming the vehicle. Check rubber mounts for melting, cracks, or deterioration. Replace as needed.
7. Install in the reverse order.

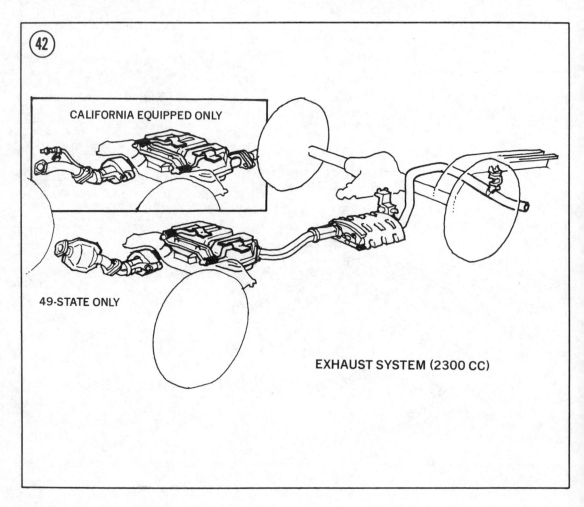

(42)

CALIFORNIA EQUIPPED ONLY

49-STATE ONLY

EXHAUST SYSTEM (2300 CC)

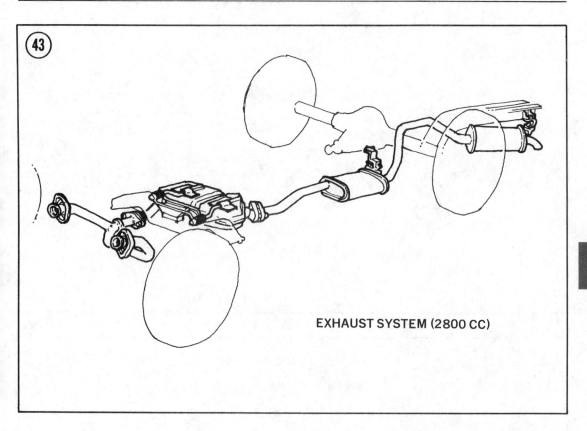

43

EXHAUST SYSTEM (2800 CC)

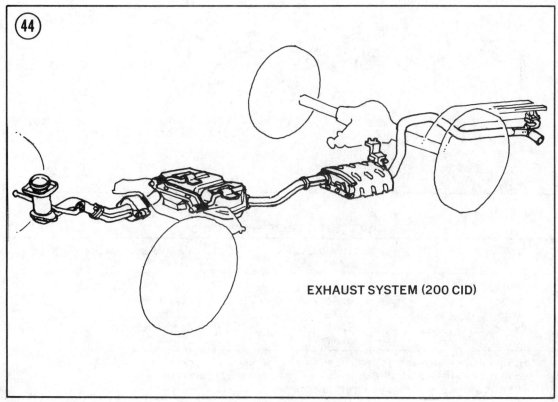

44

EXHAUST SYSTEM (200 CID)

5

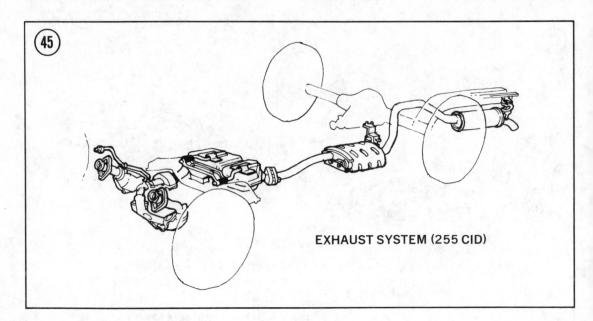

45

EXHAUST SYSTEM (255 CID)

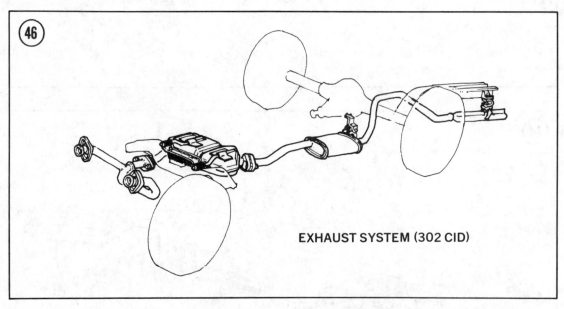

46

EXHAUST SYSTEM (302 CID)

Table 1   FUEL PUMP SPECIFICATIONS

Application	Static Pressure (psi) (1)	Min. Volume Flow (1), (3)
2300 cc	5.0-7.0 (2)	1 pt. in 25 sec.
2800 cc	3.0-6.0	1 pt. in 25 sec.
200 cid	5.0-7.0	1 pt. in 30 sec.
255 cid	6.0-8.0	1 pt. in 20 sec.
302 cid	6.0-8.0	1 pt. in 20 sec.

(1) Engine temperatures normalized, and at normal curb idle speed, transmission in neutral.
(2) With the pump-to-tank fuel return line pinched off, and a new fuel filter installed.
(3) Inside diameter of smallest passage in test flow circuit must not be smaller than 0.220 in.

NOTE: If you own a 1981 or later model, first check the Supplement at the back of the book for any new service information.

CHAPTER SIX

COOLING SYSTEM AND HEATER

6

All engines use centrifugal water pumps to pump coolant through the engine and cooling and heating systems. With all engines, a thermostat controls coolant flow, and a crossflow radiator and fan are used to cool the system.

This chapter includes service procedures for the thermostat, radiator, fan, water pump, and heater. **Table 1** and **Table 2** are at the end of the chapter.

Cooling system flushing, pressure checking and fan belt tension adjustment procedures are described.

FAN BELT TENSION ADJUSTMENT AND REPLACEMENT

Two types of fan belts are used—the V-belt or ribbed belt and the serpentine belt. Service procedures are similar and where differences occur, they are noted in the following procedure.

1. Apply parking brake and block the wheels.
2. Drive belt tension should be checked every 12,000 miles. A belt tension gauge should be used if possible. See **Figure 1**.
3. Bring the engine to normal operating temperature and turn the engine off.

4. Attach a belt tension gauge (**Figure 1**), following manufacturer's instructions. Adjust all belts to specifications (see **Table 1**).

NOTE
On single V-belts, check the tension of each belt. On dual drive V-belts, check the tension of one belt only. Compare measured tension to specifications listed in ***Table 1***.

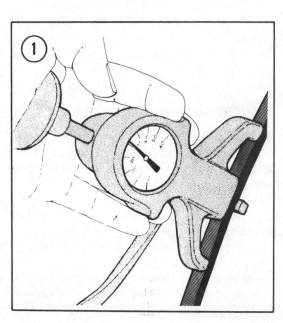

5. If belt tension adjustment is necessary, adjust the drive belts by loosening the component pivot bolts and/or adjustment slot fasteners. Move the component toward or away from the engine until the correct belt tension specification is registered on the tension gauge. Tighten all bolts and fasteners. Recheck belt tension and repeat if necessary.

CAUTION
Do not overtighten any drive belt as this will overload the component bearings and cause the belt to wear rapidly.

6. If a tension gauge is not available, press down on the belt at the middle free span between the pulleys. Belt tension deflection should be as follows:

a. For all V-belts with a free span between pulleys less than 12 inches, deflection should be between 1/8-1/4 in.

b. For all V-belts with a free span between pulleys greater than 12 inches, deflection should be between 1/8-3/8 in.

NOTE
The thumb deflection method used on V-belts cannot be used on ribbed belts because of their higher tension requirements (Figure 2).

7. On vehicles equipped with a serpentine drive belt system belt tension is automatically maintained by a back-side belt tensioner. No belt tension adjustment is required. See **Figure 3**.

V-belt Replacement

1. On vehicles with power steering, loosen the power steering pump at the mounting bracket and remove the drive belt. On vehicles with air conditioning, remove the compressor drive belt.

2. Loosen the alternator mounting and adjusting arm bolts. Move the alternator toward the engine as far as it will go so that the belt can be removed from the pulleys.

3. Installation is the reverse of Steps 1 and 2. Tighten belts to specifications as discussed earlier. See **Table 1**.

Ribbed belt

Serpentine Drive Belt Replacement

1. Insert a 16 inch drift punch in the slot of the tensioner bracket, and using the tensioner housing as a fulcrum, push down on the drift punch to force the tensioner pulley upward to relieve belt tension and remove drive belt. See **Figure 3**.

2. Remove nut securing tensioner assembly to the alternator bracket and remove the tensioner assembly.

3. To install tensioner assembly, place assembly so that tang located on rear of tensioner assembly is positioned to fit into the slot in the alternator bracket. Insert the tensioner bolt through hole in alternator bracket and torque to 40-55 ft.-lb.

NOTE
To install belt, refer to decal on top of the windshield washer coolant reservoir for proper belt routing.

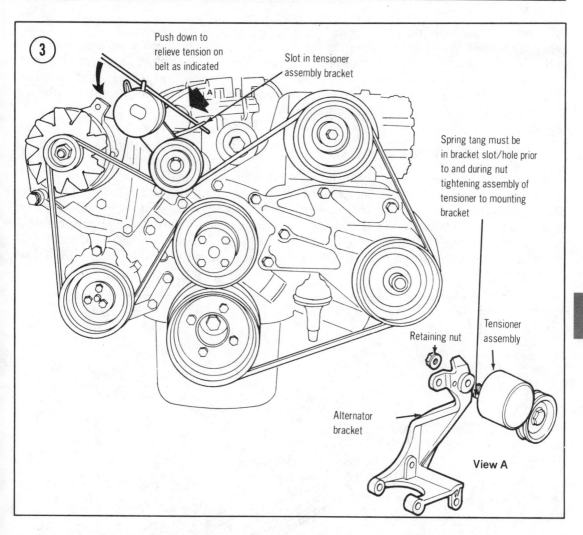

3

Push down to relieve tension on belt as indicated

Slot in tensioner assembly bracket

Spring tang must be in bracket slot/hole prior to and during nut tightening assembly of tensioner to mounting bracket

Retaining nut

Tensioner assembly

Alternator bracket

View A

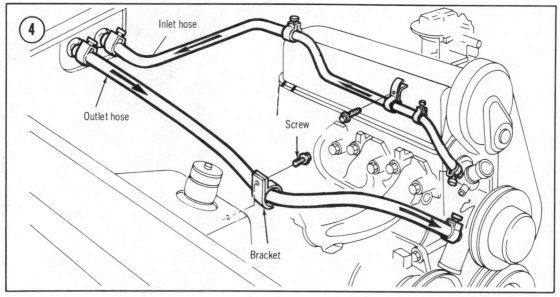

4

Inlet hose

Outlet hose

Screw

Bracket

4. Insert the 16 inch drift punch in the tensioner bracket slot, and push down on the drift to reduce tension on the tensioner pulley. Install belt along pulleys as indicated.

5. Once pulleys are routed correctly, remove drift from slot. The drive belt is automatically adjusted.

COOLING SYSTEM FLUSHING

A mixture of ethylene glycol-based antifreeze and water protects the cooling system from freezing to -20 degrees F. The system should be inspected every 12,000 miles or 12 months. If the coolant appears dirty or rusty, the system should be cleaned with a chemical cleaner, drained, flushed with clean water, and refilled. Severe corrosion may require pressure flushing, a job for a dealer or radiator shop. Flushing and coolant replacement are required every 36 months.

Flushing

1. Drain the cooling system by opening the drain tap on the lower right side of the radiator.

2. Remove the radiator cap.

3. Disconnect the heater hose from the water pump. The hose will be a drain during flushing. See **Figure 4** (2300 cc), **Figure 5** (2800 cc), **Figure 6** (200 cid), or **Figure 7** (255 cid and 302 cid) for heater hose positions on

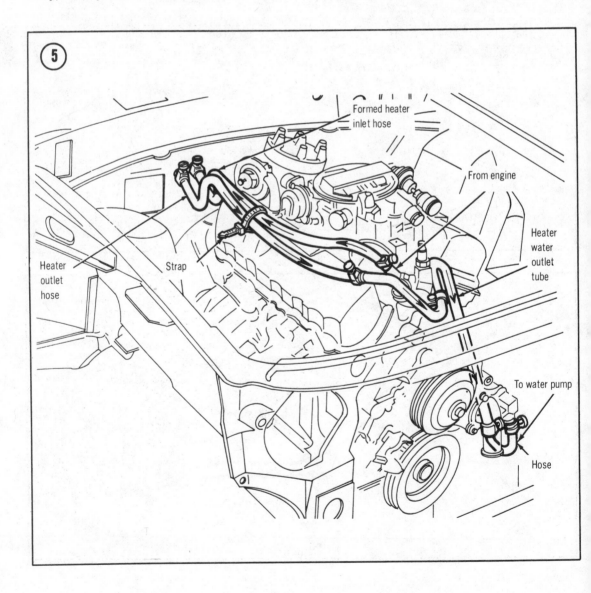

Figure 5 — labels: Formed heater inlet hose; From engine; Heater water outlet tube; To water pump; Hose; Heater outlet hose; Strap

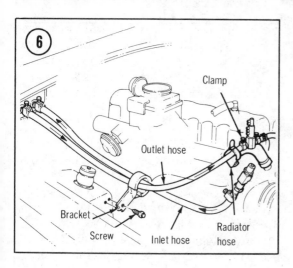

⑥

Clamp

Outlet hose

Bracket

Screw

Inlet hose

Radiator hose

non-air conditioned vehicles. Air conditioned vehicle heater hose routing is similar. For 2300 cc engines with turbocharger, see **Figure 8**.

4. Remove the thermostat as described later in this chapter, then reinstall thermostat housing.

5. Turn the heater control on the instrument panel to WARM.

6. Connect a water supply such as a garden hose to the heater hose port on the water pump. This does not have to be a positive fit, as long as most of the water enters the engine. If necessary, temporarily connect a length of heater hose to the water pump port to make the garden hose connection more convenient.

6

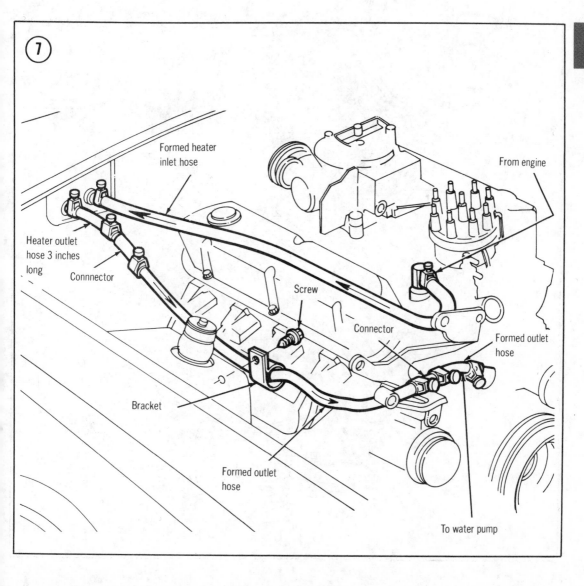

⑦

Formed heater inlet hose

From engine

Heater outlet hose 3 inches long

Connnector

Screw

Connector

Formed outlet hose

Bracket

Formed outlet hose

To water pump

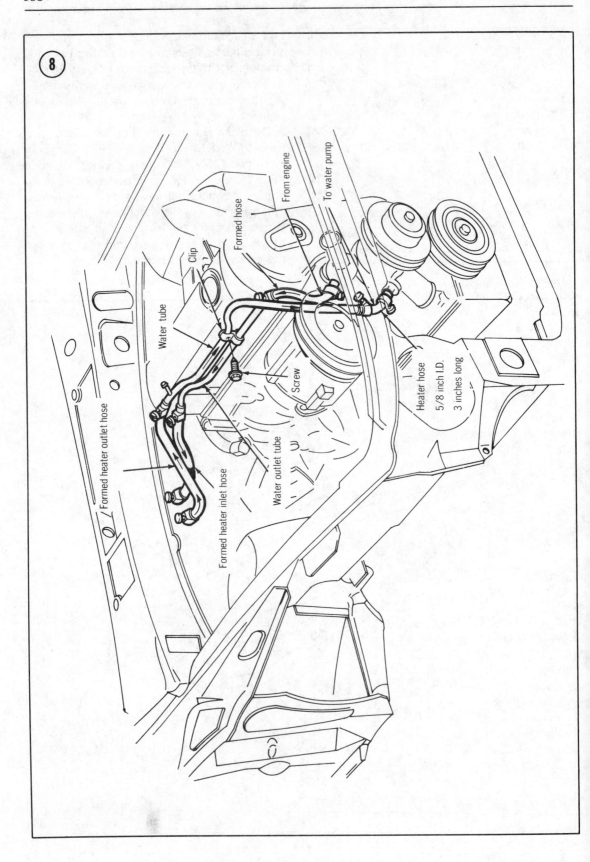

⑧

From engine

To water pump

Formed hose

Clip

Water tube

Screw

Heater hose
5/8 inch I.D.
3 inches long

Formed heater outlet hose

Formed heater inlet hose

Water outlet tube

7. Turn on water and flush for 3 to 5 minutes. Do not run the engine. During the last minute of flushing, repeatedly squeeze the upper radiator hose to expel all trapped coolant.

8. Turn off the water and reconnect the heater hose to the water pump.

9. Drain the entire system by opening the radiator drain tap, then disconnecting the lower hose from the radiator.

Refilling

1. Be sure all hoses are connected, and the instrument panel heater control is on WARM (MAXIMUM for 302 cid engines).

2. Fill the cooling system to approximately 3/4 in. below the filler neck seat with a 50/50 mixture of ethylene glycol-based antifreeze and water, even if you live in a climate that does not require this degree of freeze protection. The antifreeze is a good corrosion inhibitor. See **Table 2** for coolant capacity.

3. When the system is full, replace the radiator cap.

4. Run the engine at fast idle and recheck the coolant level in the radiator (and the reservoir bottle, if installed). Bring coolant level to approximately 1/4 in. below the filler neck seat or HOT LEVEL mark in reservoir bottle. Also check system for leaks.

5. After driving several miles, recheck the coolant level. After flushing radiator, it will take some time for all the air to be removed from the system. Normal coolant level is 2-1/2 in. to 4 in. below the filler neck seat. See **Figure 9**.

PRESSURE CHECK

If the cooling system requires repeated topping up, there is probably a leak. The following procedure requires a cooling system pressure tester (**Figure 10**). This can be done by a dealer or service station if you do not have such a tool.

1. Remove the radiator cap.

2. Wet the rubber gasket on the cap, then reinstall it tightly.

3. Detach the electrical connector from the engine temperature sender, then remove the sender. The temperature sender is located in the engine block, cylinder head, or intake manifold.

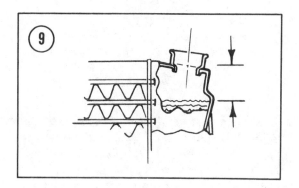

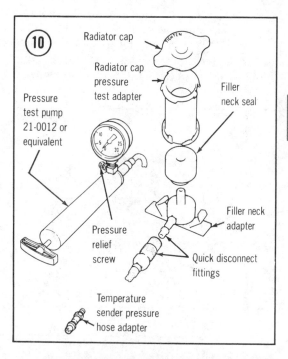

Radiator cap

Radiator cap pressure test adapter

Filler neck seal

Pressure test pump 21-0012 or equivalent

Filler neck adapter

Pressure relief screw

Quick disconnect fittings

Temperature sender pressure hose adapter

NOTE
On some engines, a small amount of coolant will be lost when the sender is removed. The radiator cap must remain in place to prevent the cooling system from draining.

4. Install an adapter (1/2 in. male pipe thread on one end and a hose fitting on the other) in place of temperature sender. Tighten securely.

5. Detach the radiator overflow hose (or overflow-to-reservoir hose) from its retaining clips (**Figure 11**). Immerse the free end of the hose in a container of water.

6. Attach the pressure tester to the hose fitting at the temperature sender and pump until bubbles appear in the container of water from the overflow hose. Keep pumping until the bubbles stop, then note the reading on the pressure tester gauge. This should range from 12-16 psi.

7. If the gauge reading exceeds 16 psi, the radiator cap must be replaced.

8. If bubbles continue and the pressure drops below 10 psi, the radiator cap is not holding pressure. Release the pressure tester. Remove the radiator cap and check for damage (**Figure 12**). If the cap appears in good condition, wash it in clean water, reinstall, and repeat Step 6. If the cap still fails to hold pressure, it must be replaced.

9. If the bubbles in the water container cease and the radiator cap holds 10-16 psi, watch the tester gauge for 2 minutes. There should be no drop in pressure. If pressure falls off, there is a leak. Inspect all hoses, freeze plugs, and connections for coolant residue.

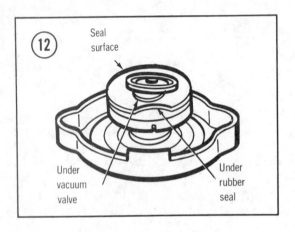

RADIATOR

Vehicles use the crossflow radiator in which the tubes are arranged for a horizontal flow of the coolant. On automatic cars, the radiator left header tank contains a heat exchanger for cooling the transmission oil. **Figure 13** shows a typical crossflow radiator.

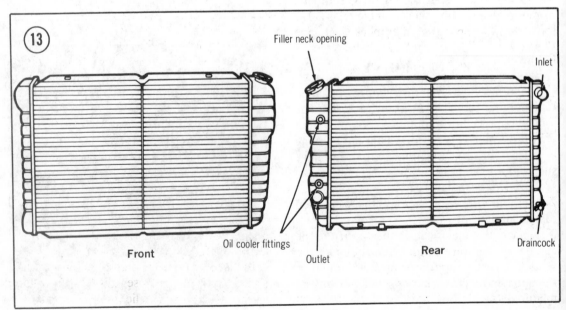

Removal

1. Remove the radiator cap. Drain the coolant by opening the tap at the lower right side of the radiator.
2. Disconnect upper and lower radiator hoses.
3. On automatic transmission models, disconnect the torque converter oil cooler lines from the side of the radiator.
4. If equipped with a fan shroud, remove 4 attaching bolts and lay the shroud back over the radiator.
5. Remove radiator securing bolts and lift the radiator out.

Installation

1. On automatic transmission models, connect the torque converter oil cooler lines before tightening the radiator support bolts.
2. After installing radiator and attaching all hoses, bleed the cooling system. To do this, disconnect the heater hose from the water pump. See **Figure 4** (2300 cc), **Figure 5** (2800 cc), **Figure 6** (200 cid), **Figure 7** (255 cid and 302 cid) or **Figure 8** (2300 cc turbocharged). Then fill the radiator until coolant flows from the heater hose. Connect the heater hose and top up the radiator.
3. Run the engine until it reaches normal operating temperature, then recheck the coolant level. Check the cooling system for leaks.

THERMOSTAT

Removal

1. Drain the cooling system by opening the radiator drain tap.
2. Disconnect the radiator hose from the thermostat housing.
3. Remove 2 bolts attaching the thermostat housing to the engine. Lift the thermostat housing away from the engine, together with the thermostat and gasket. See **Figure 14** (2300 cc), **Figure 15** (2800 cc), or **Figure 16** (200 cid, 255 cid, 302 cid).

Testing

1. Submerge the thermostat in water monitored with a thermometer. Heat the water

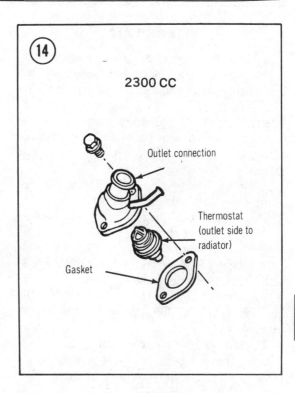

(14)

2300 CC

Outlet connection

Thermostat (outlet side to radiator)

Gasket

6

until the thermostat valve begins to open, then check the water temperature. It should range from 188 degrees to 195 degrees F. If the valve opens at the wrong temperature or fails to open, replace the thermostat.
2. Check the lift of the thermostat valve. To do this, mark a screwdriver at a point 1/4 in. from the tip. The screwdriver is used as a measuring device. Heat the water until the thermostat is fully open and measure the lift of the valve with the marked screwdriver. Replace the thermostat if the valve opens less than 1/4 in.

Installation

1. If a new thermostat is being installed, test as described in the previous procedure.
2. Remove all gasket material from thermostat housing and manifold or water pump gasket surfaces.
3. Install the thermostat in the housing.
4. Position the thermostat housing on the engine (or water pump housing), using a new gasket coated on both sides with gasket sealer. Install the housing bolt and tighten to 12-15 ft.-lb. Connect the hose and fill the cooling system as discussed earlier in this chapter.

WATER PUMP

A defective water pump is usually the problem when the engine overheats and no other cause can be found. A water pump will often warn of impending failure by making noise. Rebuilding the water pump is often impractical as it requires considerable time and effort, and is little cheaper than purchasing a rebuilt water pump.

1. Drain the cooling system by opening the tap at the lower right side of the radiator.
2. Disconnect the heater hose and lower radiator hose from the water pump. See **Figure 4** (2300 cc), **Figure 5** (2800 cc), **Figure 6** (200 cid), **Figure 7** (255 cid and 302 cid) or **Figure 8** (2300 cc turbocharged engine).
3. Remove the fan as described later in this chapter. Take the fan pulley off the water pump.
4. Loosen the alternator mounting bolts and remove the fan belt. With air conditioning, remove alternator and mounting bracket.

NOTE
On 255 cid and 302 cid engines, remove the air conditioner drive belt and idle pulley, the power steering drive belt and the power steering pump (if so equipped).

5. Remove the water pump attaching bolts, then lift the pump away from the engine.
6. Installation is the reverse of these steps. Use a new gasket coated on both sides with gasket sealer. Tighten water pump attaching bolts to 14-21 ft.-lb. (2300 cc), 7-9 ft.-lb. (2800 cc) or 12-18 ft.-lb. (200 cid, 255 cid and 302 cid).

FAN

NOTE
Ford Motor Company has indicated that the cooling fan finger guards used on the upper radiator support assembly on some 1979 models can contact the fan blades under certain conditions. In addition, flexible fan blades used on some 1979 models equipped with 302 cid V8 engines may crack if stressed. Return the vehicle to a dealer for inspection and correction, if you have not already done so.

Removal/Installation (Except 2300 cc Turbocharged Engine)

1. Loosen the fan belt.
2. If the car is equipped with a fan shroud, remove the 4 attaching bolts and lay the shroud back over the fan.
3. Remove the bolts and lockwashers attaching the fan to the water pump hub (**Figure 17**). Lift the fan away from the water pump hub.
4. Installation is the reverse of these steps. Tighten the fan bolts to 12-18 ft.-lb.

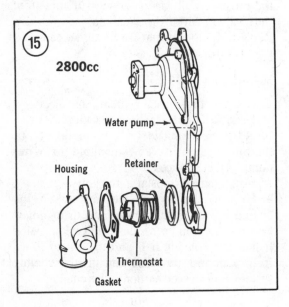

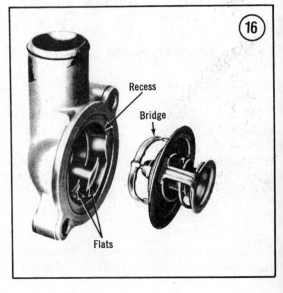

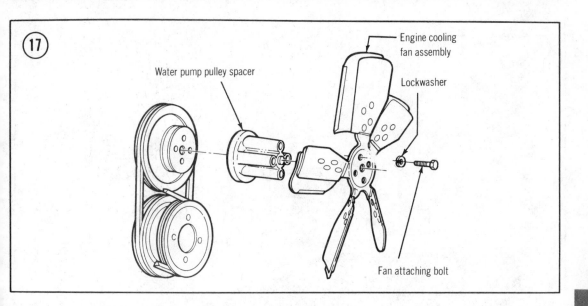

Water pump pulley spacer

Engine cooling fan assembly

Lockwasher

Fan attaching bolt

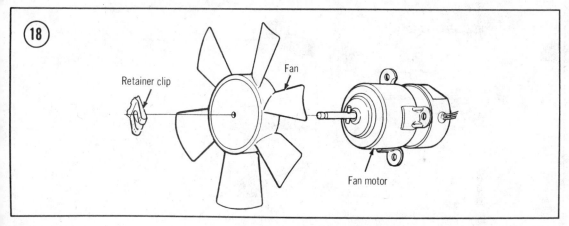

Retainer clip

Fan

Fan motor

Removal/Installation (2300 cc Turbocharged Engine)

CAUTION
Before attempting to remove the fan blade, disengage the wire harness retainer from the cooling fan and unplug the motor connector. The electric cooling fan is mounted behind the radiator and can start to operate at any time by an increase in underhood temperature, even though the ignition switch is turned off.

Refer to **Figure 18** for the following procedure.

1. Remove 4 screws securing the fan shroud to the radiator and remove the shroud-fan-motor assembly.

2. Remove the U-shaped retainer clip from the end of the motor shaft and remove the fan.
3. Remove 3 nuts attaching the motor to the shroud and remove motor assembly.
4. Installation is the reverse of these steps. Connect the electrical plug and secure the plug retainer to the shroud.

HEATER

This section covers the heater on non-air conditioned models only. Repair of the integral heater on air conditioned models requires special skills and tools, and should be left to a dealer or other competent repair shop. **Figure 19** illustrates the disassembly of the heater assembly and should be referred to as needed for the following procedures.

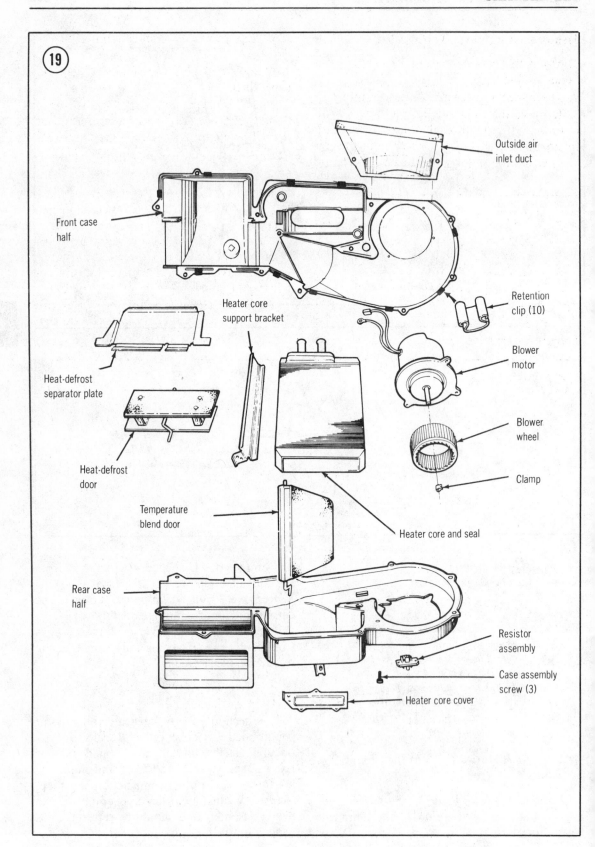

(19)

Front case
half

Outside air
inlet duct

Heater core
support bracket

Retention
clip (10)

Blower
motor

Heat-defrost
separator plate

Blower
wheel

Heat-defrost
door

Clamp

Temperature
blend door

Heater core and seal

Rear case
half

Resistor
assembly

Case assembly
screw (3)

Heater core cover

Heater Case Removal/Installation

1. Drain the cooling system by opening the radiator drain tap.

2. Disconnect the negative battery terminal.

3. Remove the right side air register duct by inserting a thin knife-blade under the register retaining tab and lifting upward until the tab pivot clears the register hole opening (**Figure 20**). Pull register assembly end out from housing.

4. Open glove box and remove glove box paper liner.

5. From beneath right side of instrument panel, remove screw securing register duct from lower instrument panel edge (**Figure 21**).

6. Remove the register duct through the glove box.

7. Remove retaining screw securing ventilator control cable lever to edge of instrument panel (**Figure 21**).

8. Detach grille cover from right ventilator assembly and remove 4 screws securing the ventilator assembly to the blower housing and remove the ventilator assembly (**Figure 21**).

9. Remove the nut securing the heater case mounting bracket to the heater case-to-cowl mounting bracket (**Figure 22**).

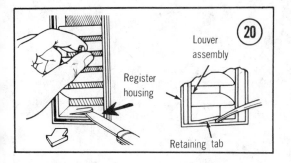

Louver assembly

Register housing

Retaining tab

6

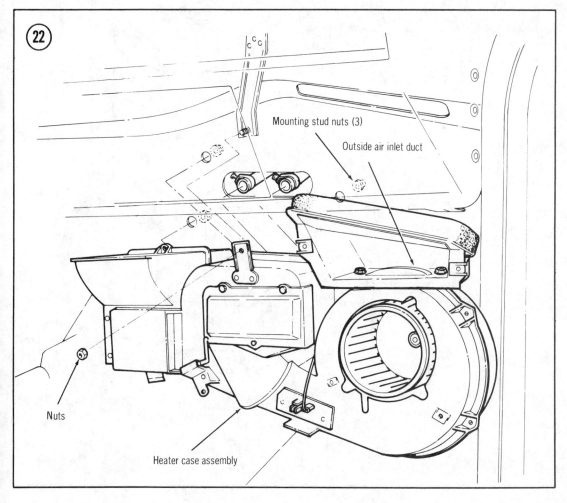

Mounting stud nuts (3)

Outside air inlet duct

Nuts

Heater case assembly

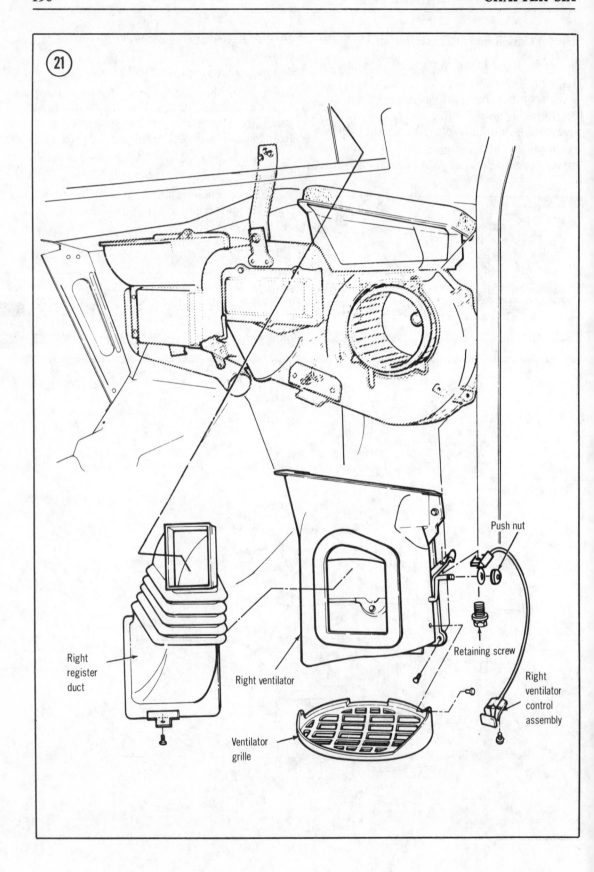

㉑

Push nut

Right register duct

Right ventilator

Retaining screw

Right ventilator control assembly

Ventilator grille

10. Remove screws securing the cowl brace to instrument panel and remove brace.

11. Disconnect both the temperature and function control cables from their control crank arms as discussed later in this chapter.

12. Disconnect the wiring harness from the resistor assembly.

13. Remove the right side cowl trim panel and disconnect the blower motor ground wire.

14. Remove the screws from the heater case-to-instrument panel bracket. Take the heater case assembly out from the instrument panel. Pull the heater hoses through the firewall, then detach them from the heater case.

15. Installation is the reverse of these steps. Refill the cooling system with antifreeze and water. Adjust the temperature and control cables as described later.

Heater Core Removal/Installation

1. Drain the cooling system by opening the radiator drain tap.

2. From inside the engine compartment, remove the heater hoses from the heater core tubes. See **Figure 4** (2300 cc), **Figure 5** (2800 cc), **Figure 6** (200 cid), **Figure 7** (255 cid and 302 cid), or **Figure 8** (2300 cc turbocharged engine) for heater hose positions.

3. Open the glove box and remove glove box liner.

4. Remove the 2 instrument panel-to-cowl brace retaining screws and remove brace.

5. Move the temperature control arm to the WARM position.

6. From inside glove box compartment, remove 4 heater core cover retaining screws and lift out cover through glove box (**Figure 23**).

6

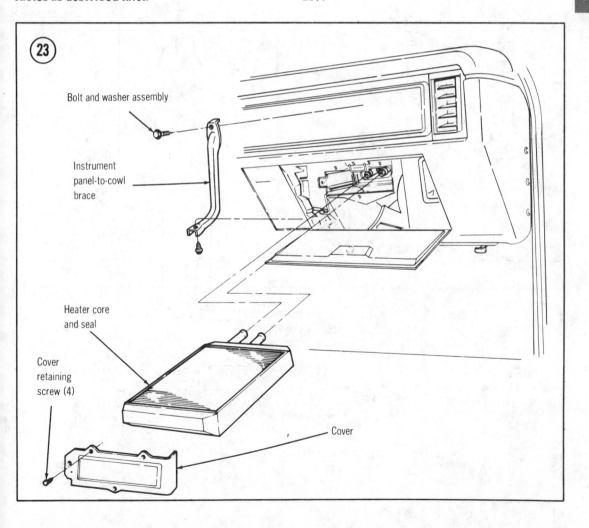

(23)

Bolt and washer assembly

Instrument panel-to-cowl brace

Heater core and seal

Cover retaining screw (4)

Cover

7. Working inside the engine compartment, remove the heater case retaining screws.

8. To loosen the heater core from the heater case, push the heater core tubes and seal toward the rear of the vehicle.

9. Lift the heater core from the case through the glove box opening (**Figure 23**).

10. Installation is the reverse of these steps. Fill the cooling system with antifreeze and water.

Blower Assembly Removal/Installlation

1. Remove the right ventilator assembly as described earlier under *Heater Case Removal/Installation*.

2. Disconnect the orange/black blower motor ground wire from spade terminal and push it back through the hole in the blower case (**Figure 24**).

3. Remove the right side cowl trim panel for access to the blower ground terminal black lug and remove the ground terminal lug retaining screw.

4. Remove 3 nuts that secure the blower motor, then lift out (**Figure 24**).

5. Installation is the reverse of these steps. When inserting the blower wheel into the blower assembly, align the flat surface on the inside diameter of the blower wheel hub with the flat surface of the motor shaft (**Figure 25**). Test system for operation.

Temperature Control Cable Adjustment

Refer to **Figure 26** for this procedure.

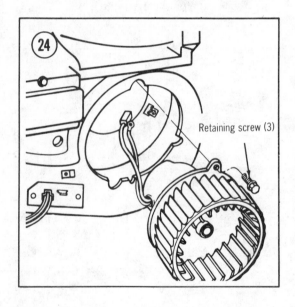

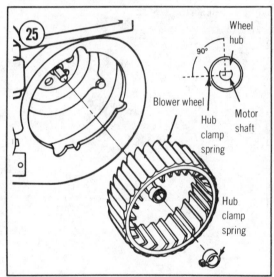

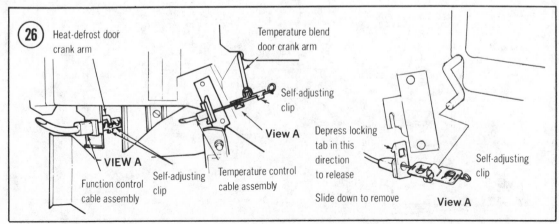

1. Move the temperature control lever on the instrument panel to COOL.

2. Hold the temperature crank arm in position, and insert the tip of a small screwdriver into the wire end loop at the end of the crank arm and pull the cable wire through the self adjusting clip until a one inch gap separates the clip and the wire end loop. See **Figure 27**.

3. Move the temperature control lever on the instrument panel to WARM to position the self-adjusting clip.

4. Check heater for proper control.

Functional Control Cable Adjustment

Refer to **Figure 26** for this procedure.

1. Move the functional control lever on the instrument panel to OFF.

2. Hold the crank arm in position, and insert the tip of a small screwdriver into the wire end loop at the end of the crank arm and pull the wire through the self-adjusting clip until one inch separates the clip and the wire end loop. See **Figure 27**.

3. Move the functional control lever on the instrument panel to DEFROST to position the self-adjusting clip.

4. Check heater for proper control.

Control Assembly/Cable Removal/Installation

On all models, the control assembly must be partly removed to gain access to control cables. Refer to **Figure 28** for this procedure.

1. Remove the instrument cluster trim panel from front of instument panel.

2. Remove the 4 control assembly mounting screws from front of instrument panel, then lower the control assembly from the instrument panel.

3. Disconnect the function and temperature control cable assemblies from the heater case assembly. **Figure 29** shows the control and cable assemblies.

4. Disconnect the electrical connectors from the blower switch, system-off switch, and illumination bulb harness.

5. Remove the control assembly with the control cables as an assembly.

6. Remove the push nuts that connect the control cables to the function lever and the frame of the control assembly as required, then remove associated cable mounting screws.

7. Remove the control cable to be replaced.

8. Installation is the reverse of these steps. After installation, adjust the control cables as described earlier.

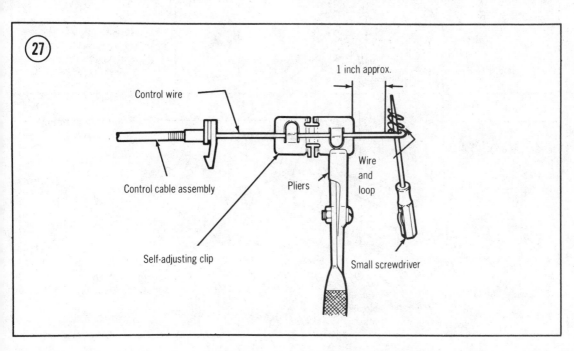

(27)

Control wire

1 inch approx.

Control cable assembly

Pliers

Wire and loop

Self-adjusting clip

Small screwdriver

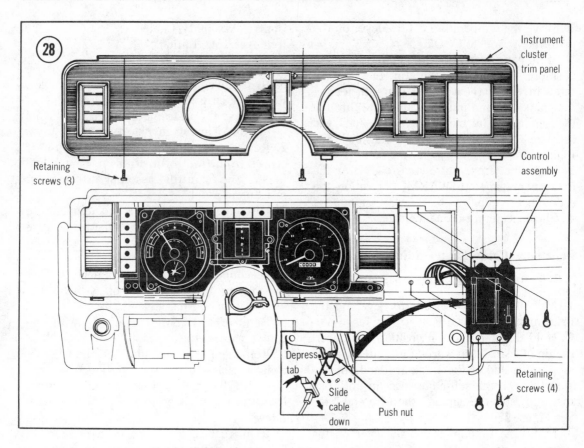

Instrument cluster trim panel

Control assembly

Retaining screws (3)

Depress tab

Slide cable down

Push nut

Retaining screws (4)

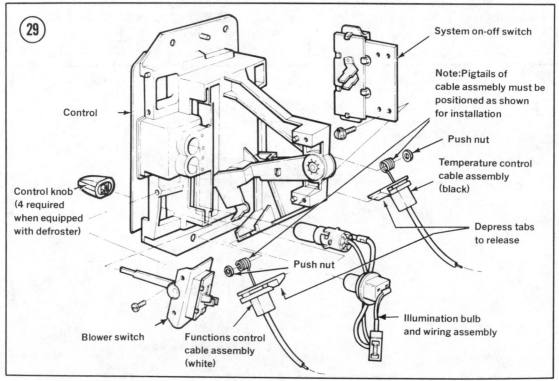

System on-off switch

Note:Pigtails of cable assmebly must be positioned as shown for installation

Push nut

Temperature control cable assembly (black)

Depress tabs to release

Control

Control knob (4 required when equipped with defroster)

Push nut

Blower switch

Functions control cable assembly (white)

Illumination bulb and wiring assembly

Table 1   DRIVE BELT TENSION

Belt Type or Size	New Belt (lb) (1)	Used Belt (lb) (2)
All except ¼ in.	120-160	75-120(2)
¼ in. only	50-80	40-60(3)
Ribbed belt, without tensioner	140-170	140-160(4)
Ribbed belt with tensioner	105-155	105-155 (5)

1. Tension is measured after belt is installed (engine has not been started).
2. If less than 75 lb., readjust to 90-120 lb.
3. If less than 40 lb., readjust to 40-60 lb.
4. If less than 110 lb., readjust to 140-160 lb.
5. If less than 105 lb., replace belt tensioner

Table 2   APPROXIMATE COOLANT CAPACITY*

	1979	1980
2300 cc	8.6 10.00**	8.6 9.0**
2300 cc Turbo	8.6 10.2**	9.2 9.2**
2800 cc	9.2 9.4**	— —
200 cid	— —	8.1 8.1**
255 cid	— —	13.4 13.7**
302 cid	14.0 14.0**	— —

*All measurements are specified in quarts. Capacity may vary (plus-minus) 15 percent.
**With air conditioning.

6

NOTE: If you own a 1981 or later model, first check the Supplement at the back of the book for any new service information.

CHAPTER SEVEN

ELECTRICAL SYSTEM

All models are equipped with a 12-volt negative ground electrical system. This chapter includes service procedures for the battery, starter, charging system, lighting system, ignition system, fuses, instruments, and windshield wipers, as well as distributor-related emission controls.

When trouble is experienced in the electrical system, Chapter Two can prove valuable as a guide to isolating problem areas as well as explaining the functions and uses of electrical test equipment. Very often, electrical trouble can be traced to a simple cause, such as a blown fuse, a loose or corroded connection, a loose alternator drive belt, or a frayed wire. But, while these problems are easily correctable and of seemingly no major importance, they can quickly lead to serious difficulty if they are allowed to go uncorrected.

If you plan to do much of your own electrical work, a multimeter (described in Chapter Two) combining the functions of an ohmmeter, ammeter, and voltmeter, is essential to locating and sorting out problems.

Above all, electrical system repair requires a patient, thorough approach to find true causes of trouble and then correct all of the faults that are involved. **Tables 1 and 2** are at the end of the chapter.

BATTERY

Care and Inspection

1. Disconnect both battery cables and remove the battery.
2. Clean the top of the battery with a baking soda and water solution. Scrub with a stiff bristle brush.

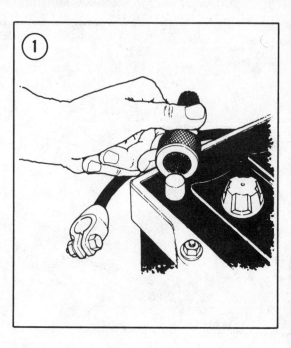

CAUTION
Keep cleaning solution out of battery cells or the electrolyte will be seriously weakened.

3. Clean battery terminals with a stiff brush or a tool made for this purpose (**Figure 1**).

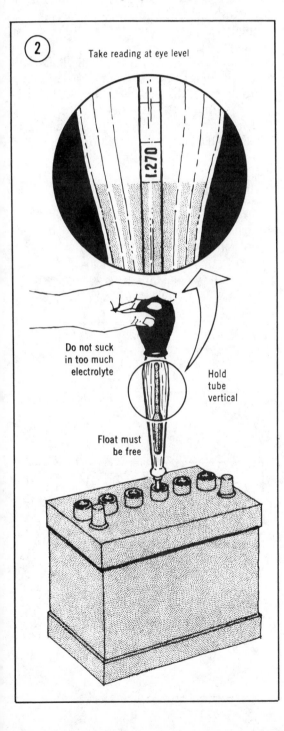

Take reading at eye level

1.270

Do not suck in too much electrolyte

Hold tube vertical

Float must be free

4. Examine entire battery case for cracks.
5. Install the battery and reconnect the battery cables.
6. Coat the battery terminals with light mineral grease or Vaseline after tightening.
7. Check the electrolyte level and top up with distilled water if necessary.

Testing

Hydrometer testing is a good way to check battery condition. Use a hydrometer with numbered graduations from 1.200 to 1.300 rather than one with just color-coded bands. To use the hydrometer, squeeze the rubber bulb, insert the tip in the cell and release the bulb (**Figure 2**). Draw enough electrolyte to float the weighted float inside the hydrometer. Note the number in line with the surface of the electrolyte. This is the specific gravity of the cell. Return the electrolyte to the cell from which it came.

The specific gravity of electrolyte in each battery cell is an excellent indicator of that cell's condition. If the reading is below 1,200, the battery needs to be charged. However, if there is a difference in specific gravity of 0.050 or more between any cells, the battery must be replaced.

NOTE
For every 10° above 80° F electrolyte temperature, add 0.004 to specific gravity reading. For every 10° below 80° F, subtract 0.004 from specific gravity reading.

CAUTION
Battery electrolyte must be fully topped up and the negative cable disconnected before charging battery.

Charging

There is no need to remove the battery from the car to charge it. Make certain the area is well-ventilated and that there is no chance of sparks or flame being in the vicinity of the battery; during charging, highly explosive hydrogen gas is produced by the battery.

Disconnect the ground lead at the battery. Remove the caps from the cells and top up each cell with distilled water. Never add electrolyte to a battery that has been in service.

Connect the charger to the battery—negative to negative, positive to positive (**Figure 3**). If the charger output is variable, select a low setting (1.5-2 amps), set the voltage selector to 12 and plug the charger in. If the battery is severely discharged (1.200 or less specific gravity) allow it to charge for at least 8 hours. Less charge deterioration requires less charging time.

After the battery has been charged for a suitable period of time, unplug the charger and disconnect it from the battery. Be extremely careful about sparks. Test the condition of each cell with a hydrometer as described above. Compare the results to **Table 1**.

If the specific gravity indicates that the battery is fully charged, and if the reading remains the same after one hour, the battery can be considered to be in good condition and fully charged. Check the electrolyte level and add water if necessary; install the caps and reconnect the ground lead.

ALTERNATOR

The alternator is belt driven from the engine. Current is supplied from the alternator-regulator system to the rotating field of the alternator through 2 brushes to 2 slip rings.

The alternator produces power in the form of alternating current. The alternating current is rectified to direct current by 6 diodes. The alternator regulator automatically adjusts the alternator field current to maintain the alternator output voltage within prescribed limits to correctly charge the battery. The alternator is self current limiting.

Alternator repairs require specialized equipment and skills. While repairs are possible, it is generally more practical for the home mechanic to have the alternator serviced by a dealer or competent repair shop. The following test procedures will tell you if repairs are necessary.

Output Test

1. Disconnect the coil wire from the distributor and ground it so the engine won't start. Turn the engine over with the starter several times, for several seconds each time.

This partially discharges the battery so the alternator will register output if it is working. After turning the engine over, reconnect the coil wire.

2. Disconnect the wire from the alternator BAT terminal. Connect an ammeter between the terminal and the wire. The ammeter must have a wide enough range to cover the alternator's rated output. See **Table 2** for output ratings.

3. Start the engine. Turn on all lights and electrical equipment. If the ammeter reading is approximately the same as the alternator's rated output, the alternator is working properly. If no currect is produced, the trouble must be isolated to the alternator or regulator. Perform the following tests.

Wiring Harness Test

The harness between the regulator plug and alternator must be tested for grounded wires before performing the next test. Otherwise the voltage regulator may be damaged.

To test, disconnect the wire connector from the regulator. Connect one test probe of an

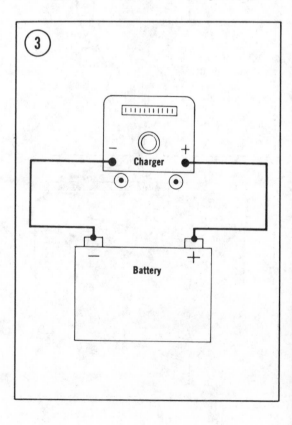

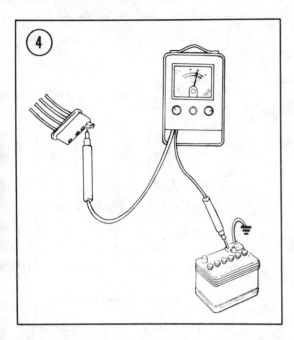

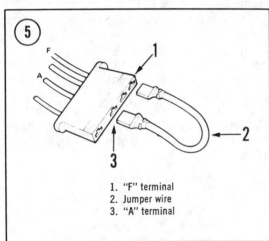

1. "F" terminal
2. Jumper wire
3. "A" terminal

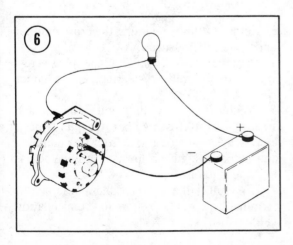

ohmmeter to the F terminal of the harness (**Figure 4** and **Figure 5**). Connect the other probe to the battery negative terminal. The ohmmeter should read between 4 and 250 ohms. If the ohmmeter does not indicate within this range, there is a ground in the harness that must be found and repaired.

Isolation Test

If the harness was OK in the previous test, connect a jumper wire between A and F terminals of the regulator wiring connector (**Figure 5**). Disconnect the wire from the alternator BAT terminal. Connect an ammeter between the wire and the terminal.

Run the engine at 1,500 rpm, with all lights and accessories on. If the ammeter indicates approximately the rated output of the alternator (see **Table 2** for output ratings), a defective regulator is indicated. If the ammeter shows a low reading, the alternator is probably at fault.

Field Circuit Test

If previous tests indicate a defective alternator, the problem can be verified by a field circuit test. This can be done with a test light or ohmmeter. The ohmmeter will give more detailed information, but either method will give a definite indication if the alternator is defective.

The test light method uses a 12-volt car battery and light bulb (**Figure 6**). Connect one test lead to the alternator frame and the other to the FLD terminal as shown. If the bulb lights brightly, the field circuit is satisfactory. If it does not, there is an internal alternator defect. Refer further testing and service to a Ford dealer or competent automotive electrical repair shop.

To test with an ohmmeter, make the connections in the same way as shown in **Figure 6**. Spin the alternator pulley by hand. The ohmmeter should read between 4 and 250 ohms, and it should fluctuate. No ohmmeter reading at all indicates an open brush lead, sticking or worn brushes, or a defective rotor. If the reading is less than 4 ohms, a grounded brush assembly, grounded field terminal, or defective rotor may be the cause.

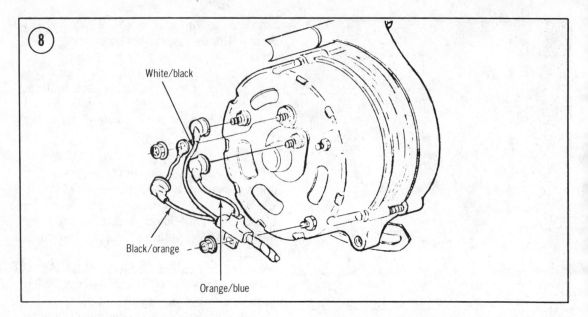

⑧

White/black

Black/orange

Orange/blue

Alternator Removal/Installation

1. Disconnect the negative battery cable.
2. Loosen the alternator mounting bolts (**Figure 7**—typical mounting bolt location). Remove the adjusting arm bolt. Detach the fan belt from the alternator pulley.
3. Carefully note the locations of the alternator wires and remove the electrical connectors from the alternator. The stator and field connectors are the push-on type. They should be pulled straight off the terminal studs to prevent damage. See **Figure 8**.
4. Remove the alternator mounting bolts, and remove the alternator.
5. Installation is the reverse of these steps. Tighten the alternator adjuster bolts to 24-40 ft.-lb., the pivot bolts to 55-70 ft.-lb. Adjust the fan belt tension (Chapter Six).

VOLTAGE REGULATOR

The electro-mechanical regulator is factory calibrated and sealed and is not to be adjusted. If a defective regulator is suspected, test it together with the alternator as described earlier in this chapter. Replace the regulator if defective.

Replacement

1. Disconnect the negative cable from battery.
2. Remove the regulator mounting screws.

The regulator is located on the left-hand, front fender apron (**Figure 9**).
3. Disconnect the regulator from the wiring harness.
4. Install by reversing Steps 1-3.

STARTER

Removal (1979 Models Only)

1. Disconnect the negative cable from battery.
2. Jack up the front end of the car and place it on jackstands.

> *NOTE*
> *Place jackstands on the longitudinal (front-to-rear) frame members of the car. Do not place the jackstands under the crossmember as this assembly must be removed during the following procedure.*

3. Remove 4 bolts retaining the crossmember under the bell housing.
4. Remove the flex coupling clamping screw at attachment point to steering gear (Chapter Nine).
5. Remove 3 nuts and bolts that attach steering gear to crossmember (Chapter Nine).
6. Disengage steering gear from flex coupling and pull steering gear down to provide access to starter motor.
7. Disconnect the starter cable at the starter terminal and note position for reinstallation (**Figure 10**).

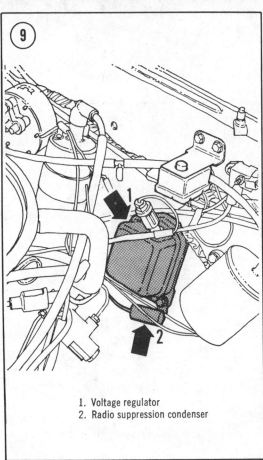

1. Voltage regulator
2. Radio suppression condenser

8. Remove the 3 starter attaching bolts and remove starter.

9. Installation is the reverse of these steps. Tighten the starter attaching bolts to 15-20 ft.-lb.

NOTE
The engine ground cable is secured by one of the starter attaching bolts. Be sure the cable is reconnected during installation.

Starter Removal/Installation (1980 Models Only)

1. Disconnect the negative cable from battery.

2. Jack up the front end of the car and place it on jackstands.

3. *255 cid only*: Remove front wishbone brace (Chapter Nine).

4. Disconnect the starter cable at the starter terminal and note position for reinstallation (**Figure 10**).

5. Remove the 2 starter attaching bolts. Pull the starter forward, then lower it away from the car. On some vehicles, it may be necessary to turn the wheels to left or right side to provide clearance.

6. Installation is the reverse of these steps. Tighten the attaching bolts to 15-20 ft.-lb.

Brush Replacement

Starter brushes should be replaced when they are worn to 1/4 in. Always install a complete set of new brushes.

1. Remove brush cover, gasket, and starter drive plunger lever cover.

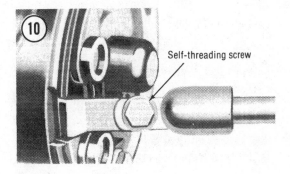

Self-threading screw

2. Remove 2 through bolts from starter frame (**Figure 11**).

3. Note position of brush leads (**Figure 12**). Remove brushes from their holders.

4. Remove drive end housing and plunger lever return spring.

5. Remove starter drive plunger lever pivot pin and lever. Remove armature.

6. Remove brush end plate. Remove ground brush retaining screws from frame and remove brushes. Cut insulated brush leads from field coils as close to field connection point as possible. Refer to **Figure 13**.

7. Install new insulated field brush lead on field coil connection. Position and crimp the clip provided with the brushes to hold brush lead to connection. Solder lead, clip, and connection together with rosin core solder and a 300-watt iron.

8. Install ground brush leads to frame with retaining screws.

9. Clean commutator with fine sandpaper. Position brush end plate to starter frame with end plate boss in frame slot (**Figure 14**).

10. Install armature in starter frame. Install starter drive gear plunger lever to frame and starter drive assembly. Install pivot pin.

11. Partially fill drive end housing bearing bore with grease. Position return spring on plunger lever and drive end housing to starter frame. Install through bolts and tighten to 55-75 in.-lb. Be certain stop ring retainer is seated properly in drive end housing.

12. Install commutator brushes in brush holders. Center brush springs on brushes.

13. Position plunger lever cover and brush cover band, with its gasket on the cover. Tighten band retaining screw.

14. Install starter as described in this chapter.

Inspection

1. Clean all parts with lint-free cloth or compressed air.

> *CAUTION*
> *Do not clean starter parts with solvent. Solvent will ruin the field coil insulation and melt the grease in the drive end bearing bore.*

2. Check electrical terminals for visible wear or damage. Replace as needed.

1. Insulated brush holders
2. Grounded brush holders

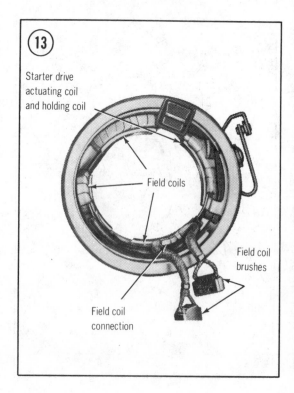

3. Check armature for visible damage such as burned wiring or a worn shaft. Replace if these can be seen.

4. Inspect the soldered connections between the armature leads and commutator. Resolder loose connections with rosin core solder.

5. Test the armature winding for shorts. To check, use an armature tester (growler). Take this to a dealer or automotive electrical shop if you don't have a tester.

6. Replace starter drives and ring gears that have milled, pitted or broken teeth or show signs of inadequate engagement or wear pattern (**Figure 15**).

Starter Relay Replacement

1. Disconnect the negative cable from the battery,

2. Carefully disconnect and identify (to ensure proper reconnection) the starter, battery, and ignition switch wires attached to

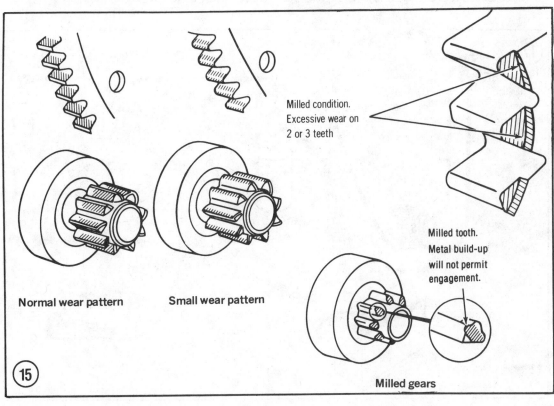

Normal wear pattern   Small wear pattern

Milled condition. Excessive wear on 2 or 3 teeth

Milled tooth. Metal build-up will not permit engagement.

Milled gears

the relay terminals. The starter relay is located on the right fender apron (**Figure 16**).

3. Remove the screws securing the relay to the fender apron. Lift the relay out.

4. Installation is the reverse of these steps.

DISTRIBUTOR

All vehicles use a solid state ignition system which uses a breakerless distributor which also employs a dual diaphragm vacuum advance feature. Refer to **Figure 17** for typical ignition system circuit.

Proper engine operation depends heavily on distributor advance characteristics. Adjustment of the advance mechanism is critical and requires special test fixtures. If timing adjustments, given in Chapter Three, do not cure the trouble, the distributor must be removed. Take the job to a dealer for repair.

Distributor Removal

To remove the distributor, refer to **Figure 18** (2300 cc), **Figure 19** (2800 cc), **Figure 20**

(200 cid) or **Figure 21** (255 cid and 302 cid), while performing the following steps.

1. Remove the air cleaner assembly (2800 cc, 255 cid and 302 cid engines only), then disconnect the distributor wiring connector (**Figure 17**) from the vehicle wiring harness.

2. *2300 cc and 200 cid engines only.* Remove one mounting bolt from the thermactor pump. Remove the pump drive belt and swing the pump to one side.

3. Remove the distributor cap and disconnect both vacuum lines from the distributor diaphragm.

4. Disconnect the distributor primary lead (**Figure 17**) at the ignition coil.

5. To make installation easier, rotate the engine until the No. 1 cylinder is at top dead center on the compression stroke. This position is reached when the 0 degree mark on the engine crankshaft damper aligns with the timing pointer and the distributor rotor points toward the No. 1 terminal in the distributor cap.

6. Scribe marks on the distributor body and the engine block where the distributor shaft enters the block.

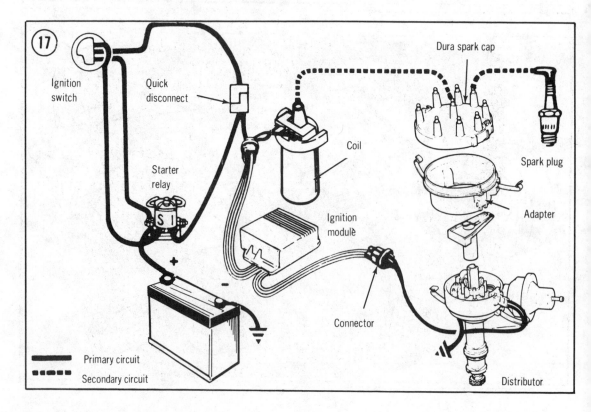

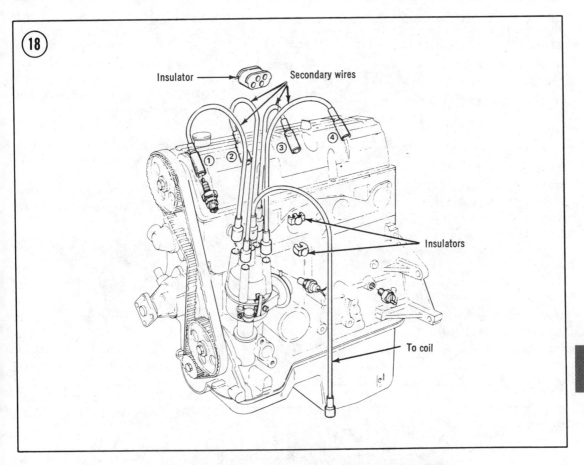

7

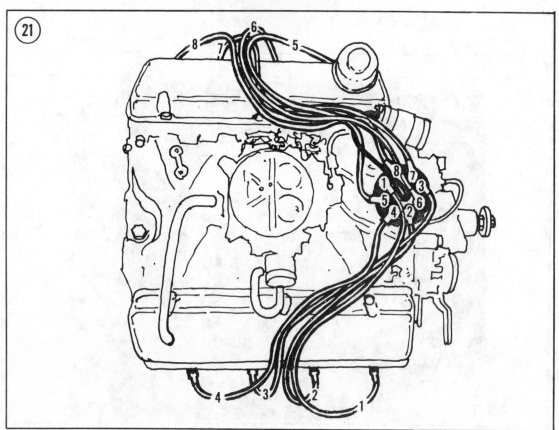

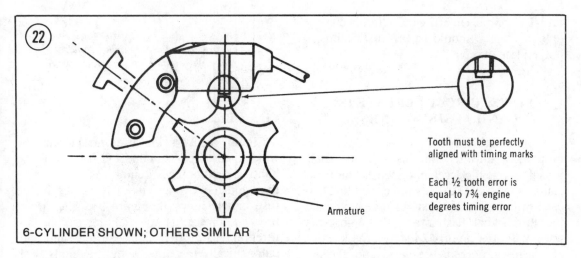

Tooth must be perfectly
aligned with timing marks

Each ½ tooth error is
equal to 7¾ engine
degrees timing error

Armature

6-CYLINDER SHOWN; OTHERS SIMILAR

7. Ensure that the armature tooth is exactly aligned with the timing mark on the distributor magnetic pickup (**Figure 22**). Each 1/2 tooth alignment error is equal to 7-3/4 degrees of engine timing error.

8. Remove the distributor hold-down bolt attaching the distributor to the engine block, then carefully lift the distributor away from the engine block.

> *NOTE*
> *Do not rotate the engine while the distributor is out of the block, or it will be necessary to time the engine.*

Distributor Installation

1. Make sure the No. 1 cylinder is at top dead center on the compression stroke. If in doubt, refer to the distributor removal procedures.

2. Make sure the armature tooth aligns exactly with the magnetic pickup timing marks with the distributor rotor pointing toward the No. 1 terminal in the distributor cap. Install the distributor in the engine block, making sure the alignment marks scribed on the distributor body and the engine block line up. Recheck the armature alignment.

3. Ensure that the distributor is fully seated in the engine block. Then install the distributor hold-down bracket and bolt and secure the distributor.

> *NOTE*
> *If the distributor fails to insert completely into the engine block, the oil pump drive shaft, located in the bottom of the distributor drive shaft, is not fully seated in*

the oil pump. Remove the distributor from the engine block, then reinstall the distributor to properly seat the oil pump drive shaft. Make sure the distributor is properly aligned with all scribed marks and timing marks as previously described.

4. Connect the distributor primary wiring connector to the vehicle wiring harness, and reconnect both vacuum hoses to the distributor vacuum diaphragm.

5. Install the distributor cap, then reconnect any hoses previously disconnected, reposition the belt-driven accessories previously moved to gain access to the distributor, and tighten all bolts to specifications.

6. Reinstall air cleaner assembly (2300 cc, 255 cid and 302 cid), then check and adjust ignition timing as described in Chapter Three.

IGNITION COIL

Removal/Installation

1. Disconnect the primary (thin) wire and the secondary (thick) wire from the coil.

2. Remove the 2 retaining screws securing the coil and bracket to the fender apron.

3. Loosen the bracket clamp and remove the coil.

4. Installation is the reverse of these steps.

Coil Resistance Test

Connect an ohmmeter between the coil terminals (**Figure 23**). Resistance should be

7

1.13-1.23 ohms. On 302 cid California engines only, resistance should be 0.71-0.77 ohms. If not, replace the coil.

FUSES, CIRCUIT BREAKERS, AND FUSIBLE LINKS

A combination fuse/circuit breaker panel is mounted beneath the instrument panel, directly above the accelerator pedal. This panel contains most of the fuses and circuit breakers used in the electrical system. It also contains the turn signal flasher and the emergency warning flasher. **Figure 24** shows the location of all fuses, circuit breakers, and flashers installed in the panel. Fuses, flasher units and circuit breakers are removed by removing the fuse panel trim cover, then pulling the failed unit directly away from the panel. No special tools are required.

Whenever a fuse blows, the cause of the trouble should be determined before replacing the fuse. Usually the trouble is a short circuit in the wiring. Always carry spare fuses of all required values in the glove compartment.

CAUTION
Never substitute tinfoil or wire for a fuse. An overload could cause major damage to the electrical system, or an electrical fire and complete loss of the car.

Circuit Breakers

Circuit breakers are used to protect the windshield wiper circuit and most of the lighting circuits. The circuit breaker protecting the windshield wiper circuit is located in the fuse panel shown in **Figure 24**. The circuit breakers protecting the lighting circuits are integral with the light switch and are automatically resetting. If the car lights flash

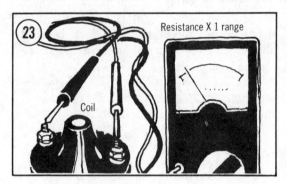

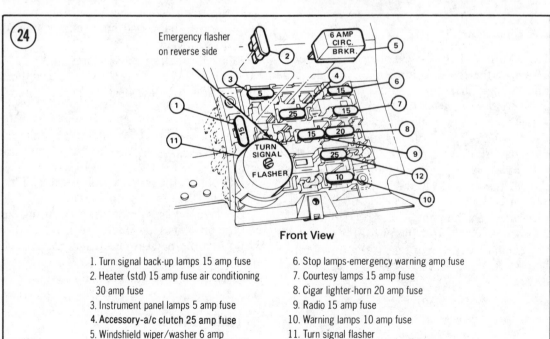

Front View

1. Turn signal back-up lamps 15 amp fuse
2. Heater (std) 15 amp fuse air conditioning 30 amp fuse
3. Instrument panel lamps 5 amp fuse
4. **Accessory-a/c clutch 25 amp fuse**
5. Windshield wiper/washer 6 amp circuit breaker

6. Stop lamps-emergency warning amp fuse
7. Courtesy lamps 15 amp fuse
8. Cigar lighter-horn 20 amp fuse
9. Radio 15 amp fuse
10. Warning lamps 10 amp fuse
11. Turn signal flasher
12. Electric choke 25 amp fuse

on and off at regular intervals, the lighting circuit is probably overloaded. Check the circuits by referring to the wiring diagrams provided at the end of this book. To remove the windshield wiper circuit breaker from the fuse panel, simply pull the breaker away from the fuse panel. To replace the circuit breakers in the headlight switch, the entire switch must be replaced. Refer to the *Headlight Switch Replacement* procedures covered under *Switches*, later in this chapter.

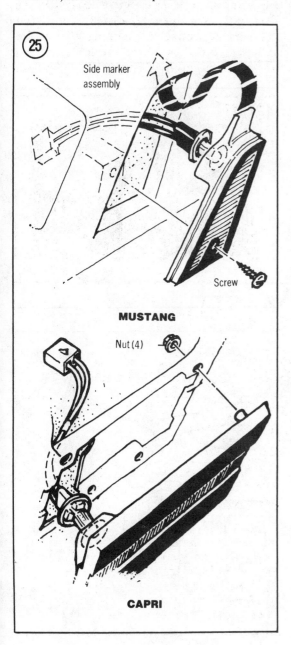

MUSTANG

CAPRI

Fusible Links

Fusible links are short sections of thin wire installed in a heavier wire. They are intended to burn out if an overload occurs, thus protecting the wiring harness and remainder of the circuit. Fusible links are incorporated in the engine compartment light circuit, the load circuit, and the heated backlight circuit. Refer to the wiring diagrams at the end of this book for the location of fusible links.

NOTE
Fusible links are a dealer replaceable item, and should be referred to your local Ford dealer or a competent garage.

LIGHTS

Headlight Replacement

1. Remove the screws securing the headlight cover.
2. Remove the 4 screws attaching the ring assembly to the adjusting ring, and remove the ring assembly.
3. Pull the headlight bulb(s) forward, out of the fender, and disconnect the wiring assembly plug.
4. Installation is the reverse of these steps. Have the headights aimed by a dealer.

Parking/Turn Signal Bulb Replacement

To replace bulbs, open the hood and locate the parking/turn signal light bulb socket. Turn the bulb socket counterclockwise until released from the light body, then remove the bulb and socket from the light body. Press in on the bulb and turn counterclockwise to remove it from the socket. Installation is the reverse of this procedure.

Side Marker Bulb Replacement

On all models, front marker bulbs are replaced by removing the exposed screw that holds the side marker lamp assembly to the fascia. Remove the lamp from the fascia and remove the bulb from the socket assembly. Installation is the reverse of this procedure. See **Figure 25**.

The rear side marker lights are removed as described under *Rear Lights Replacement*.

7

Rear Lights Replacement

The rear light assembly contains 5 bulb elements. These elements provide the functions of tail/stoplights, back-up lights, rear turn lights, hazard warning lights, and rear side marker light. On all models, the rear lights are reached through the trunk. Remove the light sockets from the lamp body, inspect the individual bulbs for proper operation, and replace bulbs as required.

Dome Light Replacement

On vehicles without sun roofs, squeeze the lens inward to release the locking tabs and remove the lens from the lamp body. Remove the bulb. Install in the reverse order. See **Figure 26**. On vehicles equipped with sun roof, the dome lamp must be removed from its mounting. Pull down on the left side of the dome lamp assembly. Using long nose needle nose pliers, remove the bulb from its socket. Install in the reverse order. See **Figure 27**.

Instrument Panel Lights

Remove the instrument panel as described later in this chapter to gain access to instrument panel lights.

SWITCHES

Headlight Switch Replacement

A combination 3-position lighting switch is mounted in the instrument panel.
1. Disconnect the battery ground cable.
2. Pull the headlamp switch out to the ON position.
3. From beneath the instrument panel, depress the headlamp knob and the shaft retainer button on the headlamp switch (**Figure 28**).
4. Remove the headlamp switch knob, shaft assembly, and retaining nut.
5. Unplug the multiple connector plug from the switch and remove the switch from the instrument panel.
6. Install in the reverse order.
7. Start vehicle and test all lights for operation.

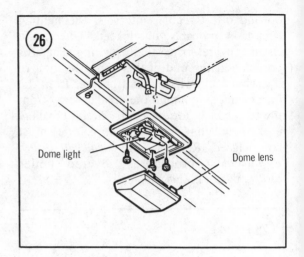

Dome light · Dome lens

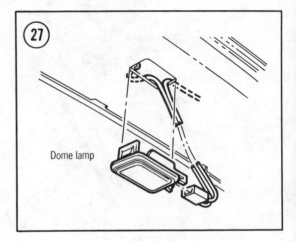

Dome lamp

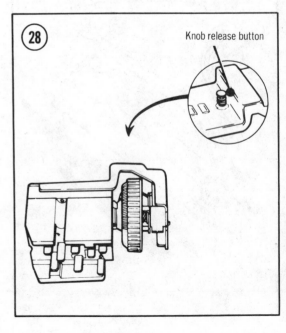

Knob release button

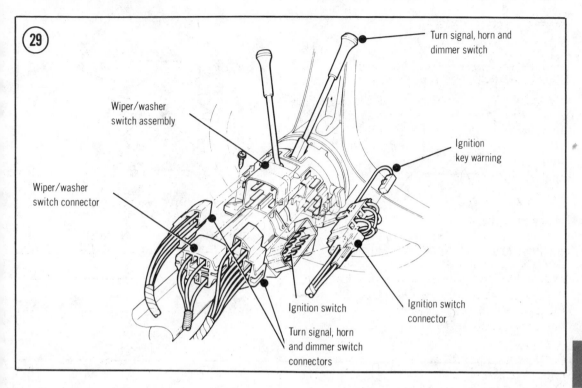

(29)

Turn signal, horn and dimmer switch

Wiper/washer switch assembly

Ignition key warning

Wiper/washer switch connector

Ignition switch connector

Ignition switch

Turn signal, horn and dimmer switch connectors

7

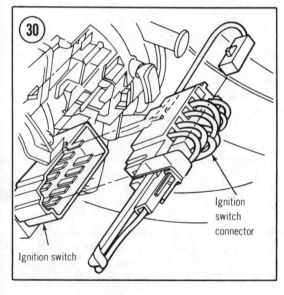

(30)

Ignition switch connector

Ignition switch

Ignition Switch Removal

Refer to **Figure 29**.

1. Disconnect the battery ground cable.
2. Remove 5 screws securing steering column trim panel to steering column, and remove the trim panel.
3. Unplug the ignition switch electrical connector by spreading apart the locking

fingers and pulling the plugs from the switch. See **Figure 30**.
4. Drill out the break-off-head bolts connecting the switch to the lock cylinder housing with a 1/8 inch drill.
5. Use an EX-3 Easy-Out tool or equivalent to remove the 2 drilled out bolts.
6. Remove the ignition switch from the actuator pin.

Ignition Switch Installation

1. Turn ignition switch to LOCK, and install ignition switch on the actuator pin.
2. Install 2 new break-off-head bolts and torque until the heads break off.
3. Plug electrical connector to the ignition switch (**Figure 30**).
4. Reinstall the steering trim shroud and support with 5 attaching screws.
5. Connect negative battery terminal.
6. Check operation of the switch after installation.

Turn Indicator/Hazard Flasher/Dimmer Switch/Wiper Switch Replacement

Refer to **Figure 29** for this procedure.

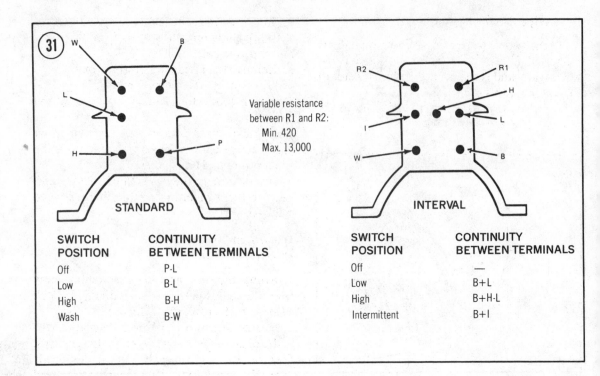

Variable resistance
between R1 and R2:
Min. 420
Max. 13,000

STANDARD	
SWITCH POSITION	CONTINUITY BETWEEN TERMINALS
Off	P-L
Low	B-L
High	B-H
Wash	B-W

INTERVAL	
SWITCH POSITION	CONTINUITY BETWEEN TERMINALS
Off	—
Low	B+L
High	B+H-L
Intermittent	B+I

1. Remove negative ground cable from battery.

2. Remove 5 screws attaching steering column trim to steering column, and remove the trim.

3. Lift out the necessary connector retainer tabs, and disconnect the connectors.

4. Remove the switch retaining screws and lift up and remove the switch assembly from the steering column.

5. Installation is the reverse of this procedure. Check operation of the switch after installation.

Switch Continuity Test

Switches can be tested for continuity with an ohmmeter. To test the wiper switch, for example, disconnect the negative cable from the battery and remove the wiper switch as discussed earlier. Test the switch if necessary (referring to the continuity diagram and terminal identification in **Figure 31**) with an ohmmeter.

FLASHER UNIT

The flasher units for the turn signal and the hazard flasher systems are found in the fuse panel (**Figure 32**). To replace a flasher, pull the old flasher straight out. When installing a new flasher, line up the metal contacts with the slots in the fuse panel, then press the flasher into place.

WINDSHIELD WIPER SYSTEM

Front Wiper Motor Replacement

The windshield wiper motor is located beneath the instrument panel on the firewall, and is replaced as follows.

1. Disconnect the negative cable from the battery.

2. Working beneath the dash, remove the retaining clip from the pin on the wiper motor pivot shaft, then disconnect the linkage arm from the pivot shaft pin (**Figure 33**).

3. Remove the 3 nuts attaching the wiper motor to the firewall.

4. Disconnect the wiper motor from the electrical connector leading into the wiring harness, then remove the wiper motor.

5. Installation is the reverse of these steps. Tighten the 3 wiper motor attaching screws to 5-7 ft.-lb.

Rear Wiper Motor Replacement

A rear wiper system is optional on 3-door models. The rear wiper motor is located inside the liftgate, and is replaced as follows. Refer to **Figure 34** for this procedure.

1. Remove the wiper arm and blade as discussed later.

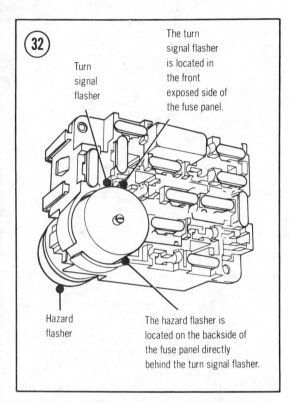

32

Turn signal flasher

The turn signal flasher is located in the front exposed side of the fuse panel.

Hazard flasher

The hazard flasher is located on the backside of the fuse panel directly behind the turn signal flasher.

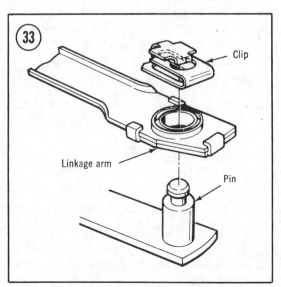

33

Clip

Linkage arm

Pin

2. Working inside the trunk, remove the pivot shaft attaching nut and spacers from the wiper motor pivot shaft.

3. Remove the liftgate inner trim panel.

4. Disconnect the wiper motor from the electrical connector leading into the wiring harness.

5. Remove the 3 screws attaching the wiper motor to the door inner skin, then remove the wiper motor and linkage assembly.

6. Installation is the reverse of these steps. Tighten the 3 wiper motor attaching screws to 5-7 ft.-lb.

Wiper Arm Replacement
(Front and Rear)

1. Swing the arm and blade assembly away from the windshield and move the slide latch away from the pivot shaft (**Figure 35**).

2. Remove the wiper arm from the pivot shaft.

3. Installation is the reverse of these steps. Position the auxiliary arm (if so equipped) over the pivot pin and push the main arm head

7

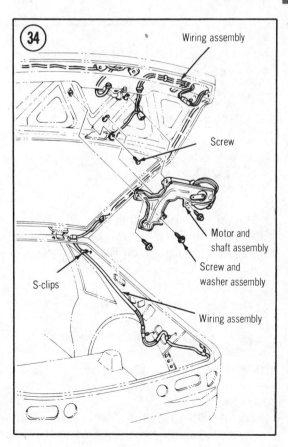

34

Wiring assembly

Screw

Motor and shaft assembly

Screw and washer assembly

S-clips

Wiring assembly

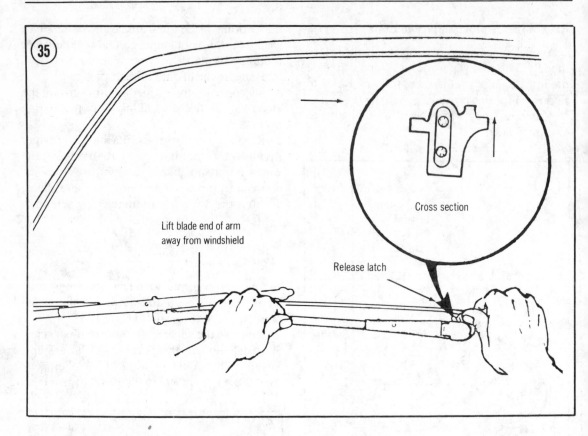

Lift blade end of arm
away from windshield

Cross section

Release latch

over the pivot shaft while holding the auxiliary arm down. Raise the blade end of the wiper arm and push the slide latch into the lock under the pivot shaft while holding the main arm head on the pivot shaft.

NOTE
Be sure the pivot shaft is in park position and the blade assembly is positioned to the correct dimension.

4. Lower the blade to the windshield. If the blade fails to touch the windshield, the slide latch is not positioned correctly.

Washer Motor Replacement

The washer motor and pump are mounted inside the washer reservoir.

Refer to **Figure 36** for this procedure.

1. *Rear Washer Motors Only*: Remove the left hand quarter trim panel, then remove the reservoir retaining screws and lift the reservoir from rear of vehicle.

2. *Front Washer Motors Only*: Remove the reservoir retaining screws and lock-tab wire,

then lift the reservoir assembly from the fender apron.

3. Disconnect the electrical connection and hose from the reservoir and remove reservoir from vehicle.

4. Using a small bladed screwdriver, pry out the retaining ring from end of washer motor.

5. Grip one end of the washer motor with pliers, and pull the motor, seal and impeller assembly out of the reservoir.

6. Installation is the reverse of this procedure plus the following. Lubricate the outside diameter of the seal with a dry lubricant, such as powdered graphite to prevent the seal from sticking to the reservoir wall during installation.

CAUTION
Do not operate the washer motor until the reservoir is filled.

INSTRUMENT PANEL GAUGES

Removal/Installation

1. Disconnect the negative cable from battery.

2. Remove the 3 screws from the instrument gauge trim cover, and remove the trim cover (**Figure 37**).

3. Remove the 2 upper and lower screws securing the instrument cluster to the instrument panel and pull the cluster away from the instrument panel.

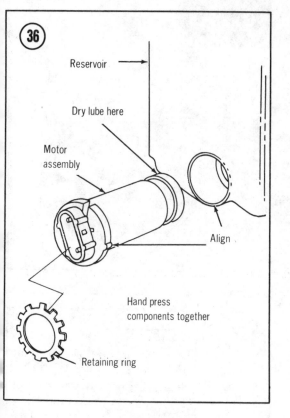

Reservoir

Dry lube here

Motor assembly

Align

Hand press components together

Retaining ring

4. From behind the instrument cluster, disconnect the speedometer cable by pressing the plastic quick connect connector, and removing the speedometer cable.

5. Pull the cluster partway out and disconnect the 2 cluster printed circuit connectors from the cluster backplate (**Figure 38**).

6. Pull the cluster panel out and remove from the instrument panel.

7. To replace a light bulb, pull the bulb socket out of the cluster.

8. To replace individual gauges, remove the screws that attach the mask and lens assembly to the cluster panel.

9. Install by reversing Steps 1-6. Before replacing the speedometer cable, apply a small amount of silicone grease in the drive hole of the speedometer head.

HORN

The horn is mounted at the front of the engine compartment, in the area of the left fender apron. To remove, disconnect the horn wire from its terminal and remove the mounting bolt. On installation, torque the mounting bolts to 12-18 ft.-lb. and connect the terminal wire.

If the horn works, but not loud enough, make sure the wires are making good contact and the horn is properly grounded to the body. To check further, connect a wire from the horn to the positive terminal of the battery. If the horn sounds normal, the wiring between the

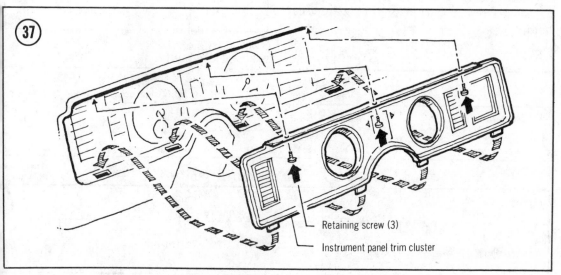

Retaining screw (3)

Instrument panel trim cluster

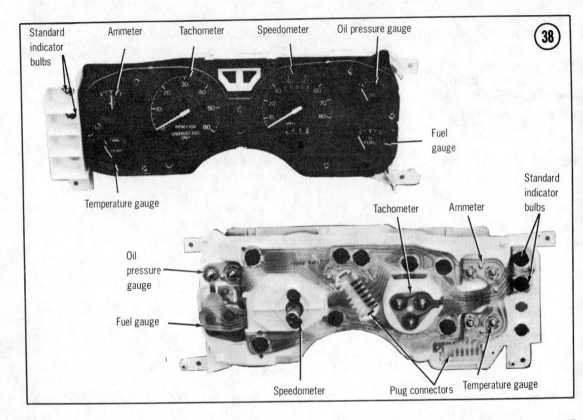

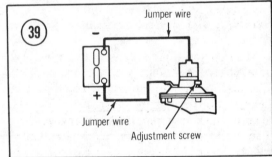

horn and the horn button or switch may be loose. If the horn does not blow, connect a wire between the negative battery terminal and the horn assembly, and connect another wire to the positive battery terminal and the horn wire terminal (**Figure 39**). If the horn fails to blow, turn the horn adjusting screw counterclockwise 1/4 to 3/8 in., then tighten adjusting screw. If horn fails to blow, replace horn.

Table 1   ELECTROLYTE SPECIFIC GRAVITY

	Permissible Value	Full Charge at 68 degrees F
Moderate climate	Over 1.20	1.26
Cold climate	Over 1.22	1.28
Warm climate	Over 1.18	1.23

Table 2   ALTERNATOR OUTPUT RATINGS

Stamp Color	Rated Output, Amperes
Orange	40
Black	65
Green	60

CHAPTER EIGHT

CLUTCH AND TRANSMISSION

Clutches are single, dry-disc types with a diaphragm spring. Pressure plate diameter is 8-1/2 in. with 2300 cc engines, 9 in. with 200 cid engines, and 10 in. with 302 cid engines. See **Table 1** for clutch specifications.

Table 1 and **Table 2** are at the end of the chapter.

Major clutch components are the disc, pressure plate, release mechanism, and linkage. The disc has friction material riveted to both facings. Coil springs in the center of the disc absorb shock and smooth clutch engagement. The release mechanism, consisting of a release lever and bearing, engages and disengages the clutch. The release mechanism is activated by a cable connected to the clutch pedal. **Figure 1** shows the clutch components for the 2300 cc engine. **Figure 2** shows the clutch components for the 200 cid engine. **Figure 3** shows the clutch components for the 302 cid engine.

CLUTCH ADJUSTMENT

The clutch pedal height should be adjusted whenever the clutch fails to disengage properly, or when new clutch parts are installed. Improper clutch pedal adjustment is a frequent cause of clutch failure and contributes to some transmission failures.

1. From inside the vehicle, measure the distance (dimension A) between the steering wheel rim and the clutch pedal pad with a tape measure. See **Figure 4**.

2. Depress the clutch pedal and measure the distance (dimension C) between the steering wheel rim and the clutch pedal pad with a tape measure (**Figure 4**). The difference between dimension A and dimension C must be within specification listed at the end of the chapter. If clutch pedal travel is not within specification, adjust the clutch pedal.

Clutch Pedal Adjustment
(2300cc and 302 cid)

1. Raise the front end of the car and place it on jackstands.

2. Remove the clutch dust shield from beneath the car. See **Figure 1, Figure 2 and Figure 3**.

3. Loosen the clutch cable locknut attached to the right side of the bellhousing. See **Figure 5**.

4. Turn the adjustment nut (clockwise to raise pedal or counterclockwise to lower pedal) and adjust clutch pedal height.

5. Clutch pedal height should be set to specifications listed in **Table 1**.

6. Tighten the locknut, depress the clutch pedal several times and check adjustment height.

8

① **CLUTCH-2300 CC**

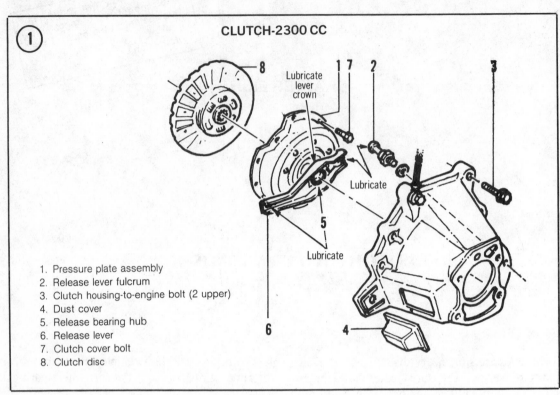

1. Pressure plate assembly
2. Release lever fulcrum
3. Clutch housing-to-engine bolt (2 upper)
4. Dust cover
5. Release bearing hub
6. Release lever
7. Clutch cover bolt
8. Clutch disc

② **CLUTCH-200 CID**

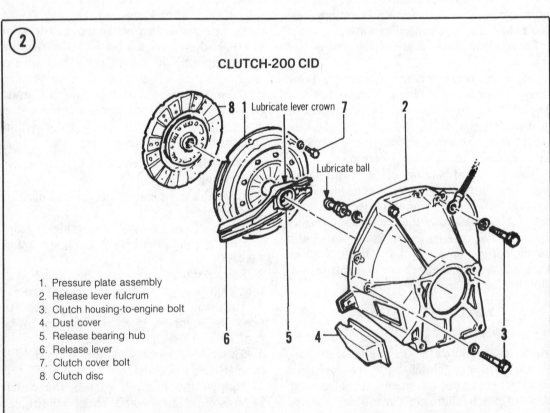

1. Pressure plate assembly
2. Release lever fulcrum
3. Clutch housing-to-engine bolt
4. Dust cover
5. Release bearing hub
6. Release lever
7. Clutch cover bolt
8. Clutch disc

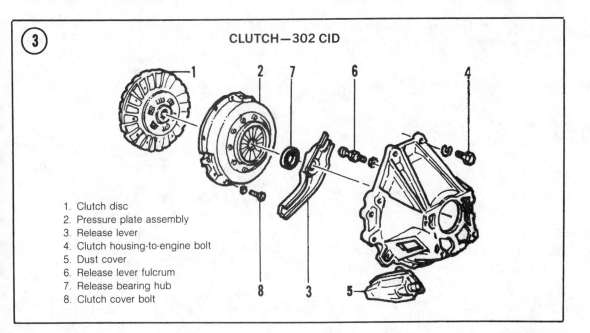

③

CLUTCH—302 CID

1. Clutch disc
2. Pressure plate assembly
3. Release lever
4. Clutch housing-to-engine bolt
5. Dust cover
6. Release lever fulcrum
7. Release bearing hub
8. Clutch cover bolt

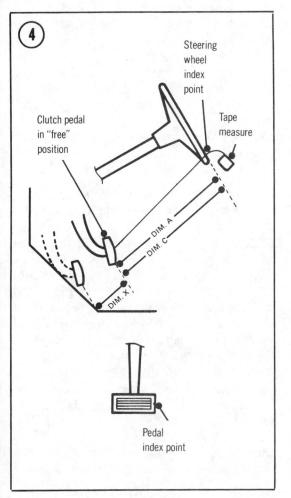

④

Steering
wheel
index
point

Tape
measure

Clutch pedal
in "free"
position

DIM. A
DIM. C
DIM. X

Pedal
index point

8

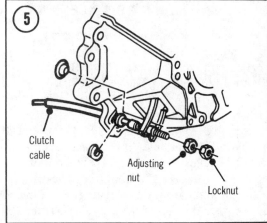

⑤

Clutch
cable

Adjusting
nut

Locknut

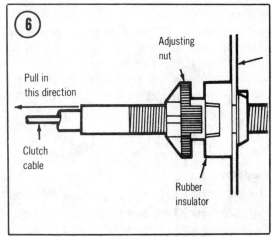

⑥

Adjusting
nut

Pull in
this direction

Clutch
cable

Rubber
insulator

7. Install dust shield and remove jackstands and lower vehicle.

Clutch Pedal Adjustment (200 cid)

1. Pull the clutch cable toward the front of the car until the adjustment nut can be rotated. See **Figure 6**.

NOTE
It may be necessary to depress the clutch pedal to release the adjusting nut from the rubber insulator.

2. Rotate the adjusting nut to obtain correct clutch pedal height adjustment (**Figure 4**) and return adjusting nut to rubber insulator.
3. Correct clutch pedal height should be 4 7/8-5 3/8 in. (dimension X, **Figure 4**). Depress clutch pedal several times to check clutch pedal adjustment.

CLUTCH CABLE REPLACEMENT

1. Disconnect the negative battery cable.
2. Remove the release lever cover from beneath the vehicle. See **Figure 1** (2800cc), **Figure 2** (200 cid), or **Figure 3** (302 cid).
3. *2300 cc and 302 cid engines only.* Loosen the locking nut and adjusting nut and remove clutch cable from the release lever (**Figure 5**).
4. *200 cid engines only.* At the dash panel, pull the nylon adjusting nut toward the front of the vehicle. Disengage the tabs from the rubber insulator and loosen the adjusting nut (**Figure 6**). Remove the cable from the release lever.
5. Remove the clutch retaining clip at the flywheel housing.
6. Remove the clutch retaining clip on the clutch pedal relay lever. Remove the cable from the vehicle along with any remaining locknuts and retracting springs.
7. Installation is the reverse of these steps. After installation, adjust the clutch as described earlier.

CLUTCH ASSEMBLY

Removal

Refer to **Figure 1** (2300 cc), **Figure 2** (200 cid), or **Figure 3** (302 cid) for this procedure.
1. Raise the vehicle on a hoist or jackstands.

2. Remove the dust shield from the flywheel housing.
3. Loosen the clutch cable adjustment nut to provide slack in the cable and remove the clutch cable from the release lever.
4. Disengage the clutch cable from the flywheel housing.
5. Remove the transmission as described in this chapter.
6. Remove the starter cable and the starter motor from the flywheel housing.
7. Remove the bolts that secure the engine rear plate to the front lower part of the flywheel housing.
8. Remove the bolts that attach the housing to the cylinder block.
9. Move the housing back just far enough to clear the pressure plate, then remove.
10. Remove the clutch release lever through the flywheel housing window until the retainer spring disengages from the pivot.
11. Loosen evenly the 6 pressure plate cover attaching bolts to release the spring tension without distortion of the cover.
12. Mark the flywheel and the edge of the pressure plate so they may be reassembled in the same relative positions. Use a sharp punch for marking.
13. Remove the pressure plate and clutch disc.

Inspection

Never replace clutch parts without considering the cause of failure. To do so only invites repeated problems.

Clean the friction surface of the flywheel with non-petroleum base cleaner such as alcohol. Inspect for cracks or scores and excessive runout. Attach a dial gauge and measure runout as described in Chapter Four. If necessary, have the flywheel reconditioned by a dealer or competent machine shop. Replace the flywheel if damage is severe.

Check the clutch disc (**Figure 7**) for oil or grease on the facings, loose or missing rivets, facings worn down to rivets, and broken springs (loose springs are okay). The disc must be replaced if any of these conditions are present. The disc should also be replaced if the facings are worn and a new pressure plate is being installed.

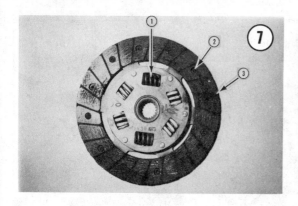

necessary to reinstall the old bearing, do not wash it in solvent; wipe with a clean cloth.

Pilot Bearing Inspection

The pilot bearing, located inside the rear end of the crankshaft, supports the transmission input shaft. **Figure 9** shows the bushing. The pilot bearing used in all vehicles is a needle roller bearing. Make sure the bearing is not loose inside the crankshaft. Also check for visible wear. If the pilot bearing is worn out-of-round or to a bell-mouthed shape, or if it is loose or sloppy, replace it as described in this chapter.

Pilot Bearing Removal

1. Remove the transmission, clutch pressure plate, and disc as described in this chapter.
2. Using Ford tool shown in **Figure 10** or equivalent, remove the pilot bearing.
3. Install new pilot bearing using Ford tool (**Figure 11**) or equivalent. On 2300 cc vehicles only, coat the pilot bore in the crankshaft with a small amount of lithium-base grease.

> *NOTE*
> *Two types of pilot bearings are used. On 2300 cc engines, the pilot bearing must be installed with the seal end of the bearing facing the transmission (**Figure 12**). On 200 cid and 302 cid engines, the pilot bearing must be installed with the collar adapter facing transmission (**Figure 13**).*

4. Install the disc, clutch pressure plate, and transmission as described in this chapter.

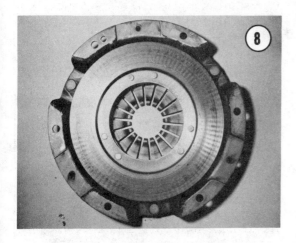

> *CAUTION*
> *Eliminate the source of any oil or grease before replacing the disc.*

Check the pressure plate (**Figure 8**) for scoring, overheating (blue-tinted areas), and cracks. Replace the pressure plate if these are evident. If inspection does not reveal the problem, take the disc and pressure plate to a competent garage and have the disc checked for deflection, and the pressure plate checked for proper diaphragm spring height and runout. Do not attempt to readjust the fingers or dismantle the pressure plate without proper tools and experience.

Check the release bearing as described later in this chapter to determine if it caused the original trouble. Never reuse a release bearing unless necessary. When other clutch parts are worn, the bearing is probably worn. If it is

8

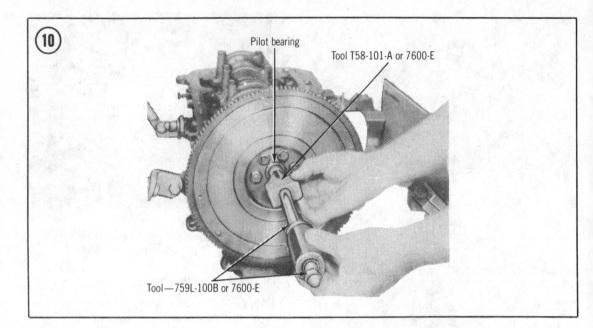

⑩

Pilot bearing

Tool T58-101-A or 7600-E

Tool—759L-100B or 7600-E

Installation

1. Be sure your hands are clean.

2. Inspect the disc facings, pressure plate, and flywheel to be sure they are free of oil, grease, or other foreign material. Do not touch the disc facings.

3. If the original pilot bearing is being reused, coat the inside of the bearing with wheel bearing grease. Wipe off any excess grease so it will not be thrown onto the clutch disc when the car is driven.

4. Place the clutch disc and pressure plate in position on the flywheel. Make sure the pressure plate fits over the dowel pins on the flywheel. If the original pressure plate is being reused, line up the punched alignment marks made during removal.

5. Start the pressure plate cover bolts, but do not tighten.

6. Center the clutch disc with an aligning tool (**Figure 14**). These can be bought at many auto parts stores. An excellent substitute is an old transmission input shaft, available from wrecking yards.

7. Tighten the pressure plate cover bolts. Tighten gradually in a diagonal pattern, then remove the aligning tool. Correct torque is 12-24 ft.-lb.

8. Install the release mechanism in the clutch housing as described in this chapter.

⑪

Pilot bearing

Tool—T71P-7137-C

Tool—T71P-7137-H

9. Position the flywheel housing on the dowels in the cylinder block.

10. Install the starting motor and connect the starter cable.

11. Install the bolts that secure the engine rear plate to the front lower part of the flywheel housing. Correct torque is 12-24 ft.-lb. (2300 cc) or 12-20 ft.-lb. (200 cid and 302 cid).

12. Connect the clutch to the flywheel housing.

13. Connect the clutch cable to the release lever and reinstall the clutch cable retaining clips.

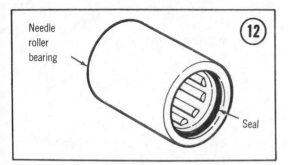

Needle roller bearing

Seal

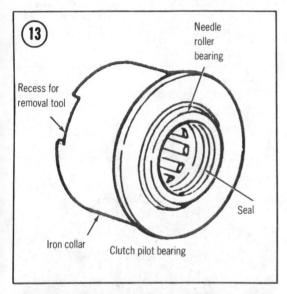

Needle roller bearing

Recess for removal tool

Seal

Iron collar   Clutch pilot bearing

14. Install the transmission as described in this chapter.

15. Install the dust cover.

CLUTCH RELEASE MECHANISM

The release mechanism removal requires that the transmission be removed first. The release mechanism is incorporated in the clutch housing, which in turn is bolted to the front of the transmission. All release bearings should be lubricated prior to installation. Refer to the following procedure for instructions on lubrication. Transmission removal procedures are described later in this chapter.

Removal

Refer to **Figure 1** (2300 cc), **Figure 2** (200 cid), or **Figure 3** (302 cid) for the following procedure.

1. Remove the release lever cover from the clutch housing.

2. Pull the end of the release lever off the fulcrum ball. The lever snaps on and off the fulcrum. Take the lever and release bearing out of the clutch housing.

3. Remove the release bearing from the release lever. The bearing is held in place by 2 spring clips. Push the bearing away from the clips to remove.

Inspection

Check release mechanism for the following:

a. Wear at the contact point of the release lever and its fulcrum ball. Replace fulcrum lever if worn.

b. Grease leaking from the release bearing. Replace the bearing if this is evident.

c. A worn release bearing. To check, hold the inner race with fingers and rotate the outer race while applying light pressure to it. If the bearing feels rough or makes noise, replace it.

Installation

1. Fill the grease groove of the release bearing hub with lithium-base grease. Clean all excess grease from inside the bore of the bearing hub.

2. Apply thin film of lithium-base grease to the bearing retainer, to both sides of the

release lever fork contacting the release bearing and hub and retaining springs, and to the release bearing surface that contacts the pressure plate fingers.

CAUTION
Be sure to clean all excess grease from components lubricated. Excess grease will be forced into the spline by the transmission input shaft bearing retainer and contaminate the clutch disc.

3. Push the release bearing into place on the release lever. When the bearing is in place, rotate it to make sure it operates smoothly.
4. Place the release lever into the clutch housing with the cable end projecting through the hole in the clutch housing.
5. Snap the release lever onto its fulcrum ball.
6. Install the release lever cover in the clutch housing.
7. Install the transmission as described later in this chapter.
8. Connect the clutch cable to the flywheel housing, connect the clutch cable to the release lever and reinstall the cable retainer.

MANUAL TRANSMISSIONS

Three types of manual transmissions are used on models discussed. The vehicle certification label on the driver's door post identifies the transmission for your vehicle. See **Figure 15**. The number "6" in the box "Trans." indicates the RAD 4-speed. The number "7" indicates both the ET 4-speed and the RUG 4-speed overdrive. To distinguish between the ET and RUG transmissions, refer to the transmission identification tag attached to the transmission housing.

The following describes shift lever and transmission removal/installation and replacement of transmission rear seals. If transmission disassembly is required, it is recommended you refer all service work to your dealer or to a qualified specialist. Transmission overhaul requires special tools and skills.

Shift Lever Removal

1. Disconnect the ground cable from the battery.

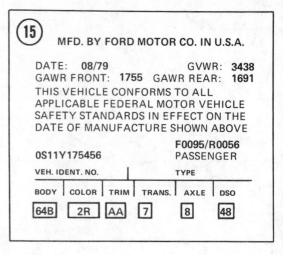

2. Place the gearshift lever in NEUTRAL position.
3. Remove the carpet and shift lever boot (**Figure 16**).
4. Remove the 3 shift lever attaching bolts and remove shift lever.

CAUTION
Bolts on RAD and Model 80ET transmissions are metric (8 mm).

Shift Lever Installation

1. Make sure the shift lever insulator is mounted directly on top of the shift rail.
2. Position the shift lever in the transmission extension housing so that the forked ends of the shift lever engage the insulator properly. See **Figure 17** (1979 2300 cc and 302 cid engines), **Figure 18** (1980 2300 cc engines) or **Figure 19** (200 cid engines).
3. Install the 3 shift lever attaching bolts (8 mm).
4. Install shift lever boot and attaching screws.
5. Position the carpet or floor mat, and install the step plates and screws.
6. Install the 2 kick panels.
7. Install the locknut and shift knob (if removed previously).

Transmission Removal
(All Models)

1. Disconnect the negative cable from the battery.
2. Place the gearshift lever in NEUTRAL, then loosen the locknut just below the gear-

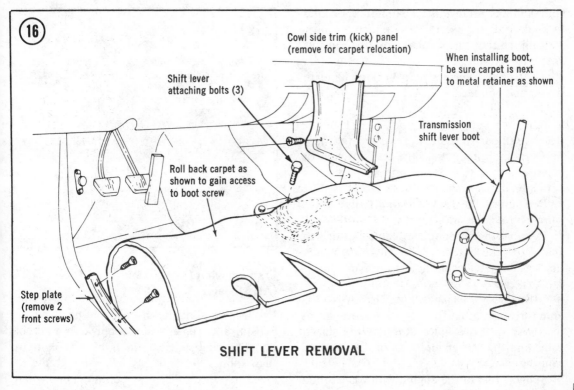

(16)

Cowl side trim (kick) panel
(remove for carpet relocation)

When installing boot,
be sure carpet is next
to metal retainer as shown

Shift lever
attaching bolts (3)

Transmission
shift lever boot

Roll back carpet as
shown to gain access
to boot screw

Step plate
(remove 2
front screws)

SHIFT LEVER REMOVAL

(17)

Shift knob

Locknut

Gearshift
lever

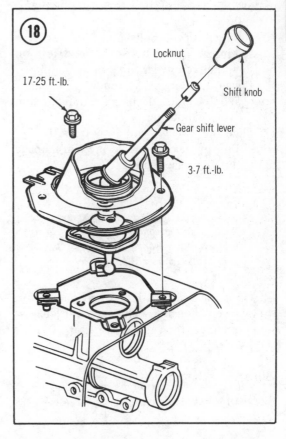

(18)

Locknut

17-25 ft.-lb.

Shift knob

Gear shift lever

3-7 ft.-lb.

8

shift knob. Unscrew the gearshift knob and locknut.

3. Remove the shift lever as described in this chapter.

4. *1980 2300 cc engines only*: Working beneath the engine hood, remove upper bolts attaching the flywheel housing to engine.

5. Raise the vehicle on a hoist or jackstands. Remove the drive shaft, as described in Chapter Ten, and either drain the transmission or insert a plug in the extension housing to prevent lubricant leakage.

6. Disconnect the back-up lamp switch wires from the transmission.

7. Remove the speedometer cable and driven gear from the extension housing, then plug the speedometer cable hole to prevent lubricant leakage.

8. *1980 2300 cc models only*: Disconnect the clutch release cable from the release lever as discussed in this chapter. Remove the starter cable and the starter motor from the flywheel housing.

9. Support rear of the engine with a jack, then remove the bolts attaching the rear crossmember to the frame.

10. Remove the 2 bolts attaching the rear crossmember to the transmission extension housing, then remove the rear crossmember.

11. Lower the engine as required, to allow removal of the bolts attaching the transmission to the flywheel housing.

12. Slide the transmission away from the flywheel housing taking care to prevent damage to the clutch release bearing.

> *NOTE*
> *On 1980 2300 cc models, it may be necessary to slide the catalytic converter heat shield bracket towards the front of the engine to allow transmission removal.*

13. Once the transmission is separated from the flywheel housing, remove the transmission from under the vehicle.

> *NOTE*
> *Leave the jack beneath the engine to support it while the transmission is out of the car.*

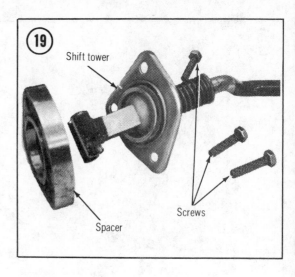

**Transmission Installation
(All Models)**

1. Clean the mating surface of the flywheel housing and transmission. Apply a thin film of wheel bearing grease to the transmission input shaft spline. Wipe off any excessive grease so the clutch disc will not be contaminated when the car is driven.

2. Make sure the clutch release mechanism is properly installed, and the clutch release bearing grease groove is full of lubricant as discussed in this chapter.

3. Move the transmission into place below the car and align the transmission input shaft splines with the clutch disc splines. Slide the transmission input shaft through the clutch release bearing, and mate the input shaft splines with the clutch disc splines. Once mated, secure the transmission attaching nuts.

> *NOTE*
> *It may be necessary to place the transmission in gear and rotate the transmission output shaft to align the input shaft splines with the clutch disc splines.*

4. *1980 2300 cc engines only*: Slide the flywheel housing firmly and squarely onto the locating dowel pins. By holding the flywheel housing in position on the dowel pins, thread the attaching bolts through the dowel pins and into the housing. Tighten the bolts to specifications listed at end of chapter. Install and tighten the center bolts to specifications. Lower the vehicle and install 2 upper bolts attaching flywheel

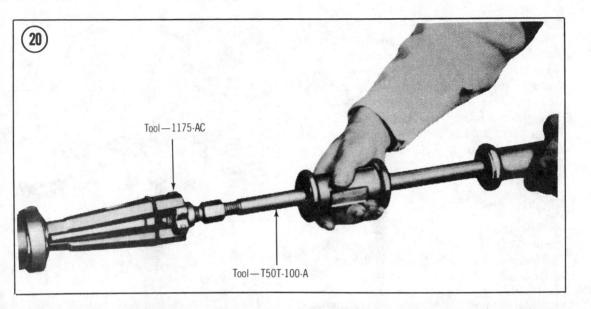

housing to engine to specifications. Raise vehicle on hoist or jackstands.

5. Use the jack supporting the engine to raise the engine until the transmission is in normal position, and secure the crossmember to frame and tighten to specifications at end of chapter.

6. Install the bolts attaching the rear crossmember to the transmission extension housing and tighten to specifications at end of chapter.

NOTE
If catalytic converter heat shield was moved on 1980 2300cc engines, move shield to original position.

7. Remove the jack from beneath the vehicle.

8. Install the speedometer cable and driven gear in the transmission housing, and tighten to specifications.

9. On 1980 2300 cc engines, install the starting motor and connect the starter cable.

10. Install the drive shaft making sure it is connected in the original position (Chapter Ten).

11. Reconnect the back-up switch on the transmission. Lower the car.

12. Working inside the vehicle, reinstall the shift lever and carpet as described in this chapter.

13. Fill the transmission with the specified lubricant (Chapter Three).

14. Move the shift lever through all gear positions to ensure freedom of movement, then check transmission for proper operation under normal driving conditions.

REAR SEAL REPLACEMENT

1. Remove transmission from vehicle as described in this chapter.

2. Remove seal from extension housing with Ford tool or equivalent shown in **Figure 20** (RAD and RUG transmissions) or **Figure 21** (ET transmissions).

3. Drive seal into extension housing with Ford tool or equivalent shown in **Figure 22** (RAD and RUG transmissions) or **Figure 23** (ET transmissions).

4. Install transmission in vehicle as discussed earlier in this chapter.

AUTOMATIC TRANSMISSIONS

Two types of automatic transmissions are used on 1979 and 1980 models. Early cars use the C3 or the C4 automatic transmission; later models are equipped with the C4. The vehicle certification label on the driver's door post identifies the transmission. The letter V in the box marked "Trans." designates the C3 transmission. The letter W designates the C4.

This section includes checks and adjustment procedures to be performed with the transmission in the car. Many problems can be corrected with the adjustment procedures described

8

here. Automatic transmission overhaul, however, requires professional skills, many special tools, and extremely high standards of cleanliness. Although procedures for removal and installation are included in this chapter, disassembly and overhaul should be left to a dealer or competent automatic transmission repair shop. **Table 2** includes torque specifications for both the C3 and C4 transmissions.

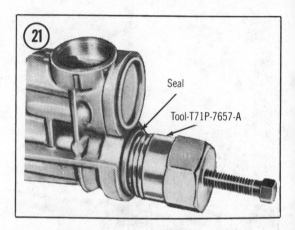

Seal

Tool-T71P-7657-A

Checking Procedures

1. With the car on a level surface, start the engine and let it idle until the transmission fluid warms to normal operating temperature (approximately 30 minutes). Proper operating temperature may also be obtained by driving the vehicle 15-20 miles under normal city type driving conditions. When normal operating temperature is obtained, park the vehicle, apply the brakes and move the shift lever through all gear positions to PARK. With the engine running, check the transmission fluid level on the dipstick. Top up if the fluid level is below the ADD mark. Do not top up if the fluid level is between the ADD and FULL marks.

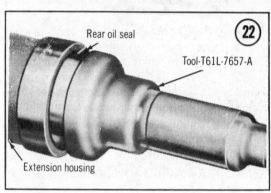

Rear oil seal

Tool-T61L-7657-A

Extension housing

CAUTION
Do not overfill the transmission. An excessive fluid level can cause the fluid to become foamy, resulting in transmission wear and damage.

2. Move the selector lever through the gears feeling for the lever detents. Make sure the selector lever pointer indicates the correct gear at each lever position. If it does not, adjust the shift linkage as described in this chapter.
3. Make sure the starter operates only in NEUTRAL or PARK. If a problem is detected, adjust the neutral start switch as described in this chapter.
4. Check idle speed as described in Chapter Three. Adjust if necessary.
5. With engine idling and brakes applied, move selector lever through the gears. The shift into gear should be noticeable, but not excessively harsh.
6. With the engine at idle, release the brakes

and check for excessive creeping in 1, 2, D, and R.

Leak Inspection

1. Check the speedometer cable connection to the transmission extension housing (**Figure 24**). Replace the rubber seal if necessary.
2. Check the transmission oil pan. If leaking is evident, try tightening the bolts to correct torque (12-16 ft.-lb. on C4 transmissions; 12-17 ft.-lb. on C3's). If necessary, remove the pan and replace the gasket.
3. Check the connection between the transmission oil filler (dipstick) tube and the transmission case. Replace the O-ring seal if a leak is detected. To replace, detach the filler tube bracket from the engine, lift the filler tube out of the transmission, install a new O-ring, then reinstall the filler tube and reconnect the filler tube bracket.
4. Check the transmission fluid cooler lines and fittings. If a leak cannot be stopped by tightening the fittings, replace the damaged parts.

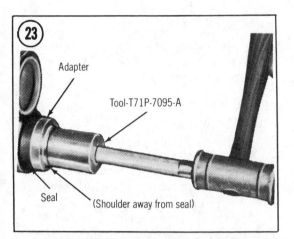

Adapter

Tool-T71P-7095-A

Seal

(Shoulder away from seal)

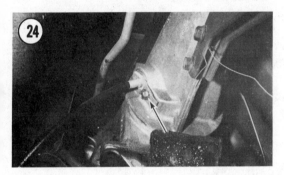

5. Remove the radiator cap and look at the engine coolant. If transmission fluid is present in the coolant, the transmission fluid cooler in the radiator is probably leaking. Consult your dealer or other competent repair shop.

6. If transmission fluid cooler leaking is suspected, disconnect the cooler lines from the cooler fitting at the lower part of the radiator. Attach a pressure gauge to one fitting and apply 50-75 psi air pressure to the other fitting. If the cooler fails to hold pressure, it is defective and must be replaced by a dealer or radiator shop.

7. Check the downshift control lever and the manual lever where they enter the left side of the transmission for leaks. Replace the seals as needed.

8. Remove the torque converter access cover at the front of the flywheel housing, and check the torque converter drain plug (**Figure 25**) for leakage. If the plug leaks, remove it and coat the threads with gasket sealer. Reinstall and tighten to 27-39 ft.-lb. (C3 transmission) or 28-40 ft.-lb. (C4 transmission).

8

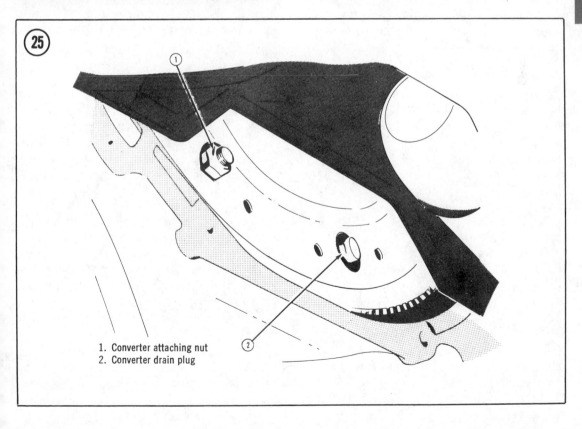

1. Converter attaching nut
2. Converter drain plug

9. After inspection for leaks is complete, fill the transmission with fluid.

> *NOTE*
> *The following 3 procedures — manual linkage adjustment, downshift linkage adjustment, and neutral start switch adjustment — must be performed in the order in which they are listed.*

Manual Linkage Adjustment

1. Place the transmission shift lever in DRIVE. Apply the handbrake firmly. Raise the front end of the vehicle and place it on jackstands.
2. Working beneath the car, loosen the nut securing the manual linkage rod to the base of the shift lever (**Figure 26**).
3. Move the transmission manual lever (**Figure 26**) to DRIVE position (second detent from rear of the transmission).
4. Have an assistant press the transmission shift lever firmly against the rear DRIVE stop, then tighten the nut securing the manual linkage rod to the base of the shift lever to 10-20 ft.-lb.
5. Lower the car from the jackstands, and check the operation of the transmission in each shift lever position.

Downshift Linkage Adjustment

The manual linkage adjustment must be accomplished before attempting the downshift linkage adjustment.

1. Referring to **Figure 27** (2300 cc), **Figure 28** (2800 cc, 255 cid and 302 cid) or **Figure 29** (200 cid), disconnect the return spring from the downshift rod.
2. With an assistant pressing the accelerator pedal to the floor, or holding the carburetor throttle wide open, hold the downshift rod fully depressed (through the detent).
3. Adjust the downshift screw for a 0.010-0.080 in. clearance (2300 cc, 2800 cc 255 cid, or 302 cid) or 0.050-0.080 in. clearance (200 cid) between the screw tip and the throttle arm.
4. Release the throttle and reconnect the downshift rod return spring.

Neutral Start Switch Adjustment (C4 Transmission Only)

Both the manual linkage adjustment and the downshift linkage adjustment must be performed prior to this procedure.

1. Place the shift lever in NEUTRAL. Firmly apply the handbrake. Raise the car and place it on jackstands.

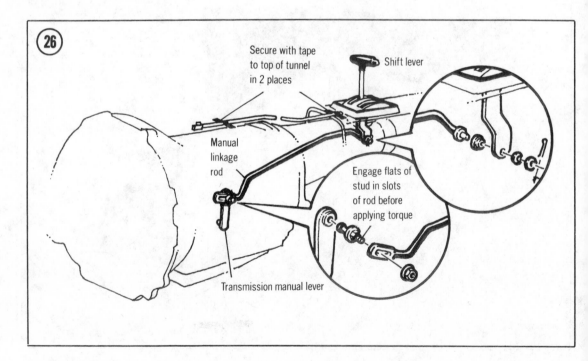

(26)

Secure with tape to top of tunnel in 2 places

Shift lever

Manual linkage rod

Engage flats of stud in slots of rod before applying torque

Transmission manual lever

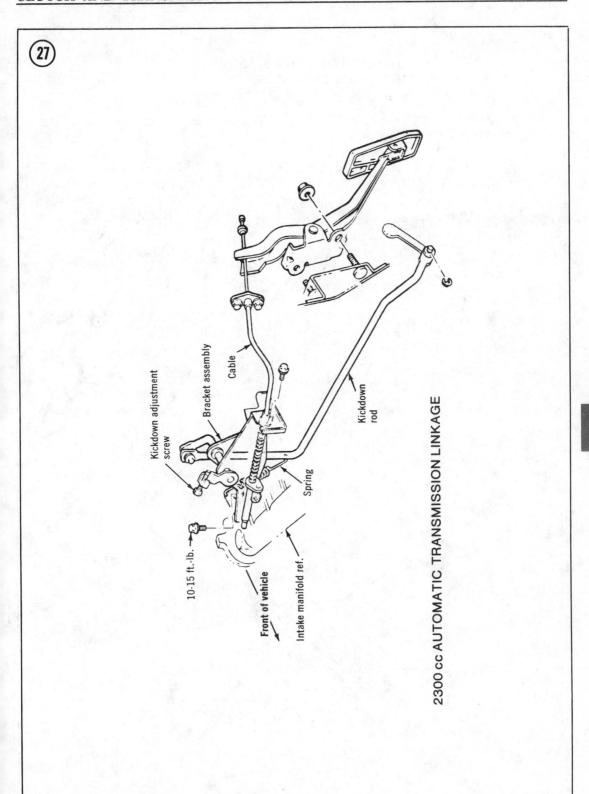

㉗

Kickdown adjustment screw

Bracket assembly

Cable

Kickdown rod

10-15 ft.-lb.

Spring

Front of vehicle

Intake manifold ref.

2300 cc AUTOMATIC TRANSMISSION LINKAGE

8

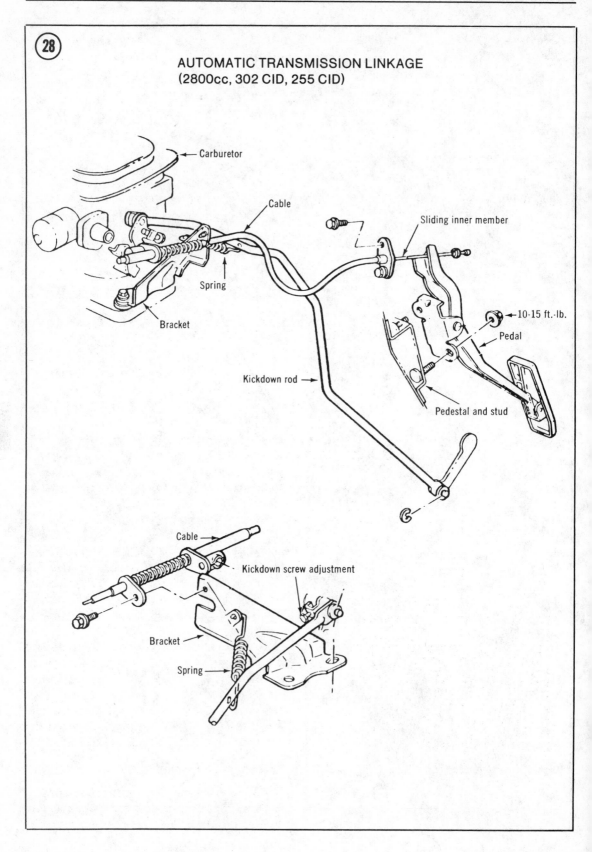

(28)

AUTOMATIC TRANSMISSION LINKAGE
(2800cc, 302 CID, 255 CID)

Carburetor

Cable

Sliding inner member

Spring

Bracket

10-15 ft.-lb.

Pedal

Kickdown rod

Pedestal and stud

Cable

Kickdown screw adjustment

Bracket

Spring

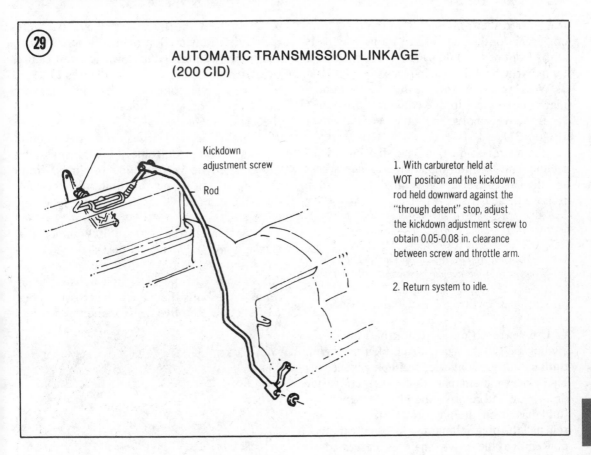

29

AUTOMATIC TRANSMISSION LINKAGE
(200 CID)

Kickdown
adjustment screw

Rod

1. With carburetor held at
WOT position and the kickdown
rod held downward against the
"through detent" stop, adjust
the kickdown adjustment screw to
obtain 0.05-0.08 in. clearance
between screw and throttle arm.

2. Return system to idle.

8

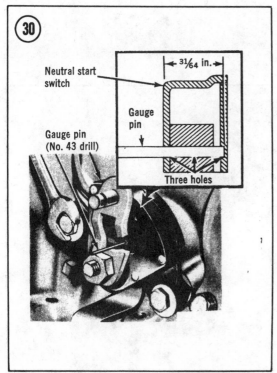

30

Neutral start
switch

Gauge pin
(No. 43 drill)

31/64 in.

Gauge
pin

Three holes

2. Loosen the 2 neutral start switch attaching bolts on the left side of the transmission. See **Figure 30**.

3. Insert a gauge pin (shank end of a No. 43 drill) in each of the switch adjustment holes, as shown in **Figure 30**. Rotate the switch body until the gauge pin can be inserted the full 31/64 in., and go through all 3 holes in the switch. **Figure 30** is a cross-sectional view of the switch with the gauge pin properly inserted.

4. Once the switch is properly adjusted, and the gauge pin is in place, tighten the switch installation bolts to 55-75 in.-lb., then remove the gauge pin.

5. Lower the car from the jackstands, and verify that the starter operates only when the transmission is in NEUTRAL or PARK.

Transmission Removal

1. Raise the vehicle on a hoist or jackstands.

2. Place a drain pan under the transmission fluid pan. Loosen the fluid pan bolts from the

rear toward the front and drain the fluid from one corner of the pan. Secure 2 attaching bolts at the front of the fluid pan and 2 at the rear to temporarily hold the pan in place.

3. Working at the front of the flywheel housing, remove the 2 torque converter drain plug access cover bolts and the access cover (**Figure 31**).

4. Use a wrench on the crankshaft pulley attaching bolt to crank the engine to gain access to the 3 converter attaching bolts, then remove these bolts.

> *CAUTION*
> *On belt-driven overhead camshaft engines, never turn the engine backward. This will cause the cam belt to jump teeth.*

5. Use a wrench on the crankshaft pulley attaching bolt once again to crank the engine until the torque converter drain plug is accessible. Place a drain pan under the converter drain plug and remove the plug. After all the fluid has been drained from the converter, reinstall the plug and tighten to specifications.

6. Remove the drive shaft as described in Chapter Ten and plug the rear end of the extension housing to prevent lubricant leakage.

7. Disconnect the speedometer cable (**Figure 24**) from the transmission extension housing.

8. Disconnect the transmission manual shift rod at the transmission manual lever (**Figure 26**), and disconnect the downshift rod at the transmission downshift lever (**Figures 27-29**).

9. Remove the bolts attaching the starter to the torque converter housing, and position the starter out of the way.

10. Disconnect the wires from the neutral start switch on the left side of the transmission.

11. Detach the vacuum line (or lines) from the transmission vacuum unit, then disconnect the vacuum lines from their retaining clips.

12. Position a transmission jack under the transmission fluid pan and raise slightly.

13. Remove the nuts that attach the rear crossmember to the extension housing, then remove the bolts that attach the crossmember to the frame. Remove the crossmember.

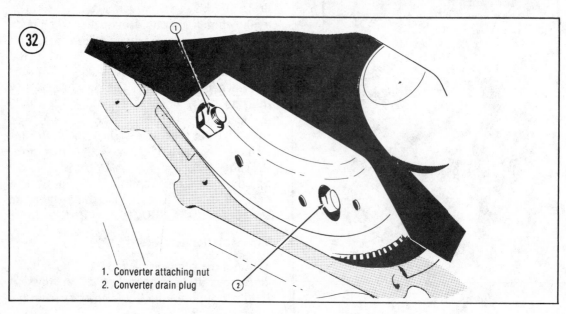

1. Converter attaching nut
2. Converter drain plug

14. Disconnect the muffler inlet pipe at the exhaust manifold and secure it in a raised position to the right side of the vehicle.

15. Lower the jack under the transmission fluid pan and allow the transmission to hang.

16. Position a jack to the front of the engine and raise the engine to gain access to the 2 upper converter housing-to-engine attaching bolts.

17. Disconnect the oil cooler lines at the transmission, then remove the lines from the retaining clips at the cylinder block and position out of the way. Plug all openings to keep dirt out.

18. Remove the remaining converter housing-to-engine attaching bolts.

19. Disconnect the transmission filler tube from the cylinder block and lift the filler tube from the transmission case. Plug the opening to keep out dirt.

20. Secure the transmission to the supporting jack with safety chain.

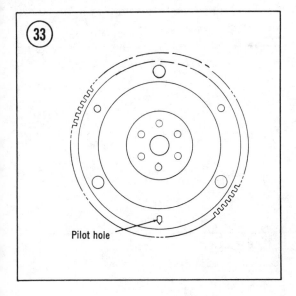

(33)

Pilot hole

21. Remove the 2 upper converter housing-to-engine attaching bolts.

22. Carefully move the transmission to the rear and down to remove it from under the vehicle.

Installation

Installation is the reverse of the removal procedure plus the following steps.

1. On C3 transmissions, turn the flywheel so the pilot hole (**Figure 33**) is at the bottom (6 o'clock position). On 2300 cc engines, because the flywheel has only one converter drain plug access hole, turn the converter so that the drain plug is at the 4 o'clock position. The first flywheel-to-torque converter bolt that is installed must go through the pilot hole and be tightened to specifications. Install the remaining 2 bolts and tighten to specifications. If the first bolt is installed in one of the other 2 holes, the flywheel and torque converter may be misaligned.

2. Tighten all bolts and nuts to specifications listed at end of chapter.

3. Fill the transmission with automatic transmission fluid (see Chapter Three). Run the engine as described in this chapter until the transmission warms to normal operating temperature. Check the transmission fluid level and top up as needed. Do not overfill the transmission.

> *CAUTION*
> *Do not race the engine at any time during the filling procedure.*

4. Check the transmission, torque converter, and all lines and points of attachment for leaks.

5. Perform the manual linkage, downshift linkage, and neutral start switch (C4 transmissions only) adjustments as described earlier.

Tables are on the following page.

Table 1   CLUTCH SPECIFICATIONS

Type (all)	Single dry plate, diaphragm spring
Size	
2300cc engine	8 1/2 in.
2300cc turbo engine	8 1/2 in.
200 cid engine	9 in.
302 cid engine	10 in.
Torque—Flywheel housing to engine bolts	
2300cc engine	28-38 ft.-lb.
2300cc turbo engine	28-38 ft.-lb.
200 cid and 302 cid engines	38-55 ft.-lb.
Torque—Pressure plate to flywheel bolts	
2300cc engine	12-24 ft.-lb.
2300cc turbo engine	12-24 ft.-lb.
200 cid and 302 cid engines	12-20 ft.-lb.
Clutch Pedal Free Travel	
2300cc	5 1/4 in.
200 cid	5 1/4 in.
302 cid	6 1/2 in.

Table 2   AUTOMATIC TRANSMISSION TIGHTENING TORQUES

Item	C-3 (Ft.-lb.)	C-4 (Ft.-lb.)
Flywheel to converter housing	27-49	20-30
Oil pan to transmission case	12-17	12-16
Converter housing to engine	27-39	28-38
Filler tube to oil pan	28-38	32-42
Neutral start switch	12-15	55-75 in.-lb.
Cooler line to transmission case	7-10	12-18
Band adjusting screws to transmission case	35-45	35-45

NOTE: If you own a 1981 or later model, first check the Supplement at the back of the book for any new service information.

CHAPTER NINE

FRONT SUSPENSION AND STEERING

The vehicles covered in this manual use a MacPherson strut front suspension. Shock struts with coil springs are mounted between the lower arm and a spring pocket in the No. 2 crossmember. A stabilizer bar connects the lower control arms. **Figure 1** and **Figure 2** show the front suspension.

Rack-and-pinion steering is used. The steering mechanism is controlled through a 2-section steering column, the upper steering shaft is a machined rod, and the lower shaft is a formed tube which fits over the upper shaft and insulator clips. An intermediate shaft and U-joint assembly attaches to the lower steering gear at the other end.

Table 1 provides steering specifications; **Tables 2-4** provide torque specifications. They are found at the end of the chapter.

WHEEL ALIGNMENT

Several front suspension angles affect the running and turning of the front wheels. These angles must be properly aligned to prevent excessive tire wear, as well as to maintain directional stability and ease of steering. They are:

  a. Caster
  b. Camber
  c. Toe-in
  d. Steering axis inclination
  e. Steering angle

> NOTE
> Angles (a) and (b) are not adjustable. Each is set at the factory and cannot be changed. Angles (d) and (e) are not adjustable. They are measured to check for bent suspension and steering parts. These adjustments should be left to a front-end specialist. Toe-in, however, is easily measured with a good steel tape measure.

Pre-Alignment Check

The steering and various suspension angles are affected by several factors. Perform the following steps before checking or adjustment.

1. Check tire pressure and wear. See *Check Tire Pressure,* Chapter Three.
2. Check play in front wheel bearings. Adjust if necessary, using procedures discussed later in this chapter.
3. Check play in ball-joints as described later in this chapter.
4. Check for broken springs.
5. Remove any excessive load.
6. Check shock struts as described later in this chapter.

9

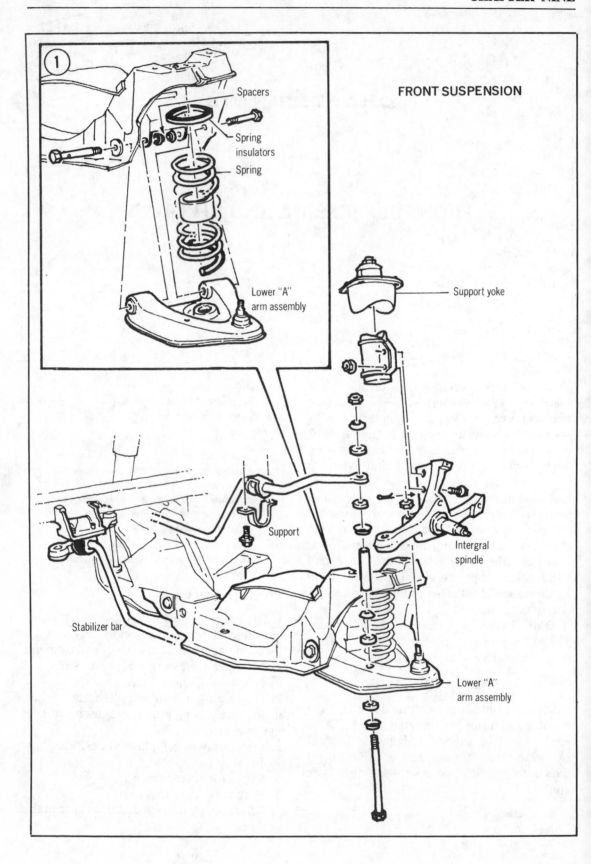

FRONT SUSPENSION

Spacers

Spring insulators

Spring

Lower "A" arm assembly

Support yoke

Intergral spindle

Support

Stabilizer bar

Lower "A" arm assembly

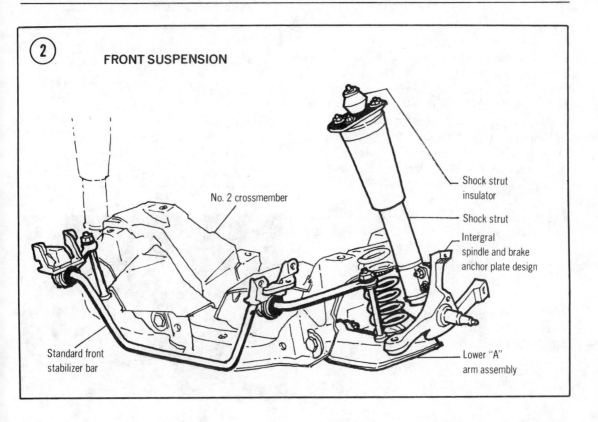

② **FRONT SUSPENSION**

No. 2 crossmember

Shock strut insulator

Shock strut

Intergral spindle and brake anchor plate design

Standard front stabilizer bar

Lower "A" arm assembly

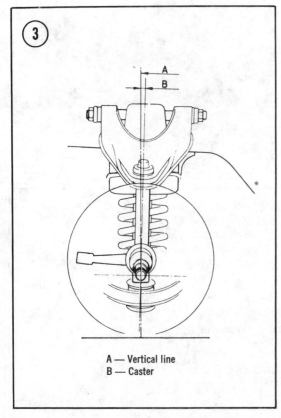

③

A — Vertical line
B — Caster

7. Check tie rods for looseness as described in this chapter. Check rack-and-pinion mechanism for looseness (3/8 in. free play at wheel rim).

8. Check wheel balance.

9. Check rear suspension for looseness.

> *NOTE*
> *Front tire wear patterns can indicate several alignment problems. These are discussed and illustrated under **Tire Wear Analysis**, Chapter Two.*

Caster and Camber

Caster is the inclination of the line through the ball-joints from vertical. See **Figure 3**. Positive caster shifts the wheel forward; negative caster shifts the wheel rearward. Caster causes the wheel to return to a straight ahead position after a turn. It also prevents the wheel from wandering due to wind, potholes, or uneven road surfaces.

Camber is the inclination of the wheel from vertical. With positive camber, the top of the tire leans outward. With negative camber, the top of the tire leans inward.

9

Toe-in

Toe-in should range from 3/16-7/16 in. on 1979 models and from 1/16-5/16 in. on 1980 models. This means distance A in **Figure 4** should be equal to or 7/16 in. less than distance B for 1979 models, and be equal to or 5/16 in. less than distance B for 1980 models. If toe-in is incorrect, adjust as follows.

1. Make sure the steering wheel and column alignment marks are lined up (**Figure 5**).

2. Loosen the clamp screw on the tie rod bellows (**Figure 6**). Make sure the bellows can rotate freely on the tie rod. Otherwise the bellows will be twisted and damaged.

3. Hold the tie rod socket with an open end wrench and loosen the jam nut (**Figure 7**).

4. While holding the tie rod socket steady, turn the tie rod with Vise Grips to increase or reduce toe-in. See **Figure 7**. Tie rod lengths should be equal after adjustment.

> *CAUTION*
> *Do not grip the tie rod threads with the Vise Grips.*

5. Once toe-in is correct with the steering wheel in the straight ahead position, hold the tie rod socket with an open end wrench and tighten the jam nut to 35-50 ft.-lb. Securely tighten the screws on the tie rod bellows clamps.

Steering Axis Inclination

Steering axis inclination is the inward or outward lean of the line through the ball-joints. It is not adjustable.

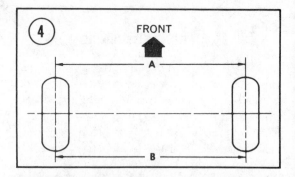

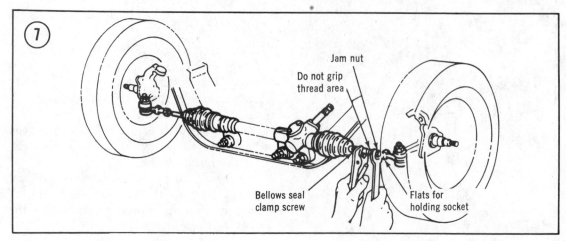

Turning Angle

When a car turns, the inside wheel makes a smaller circle than the outside wheel. Because of this, the inside wheel turns at a greater angle than the outside wheel. When the inside wheel is turned 20 degrees from straight ahead, the outside wheel should be turned 19.74 degrees. Turning angle is the result of a combination of caster, camber, and toe-in adjustments. If the turning angle is incorrect after these adjustments have been made, check for bent suspension parts.

WHEEL BEARINGS

Removal/Installation

Refer to **Figure 8** for this procedure.
1. Loosen the front wheel nuts, jack up the front end of the car, place it on jackstands, and remove the front wheels.

2. Detach the disc brake caliper from the spindle. Hang it from the frame with wire. Do not allow it to hang from the brake line.

3. Remove the grease cap from the hub. Tap lightly with the mallet to free cap.

4. Remove the cotter pin, nut lock, wheel bearing adjusting nut, and washer from the wheel spindle.

5. Pull the hub and disc out about one inch, then push it back onto the spindle. This will loosen the outer wheel bearing so it can be removed.

6. Pull the brake hub and disc off the spindle, together with the inner wheel bearing and grease seal.

7. Working through the center of the hub, drive the grease seal out with a drift or screwdriver. Remove the inner wheel bearing.

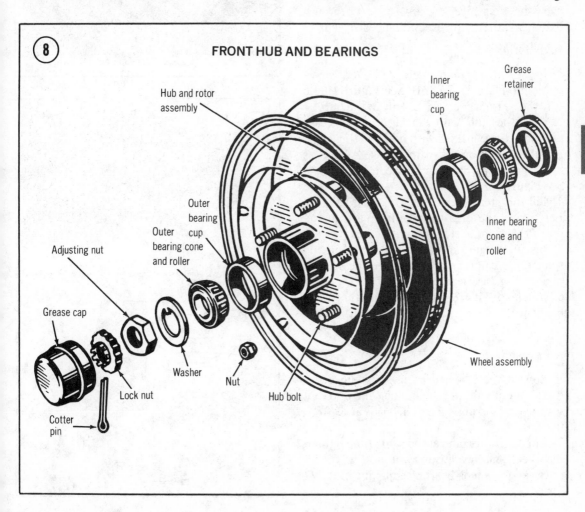

(8) **FRONT HUB AND BEARINGS**

Grease retainer
Inner bearing cup
Hub and rotor assembly
Inner bearing cone and roller
Outer bearing cup
Outer bearing cone and roller
Adjusting nut
Grease cap
Washer
Nut
Hub bolt
Lock nut
Cotter pin
Wheel assembly

9

Inspection

1. Clean all parts throughly in solvent before inspection. Be sure all old grease is removed from wheel bearings (inner and outer).

2. Check the wheel bearing cups (outer races). Look for signs of wear, scoring, chipping, rust, or the bluish tint that indicates overheating. If any of these defects can be seen, remove the bearing cups with Ford tool shown in **Figure 9**.

CAUTION
If a bearing cup is replaced, the corresponding bearing must also be replaced.

3. Inspect the inner and outer bearing assemblies for rust, galling, wear, and bluish tint that indicates overheating. Rotate the bearings and check for roughness and excessive noise. Replace any suspect bearings, together with the corresponding bearing cups.

Installation

1. If the bearing cups were removed, drive them into place with a drift. See **Figure 10**. Be sure the bearing cups seat evenly in the hub.

2. Pack the hub with wheel bearing grease until the grease is flush with both bearing cups.

3. Pack the bearings with grease. Work as much grease as possible between the rollers. See **Figure 11**.

4. Fill the grease seal lip with grease (**Figure 12**). Drive the grease seal into place in the hub. Be sure the seal is properly seated.

5. Install the hub and disc assembly on the spindle. Be careful not to damage the spindle threads or grease seal.

6. Refer to **Figure 8** and install the outer bearing, flat washer, and adjusting nut on the wheel spindle.

Adjustment

1. Loosen the wheel bearing adjusting nut 3 turns, then pull the brake disc in and out several times to push the brake pads away from the disc.

2. Rotate the disc and at the same time tighten the wheel bearing adjusting nut to 17-25 ft.-lb.

3. Back off wheel bearing adjusting nut 1/2 turn.

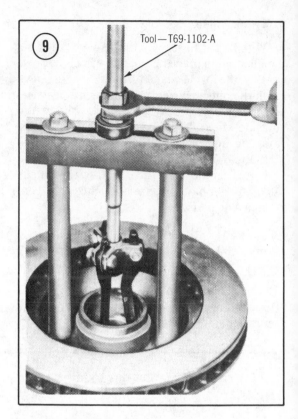

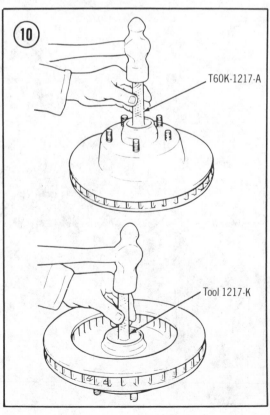

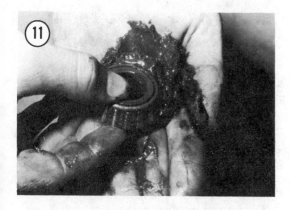

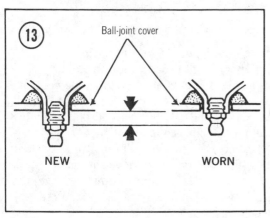

Ball-joint cover

NEW   WORN

4. If an in.-lb. torque wrench is available, tighten the adjusting nut to 10-15 in.-lb. Otherwise tighten nut finger-tight.

5. Install the nut lock and a new cotter pin. Bend over both ends of the cotter pin.

6. Grasp the hub firmly in both hands and shake it up, down, and sideways. There should be no play in the bearing.

7. Install the grease cap, then the wheel. Spin the wheel and check for bearing noise or roughness. If these are evident, clean or replace the bearings as needed.

8. Pump the brake pedal several times to release the brake pads.

STABILIZER BAR

Removal/Installation

Refer to **Figure 2**.

1. Jack up the front end of the car and support with jackstands.

2. Remove the nut from the upper end of the stabilizer attaching stud. Repeat this step at the other side of the car.

3. Detach the stabilizer bar insulator brackets from the car frame.

4. Disassemble the insulator brackets and end bushings. Replace any worn or damaged components, especially rubber insulators.

5. Installation is the reverse of these steps. Tighten all nuts and bolts to the specifications listed at the end of the chapter.

BALL-JOINTS

Ball-joints are not replaceable on vehicles covered in this manual. The control arm, bushing and ball-joint must be replaced as an assembly if the ball-joint is worn.

Inspection

1. Stop vehicle in normal driving position with ball-joints loaded.

2. Clean grease fitting and checking surface.

NOTE
The checking surface is the round boss where the grease fitting is threaded (Figure 13).

3. Examine checking surface. The surface should project outside the cover (**Figure 13**). If the checking surface is inside the cover, replace the lower arm assembly as described in this chapter.

CONTROL ARMS

Control arm service removal requires special tools and service procedures to remove both control arm and coil springs. Control arm service should, therefore, be referred to a dealer or a competent garage.

9

SHOCK STRUT AND SPINDLE

Shock Strut Replacement

1. From inside the engine compartment, remove the 16 mm strut to upper mount attaching nut. A screwdriver placed in the upper slot will hold rod stationary while removing nut. Refer to **Figure 1** and **Figure 2**.

2. Loosen the front wheel nuts, jack up the front end of the car by the lower control arms, place it on jackstands, and remove the front wheels.

3. Remove the brake caliper, disc assembly and dust shield (Chapter Eleven).

4. Remove 2 lower nuts and bolts attaching shock strut to spindle.

5. Lift the shock strut up from the spindle to compress the strut rod, then pull down and remove.

6. Installation is the reverse of these steps. Tighten all nuts and bolts to specifications listed at end of chapter.

Spindle Replacement

1. Loosen the front wheel nuts, jack up the front end of the car, place jackstands under both sides at the jacking pads behind the lower arms, and remove the front wheels.

2. Remove the brake caliper, disc assembly, and dust shield (Chapter Eleven).

3. Remove the stabilizer bar as described earlier in this chapter.

4. Detach the steering tie rod from the spindle arm with a tie rod separator (**Figure 14**).

5. Remove the cotter pin from the ball-joint stud nut. Loosen the nuts one or two turns. Do not remove the nuts yet.

6. Tap the spindle near each stud to relieve the stud pressure (**Figure 2**).

7. Place a jack beneath the lower arm. Compress the coil spring and remove the stud nut.

8. Remove 2 bolts attaching the spindle to the shock strut (**Figure 1**).

9. Compress the shock strut enough to remove the spindle. Take out the spindle.

10. Installation is the reverse of these steps. Tighten all nuts and bolts to the specifications listed at end of chapter.

STEERING WHEEL AND COLUMN

Steering Wheel Removal/Installation

1. Turn the steering wheel to the straight ahead position. Check for factory alignment marks. Make your own if these are not available. See **Figure 5**.

2. Disconnect the battery ground cable.

3. Remove steering wheel hub cover by pulling outwards (2- and 3-spoke wheels) or by pushing out the emblem from the back side of the steering wheel (4-spoke wheels).

4. Disconnect the horn wires.

5. Remove the steering wheel nut.

6. Remove the steering wheel with a puller. See **Figure 15**. The puller bolts must have 5/8-18 in. threads.

CAUTION
Do not use a knock-off type puller or strike the steering column while removing the steering wheel, as damage to the steering shaft or bearings may result.

7. Installation is the reverse of these steps. Line up the steering wheel and column alignment marks shown in **Figure 5**. Tighten the steering wheel nut to 30-40 ft.-lb. Then install the steering wheel cover.

Steering Column Removal/Installation

Refer to **Figure 16** for this procedure.

1. Disconnect the battery ground cable.

2. Remove 2 nuts attaching flexible coupling to flange on steering wheel input wheel. Disengage the safety strap and bolt assembly from the flexible coupling.

3. Remove steering column trim shrouds attaching screws, and remove shrouds.

4. From beneath the column, remove the steering column cover and hood release mechanism.

5. Disconnect all electrical connections and lay aside.

6. Remove screws attaching dust boot to dash panel and remove dust boot.

7. Remove nuts securing column to the brake pedal support.

8. Carefully withdraw the steering column into the passenger compartment.

9. Installation is the reverse of these steps. Tighten all fasteners to specifications at end of chapter.

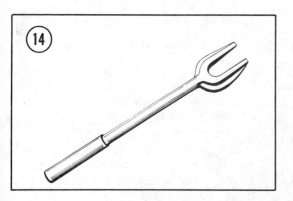

14

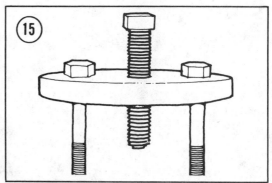

15

16

STEERING COLUMN

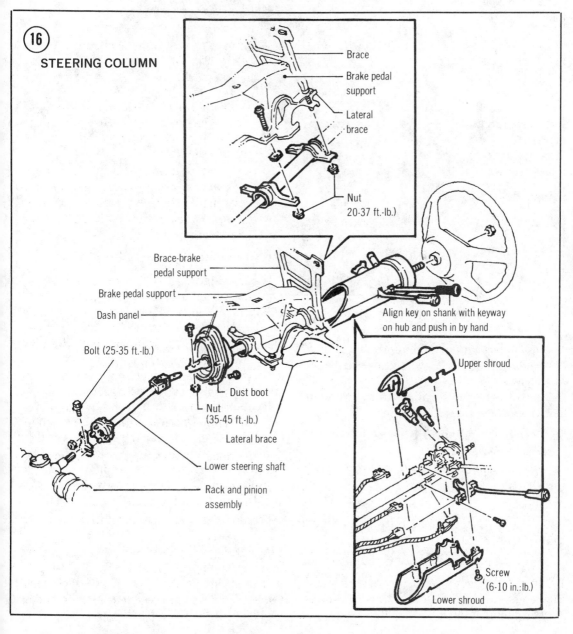

Brace

Brake pedal
support

Lateral
brace

Nut
20-37 ft.-lb.)

Brace-brake
pedal support

Brake pedal support

Dash panel

Bolt (25-35 ft.-lb.)

Dust boot

Nut
(35-45 ft.-lb.)

Lateral brace

Lower steering shaft

Rack and pinion
assembly

Align key on shank with keyway
on hub and push in by hand

Upper shroud

Screw
(6-10 in.:lb.)

Lower shroud

9

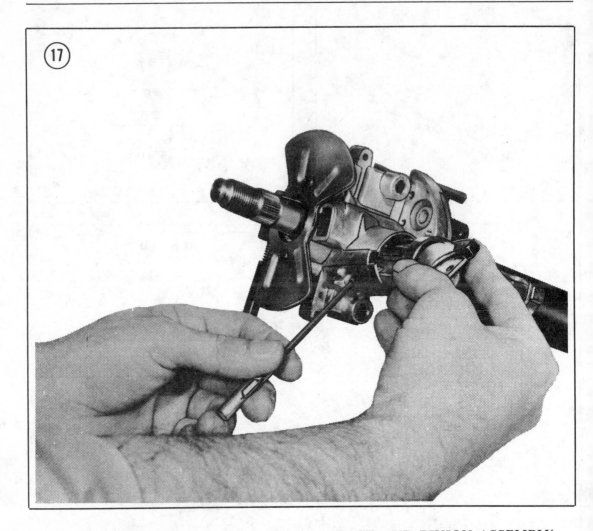

Lock Cylinder Replacement

1. Disconnect battery ground cable.
2. Remove the steering wheel as described in this chapter.
3. Remove screws securing trim shroud to column and remove trim shroud.
4. Detach the electrical connector from the key warning switch.
5. Position gearshift lever in PARK (column shift only) and turn ignition key to RUN position.
6. Insert a 1/8 in. wire pin in the lock cylinder hole (**Figure 17**).
7. Push on the wire pin and pull the lock cylinder out of the steering column. Remove wire pin.
8. Installation is the reverse of these steps.

RACK AND PINION ASSEMBLY

Removal/Installation
(Manual and Power Steering)

1. Disconnect the battery ground cable. Turn the ignition key to the unlocked position.
2. Turn the steering wheel to the straight ahead position. Line up the steering wheel and column alignment marks (**Figure 5**). Make your own marks if there are none. Leave the ignition key in the ON position.
3. Jack up the front end of the car and place it on jackstands.
4. Detach the tie rods from the wheel spindle arms (**Figure 18** and **Figure 19**).
5. Detach the lower steering shaft from the rack-and-pinion assembly (**Figure 16**).
6. Remove the No. 2-A crossmember to allow removal of steering gear attaching bolts.

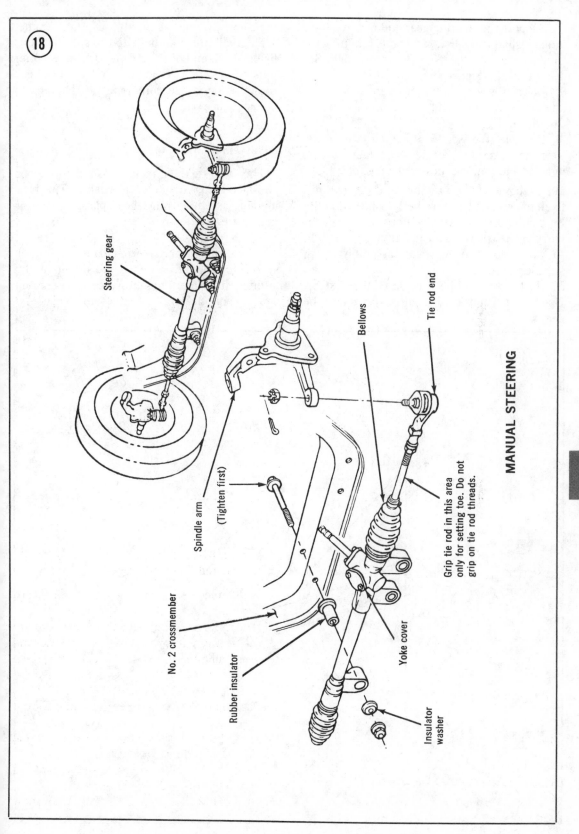

MANUAL STEERING

9

7. Support the steering gear and remove the 2 nuts, insulator washers, and bolts retaining the steering gear to the No. 2 crossmember. See **Figure 18** and **Figure 19**.

8. Lower the gear slightly to permit access to the pressure and return line fittings (power steering only).

9. Remove the screw attaching the power steering hose bracket to the steering gear bracket and remove (power steering only).

10. Disconnect the pressure and return lines from the steering gear valve housing. Plug the lines and ports in the valve housing to prevent entry of dirt (power steering only).

11. Remove steering gear assembly from vehicle.

12. Installation is the reverse of these steps. Use 2 new self-locking nuts to attach the rack-and-pinion assembly to the frame. Tighten all nuts and bolts to the specifications listed at the end of the chapter. Use new cotter pins to secure the tie rod end nuts. Check toe-in as described earlier in the chapter and adjust if necessay.

Disassembly

The inner tie rods, rack, housing, and upper pinion bearing are not replaceable. The rack housing assembly must be replaced if any of these parts is defective.

Disassembly of steering units requires special tools and experience and should not be attempted. Refer maintenance of steering units to your dealer or a competent garage.

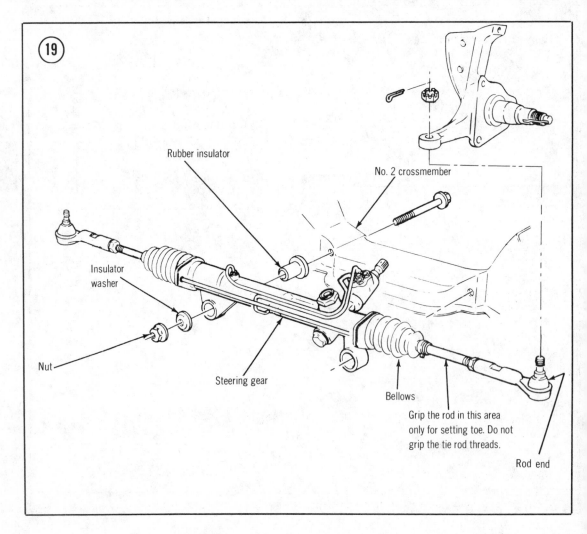

(19)

Rubber insulator

No. 2 crossmember

Insulator washer

Nut

Steering gear

Bellows

Grip the rod in this area only for setting toe. Do not grip the tie rod threads.

Rod end

Table 1   STEERING SPECIFICATIONS

Type	Rack and pinion
Gear ratio (manual)	
At straightahead position	24.9
At full turn	21.7
Gear ratio (power)	
At straightahead position	20.1
At full turn	14.2
Number of turns	
Manual	4.08
Power	3.05
Lubricant capacity	
Manual	Approximately 5 oz. or 0.31 pints
Power (steering pump)	Approximately 2.5 pints
Steering wheel play wheel	$\frac{3}{8}$ in. or less (at rim)

Table 2   MANUAL STEERING TIGHTENING TORQUES

Item	Ft.-lb.
Support yoke cover bolts	15-20
Pinion cover bolts	15-20
Steering gear to crossmember	80-100
Tie rod end to inner tie rod	35-50
Tie rod end to spindle arm	35-47*
Pinion shaft to flexible coupling	20-37
Ball housing to rack	40-60

*Tighten to 35 ft.-lb., then to nearest cotter pin slot.

Table 3   POWER STEERING TIGHTENING TORQUES

Item	Ft.-Lb.
Pressure line fitting (pump-to-gear ½ hex)	10-15 (1979)
	15-20 (1980)
Return line fitting	10-15 (1979)
	15-20 (1980)
Gear-to-crossmember mounting bolt nut	80-100
Tie rod end-to-spindle arm nut	35-47*
Tie rod end-to-tie rod jam nut	35-50
Steering flex coupling bolt	20-30
Yoke plug locknut	44-66
Pressure line fittings at valve	10-15 (1979)
	19-28 (1980)
Pressure line fittings at power cylinder (gear housing)	10-15 (1979)
	19-28 (1980)
Valve housing to gear housing bolts	10-15
Pinion bearing locknut	23-34 (1979)
	27-45 (1980)
Pinion bearing plug	40-60
Tie rod socket locknut	55-60

*Tighten to minimum specification, then tighten to nearest cotter pin slot and insert cotter pin.

9

Table 4   TIGHTENING TORQUES, FRONT SUSPENSION

Item	Ft.-Lb.
Lower arm to No. 2 crossmember	150-220 (1979)
	200-220 (1980)
Stabilizer bar mounting clamp to bracket	14-26
Stabilizer bar to lower arm	6-12 (1979)
	9-12 (1980)
Spindle to shock strut	120-180 (1979)
	150-180 (1980)
Shock strut to upper mount (1 nut)	50-75 (1979)
	60-75 (1980)
Stabilizer bar mounting bracket to underbody	35-50
Ball-joint to spindle	80-120
Shock upper mount to body (3 nuts)	50-75 (1979)
	60-75 (1980)
Steering gear to No. 2 crossmember	90-100
Tie rod end to spindle	35-47

NOTE: If you own a 1981 or later model, first check the Supplement at the back of the book for any new service information.

CHAPTER TEN

REAR SUSPENSION

The rear suspension consists of a 4 link coil spring design controlled by conventional telescopic shock absorbers. The rear axle attaches to the body by 2 upper arms that control side to side movement, and 2 lower arms which control forward and rear movement. One coil spring is used on each side and mounted between an upper seat welded to the body and a lower seat which is part of the lower arm assembly. The drive shaft is a one-piece tube supported at front and rear by universal joints. The front yoke has internal splines that slide on the transmission main shaft, allowing the drive shaft to change length to compensate for axle movement.

This chapter includes service procedures for the rear suspension, axle shafts, wheel bearings, and drive shaft. Inspection procedures are included to tell you if differential repairs are necessary.

Table 1 provides differential and rear suspension specifications; **Table 2** provides torque specifications. They are found at the end of the chapter.

REAR SUSPENSION

Shock Absorber Replacement

1. From inside trunk on 2-door models, remove rubber cap from upper shock absorber T-stud and remove attaching nut, washer, and insulator. On 3-door models, remove side panel trim covers and remove upper shock absorber attaching nut, washer, and insulator. See **Figure 1**.

2. Securely block both front wheels so the car will not roll in either direction. Jack up the rear end of the car and place it on jackstands.

3. Working beneath the car, compress the shock absorber, then remove from upper hole in shock tower.

4. Remove bolt securing shock absorber to lower shock mounting stud (**Figure 1**).

5. Lift shock absorber straight up and out of bracket.

6. Install in the reverse order. Tighten the lower bolt to 40-55 ft.-lb. Tighten the upper nut to 14-16 ft.-lb.

Rear Spring Replacement

NOTE
If vehicle is equipped with rear stabilizer bar, remove stabilizer bar as discussed later in this chapter before beginning rear spring removal.

1. Securely block both front wheels so the car will not roll in either direction. Jack up the rear end of the car until the rear shocks are fully suspended.

2. Place a jack beneath the center of the rear axle.

10

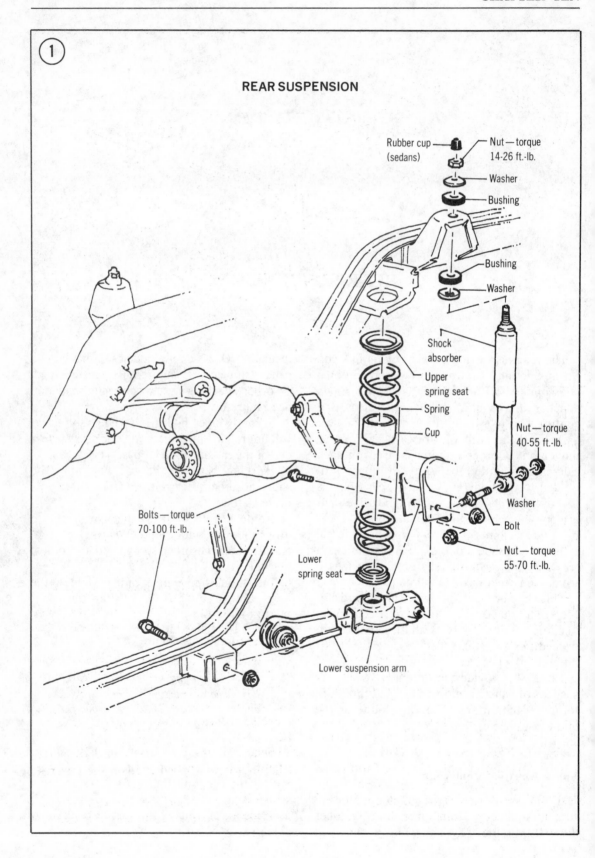

① REAR SUSPENSION

Rubber cup (sedans) — Nut — torque 14-26 ft.-lb.
Washer
Bushing
Bushing
Washer
Shock absorber
Upper spring seat
Spring
Cup
Nut — torque 40-55 ft.-lb.
Washer
Bolt
Nut — torque 55-70 ft.-lb.
Bolts — torque 70-100 ft.-lb.
Lower spring seat
Lower suspension arm

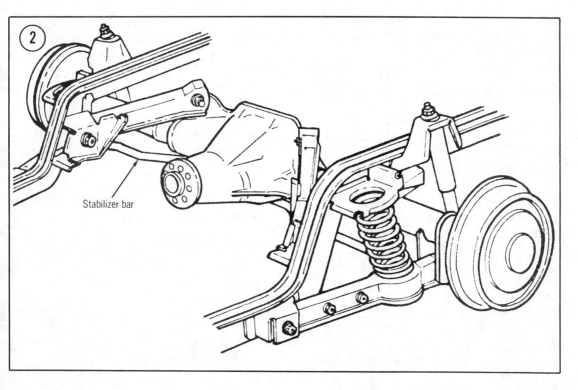

Stabilizer bar

3. Place a second jack beneath the lower arm pivot bolt. Loosen and remove the nut and bolt.

4. Lower the second jack to relieve spring load, then remove 2 bolts securing the lower spring arm to the lower arm. Remove spring, and 2 spring coil insulators from vehicle (**Figure 1**).

Rear Spring Installation

New locknuts and bolts must be used whenever a spring has been removed. Refer to **Figure 1** for this procedure.

1. Insert upper spring coil insulator into spring seat in upper bracket. It may be necessary to tape the spring coil insulator in position.

2. Position lower spring insulator on lower spring arm assembly.

3. Place the coil spring on the lower arm spring seat so that end of spring faces toward left rear of vehicle.

4. Raise second jack until the lower arm is in position. Ensure spring is seated in both insulators, then insert the 2 spring bolts from the outboard side. Install the locknut and tighten finger-tight only.

5. Lower second jack and remove from beneath vehicle. Raise the axle with first jack to curb height.

6. Tighten lower arm pivot bolt to 70-100 ft.-lb.

NOTE
Replace rear stabilizer bar as discussed later in this chapter if so equipped.

7. Remove the jackstands and lower the car.

Rear Stabilizer Bar Replacement

Refer to **Figure 2** for this procedure. New nuts and bolts must be used whenever the stabilizer bar is removed.

1. Securely block both front wheels so the car will not roll in either direction. Jack up the rear end of the car and place it on jackstands.

2. Remove 4 bolts securing stabilizer bar to brackets on lower arm and remove stabilizer bar.

3. Install in the reverse order. Position stabilizer bar with color code on bar towards right side of vehicle.

Align 4 holes in stabilizer bar with holes in lower arm brackets. Install 4 bolts and tighten to 15-20 ft.-lb.

10

NOTE
Ensure that adequate clearance is maintained between the stabilizer bar and lower arm when installing stabilizer bar.

4. Remove the jackstands and lower the car.

DRIVE SHAFT

Removal/Installation

1. Securely block both front wheels so the car will not roll in either direcion. Jack up the rear end of the car and place it on jackstands.
2. Check for factory alignment marks on the drive shaft and the companion flange on the differential (**Figure 3**). Make your own marks if they are not visible. The drive shaft must be installed in its original position to prevent imbalance and vibration.
3. Remove 5 bolts attaching the drive shaft to the companion flange (**Figure 4**). Lower the shaft away from the differential. Wrap tape around the loose U-joint bearings so they do not fall out.
4. Pull the drive shaft toward the rear of the vehicle until the slip yoke clears the transmission extension housing and the seal. Either drain the transmission or plug the extension housing to prevent lubricant leakage.
5. Installation is the reverse of these steps. Tighten the companion flange U-bolts to 8-15 ft.-lb. Check the extension housing oil seal and replace if necessay. Be sure to match the alignment marks during installation.

Inspection

1. Check the drive shaft for bending. Rotate it between accurate centers, such as V-blocks or a lathe, and measure runout with a dial gauge. Measure at front, center, and at the rear between balance weights and yoke welds. Maximum allowable runout is 0.035 in.
2. Inspect the universal joints. If the spiders or bearings show signs of wear, replace them.

Universal Joint Repair

Refer to **Figure 5**.

1. Lightly scribe or punch alignment marks on the yoke (or coupling flange) and drive shaft before disassembly.

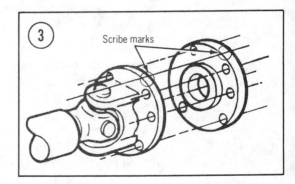

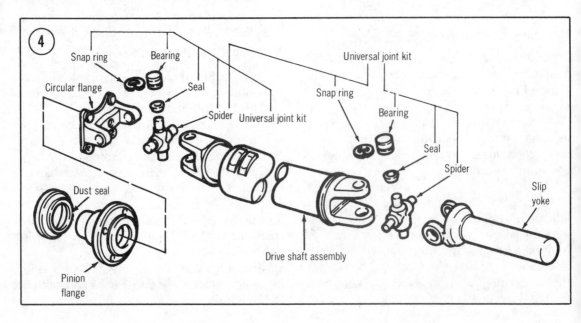

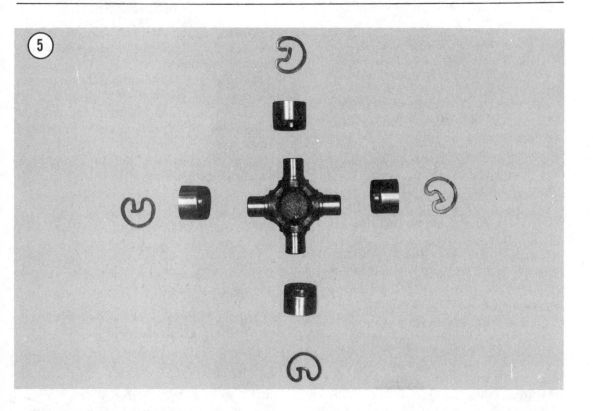

2. Place the drive shaft in a vise as near the U-joint as possible. Be careful not to distort the shaft.

3. Remove the snap rings that retain the U-joint bearings. See **Figure 6**.

4. Press out one bearing, using a C-clamp and 2 sockets as shown in **Figure 7**. One socket must be small enough to fit inside the bearing hole in the yoke. The other socket must be large enough so that the bearing will fit inside it. When the C-clamp is tightened, one bearing is pressed out of the yoke and into the large socket.

> *NOTE*
> *If the bearing comes out only part way, pull it the rest of the way with pliers or Vise Grips.*

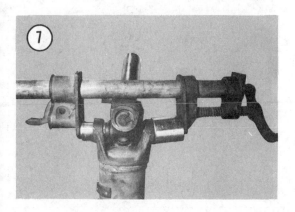

5. Using the same method as Step 4, press the spider in the other direction to remove the opposite bearing. Take out the thrust bearings and seals.

6. Remove the spider from the yokes.

7. Assemble in the reverse order. Pack the bearing cups with grease.

10

NOTE
If the U-joints bind after assembly, rap sharply on the yokes with a brass or other soft metal hammer. Be careful not to hit the bearings.

REAR AXLE

Four types of rear axles are used on 1979-1980 models. The rear axle identification tag, fastened to one of the rear cover-to-housing bolts identifies the rear axle. The rear axle designations are WGF, WGG, WGX, or WGZ. Before servicing your vehicle's rear axle, refer to the identification label to determine rear axle type. The rear axle designations will be referred to in the following procedures.

Shaft Removal
(WGF and WGG Rear Axles)

The rear axle shafts, wheel bearings, and oil seal can be replaced without removing the differential assembly from the axle housing.

Figure 8 shows a typical axle shaft and related parts. Refer to it as needed for this procedure.

1. Securely block both front wheels so the car will not roll in either direction. Jack up the rear end of the car and place it on jackstands.
2. Remove the wheels and brake drums. See Chapter Eleven.

3. Working through the hole provided in each axle shaft flange, remove the nuts that secure the wheel bearing retainer plate (**Figure 9**).
4. Mark the axle shafts for location (right and left) and pull them from the housing. If necessary, use a slide hammer and adapter (**Figure 10**). These are available from tool rental dealers.
5. Once the axle shafts are loose, withdraw them from the housing.

CAUTION
Removal and insertion of rear axle shafts must be performed with caution. The entire length of the shaft (including spline) must pass through the axle oil seal without contact. Roughing or cutting the seal element will result in early seal failure.

6. Remove the brake backing plates and attach them to the frame rail with wire.

Shaft Installation

Installation is the reverse of the removal procedure, plus the following.

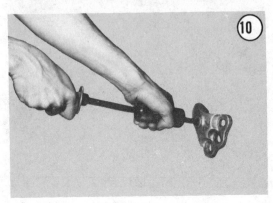

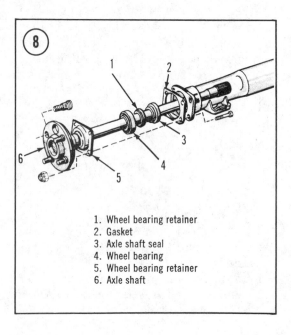

1. Wheel bearing retainer
2. Gasket
3. Axle shaft seal
4. Wheel bearing
5. Wheel bearing retainer
6. Axle shaft

1. Pack the wheel bearings with grease.
2. Use a new flange gasket coated on both sides with gasket sealer.
3. Install a new oil seal as described later in this chapter. Tighten the axle shaft retainer nuts to 20-40 ft.-lb.

Oil Seal Replacement

The rear axle oil seals must be replaced whenever the axle shafts are removed.
1. Remove the axle shaft as described earlier in this chapter.
2. Remove the old oil seal with Ford puller (**Figure 11**) or equivalent.

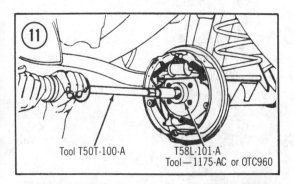

Tool T50T-100-A   T58L-101-A
Tool—1175-AC or OTC960

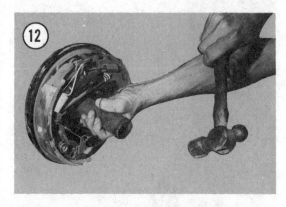

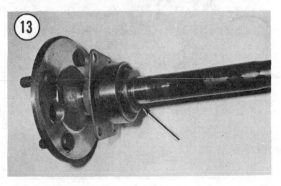

3. Lightly coat the outer edge of a new seal with oil resistant gasket sealer (No. 2 Permatex).

NOTE
Do not put gasket sealer on the sealing lip.

4. Tap the seal into place with a suitable drift (**Figure 12**). Be careful not to distort the seal.
5. Coat the seal lip with grease.

Rear Wheel Bearing Replacement

The following procedure requires a press and special support stands. Rather than improvise tools, the job should be taken to a machine shop or dealer, which has the equipment to replace the bearing safely. A great deal of expense can be saved by removing the axle shaft yourself and taking it to the repair shop. However, if press tools are available, the bearing can be replaced by performing the following procedure.
1. Remove the axle shaft as described earlier.
2. Using a hammer and cold chisel, make several deep nicks in the bearing retainer ring (**Figure 13**). The retainer ring will then slide off easily.

CAUTION
Do not hit the axle shaft with the chisel when removing the retainer ring.

3. Place the axle shaft in a press stand. Press the retainer bearing off, then take off the retainer plate.

CAUTION
Never attempt to use heat to remove or install bearing or retainer as heat will weaken the axle shaft.

4. Place the retainer plate and new bearing on the axle shaft. Place the assembly on a press stand. Press the bearing on until it seats firmly against the shaft shoulder.
5. Press a new retainer ring onto the shaft until it seats firmly against the bearing.

CAUTION
Do not attempt to press the bearing and retainer ring on at the same time.

6. Pack the bearing with multipurpose grease.

10

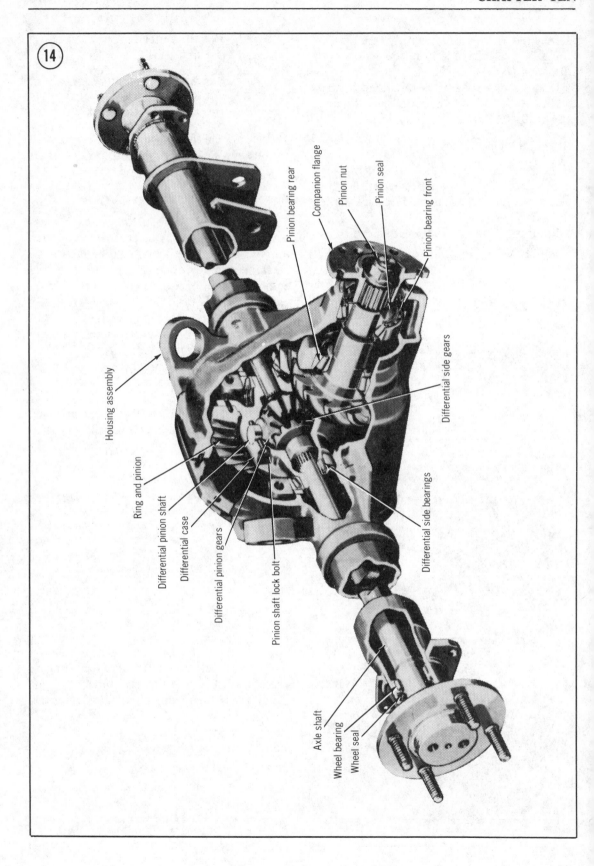

(14)

Pinion bearing rear

Companion flange

Pinion nut

Pinion seal

Pinion bearing front

Housing assembly

Differential side gears

Ring and pinion

Differential pinion shaft

Differential case

Differential pinion gears

Pinion shaft lock bolt

Differential side bearings

Axle shaft

Wheel bearing

Wheel seal

Shaft Removal
(WGX and WGZ Rear Axles)

The rear axle shafts, wheel bearings, and oil seal can be replaced without removing the differential assembly from the axle housing.

Figure 14 shows a typical axle housing assembly. Refer to it as needed for this procedure.

1. Securely block both front wheels so the car will not roll in either direction. Jack up the rear end of the car and place it on jackstands.
2. Remove the wheels and brake drums. See Chapter Eleven.
3. Drain rear axle lubricant by removing 10 screws securing rear cover to axle housing assembly and remove cover. Place pan beneath axle housing to catch lubricant.

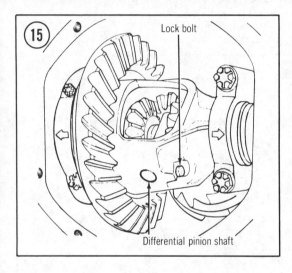

Lock bolt

Differential pinion shaft

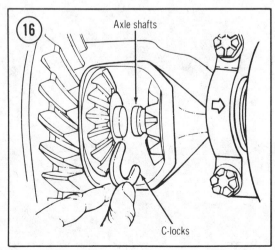

Axle shafts

C-locks

4. From inside rear of axle housing, remove differential pinion shaft lock screw and differential pinion shaft. See **Figure 15**.
5. Push flanged end of axle shafts toward center of axle housing. Remove C-lock from end of axle shaft (**Figure 16**).
6. Once the axle shafts are loose, withdraw them from the housing.

CAUTION
Removal and insertion of rear axle shafts must be performed with caution. The entire length of the shaft (including spline) must pass through the axle oil seal without contact. Roughing or cutting the seal element will result in early seal failure.

Shaft Installation

NOTE
Install a new oil seal as discussed later in this chapter.

1. Pack the wheel bearing with grease.
2. Carefully insert the axle into the housing and mate end of axle splines with splines in side gear. Push axle firmly until end of axle can be viewed in differential case.
3. Insert the C-lock on end of axle shaft. Push axle shaft outboard until shaft splines engage and C-lock seats in counterbore of differential side gear.
4. Install the differential pinion shaft through case and pinion gears, ensuring that the shaft hole is aligned with lock screw hole (**Figure 15**).
5. Install lock screw and tighten to 15-22 ft.-lb.
6. Apply silicone sealer (Ford specification DAZ-19562-B or equivalent) to housing cover as shown in **Figure 17** and install housing cover. Tighten bolts to 25-35 ft.-lb.
7. Fill rear axle with 3-1/2 pints of Ford rear axle lubricant ESW-M2C-154-A or equivalent.

Oil Seal and Rear Wheel
Bearing Replacement

The rear axle oil seal must be replaced whenever the axle shafts are removed.
1. Remove the axle shaft as described earlier in this chapter.

10

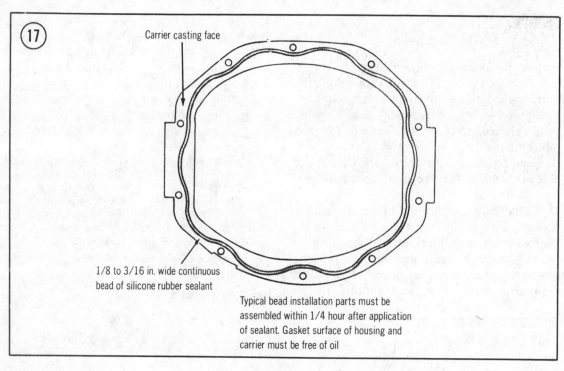

(17) Carrier casting face

1/8 to 3/16 in. wide continuous
bead of silicone rubber sealant

Typical bead installation parts must be
assembled within 1/4 hour after application
of sealant. Gasket surface of housing and
carrier must be free of oil

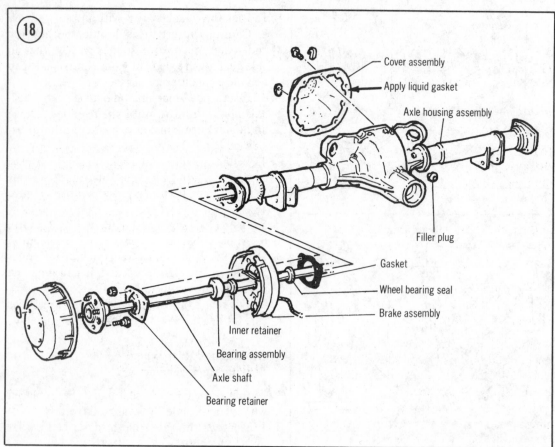

(18)

Cover assembly

Apply liquid gasket

Axle housing assembly

Filler plug

Gasket

Wheel bearing seal

Brake assembly

Inner retainer

Bearing assembly

Axle shaft

Bearing retainer

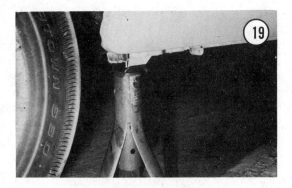

2. Using Ford tool (**Figure 11**) or equivalent, remove oil seal and bearing as a unit. Insert tool so tangs on tool end engage bearing outer race.

3. Pack the bearing with multipurpose grease and install using Ford tool (**Figure 12**) or equivalent into housing bore.

4. Lightly coat the outer edge of a new seal with oil resistant gasket sealer (No. 2 Permatex).

NOTE
Do not put gasket sealer on the sealing lip.

5. Tap the seal into place with a suitable drift (**Figure 12**). Be careful not to distort the seal.

6. Coat the seal lip with grease.

Axle Shaft Inspection (All Models)

1. Carefully examine the machined surfaces of the axle shaft and axle housing for wear. Check the shaft for bends, signs of twisting, or other damage. If necessary, smooth the splines with fine emery paper.

2. Inspect the rear wheel bearing. Rotate it and check for noise, roughness, or looseness. If in doubt, replace it as described earlier in this chapter.

Differential Carrier and Axle Housing Removal/Installation (Integral Carrier Axle)

The rear axle assembly on some models is an integral type housing, hypoid design. The differential carrier and axle housing are permanently combined into a single unit (**Figure 18**). A cover on the rear of the differential carrier provides access for inspection.

1. Securely block both front wheels so the car will not roll in either direction. Jack up the rear end of the car and place it on jackstands, beneath the underbody as shown in **Figure 19**.

2. Drain the rear axle oil.

3. Disconnect the drive shaft from the differential companion flange as described earlier. Leave the front end of the drive shaft in the transmission.

4. Disconnect the lower ends of the shock absorbers as described earlier in this chapter.

5. Remove the brake drums (Chapter Eleven).

6. Remove the axle shafts as described in this chapter.

7. Remove vent hose, then remove vent tube from brake tube junction and axle housing.

8. Detach the hydraulic brake line T-connection from the axle housing.

CAUTION
Do not open any brake lines or the brakes will have to be bled.

9. Detach the brake line from its retaining clip on the axle housing.

10. Remove both brake backing plates from the axle housing. Hang them from the frame with wire. Leave the brake lines and handbrake cables attached.

11. Place a jack beneath the axle housing to support it.

12. Remove the nuts and bolts securing the upper arms from the axle housing bracket mountings and disconnect the upper arms.

13. Lower the axle housing assembly until the coil springs are released from their insulators.

14. Remove bolts attaching the suspension lower arms to the axle housing. Disconnect both arms from the axle housing.

15. Lower the axle housing away from the car.

16. Installation is the reverse of these steps. Fill the axle with a lubricant recommended in Chapter Three.

Differential Carrier Inspection (Integral Carrier Housing)

1. The axle housing need not be removed from the car for inspection. Drain the oil and disconnect the drive shaft from the differential.

10

2. Clean dirt and other debris from around inspection cover with wire brush and solvent. Remove 10 bolts securing cover to housing, and remove cover (**Figure 18**).

3. Clean the teeth on the gears. Look for visible wear or damage. Check the gears for chipped or missing teeth.

4. Rotate the gears and check for rough movement that may indicate defective bearings or chipped gears. Turn the gears with a wrench on the differential case bolts. See **Figure 20**.

5. Check the tooth contact pattern on the pinion and ring gear. To do this, apply a thin, even coat of lead oxide to the ring gear teeth. Turn the gear several turns in both directions so the contact pattern of the teeth is pressed into the coat of lead oxide. The contact pattern should have the following characteristics:

a. Both drive and coast patterns should be fairly well centered on the teeth.

b. Some clearance between the top of the teeth and the top of the pattern is desirable.

c. There should be no distinct lines (indicating areas where pressure is high).

d. Marks on adjoining gear teeth should be directly opposite each other.

Figure 21 shows typical contact patterns. The pattern need not be exactly as shown or described to be acceptable. An erratic pattern indicates that repairs are needed.

6. Measure gear backlash at several points around the ring gear. Attach a dial gauge as shown in **Figure 22**. Hold the pinion from turning with one hand and move the ring gear

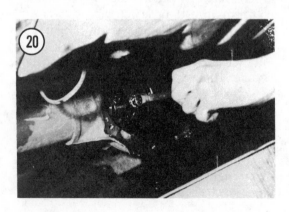

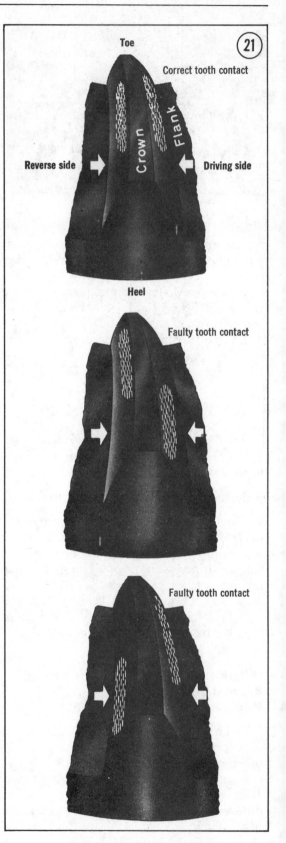

against the dial gauge as much as possible. The reading on the gauge is gear backlash. All readings should be within 0.008-0.012 in. Maximum variation between readings is 0.004 in.

7. Connect the dial gauge as shown in **Figure 23** and measure ring gear runout. Turn the ring gear through one full turn and note the indicator reading. This must be less than 0.003

in. If the reading exceeds this figure, disassembly and repair of the differential are necessary.

NOTE
If the inspection procedures indicate defects, take the axle housing to a dealer or competent garage. Do not disassemble the differential carrier further without the necessary tools and experience.

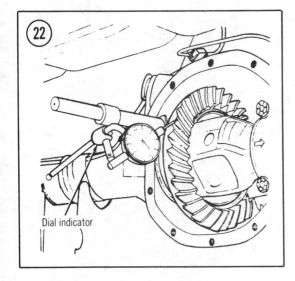

Dial indicator

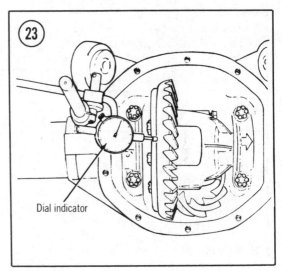

Dial indicator

Tables are on the following page.

10

Table 1   DIFFERENTIAL AND REAR SUSPENSION SPECIFICATIONS

Differential type	Hypoid, integral carrier
Ring gear diameter	
WGF/WGG	6 3/4 in.
WGX/WGZ	7 1/2 in.
Ring gear runout, maximum	0.003 in.
Ring gear backflash*	
WGF/WGG	0.008-0.012 in. (1979)
	0.008-0.015 in. (1980)
WGX/WGZ	0.0012 in.
Lubricant capacity (approximate)	
WGF/WGG	2.5 pints
WGX/WGZ	3.5 pints
Rear suspension type	Coil springs, tubular shock absorbers

*Maximum variation between readings 0.003 in.

Table 2   TIGHTENING TORQUES

Item	Torque
Axle shaft bearing retainer nuts	20-40 in.-lb.
Differential cover bolts	25-35 in.-lb.
Oil filler plug	
WGF/WGG	25-40 in.-lb.
WGX/WGZ	24-45 in.-lb.
Shock absorber nuts	
Upper	14-26 ft.-lb.
Lower	40-55 ft.-lb.
Upper arm to frame	70-100 ft.-lb.
Upper arm to axle	70-100 ft.-lb.
Lower arm to axle	70-100 ft.-lb.
Lower arm to frame	70-100 ft.-lb.
Drive shaft circular flange bolts	70-95 ft.-lb.
Drive shaft U-bolt nuts	8-15 ft.-lb.

NOTE: If you own a 1981 or later model, first check the Supplement at the back of the book for any new service information.

CHAPTER ELEVEN

BRAKES

All vehicles use front disc brakes and rear drum brakes. The front disc brakes are ventilated, and use a single-piston, sliding caliper. All brakes are self-adjusting. The handbrake is a mechanical type which operates the rear brakes through a cable linkage.

Tables 1 and 2 provide brake specifications. **Table 3** provides torque specifications. They are found at the end of the chapter.

BRAKE FAILURE

Failure of one of the brake circuits will normally be indicated by the brake warning light turning on. However, if the light is burned out or the wiring faulty, the first indication of a brake failure may occur when the brakes are applied. If the warning light comes on, carefully slow and stop the vehicle, taking into account that the braking effectiveness is greatly reduced. Remove the cap from the master cylinder reservoir (**Figure 1**) and check to see if there is fluid in both reservoirs. If the level is low in one, or it is empty, check further for leaks along the brake lines and at each wheel. If the level is correct in both reservoirs, the fault may lie in the switch, wiring, or the differential pressure valve in the master cylinder. In any case, drive the vehicle with extreme care until the system can be checked and the trouble corrected.

BRAKE BLEEDING

The hydraulic system should be bled whenever air is suspected of entering it or when braking effectivness is reduced. If the pedal feels soft, or if pedal travel increases considerably, bleeding is usually called for. Bleeding is also necessary whenever a hydraulic line is disconnected, or the braking system is repaired.

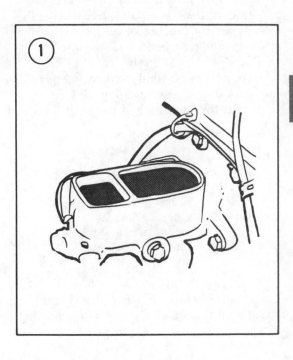

①

11

Because this procedure requires handling brake fluid, be careful not to contaminate brake pads, shoes, discs, or drums with fluid. Clean all dirt from bleeder screws before beginning. Two people are required to bleed the system—one to operate the brake pedal, and the other to open and close the bleed valves.

Bleeding should be conducted in the following order: master cylinder, right rear, left rear, right front, left front.

1. Clean away all dirt around the master cylinder. Top up the reservoir with brake fluid (Ford Extra Heavy Duty or DOT 3). Leave the top off the reservoir and cover with a clean shop rag.

2. Attach a rubber hose to the bleeder screw. Be sure the tube fits snugly. Dip the other end of the tube in a jar containing several inches of clean brake fluid (**Figure 2**).

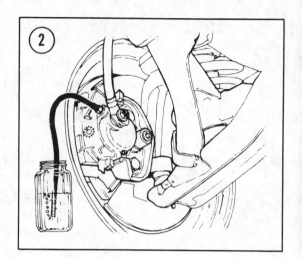

> *CAUTION*
> *Do not allow the end of the tube to come out of the brake fluid during bleeding. This could allow air into the system, requiring that the bleeding procedure be done over.*

3. Use a 3/8 in. box-end wrench and open the bleeder screw about 3/4 turn.

4. Have an assistant press the brake pedal slowly to the floor. When the pedal reaches the floor, close the bleeder valve. Do not let the pedal up until the bleeder screw is closed.

5. Release the pedal slowly.

6. Repeat Steps 3-5 until the fluid entering the jar from the tube is free of air bubbles.

7. Repeat this procedure at the other bleeder screws.

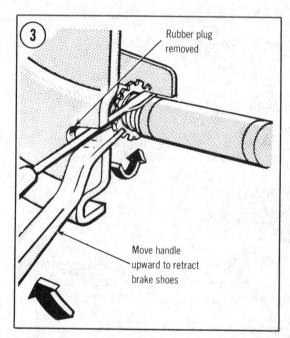

> *NOTE*
> *Watch the brake fluid level in the master cylinder throughout the bleeding procedure. If either of the reservoirs are allowed to become empty, air will be sucked into the hydraulic system and the bleeding procedure must be repeated.*

8. Road test the vehicle to ensure that the brakes operate correctly. Begin checking at low speed until you are confident that the braking action is good.

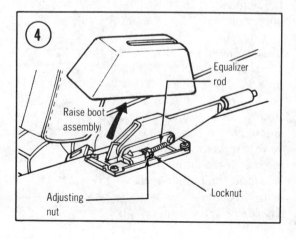

BRAKE ADJUSTMENT

Disc Brakes

The front disc brakes do not require adjustment.

Drum Brakes

The rear drum brakes are self-adjusting. Manual adjustment is unnecessary unless the brakes have been repaired. In such case use the following procedure.

1. Loosen the rear wheel nuts, jack up the rear end of the car and place it on jackstands.
2. Pry the rubber cover from the rear brake backing plate.
3. Insert a narrow-bladed screwdriver through the backing plate and push the self-adjuster lever away from adjusting wheel (**Figure 3**).
4. Turn the adjusting wheel upward with a brake adjusting tool until the brakes lock the drum.
5. Back off the adjusting wheel until the brake drum can be turned with very slight drag.
6. Repeat this procedure for the opposite wheel.

HANDBRAKE

Adjustment

1. Securely block both front wheels so the car will not roll in either direction.

2. Fully release the handbrake and place the transmission in NEUTRAL.
3. Jack up the rear end of the car until the tires are clear of the ground. Support car with jackstands.
4. From inside the vehicle, remove the handbrake boot cover and tighten the handbrake cable adjusting nut (**Figure 4**) until the rear brakes drag when the wheels are turned by hand.
5. Loosen the adjusting nut until the brakes just stop dragging.
6. Remove the jackstands, lower the car, and make sure the handbrake operates properly.

Handbrake Removal/Installation

Refer to **Figure 5** for this procedure.
1. Completely remove the handbrake adjusting nut shown in **Figure 4**.
2. Remove the 2 screws attaching the handbrake lever to the transmission tunnel. Lift the handbrake lever out.
3. Installation is the reverse of these steps. Tighten the handbrake attaching bolts to 10-16 ft.-lb. Adjust the handbrake linkage as described earlier.

Handbrake Cable Removal

Refer to **Figure 5** for this procedure.

11

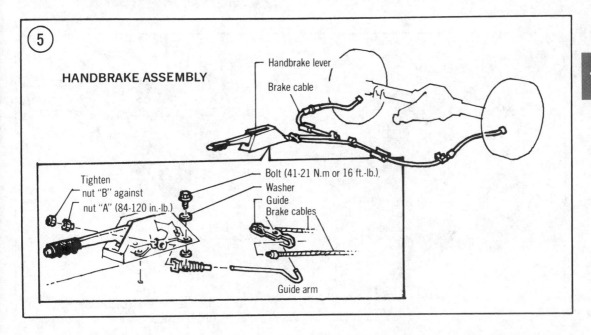

⑤

HANDBRAKE ASSEMBLY

Handbrake lever

Brake cable

Tighten nut "B" against nut "A" (84-120 in.-lb.)

Bolt (41-21 N.m or 16 ft.-lb.)
Washer
Guide
Brake cables

Guide arm

1. Securely block both front wheels so the car will not roll in either direction.

2. Release the handbrake and loosen the attaching nuts (**Figure 4**).

3. Jack up the rear end of the car until the tires are clear of the ground. Place jackstands beneath the car.

4. Unhook the handbrake cable from the equalizer.

5. Use pliers to compress the cable retainer prong and release the cable from the bracket attaching it to the car frame.

6. Open the ends of the floor pan cable clips and remove the clip that attaches the conduit to its bracket, and remove clip attaching cable to underbody.

7. Remove the rear wheels and brake drums as described later in this chapter.

8. Detach the cable ends from the parking brake levers on the secondary brake shoes.

9. Compress the retainer prong and pull the cable ends through the parking plate and withdraw from the car.

Cable Installation

Refer to **Figure 5** for this procedure.

1. Insert the cable ends into the backing plate. Pull the ends in until the retainer prongs lock the cable in place.

2. Connect the cable ends to the handbrake levers.

3. Install self-adjuster springs.

4. Place the cable in the retaining clip fastened to the underbody and through the conduit bracket.

5. Thread cable through plastic guide block.

6. Hook cable into equalizer.

7. Install rear brake drums and wheels, then lower car and tighten wheel nuts to 80-105 ft.-lb.

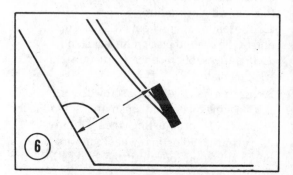

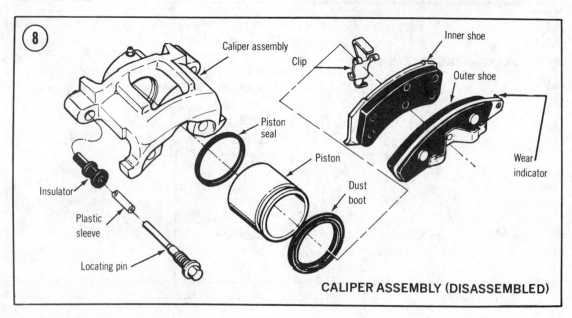

CALIPER ASSEMBLY (DISASSEMBLED)

8. Adjust handbrake linkage as described earlier.

BRAKE PEDAL

NOTE
Ford Motor Company has indicated that some 1979 models may have a defective retaining pin holding the brake pushrod to the brake pedal. Return the vehicle to a dealer for inspection and correction, if you have not already done so.

Adjustment

1. With the handbrake fully released (engine running for power brake installations), measure the distance from the top of the brake pedal pad to the floorboard sheet metal (through the carpet and sound deadener) as shown in **Figure 6**. Pedal height should be as specified in **Table 1**.
2. If brake pedal height is not within specification, check at the pedal mounting point for missing, worn, or damaged bushings. Replace as needed.
3. If the pedal bushings are in good condition, make sure the master cylinder is securely attached to the firewall.
4. Hook a tape measure over the top of the brake pedal and measure the distance from the pedal to the 6 o'clock position on the steering wheel rim. Press the brake pedal firmly with about 25 lb. pressure and measure again. The difference between these 2 measurements is the pedal travel. The distance should not exceed the specifications in **Table 1**.
5. If pedal travel is excessive, pump the brake pedal rapidly, several times. If pedal travel is reduced significantly (pedal pump up), there is probably air in the hydraulic system. Bleed the brakes as described in this chapter.
6. If pumping the brake pedal does not reduce pedal travel, adjust the brakes using the self-adjuster mechanism. To do this, drive the car forward about 10 feet, then press the brake pedal firmly (25 lb. pressure) and hold down until the car stops. Drive the car backward about 10 feet and stop it in the same manner. Repeat this procedure several times.
7. If pedal travel is still excessive, check the pedal attachment point for worn or missing pedal bushings. Replace as needed.
8. If pedal bushings are in good condition, remove the brake drums and inspect the self-adjuster mechanisms as described under *Brake Shoes, Installation.*

PRESSURE DIFFERENTIAL VALVE AND WARNING LIGHT SWITCH

The pressure differential valve and warning light switch are combined into a single unit located in front of the master cylinder on the fender apron. If hydraulic pressure drops severly in either the front or rear brake system, the valve operates the switch activating the warning light in the passenger compartment. The pressure differential valve must be centered whenever the brakes are bled. To center, turn the ignition switch to ACC or ON (but do not start the engine). Press the brake pedal firmly until the warning light goes out (if illuminated). Turn ignition switch OFF.

If the pressure differential valve is defective, replace it. Do not attempt to repair the valve. Refer to **Figure 7** while performing the following procedure.
1. Disconnect the brake warning light wiring connector from the valve.
2. Detach the hydraulic lines from the valve.
3. Remove 2 bolts and nuts attaching the valve to the front fender apron. Lift the valve out of the car.
4. Installaton is the reverse of these steps. Bleed the brakes and center the new valve, as described in this chapter, before driving vehicle.

DISC BRAKE PADS

Removal

1. Remove cap from master cylinder and remove brake fluid until reservoir is half full. Discard this fluid. See **Figure 1**.
2. Loosen the front wheel nuts, jack up the front end of the car, place it on jackstands, and remove the front wheels.
3. Remove 2 caliper locating pins from caliper assembly (**Figure 8**).

11

4. Discard rubber caliper insulators and plastic sleeves.

5. Remove the caliper assembly from the integral spindle/anchor plate and rotor (**Figure 9**).

6. Detach both outer and inner brake pads from caliper assembly. See **Figure 10**.

7. Hang the caliper from the upper suspension arm with wire.

Inspection

1. Inspect the pads for wear and damage caused by overheating. Check for grease, oil, or brake fluid on the friction material. If the pads are overheated (indicated by blue-tinted areas), replace them. Pads must also be replaced if they have been contaminated by grease, oil or brake fluid.

WARNING
If pads are being replaced on one wheel, they must also be replaced on the other wheel to maintain equal brake action, and avoid excessive brake pull under normal driving conditions.

2. Carefully clean the outside of the caliper. Look for brake fluid leaks, and overhaul the caliper assembly as described later in this chapter if leaks are detected.

3. Inspect the flexible brake hose attached to the caliper. Replace the brake hose if it is swollen, cracked, or leaking.

Installation

1. If new pads are being installed, press the caliper piston into its bore to provide clearance for the brake pads. Use a 4 in. C-clamp and a

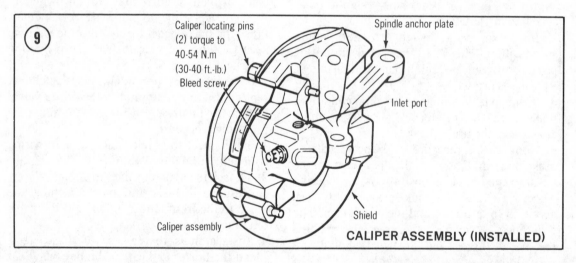

(9) Caliper locating pins (2) torque to 40-54 N.m (30-40 ft.-lb.)
Bleed screw
Spindle anchor plate
Inlet port
Shield
Caliper assembly
CALIPER ASSEMBLY (INSTALLED)

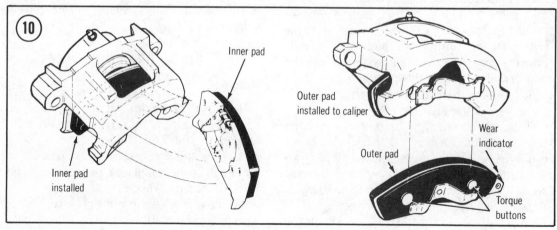

(10) Inner pad
Inner pad installed
Outer pad installed to caliper
Outer pad
Wear indicator
Torque buttons

block of wood 2-3/4 x 1 x 3/4 in. thick to compress the piston.

2. Install new locating pin insulators and plastic sleeves in the caliper housing with tool shown in **Figure 11**. When installed, examine to see that both insulator flanges straddle the housing holes and the plastic sleeves are bottomed in the insulators and slipped under the upper lip. See **Figure 12**.

3. Make sure the anti-rattle clips are in position, then install the inner and outer brake pads.

NOTE
*The outer pad can be identified as right or left hand by the wear indicator which always must face toward the front of the vehicle (**Figure 10**).*

4. Remove the C-clamp and block of wood (if used) from the brake caliper. Remove the wire attaching the caliper to the upper suspension arm.

5. Install the caliper assembly over the rotor with the outer brake shoe against the rotor braking surface.

WARNING
*Ensure that each round torque button on the outer pad is seated solidly in one of the holes of outer leg, and the pad is held tightly against caliper housing by the spring clip. If buttons are not seated, brake failure will occur (**Figure 10**).*

6. Install 2 locating pins to the integral spindle/anchor plate and caliper insulators, and tighten to 30-40 ft.-lb. See **Figure 8**.

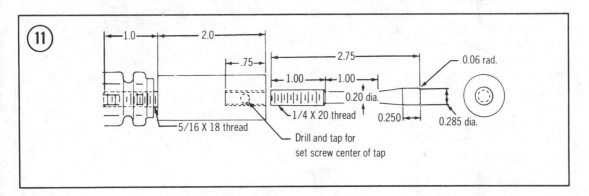

⑪ 5/16 X 18 thread — Drill and tap for set screw center of tap — 1/4 X 20 thread — 0.20 dia. — 0.250 — 0.285 dia. — 0.06 rad.

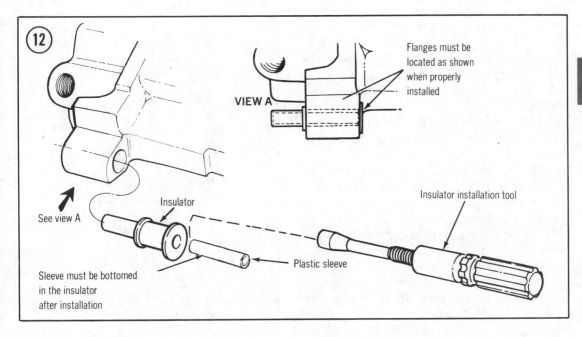

⑫ Flanges must be located as shown when properly installed

VIEW A

Insulator installation tool

See view A

Insulator

Plastic sleeve

Sleeve must be bottomed in the insulator after installation

11

7. Clean dirt away from around master cylinder and fill reservoir as required to within 1/4 in. from top with Ford Extra Heavy or DOT 3 brake fluid (**Figure 1**).

8. Pump the brake pedal several times to seat the brake caliper and pads. Recheck the caliper and brake hose for leaks.

9. Install the wheel and wheel nuts. Lower the car from the jackstands and tighten the wheel nuts to 80-105 ft.-lb.

DISC BRAKE CALIPER

Caliper Removal

Refer to **Figure 8** for this procedure.

1. Loosen the front wheel nuts, jack up the front end of the car, place it on jackstands and remove the wheel.

2. Unscrew the tube fitting that connects the brake hose to its bracket on the frame (**Figure 13**). Pull out the horseshoe-type clip and detach the hose from the brakets. Plug the brake tube.

3. Unscrew the entire hose assembly from the caliper.

4. Perform Steps 2-5 under *Disc Brake Pad Replacement* to remove the caliper.

Installation

1. To install the caliper, perform Steps 2-6 under *Disc Brake Pad Replacement*, plus the following.

2. Install the flexible brake hose into the fitting on the caliper. This fitting is self-sealing and does not require a gasket. Tighten hose fitting to 20-30 ft.-lb.

3. Attach the top end of the brake hose into its bracket and install the retaining clip. Do not twist the hose.

4. Remove the plug sealing the brake tube and connect the tube to the hose with the tube fitting nut. Tighten nut assembly to 10-18 ft.-lb.

5. Bleed the brake system, and centralize the brake pressure differential valve as described earlier in this chapter.

6. Pump the brake pedal several times to seat the brake caliper and pads. Recheck the caliper and brake hose for leaks.

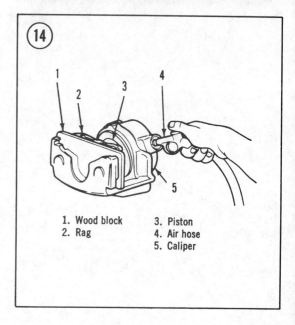

1. Wood block   3. Piston
2. Rag   4. Air hose
                   5. Caliper

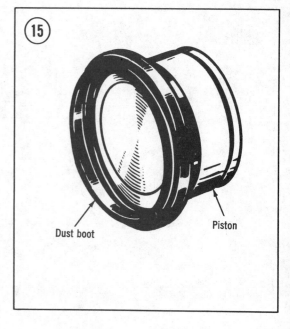

Dust boot   Piston

7. Install the wheel and wheel nuts. Lower car from jackstands and tighten the wheel nuts to 80-105 ft.-lb.

Caliper Disassembly

1. Place several layers of cloth or a block of soft wood over the caliper piston, then blow compressed air into the brake hose fitting (**Figure 14**) to force the caliper piston out of its bore. Service station air hoses will work well if you do not have an air compressor. If the caliper piston is difficult to remove, tap it lightly around the edges, while applying compressed air, to free the piston in its bore.

> *WARNING*
> *The caliper piston may come out of its bore with considerable force. Point the piston away from your body when removing to prevent injury.*

2. Remove the dust boot from the caliper.
3. Remove the piston seal from the piston bore, and discard it.

Cleaning and Inspection

1. Remove rust or corrosion from machined surfaces of the caliper housing with a wire brush.

> *CAUTION*
> *Do not use a wire brush on the cylinder bore or damage to the machined surfaces will result.*

2. Clean caliper housing and piston with denatured alcohol. Clean and dry the grooves and passages with clean compressed air. Be sure that cylinder bore is free of foreign matter.
3. Check cylinder bore, seal groove and boot groove in the bore and piston for damage or excessive wear. Replace piston if it is pitted, scored, or worn.
4. Remove corrosion from the boot groove.

> *NOTE*
> *If you have any doubts about your own ability to determine wear or damage, take the disassembled caliper to your dealer.*

5. Replace the anti-rattle clip, plastic sleeve, piston seal, and dust boots with new components.

Caliper Assembly

1. Dip a new piston seal in clean brake fluid and install in the cylinder bore. Be sure the seal is fully seated in its groove and is not twisted in any way.

> *NOTE*
> *Never reuse a caliper piston seal. In addition to preventing brake fluid leaks, the seal retracts the caliper piston when the brake pedal is released. Very minor damage or age deterioration can make the seal totally inoperative.*

2. Insert piston through dust boot until boot is around the bottom (closed end) of the piston (**Figure 15**).
3. Hold piston and dust boot above the caliper cylinder bore, then work the bead of the dust boot into the groove near the top of the cylinder bore with your fingers.
4. After bead is seated in groove, press straight down on piston until it bottoms in the bore. If necessary, bottom the piston with a C-clamp and a block of wood inserted between the clamp and piston.

> *CAUTION*
> *Do not cock piston in bore.*

5. Install caliper as outlined previously.
6. Bleed hydraulic brake system (refer to *Brake Bleeding* section in this chapter).

Anchor Plate Removal

The anchor plate is an integral part of the spindle. Refer to Chapter Nine for its removal.

BRAKE DISCS

Inspection

1. Loosen the front wheel nuts, jack up the front end of the car, place it on jackstands and remove the wheels.
2. Check the front wheel bearing adjustments as described in Chapter Nine. Adjust if needed.

11

3. Remove the caliper as described earlier. Leave the brake hose connected and hang the caliper from the upper suspension arm with wire. Do not allow it to hang from the brake line.

4. Inspect the disc surface for deep scratches. Small marks are not important, but deep scratches reduce braking efficiency and increase brake pad wear. If the disc is deeply scratched, it can be turned on a lathe to smooth the surfaces. However, the disc must not be cut thinner than 0.810 in.

5. With a dial gauge contacting the swept area of the disc (**Figure 16**), rotate the disc one full turn and measure runout. Normal runout is 0.003 in. or less. Replace or turn the disc if runout is in excess of this amount.

6. Use a micrometer to measure the thickness of the disc at several points around the circumference, and at varying distances from the center of the disc. Standard disc thickness is 0.870 in. If the disc is less than 0.810 in. at any point, replace it.

Removal

1. Loosen the front wheel nuts, jack up the front end of the car, place it on jackstands, and remove the front wheels.

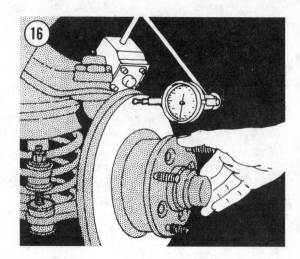

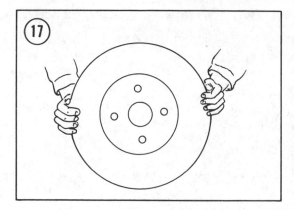

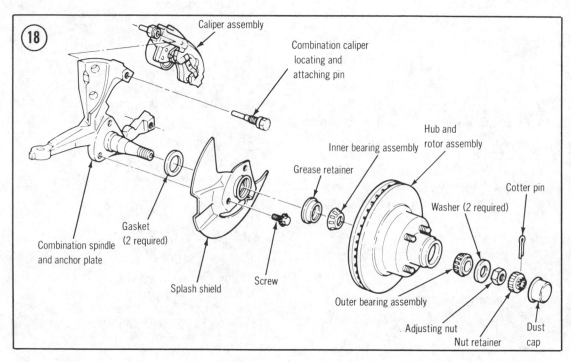

2. Remove the caliper assembly as described earlier. Do not remove the anchor plate. It is not necessary to detach the brake hose attached to the caliper. Hang the caliper assembly from the front suspension arm with wire. Do not allow it to hang from the brake line.

CAUTION
Do not stretch or twist the brake hose.

3. Remove the wheel bearing grease cap cotter pin, nut lock, and adjusting nut as described in Chapter Nine.

4. Grasp the disc in both hands (**Figure 17**) and pull it off the spindle far enough to loosen the wheel bearing washer and outer wheel bearing. See **Figure 18**.

5. Push the disc back onto the spindle and take the washer and outer wheel bearing off the spindle.

6. Pull the brake disc off the spindle together with the inner wheel bearing and grease seal.

Installation

1. If a new disc is being installed, remove the protective coating on the disc surfaces with carburetor degreaser. New wheel bearings must be installed, using procedures described in Chapter Nine.

2. If the original disc is being installed, pack the wheel bearings with grease as described in Chapter Nine. The wheel bearing and grease seal must be in good condition. The braking surfaces of the disc should be cleaned prior to installation.

3. Slide the brake disc, together with the inner wheel bearing and grease seal onto the spindle.

CAUTION
Keep the disc centered on the spindle to prevent damage to the grease seal and spindle threads.

4. Install the outer wheel bearing and washer, then install the wheel bearing adjusting nut and tighten it finger-tight. Make sure the disc rotates freely.
5. Install the caliper assembly as described in this chapter.
6. Adjust the wheel bearings as described in Chapter Nine.
7. Lower the car and tighten all wheel nuts to 80-105 ft.-lb.
8. Bleed the brakes and center the pressure differential valve if the caliper brake hose was disconnected.
9. Pump the brake pedal seveal times to seat the brake pads and caliper, then drive the car to make sure the brakes operate properly.

BRAKE DRUMS

Removal

1. Loosen the rear wheel nuts, jack up the rear end of the car, place it on jackstands and remove the rear wheels.
2. Use pliers to remove 3 drum retainer nuts securing the brake drum to the axle shaft studs (**Figure 19**).
3. If the brake drum is free, pull it off the axle studs. If the brake shoes are holding the brake drum, preventing its removal, pry the rubber cover from the backing plate. Insert a narrow screw driver through the hole in the backing plate (**Figure 3**) and disengage the adjusting lever from the adjusting screw. While holding the adjusting lever away from the adjusting screw, back off on the adjusting screw with a brake adjusting tool until the drum is free of the brake shoes.

CAUTION
Do not damage the notches in the adjusting screw while turning. The self-adjusting mechanism will not operate properly if the adjusting screw notches are damaged.

Inspection

1. Clean the brake drum inner surfaces with solvent before inspection.

2. Check the drum surface for scoring, excessive or uneven wear, corrosion, or heat spots (blue-tinted areas). Minor scratches can be removed with fine emery paper. If heat spots are visible, the drum must be replaced.

3. If you have a micrometer, measure the drum for wear and out-of-roundness. This measurement can be most easily done by a dealer or machine shop. The maximum permissible out-of-roundness is 0.007 in. Maximum permissible drum diameter is 9.060 in. If the drum is out-of-round, scored, or worn, it can be turned on a lathe to repair it. However, the inside diameter of the drum must not be increased to more than 9.060 in.

NOTE
If the drum diameter is less than 0.030 in oversize after turning, standard brake linings can be used. If the drum diameter is 0.030-0.060 in. oversize, oversized linings must be installed.

Installation

1. If a new brake drum is being installed, remove the brake drum protective coating with carburetor degreaser. Lightly sand the brake surface with fine sandpaper to make sure that no coating residue remains. Wipe the drum clean with a cloth soaked in alcohol. Install new wheel bearings as described in Chapter Ten.

2. If the original brake drum is being reinstalled, the original wheel bearings may be used. However, clean and pack them with grease as described in Chapter Ten.

3. If the brake adjusting screw was backed off to remove the brake drum, readjust the screw until the brake drum will just fit over the brake shoes (**Figure 3**).

4. Install the brake drum and 3 retainer nuts.

5. Adjust the brakes as described in this chapter. Install the wheel and wheel nuts. Lower the car and tighten the wheel nuts to 80-105 ft.-lb.

BRAKE SHOES

Inspection

1. Loosen the rear wheel nuts, jack up the rear end of the car, place it on jackstands and remove the rear wheels.

2. Remove brake drums as described earlier.

3. Brush all dust from the brake drum inner surface and the brake shoes.

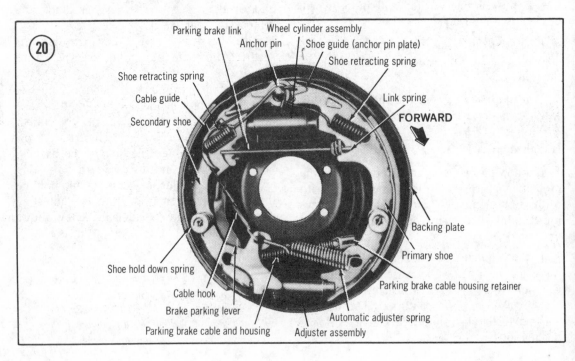

4. Inspect the lining material on the brake shoes. Make sure it is not cracked, unevenly worn, or separated from the brake shoes. Replace the brake shoes if the linings are worn to within 1/32 in. of any rivet head. The brake shoes must also be replaced if there is oil, grease or brake fluid on the linings. If blue-tinted areas are visible on brake shoes (indicating overheating), replace the shoes.

NOTE
Replacement of the hold-down and retracting springs is strongly recommended

if the brake shoes have been overheated. Heat weakens the springs and could cause premature lining wear.

Removal

Refer to **Figure 20** for this procedure.
1. Loosen the rear wheel nuts, jack the rear end of the car up, place it on jackstands, and remove the rear wheels.
2. Remove the rear brake drums as described earlier.
3. Place a clamp over the ends of the wheel cylinder (**Figure 21**).
4. Remove the brake retracting springs with a spring removal tool (**Figure 22**). Place the socket end of the tool over the anchor pin and twist the tool to remove the spring. Remove the secondary (rearmost) spring, then the primary spring.
5. Lift the self-adjusting cable off the anchor pin (**Figure 23**). Unhook the other end of the cable from the self-adjuster lever and lay cable aside.
6. Remove the hold-down springs as shown in **Figure 24**. Press the spring retaining collars inward and twist until the pins fit through the slots in the retaining collars. Collect the pins, retainer collars, and springs.

11

7. Spread the upper end of the brake shoes away from the wheel cylinders (**Figure 25**). Pull the shoes off, together with the adjusting screw, self-adjuster spring, and self-adjuster lever.

8. Separate the handbrake lever from the secondary shoe (**Figure 20**). Detach the handbrake cable from the lever, then remove the handbrake and link spring.

Installation

1. Attach the handbrake lever to the secondary (rearmost) brake shoe.

2. Apply a thin coat of high-temperature grease to the friction points between the brake shoes and backing plate.

> *CAUTION*
> *Do not contaminate the brake linings by getting grease on them.*

3. Position the brake shoes on the backing plate and secure them with the hold-down springs (**Figure 26**).

4. Install the handbrake link and spring (**Figure 26**). Back off the handbrake adjusting nut, as described under *Handbrake Adjustment*, then reconnect the handbrake cable to the handbrake lever.

5. Place the loop of the self-adjuster cable over the anchor pin (**Figure 27**). Note that one side of the cable loop is crimped. This side must face the backing plate.

6. Install the self-adjuster cable guide in the secondary (rearmost) brake shoe (**Figure 28**). Lay the cable in the cable guide groove.

> *NOTE*
> *The cable must be properly placed in the cable groove. Do not let the cable get between the cable guide and the brake shoe.*

7. Install the primary (frontmost) brake retracting spring. Use the brake spring tool as shown in **Figure 29**.

8. Install the secondary brake retracting spring. Make sure the self-adjuster cable and spring ends are flat on the anchor pin.

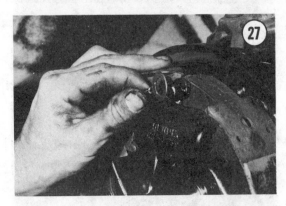

9. Remove the clamp from the wheel cylinder.
10. Apply a light, even coat of high-temperature grease to the adjusting screw threads (**Figure 30**). Turn the adjusting screw all the way into the pivot nut, then back off 1/2 turn.
11. Place the socket of the spring removal tool on the adjusting screw. Install the adjusting screw assembly between the bottom ends of

the brake shoes. The socket end faces the rear of the car and the pivot nut end faces the front.

NOTE
*If the adjusting screw assembly is installed on the wrong side of the car, the brake shoes will be retracted instead of expanded when the self-adjusting mechanism operates. This will cause the rear brakes to be inoperative. The adjusting screws and levers are stamped "R" and "L" for left and right sides (**Figure 30**).*

12. Hook the self-adjusting lever into the hole in the secondary shoe (**Figure 31**).
13. Install the adjuster spring in the primary brake shoe web (**Figure 32**). The hook end of the spring must be completely into the hole, and the last coil of the spring should be at the edge of the hole.
14. Attach the other end of the self-adjuster spring to the oval hole in the self-adjuster lever.
15. Hook the self-adjuster cable into the self-adjuster lever (**Figure 33**).

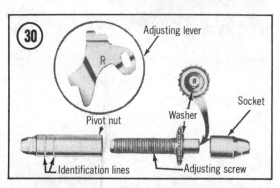

11

16. After installation, check the self-adjuster assembly for proper installaton. To do this, pull the self-adjuster cable far enough to lift the self-adjuster lever past one tooth on the adjusting wheel (**Figure 34**). Watch the self-adjuster lever. It should snap into place behind the next tooth. When the cable is released, the self-adjuster should rotate the adjusting wheel one tooth and the lever should return to its original position. If the adjusting lever movement is slow, or the adjusting wheel fails to turn, perform Steps 17-23 to determine the cause. If the adjusting mechanism works properly, go to Step 23.

17. Make sure the adjusting screw socket (**Figure 30**) is properly seated in its notch in the secondary brake shoe.

18. Make sure the self-adjuster lever contacts the adjusting wheel at a point 5/32-7/32 in. above the center line of the adjusting screw. If the contact point is too low, the lever will not turn the adjusting screw properly.

19. Check the ends of the self-adjuster cable where the wire enters the hook and loop. The wire should extend all the way through, or slightly beyond, the crimped portion of the hook and loop. If the wire does not extend all the way through, the cable must be replaced.

1. Self-adjuster cable   3. Self-adjuster lever
2. Cable guide   4. Adjusting wheel

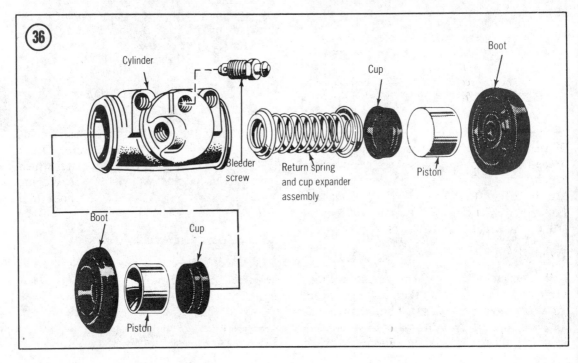

20. Measure the cable length. Correct cable length is 8-13/32 in. from the end of the hook to the end of the loop. Replace the cable if it is too long.

21. Check the cable guide for damage. The guide must lie flat on the brake shoe, and the cable groove must be parallel to the brake shoe. Replace the cable guide if damage is evident.

22. Check the self-adjuster lever for wear or damage at the hook that attaches it to the brake shoe. Replace the lever if wear or damage is evident.

23. Install the brake drum and adjust the brakes as described in this chapter.

24. Install the wheels and wheel nuts. Lower the car and tighten the wheel nuts to 80-105 ft.-lb.

WHEEL CYLINDERS

Removal/Installation

1. Remove the brake drums and shoes as described earlier.

2. Unscrew the brake line nut from the wheel cylinder (**Figure 35**). Remove 2 bolts and lockwashers attaching the wheel cylinder to the backing plate, then lift the cylinder away from the plate.

> *CAUTION*
> *Do not bend rear brake lines away from the wheel cylinders after unscrewing the nut. Bending the brake line will make it difficult to reconnect. The wheel cylinder will separate from the brake line when it is lifted out.*

3. Installation is the reverse of these steps. Wipe the ends of the brake lines clean before reconnecting. Tighten the wheel cylinder attaching bolts to 110 to 160 in.-lb. Bleed the brakes and center the pressure differential valve as described earlier in this chapter.

Overhaul

Wheel cylinders can be rebuilt without removing them from the backing plate. However, extreme care must be taken not to let any dirt or foreign material enter the cylinders during rebuilding. **Figure 36** is an exploded view of one wheel cylinder. Refer to it as needed during the following procedure.

1. Remove the rubber boot from each end of the wheel cylinder. Discard the boots.

2. Take out the pistons, piston cups, and return springs. Discard the piston cups.

3. Remove the bleeder screw from the cylinder.

4. Throughly clean all parts with brake fluid, then blow dry with compressed air.

5. Inspect the piston and replace it if it is scored, worn, or damaged.

6. Check the cylinder bore for scoring, corrosion or excessive wear. If any of these conditions are visible, the bore may be honed smooth. However, the cylinder may not be honed more than 0.003 in. over the standard wheel cylinder diameter (**Table 2**). If the wheel cylinder bore would have to be honed more than 0.003 in. oversize to smooth it, the wheel cylinder must be replaced.

7. Make sure the bleeder screw hole is unobstructed.

8. Coat the cylinder bore, return spring, new piston cups, and pistons with brake fluid.

9. Refer to **Figure 36**. Install the return spring in the cylinder. Install both piston cups, taking care not to bend back the lips of the cups. Install the pistons with the flat ends facing into the cylinder and the hollow ends facing outward. Install a new rubber boot over each end of the wheel cylinder.

SPLASH SHIELD/ BACKING PLATE

Disc brakes are provided with splash shields to protect them from dirt and water. Drum brakes are equipped with backing plates which hold the brake assembly, as well as keeping contaminants off of the brake shoes and drums.

Splash Shield Removal/Installation

1. Remove caliper and hub/rotor assembly as described in this chapter.

2. Remove the 3 bolts attaching the splash shield to the spindle (**Figure 18**). Lift the splash shield clear of the car.

3. Installation is the reverse of these steps.

11

Backing Plate
Removal/Installation

Refer to **Figure 20** for the following procedure.

1. Remove the brake shoes, adjuster assembly, handbrake mechanism, and wheel cylinder as described earlier in this chapter.
2. Remove the rear axle shaft as described in Chapter Ten.
3. Pry the prongs on the handbrake cable retainer and housing away from the backing plate.
4. Remove the backing plate and gasket from the axle housing.
5. Installation is the reverse of these steps. Use a new backing plate gasket.

MASTER CYLINDER

Removal

1. Disconnect the negative battery cable.
2. Disconnect the stoplight switch wires from the connector at the brake pedal (**Figure 37**).
3. Remove the stoplight switch retaining clip.

Slide the stoplight switch off the brake pedal pin just far enough to clear the pin, then lower the switch out of the way, and remove it.

4. Loosen the master cylinder attaching bolts from the engine compartment, and slide the master cylinder pushrod, its bushings, and nylon spacers off the brake pedal pin.
5. Refer to **Figure 38**. Disconnect the primary and secondary brake lines from master cylinder.

> *NOTE*
> *Brake fluid will damage paint. Place rags beneath the master cylinder. If any brake fluid spills onto the paint, immediately wipe the area, then wash with soapy water.*

6. From inside the engine compartment, remove the 2 bolts and lockwashers attaching the master cylinder to the firewall. Lift the master cylinder forward and upward to remove it from vehicle.

Disassembly

1. Clean the outside of the master cylinder before taking it apart. Refer to **Figure 38**.

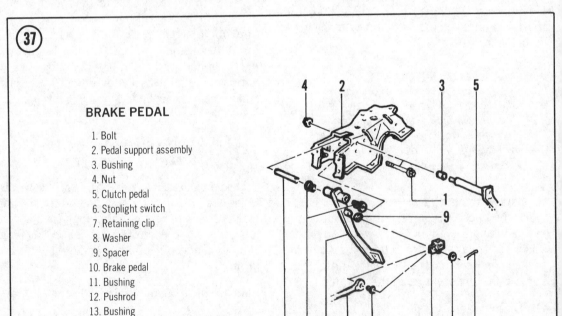

(37)

BRAKE PEDAL

1. Bolt
2. Pedal support assembly
3. Bushing
4. Nut
5. Clutch pedal
6. Stoplight switch
7. Retaining clip
8. Washer
9. Spacer
10. Brake pedal
11. Bushing
12. Pushrod
13. Bushing
14. Sleeve

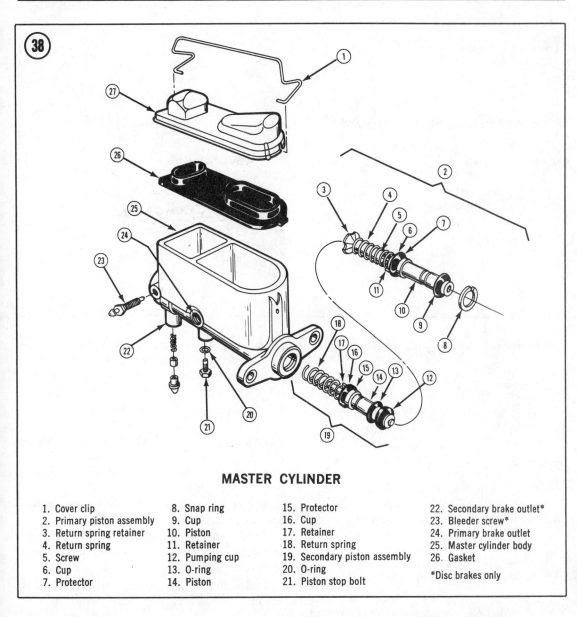

MASTER CYLINDER

1. Cover clip	8. Snap ring	15. Protector	22. Secondary brake outlet*
2. Primary piston assembly	9. Cup	16. Cup	23. Bleeder screw*
3. Return spring retainer	10. Piston	17. Retainer	24. Primary brake outlet
4. Return spring	11. Retainer	18. Return spring	25. Master cylinder body
5. Screw	12. Pumping cup	19. Secondary piston assembly	26. Gasket
6. Cup	13. O-ring	20. O-ring	
7. Protector	14. Piston	21. Piston stop bolt	*Disc brakes only

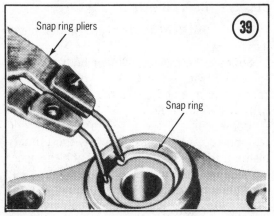

2. Remove the filler cover and gasket. Pour out any brake fluid left in the master cylinder.

3. Remove the secondary piston stop bolt and O-ring from the bottom of the master cylinder.

4. Press the primary piston into the cylinder, then remove the snap ring from its groove (**Figure 39**).

5. Remove the pushrod and primary piston from the master cylinder bore.

NOTE
Do not take apart the primary piston assembly. The assembly is preadjusted at the factory and is replaced as a unit.

11

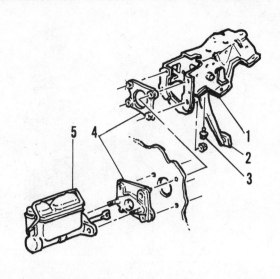

BRAKE ASSEMBLY (NON-POWER)

1. Pedal support assembly
2. Brake pedal
3. Bolt
4. Spacer
5. Master cylinder

6. Remove the secondary piston assembly.

NOTE
Do not remove the outlet tube seats, outlet check valves, or check valve springs from the master cylinder.

Inspection

1. Clean all parts in isopropyl alcohol.
2. Inspect the pistons for wear, chipping, or other visible defects. Replace as needed.

NOTE
When using a master cylinder repair kit, install all parts supplied with kit.

3. Make sure all passages and openings are unobstructed. Blow the cylinder bore out with compressed air.
4. Check the cylinder bore for scores, pitting, corrosion, or wear. If these conditions are visible, the bore may be honed smooth. However, the bore diameter must not be increased by more than 0.003 in. over the standard diameter of 0.875 in.

Assembly

1. Dip all parts except the master cylinder body in clean brake fluid.
2. Assemble the return spring and secondary

piston assembly. Carefully insert this assembly in the master cylinder bore.
3. Install the primary piston assembly in the cylinder bore. Press the piston into the bore and secure with a snap ring (**Figure 39**).
4. Install the rubber boot and retainer on the pushrod. Install the pushrod in the primary piston. Stretch the pushrod boot over the master cylinder body, then seat the lip of the boot in its groove.
5. Install the piston stop bolt O-ring in the bottom of the master cylinder.
6. Install the gasket in the master cylinder cover. Make sure the gasket is properly seated in the cover.
7. Install the master cylinder cover and gasket on the cylinder. Secure with the cover clip.

Master Cylinder Bleeding

Prior to installing the master cylinder, bleed it as follows.
1. Support the master cylinder body in a vise (protect it with soft pieces of wood placed on each side of the body). Fill the master cylinder with fresh brake fluid.
2. Loosely install the plugs in the front and rear brake outlet bores. Depress the primary piston a few times until no air bubbles appear in the brake fluid.
3. Tighten the plugs. Attempt to depress the piston. If there is still piston travel, air is still

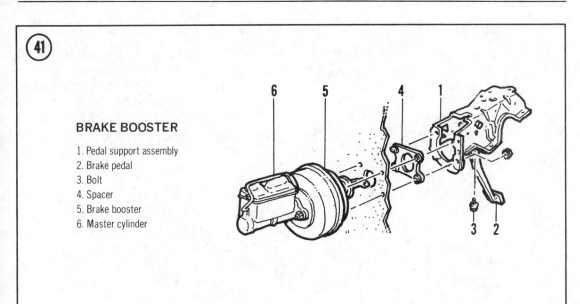

(41)

BRAKE BOOSTER

1. Pedal support assembly
2. Brake pedal
3. Bolt
4. Spacer
5. Brake booster
6. Master cylinder

present in the master cylinder. Bleed again until piston travel is restricted.

4. Remove the plugs and install the cover and diaphragm assembly. Be sure that the cover retainer is tightened securely.

**Installation
(Cars Without Power Brakes)**

Refer to **Figure 40** for the following procedure.

1. Insert the master cylinder pushrod and boot through the firewall.

2. Install the master cylinder retaining bolts but do not tighten.

3. Coat the nylon washers and bushing with SAE 10W-40 engine oil. Place the nylon washer on the brake pedal pin.

4. Slide the end of the master cylinder pushrod over the brake pedal pin, then install the bushing in the pushrod. Install the stoplight switch, then install the other nylon washer and secure with the spring clip.

5. Connect stoplight switch wiring connector (**Figure 37**).

6. Tighten the master cylinder retaining bolts to 13-25 ft.-lb.

7. Connect the brake lines to the master cylinder.

8. Fill the master cylinder with brake fluid. Use Ford Extra Heavy Duty Brake Fluid, or a

brake fluid marked DOT 3 on the label. Fill to within 1/4 in. of the top of the reservoirs. See **Figure 1**.

9. Bleed the brakes and center the pressure differential valve as described earlier in this chapter.

10. Press the brake pedal several times, then check the master cylinder for brake fluid leaks.

**Installation
(Cars With Power Brakes)**

Refer to **Figure 41** for the following procedure.

1. Check brake booster pushrod length as described under *Brake Booster* in this chapter.

2. Position the master cylinder on the brake booster studs. Install the retaining bolts and tighten to 13-25 ft.-lb.

3. Connect the brake lines to the master cylinder. Tighten the nuts to 10-15 ft.-lb.

4. Fill the master cylinder with Ford Extra Heavy Duty Brake Fluid, or a brake fluid marked DOT 3 on the label. Fill to within 1/4 in. of the top of the reservoirs. See **Figure 1**.

5. Bleed the brakes and center the pressure differential valve as described earlier in this chapter.

6. Press the brake pedal several times and check for brake fluid leaks.

11

BRAKE BOOSTER

A vacuum-operated brake booster is optional on all models. **Figure 41** shows the booster and related parts.

If a faulty brake booster is suspected, the unit should be tested by a dealer or other competent service shop. If testing indicates a defective booster, it must be replaced.

Booster Pushrod Measurement

1. Make a measuring tool out of 16 gauge steel. **Figure 42** gives the dimensions.
2. Place the tool over the pushrod (**Figure 43**). Press it toward the brake booster. The tool should touch the booster when about 5 pounds of pressure is applied.
3. If necessary, turn the pushrod adjusting screw to change its length.

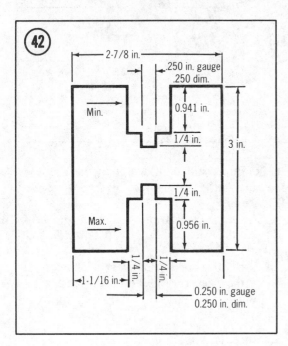

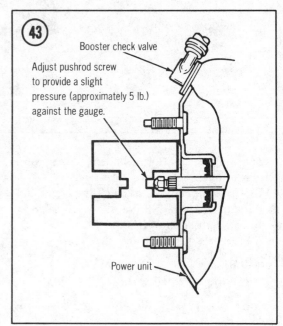

Table 1 BRAKE PEDAL HEIGHT AND TRAVEL SPECIFICATIONS

	Pedal Height		
Brake Type	Maximum	Minimum	Pedal Travel
1979 non-power	8.8 in.	7.5 in.	$2\frac{3}{4}$ in.
1979 power	7.4 in.	6.6 in.	$2\frac{1}{4}$ in.
1980 non-power	8.8 in.	7.6 in.	3.0 in.
1980 power	7.0 in.	6.0 in.	2.0 in.

Table 2 BRAKE SPECIFICATIONS

Pedal	
Free height	See Table 1
Stroke, maximum	See Table 1
Master Cylinder Bore Diameter	
1979	0.938 in.
1980	0.875 in.
Wheel Cylinder Diameter	
Disc brakes	2.60 in. (1979)
	2.36 in. (1980)
Rear drum brakes	0.875 in.
Disc	
Diameter	9.3 in.
Thickness	
Standard	0.870 in.
Minimum	0.810 in.
Drums	
Diameter	
Standard	9.000 in.
Minimum	9.060 in.
Maximum out-of-round	0.007 in.

Table 3 TIGHTENING TORQUES

Item	Torque
Caliper bleed screw	6-15 ft.-lb.
Caliper locating pins (disc brakes)	30-40 ft.-lb.
Master cylinder to dash panel screw	13-25 ft.-lb.
Master cylinder to power booster	13-25 ft.-lb.
Power booster to panel	13-25 ft.-lb.
Pressure differential valve bracket bolts and nuts	7-11 ft.-lb.
Wheel cylinder bleeder screw	32-65 in.-lb.
Brake pedal pivot shaft nut	**10-20 ft.-lb.**
Wheel cylinder to backing plate screws (drum brakes)	110-160 in.-lb.
Wheel to hub and drum (drum brakes)	70-115 ft.-lb.
Rear brake backing plate to axle housing	20-40 ft.-lb.
Handbrake lever mounting bolts	10-16 ft.-lb.
Brake line connection to rear axle housing	12-19 ft.-lb.
Hydraulic brake tube connections	10-18 ft.-lb.

11

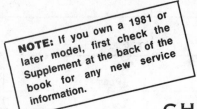
NOTE: If you own a 1981 or later model, first check the Supplement at the back of the book for any new service information.

CHAPTER TWELVE

TURBOCHARGER

A turbocharged engine is optional for 1979 and 1980 model 2300 cc vehicles covered in this manual. Except for the turbocharger unit, and necessary component hardware, the turbocharged and non-turbocharged 2300 cc engines are alike. Emission systems for the 2300 cc turbocharged engine are similar to those described for normally aspirated 2300 cc engines in Chapter Four. However, the addition of a dual wall exhaust pipe from the light-off catalyst to the underbody catalyst has been added to all 2300 cc tubocharged engines. The dual wall pipe is used to maintain high exhaust temperature to the underbody catalyst to maintain conversion temperature.

On 1980 models, turbocharged engines are programmed to use an Electrodrive Cooling System. This system replaces the conventional engine accessory belt driven cooling fan by using an electric motor driven fan. The Electrodrive Cooling System will reduce engine fan noise, improve hot fuel handling and improve the turbochargers cooling requirements.

The turbocharger boosts engine output by approximately 35 percent horsepower and 25 percent torque compared to normally aspirated 2300 cc engines. The turbocharger is an "on demand" system, which boosts engine output during high-load/high speed conditions, but has little effect on fuel economy at moderate-to-light load conditions. Tightening torques for the turbocharger are given in **Table 1** at the end of the chapter.

SYSTEM COMPONENTS

The turbocharging system is shown in **Figure 1**. The basic components are:
a. Compressor
b. Center housing
c. Outlet elbow with wastegate
d. Turbine
e. Wastegate actuator

With **Figure 2** as a guide, begin with the compressor and locate each of the components in turn.

Compressor

The compressor is a centrifugal, radial outflow type. It comprises a cast compressor wheel, backplate assembly, and specially designed housing that encloses the wheel and directs the air/fuel mixture through the compressor.

Center Housing

The center housing supports the compressor and turbine wheel shaft in bearings containing oil holes for directing lubrication to the bearing bores and shaft journals.

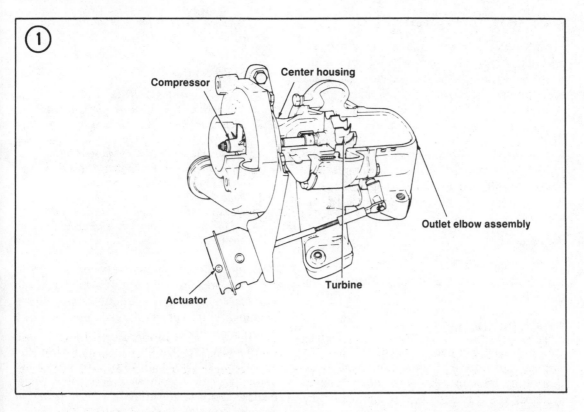

Compressor

Center housing

Outlet elbow assembly

Turbine

Actuator

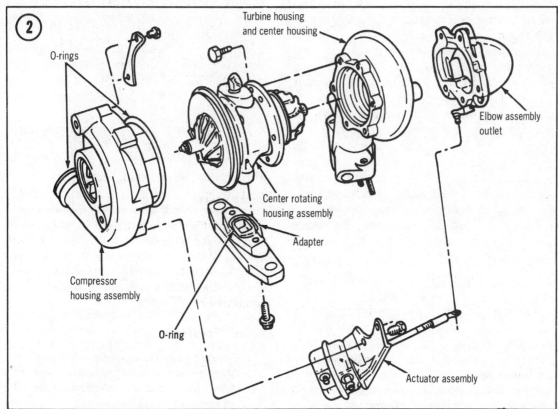

O-rings

Turbine housing
and center housing

Elbow assembly
outlet

Center rotating
housing assembly

Adapter

Compressor
housing assembly

O-ring

Actuator assembly

12

Outlet Elbow with Wastegate

The outlet elbow contains the wastegate assembly, or bypass valve, which in operation allows a portion of the exhaust gas to bypass the turning wheel so boost pressure can be controlled.

Turbine

The turbine is a centripetal, radial inflow type. It is comprised of a cast turbine wheel, wheel shroud, and specially-designed housing which directs the exhaust gas through the turbine.

Actuator

The actuator is a spring-loaded diaphragm device that senses the outlet pressure of the compressor.

TURBOCHARGER SERVICE

The efficiency of your turbocharger depends in great part on the efficiency of your engine lubricating system. As with other engine systems, the turbocharger is lubricated by engine lubricating oil. Thus, the engine oil and oil filter must be changed every 3,000 miles. See **Figure 3** and **Figure 4**.

By changing both the engine oil and oil filter every 3,000 miles, along with following service procedures mentioned in Chapter Three, the turbocharger unit should operate efficiently. However, if turbocharger service is necessary, we will stress that service and repair is best left to your dealership which possesses the necessary special tools and experience to service your unit. However, should the need arise that makes it necessary for you to perform basic component replacement, the following procedures are well within the ability of the experienced enthusiast-mechanic.

> *NOTE*
> *It is important not to accelerate the turbocharged engine to top rpm immediately after starting because of possible damage to the engine and turbocharger unit due to inadequate lubrication. In the same respect, immediately shutting off the engine which has been operating at top rpm for an*

extended period of time can also damage the engine and turbocharger unit.

Service Precautions

> *WARNING*
> *When working in the engine compartment, keep hands and other objects clear of the radiator fan blades. The electric cooling fan on the 2300 cc turbocharger engine can start to operate at any time by an increase in underhood temperature, even though the ignition switch may be turned off. Thus, it is necessary to disconnect the electric fan motor before working under the hood.*

1. Before attempting any turbocharger repair, clean the area around the turbocharger with a non-caustic cleaning solution. Cover engine openings with clean shop rags to prevent entry of foreign material.
2. When removing the turbocharger assembly, take precautions not to bend, nick, or damage the compressor or turbine wheel blades. Damage to either part can result in rotating assembly imbalance, and failure of the center housing, compressor and/or turbine housings. See **Figure 2**.
3. Before disconnecting the center housing from the compressor or turbine housing, scribe the components in order of disassemby to assure each may be reinstalled in the same relative position.
4. If silicone sealer or a similar sealer is found at any point during disassembly, the area should be examined, cleaned and sealed with an equivalent sealer during reassembly.
5. If any individual parts of the turbocharger are replaced with new parts, the wastegate actuator must be recalibrated by a dealer or turbocharger specialist.

> *NOTE*
> *At any time the engine is damaged due to component failure (main bearing, connecting rod bearing, camshaft bearing, piston breakage, etc.) the entire engine assembly should be thoroughly cleaned, and the oil and oil filter changed as a part of the repair procedure. In addition, the turbocharger should be flushed with clean engine oil to reduce contamination.*

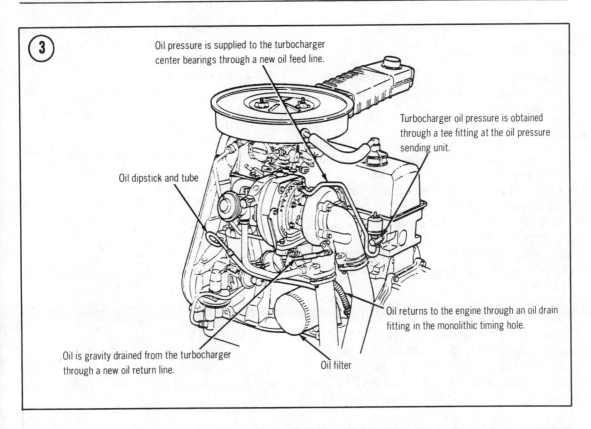

3

Oil pressure is supplied to the turbocharger center bearings through a new oil feed line.

Turbocharger oil pressure is obtained through a tee fitting at the oil pressure sending unit.

Oil dipstick and tube

Oil returns to the engine through an oil drain fitting in the monolithic timing hole.

Oil is gravity drained from the turbocharger through a new oil return line.

Oil filter

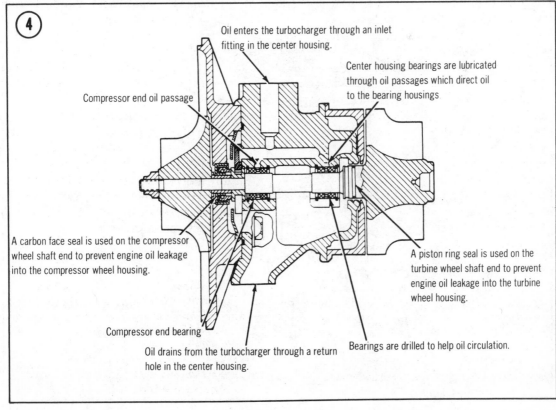

4

Oil enters the turbocharger through an inlet fitting in the center housing.

Center housing bearings are lubricated through oil passages which direct oil to the bearing housings.

Compressor end oil passage

A carbon face seal is used on the compressor wheel shaft end to prevent engine oil leakage into the compressor wheel housing.

A piston ring seal is used on the turbine wheel shaft end to prevent engine oil leakage into the turbine wheel housing.

Compressor end bearing

Oil drains from the turbocharger through a return hole in the center housing.

Bearings are drilled to help oil circulation.

12

TURBOCHARGER

Removal/Installation

1. Raise the vehicle on a hoist or jackstands.

2. From beneath the vehicle, remove the 4 exhaust outlet nuts and crossover pipes leading to the turbocharger.

3. From the right side of the intake manifold, remove the crossover pipe retaining nuts, and lower the crossover pipe.

4. Remove the retaining exhaust outlet pipe to catalyst inlet and outlet pipe.

5. Remove the turbocharger rear mounting brace bolts (**Figure 5**).

6. Lower vehicle from hoist or jackstands and remove the air cleaner and duct assembly. See **Figure 6**.

7. Disconnect the oil supply line from the oil line fitting attached to the turbo center housing. Plug both the oil line and fitting to prevent entry of foreign material. See **Figure 7**.

8. Remove 2 bolts securing the accelerator cable bracket to the intake manifold, and remove accelerator cable bracket (**Figure 8**).

9. Remove 2 nuts securing the turbo heat shield to the turbo center housing and the turbine housing. Remove the heat shield (**Figure 8**).

10. Disconnect the turbocharger vacuum line at the intake manifold and the wastegate actuator diaphragm hoses.

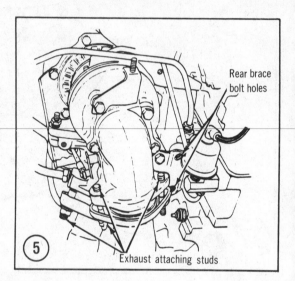

Rear brace bolt holes

Exhaust attaching studs

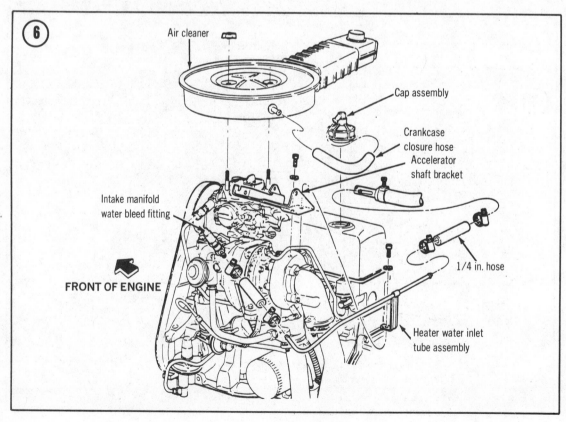

Air cleaner

Cap assembly

Crankcase closure hose
Accelerator shaft bracket

Intake manifold water bleed fitting

1/4 in. hose

FRONT OF ENGINE

Heater water inlet tube assembly

11. Remove bolt securing the oil dipstick tube to make room for turbocharger removal (**Figure 9**).

12. Disconnect and plug the EGR tube from the turbine housing (**Figure 7**).

13. Remove 4 nuts securing the turbocharger housing to the intake manifold and to the rear mounting turbocharger brace (**Figure 10**).

14. Remove all remaining attached fasteners and hoses leading to the turbocharger assembly.

15. Referring to **Figure 5**, remove 2 bolts securing the turbocharger rear brace and remove the turbocharger assembly from the engine.

16. Installation is the reverse of the removal procedure, plus the following. Replace O-rings installed at the compressor inlet to the intake manifold; compressor outlet to intake manifold; and the oil drain adapter to the intake manifold. See **Figure 11** and **Figure 12** for O-ring locations. Tighten all nuts and bolts to specifications.

NOTE
To ease installation of O-rings, apply a small amount of grease to the compressor assembly.

WASTEGATE ACTUATOR ASSEMBLY

Actuator (Original Equipment) Removal/Installation

1. Remove the heat shield (**Figure 8**) and clip, attaching the actuator rod to the wastegate arm (**Figure 7**).

2. Detach and remove all vacuum lines leading to the actuator assembly. Plug all detached lines to prevent entry of foreign material.

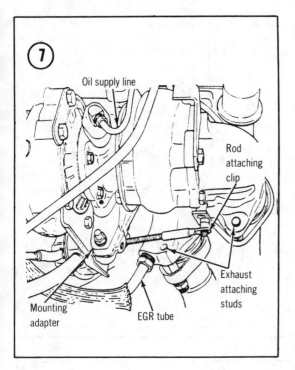

Oil supply line

Rod attaching clip

Exhaust attaching studs

Mounting adapter

EGR tube

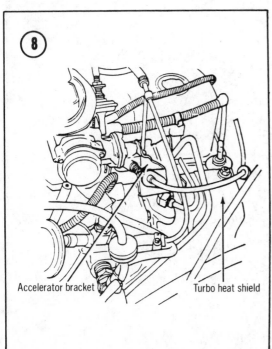

Accelerator bracket

Turbo heat shield

O-rings

12

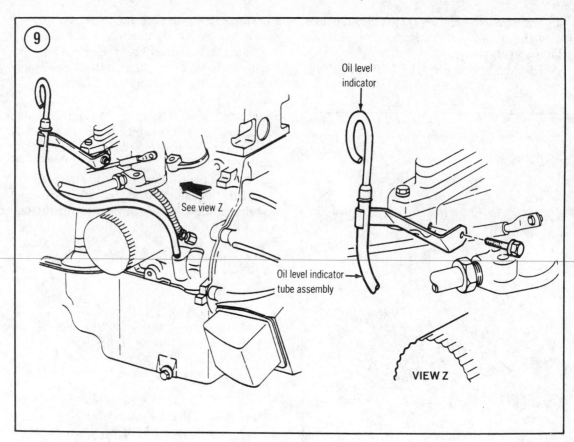

⑨ See view Z

Oil level indicator

Oil level indicator tube assembly

VIEW Z

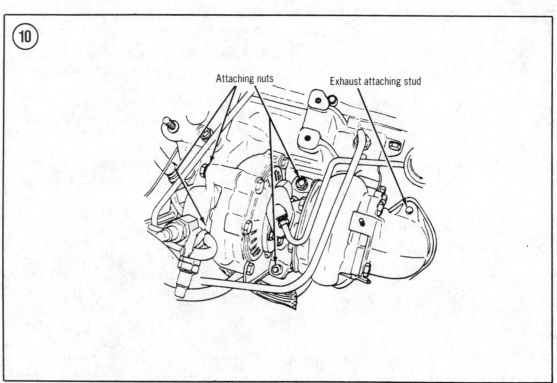

⑩ Attaching nuts   Exhaust attaching stud

3. Remove 2 bolts attaching actuator diaphragm assembly to the compressor housing (**Figure 2**).

4. Installation is the reverse of these steps. Tighten all of the attaching bolts to specifications.

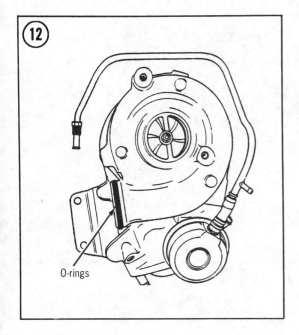

O-rings

Actuator Service Replacement (New)

1. Remove the actuator assembly as previously described.

2. Install 2 bolts securing the actuator diaphragm assembly to the compressor housing.

3. Unscrew the actuator rod until it justs fits over the pin on the wastegate arm. (Wastegate arm is positioned full forward.)

4. **Insert the clip securing the actuator rod to the wastegate arm and apply Loctite to the threads on the rod.**

5. Tighten all of the attaching bolts to specifications.

COMPRESSOR ASSEMBLY

Removal/Installation

Refer to **Figure 13** for the following procedure.

1. Remove the turbocharger assembly from the engine as previously described and place on workbench.

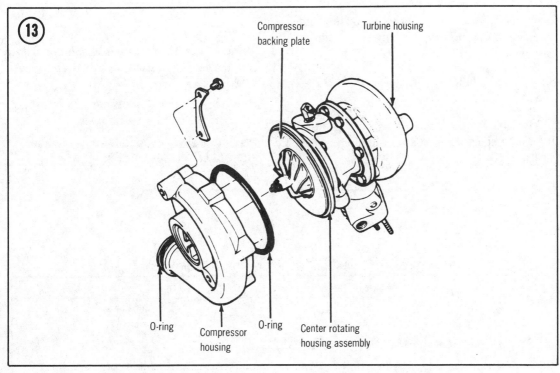

Compressor backing plate

Turbine housing

O-ring

Compressor housing

O-ring

Center rotating housing assembly

12

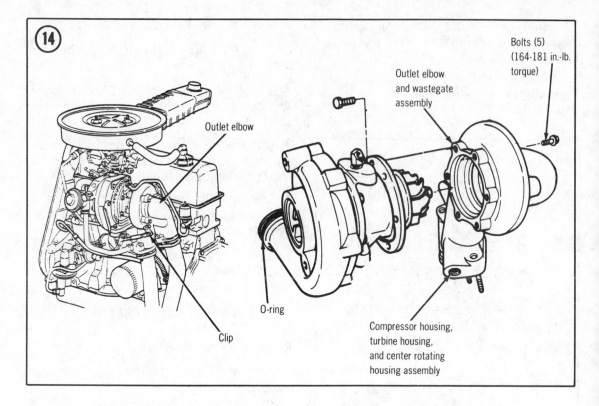

2. Remove the wastegate actuator rod retaining clip and remove rod from the wastegate arm (**Figure 7**).

3. Scribe a line across compressor housing and center rotating housing assembly to aid in reassembly.

4. Remove 6 bolts securing the compressor housing to the backing plate.

5. Assemble by reversing Steps 1-4. Tighten all bolts to specifications after aligning match marks.

TURBINE HOUSING

Removal/Installation

Refer to **Figure 14** for the following procedure.

1. Remove the turbocharger assembly from the engine as previously described and place on workbench.

2. Remove 5 bolts securing the turbine assembly to the compressor housing.

3. Assemble by reversing Steps 1 and 2. Tighten all bolts to specifications.

Table 1   TURBOCHARGER TIGHTENING TORQUES

Item	Torque
Compressor housing bolts	145-165 in.-lb.
Turbine housing bolts	164-181 in.-lb.
Outlet elbow and wastegate assembly bolts	164-181 in.-lb.

SUPPLEMENT

1981 AND LATER SERVICE INFORMATION

> The following supplement provides additional information for servicing 1981 and later Ford Mustangs and Mercury Capris.
>
> The chapter headings in this supplement correspond to those in the main portion of this manual. If a procedure is not included in this supplement, then there are no changes affecting 1981 and later models.
>
> If your vehicle is covered by this supplement, carefully read the supplement and then read the appropriate chapter in the basic book before beginning any work.

CHAPTER THREE

LUBRICATION, MAINTENANCE AND TUNE-UP

SCHEDULED MAINTENANCE

Table 1 provides a summary of periodic maintenance required for 1981 models. **Table 2** provides a summary of periodic maintenance for 1982-on models.

> *NOTE*
> *Use Schedule A for Canadian vehicles and Schedule B for all vehicles sold in the United States.*

Automatic Transmission Fluid

Ford Motor Co. changed its fluid recommendation for the C3 automatic transmission to DEXRON II, beginning with 1982 model year. The C5 automatic transmission requires the use of Type H fluid.

Crankcase Emission Filter (2300 cc)

Starting with 1981 models, the crankcase emission filter is the oil filler cap. At the intervals specified in **Table 1** or **Table 2**, remove the closure hose at the oil filler cap. Install a new cap and reconnect the closure hose at the cap.

AUTOMATIC TRANSMISSION

Procedures for changing the fluid in automatic transmissions remains the same as for 1980 and earlier models. The fluid capacity has changed. See **Table 3**.

Power Steering Fluid Leaks

A new center vent power steering pump dipstick/cap assembly (part No. E6DZ-3A006-A) with additional baffling is available to combat the problem of power steering fluid leakage caused by fluid spilling past the dipstick cap assembly on 1983-1985 models. When used with 302 cid HO and 2.3L EFI turbo engines, an additional rubber baffle (part No. E5SZ-3E550-A) should also be installed.

TUNE-UP

Tune-up procedures remain the same as for 1980 and earlier models. Refer to the *Tune-up* section in Chapter Three of the basic book. Because of emission requirements, vehicles are

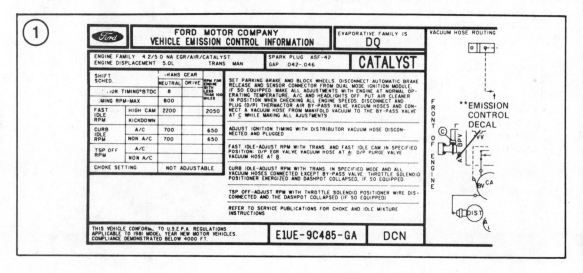

equipped with a varying range of emission control systems and calibrations which determine the ignition timing and carburetor adjustments. When performing engine tune-ups, refer to your car's Vehicle Emission Control Information (VECI) label in the engine compartment for tune-up specifications and adjustment procedures. See **Figure 1** for a typical label.

Cylinder Head Bolts (230 V6)

The 230 cid V6 uses stretch-type cylinder head bolts. Once these bolts have been torqued to specification, they cannot be reused. Torquing the bolts stretches them and they cannot hold the specified torque if reused.

> *NOTE*
> *Power or air-driven tools should **not** be used for removing or installing cylinder head bolts.*

Follow the pattern shown in Figure 2 and tighten the cylinder head bolts as follows:

a. First stage—47 ft.-lb. (65 N•m).
b. Second stage—55 ft.-lb. (75 N•m).
c. Third stage—63 ft.-lb. (85 N•m).
d. Fourth stage—74 ft.-lb. (101 N•m).
e. Final torque—Back off all bolts 2-3 turns and repeat the 4-stage sequence.

Dual Oil Sump

A dual sump oil pan is used with 1984 and later 302 cid V8 engines. One drain plug is located at the front of the oil pan; the other is found on the left side of the pan. Be sure to remove both plugs when changing the crankcase oil. If you do not, the pan will not drain completely and filling the crankcase with the specified amount of oil will create an excessively high oil level which can result in engine damage.

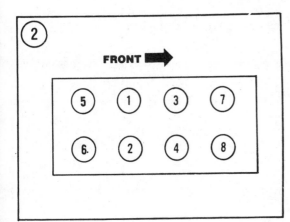

TABLE 1   SCHEDULED MAINTENANCE—1981

Every 5,000 miles or 5 months, whichever comes first **A Schedule** • Have dealer check idle speed and adjust if required • Adjust automatic transmission bands[1]

Every 10,000 miles or 10 months, whichever comes first
A Schedule
  • Change engine oil and filter[1,2]
  • Check clutch pedal free play
B Schedule
  • Change engine oil and filter[1,2]
  • Check drive belt condition and tension. Adjust and/or replace belt as required
  • Have dealer check idle speed
  • Check clutch pedal free play

Every 15,000 miles or 15 months, whichever comes first
A Schedule
  • Check and lubricate exhaust heat control valve
  • Replace spark plugs on 2300 cc turbocharged engines
 	
(continued)

13

TABLE 1   SCHEDULED MAINTENANCE—1981 (continued)

Every 20,000 miles or 20 months, whichever comes first
A Schedule
- Replace spark plugs[1,3]
- Check drive belt condition and tension; adjust and/or replace belt as required
- Check choke operation
- Have dealer check thermactor delay valve
- Replace PCV valve[3]
- Have dealer check idle mixture after installing new PCV valve
- Replace automatic transmission oil if vehicle operated under severe service[1]

Every 30,000 miles or 30 months, whichever comes first
A Schedule
- Replace carburetor air cleaner element[4]
- Check cooling system
- Replace engine coolant
- Inspect exhaust system heat shields[5]
- Lubricate front suspension and steering linkage
- Check brake master cylinder fluid

B Schedule
- Replace carburetor air cleaner element[4]
- Replace crankcase emission filter (6-cylinder)
- Check choke operation
- Check cooling system
- Replace engine coolant
- Inspect exhaust system heat shields[5]
- Lubricate front suspension and steering linkage
- Check brake master cylinder fluid

Every 50,000 miles or 50 months, whichever comes first
B Schedule
- Replace crankcase emission filter (4-cylinder)

A and B Schedules
Annually regardless of mileage
- Check coolant condition and protection[6]

NOTES
1. Severe service operation: When operating the vehicle under any of the following conditions, change engine oil every 3 months or 3,000 miles (4,800 km), replace the filter at alternate oil changes, and clean and regap the spark plugs every 6,000 miles.
   a. Extended periods of idling or low-speed operation.
   b. Towing trailers over 1,000 pounds gross trailer weight for long distances.
   c. Operation when outside temperatures remain below 10° F (-12° C) for 60 days or more and most trips are less than 10 miles (16 km).
   d. Operation in severe dust conditions.
2. All 2300 cc turbocharged engines require an oil and oil filter change every 3,000 miles (4,800 km).
3. Consult the Vehicle Emission Control Information Decal for the appropriate specifications.
4. Perform more often if the vehicle is operated in severe dust conditions.
5. Remove shield attachment and clean off all accumulated debris. Inspect shield condition. Perform every 10,000 miles (16,000 km) if the vehicle is operated in severe conditions over unpaved roads or off-road.
6. If coolant is dirty or rusty, drain, clean and refill the system with the prescribed solution of coolant and water. Use only a permanent type antifreeze.

Table 2 SCHEDULED MAINTENANCE (1982-ON)

Every 7,500 Miles or 12 Months
A Schedule
- Change engine oil[1,2]
- Replace oil filter[1,2]
- Check drive belt tension and condition
  (2300 cc only)
- Have dealer check idle speed

B Schedule
- Change engine oil[1,2]
- Replace oil filter[1,2]
- Check drive belt tension and condition
  (except 255 cid V8 engine)
- Have dealer check idle speed
- Check and lubricate manifold heat control valve
  (255/302 cid V8 with model 2150 carburetor only)
- Drain and refill Traction-Lok rear axle
  (severe service only)

Every 12 Months
A and B Schedules
- Check coolant protection and condition

Every 18,000 Miles
A Schedule
- Replace spark plugs
  (Canadian turbocharged 2300 cc engine only)

Every 22,500 Miles
A Schedule
- Replace spark plugs[1]
- Check drive belt tension
  (302 cid V8 engine only)
- Check and clean choke linkage

Every 30,000 Miles
A Schedule
- Replace air cleaner filter

B Schedule
- Replace spark plugs[1]
- Have dealer check idle speed
- Replace air cleaner filter
- Replace crankcase emission filter
  (200 cid engine only)
- Check and clean choke linkage
- Check and lubricate manifold heat control valve
  (255/302 cid V8 with model 2150 carburetor only)

A and B Schedules
- Check exhaust heat shields
- Lubricate steering linkage
- Lubricate front suspension
- Check master cylinder fluid level
- Check brake hose and lining condition
- Check front wheel bearings

(continued)

13

Table 2 SCHEDULED MAINTENANCE (1982-ON) (continued)

Every 42,500 Miles or 36 Months
A Schedule
- Drain and refill engine coolant
  (Canadian turbocharged 2300 cc engine only)
- Check cooling system hoses and clamps
  (Canadian turbocharged 2300 cc engine only)

Every 45,000 Miles
B Schedule
- Check and lubricate manifold heat control valve
  (255/302 cid V8 with model 2150 carburetor only)

Every 52,500 Miles
A and B Schedules
- Drain and refill engine coolant
- Check cooling system hoses and clamps
- Replace crankcase emission filter
  (all except 200 cid and Canadian turbocharged
  2300 cc engines)

Every 54,000 Miles
A Schedule
- Replace crankcase emission filter
  (Canadian turbocharged 2300 cc engine only)

1. Severe service operation: If the vehicle is operated under any of the following conditions, change engine oil and oil filter at 3,000 mile or 3 month intervals. Check and regap spark plugs every 6,000 miles. Change Traction-Lok rear axle fluid every 7,500 miles. Change automatic transmission fluid and filter every 22,500 miles.
   a. Extended idle or low-speed operation (short trips, stop-and-go driving)
   b. Trailer towing
   c. Operation at temperatures below 10° F for 60 days or more with most trips under 10 miles
   d. Sustained high-speed driving in hot weather
   e. Very dusty conditions
2. Canadian turbocharged 2300 cc engine: Change oil and filter every 6,000 miles for normal service; every 3,000 miles for severe service.

Table 3 AUTOMATIC TRANSMISSION FLUID

Transmission/Engine	Fluid Type	Capacity*
1981 C-4 transmission		
2300 cc	DEXRON II	7.25 qt.
200 cid	DEXRON II	7.7 qt.
255 cid	DEXRON II	10.0 qt.
1982-on C-3 transmission		
2300 cc/200 cid	DEXRON II	8.0 qt.
1982-on C-5 transmission		
200/230/255 cid	Type H	11.0 qt.

* Approximate fluid capacity. Final fluid capacity to be determined by dipstick reading.

CHAPTER FOUR

ENGINE

Engine service procedures are the same as for earlier models. However, some service and torque specifications have changed for the 255/302 cid engines. These are listed in **Table 4** and **Table 5**.

The 302 cid HO (high output) V8 engine is optional in 1983 and later models. The HO version differs from the standard 302 cid engine primarily in the use of the 351 cid marine camshaft with higher lift, longer duration and increased valve overlap. Use of this camshaft changes the firing order from 1-5-4-2-6-3-7-8 to 1-3-7-2-6-5-4-8. Specifications for the 302 HO engine that differ from the standard 302 cid are provided in **Table 6**.

The 2300 cc 4-cylinder engine incorporates integral dampers on intake and exhaust valves on 1983 applications. See **Figure 3**.

230 CID V6

The 230 cid V6 replaces the 200 cid inline 6-cylinder in 1983 models. This engine is similar to the V8 engines in construction and components. It can be serviced using the procedures provided for V8 models with the exceptions noted below. Specifications and tightening torques for the 230 cid V6 are provided in **Table 7** and **Table 8**. See **Figure 4** and **Figure 5** for internal and external engine construction. See **Figure 6** for ignition wire routing.

Cylinder Head

The 230 cid V6 engine uses aluminum cylinder heads. The head used on 1984 and later models has a shrouded intake valve to increase swirling of the air-fuel mixture as it enters the cylinder. This cylinder head is not interchangeable with that used on 1983 models.

The use of aluminum cylinder heads requires the use of a special coolant containing a corrosion inhibitor to avoid engine and radiator damage. Prestone II is one of the recommended coolants which meets Ford specification ESE-M97B43-A.

Spark plugs must not be removed when the head is hot or the plug hole threads in the cylinder head may be stripped. If plug hole threads are damaged or stripped, they can be repaired by a dealer using a Tapersert kit.

The procedure involves cutting new threads in the spark plug hole. After the hole is rethreaded, a sleeve with inside and outside threads is installed in the hole. The outside of

13

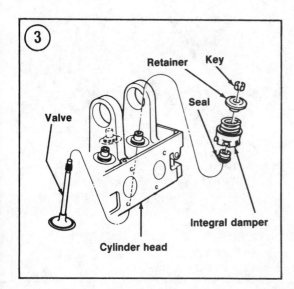

③ Retainer Key
Seal
Valve
Integral damper
Cylinder head

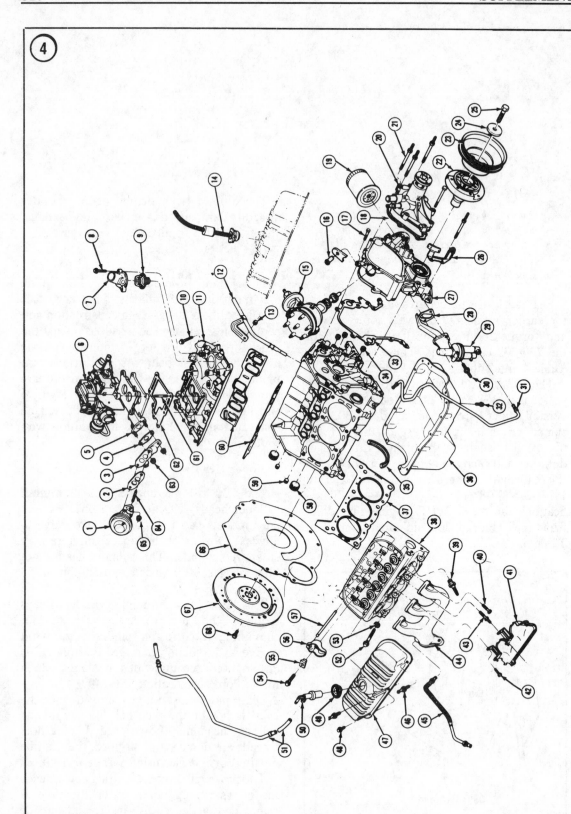

230 CID V6 ENGINE
EXTERNAL CONSTRUCTION

1. EGR valve
2. Valve gasket
3. EGR valve adapter
4. Adapter gasket
5. Carburetor spacer
6. Carburetor
7. Thermostat housing
8. Housing attaching bolt (3)
9. Thermostat
10. Manifold attaching bolt (14)
11. Intake manifold
12. Oil level indicator tube
13. Tube attaching nut (1)
14. Tube and filter assembly oil fill cap
15. Ignition distributor
16. Distributor hold-down clamp and bolt
17. Cover attaching bolt (7)
18. Pump gasket (water)
19. Oil filter
20. Water pump
21. Water pump attaching bolts (8)
22. Crankshaft damper
23. Crankshaft pulley
24. Damper bolt washer
25. Damper attaching bolt
26. Ignition timing indicator
27. Front cover
28. Pump gasket
29. Fuel pump
30. Pump attaching stud/bolt (2)
31. Fuel line-pump to carburetor
32. Pan attaching bolt (14)
33. Cover gasket
34. Oil gallery plug

35. Oil pan rear seal
36. Oil pan
37. Cylinder head gasket
38. Cylinder head
39. Spark plug
40. Manifold attaching bolts (6 each side)
41. Hot air intake shroud
42. Shroud and manifold attaching stud bolt
43. Manifold and shroud attaching bolt with stud
44. Exhaust manifold
45. EGR tube
46. Cover attaching bolt with stud (2 each side)
47. Valve cover
48. Cover attaching bolt (3 each side)
49. Valve grommet
50. PCV valve
51. PCV valve hose and tube
52. Cylinder head attaching bolt (8 each side)
53. Cylinder head bolt washer
54. Fulcrum attaching bolt (12 each side)
55. Rocker arm fulcrum
56. Rocker arm
57. Pushrod
58. Water jacket plug
59. Oil gallery plug
60. Manifold gasket
61. Carburetor attaching stud (4)
62. Carburetor gasket
63. Adapter attaching nut (2)
64. Valve attaching stud (2)
65. Valve attaching nut (2)
66. Rear cover plate
67. Drive plate
68. Plate attaching bolt (5)

13

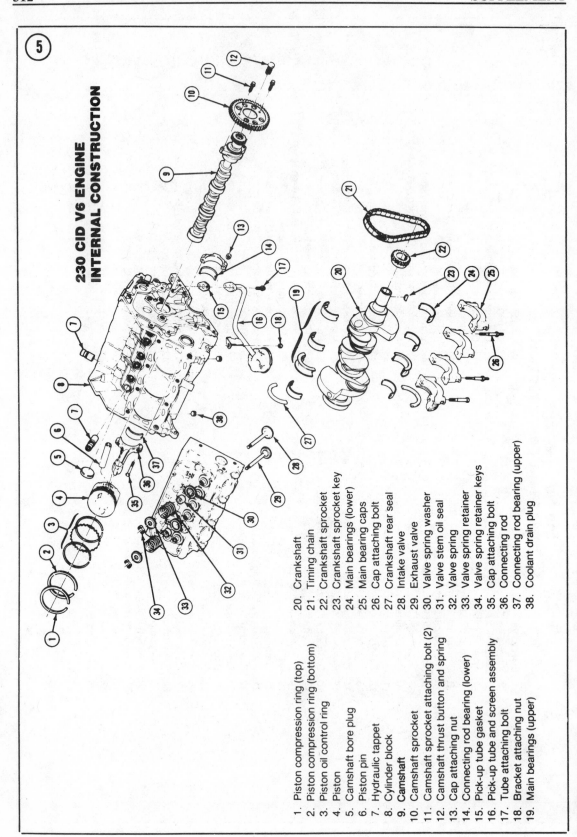

230 CID V6 ENGINE
INTERNAL CONSTRUCTION

1. Piston compression ring (top)
2. Piston compression ring (bottom)
3. Piston oil control ring
4. Piston
5. Camshaft bore plug
6. Piston pin
7. Hydraulic tappet
8. Cylinder block
9. Camshaft
10. Camshaft sprocket
11. Camshaft sprocket attaching bolt (2)
12. Camshaft thrust button and spring
13. Cap attaching nut
14. Connecting rod bearing (lower)
15. Pick-up tube gasket
16. Pick-up tube and screen assembly
17. Tube attaching bolt
18. Bracket attaching nut
19. Main bearings (upper)
20. Crankshaft
21. Timing chain
22. Crankshaft sprocket
23. Crankshaft sprocket key
24. Main bearings (lower)
25. Main bearing caps
26. Cap attaching bolt
27. Crankshaft rear seal
28. Intake valve
29. Exhaust valve
30. Valve spring washer
31. Valve stem oil seal
32. Valve spring
33. Valve spring retainer
34. Valve spring retainer keys
35. Cap attaching bolt
36. Connecting rod
37. Connecting rod bearing (upper)
38. Coolant drain plug

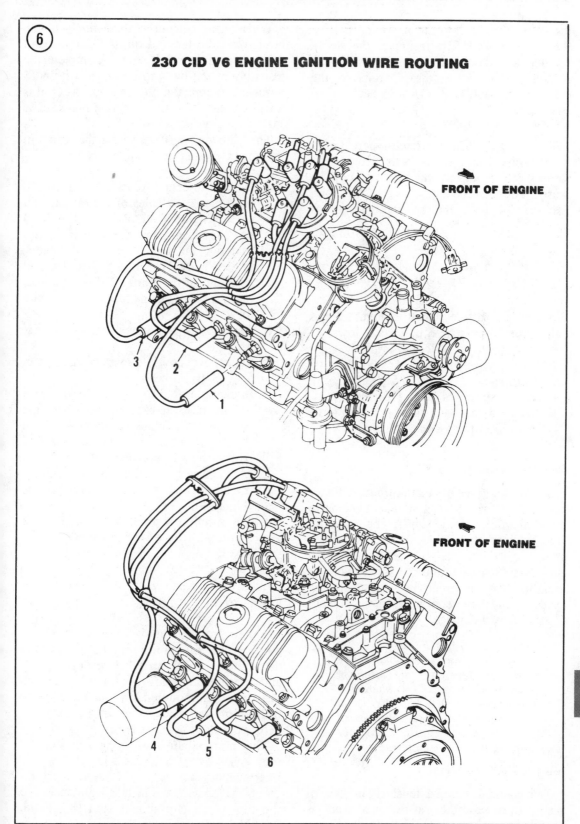

230 CID V6 ENGINE IGNITION WIRE ROUTING

FRONT OF ENGINE

FRONT OF ENGINE

13

the sleeve threads into the reworked hole in the cylinder head. The inside of the sleeve provides new threads to accept the spark plug. If this service is necessary, remove the cylinder head and take it to a dealer.

Cylinder Head Torque

The 230 cid V6 uses stretch-type cylinder head bolts. Once these bolts have been torqued to specification, they cannot be reused. Torquing the bolts stretches them and they cannot hold the specified torque if reused.

NOTE
*Power or air-driven tools should **not** be used for removing or installing cylinder head bolts.*

Follow the pattern shown in **Figure 2** and tighten the cylinder head bolts as follows:
  a. First stage—47 ft.-lb. (65 N•m).
  b. Second stage—55 ft.-lb. (75 N•m).
  c. Third stage—63 ft.-lb. (85 N•m).
  d. Fourth stage—74 ft.-lb. (101 N•m).
  e. Final torque—Back off all bolts 2-3 turns and repeat the 4-stage sequence.

Aluminum Components

In addition to the use of aluminum cylinder heads, the 230 cid V6 engine makes extensive use of aluminum components. The accessory brackets, intake manifold, front cover, water pump, pistons and oil pump are all aluminum. Since aluminum is softer than cast iron, use care in removing and installing fasteners in these components to prevent possible thread damage.

NOTE
*Power or air-driven tools should **not** be used for removing or installing fasteners which thread into aluminum components. All such fasteners should be removed and installed with hand tools to avoid cross-threading or stripping the aluminum threads.*

Silicone Rubber Sealant

This material is used extensively in place of gaskets during assembly at the factory and is specified for repair procedures.

When using silicone sealant, apply in the bead size indicated and run the bead around the *inside* of any bolt holes. Complete the assembly of the parts to be joined within 15 minutes of applying the sealant. After this time, the sealant begins to set and may lose its sealing qualities as a result.

The following surfaces should be sealed in this manner using the bead size indicated.

  a. Oil pan-to-engine block: Run a 1/8 in. bead along the sides of the oil pan rail on the engine block. Run a 1/4 in. bead on the front cover rail with extra material on the front cover-to-block joint (**Figure 7**). Run a 1/8 in. bead at each end of the rear seal where the rear main cap and engine block meet (**Figure 8**).
  b. Thermostat housing: Run a 1/16 in. bead.
  c. Rocker arm cover-to-cylinder head: Run a 1/3-3/16 in. bead.
  d. Intake manifold-to-engine block: Run a 1/8 in. bead at each corner where the head joins the block and at each end of the block where the intake manifold seats against it. Force an extra bead into each corner junction of the intake manifold and cylinder head gaskets (**Figure 9**).
  e. Air injection secondary cover-to-intake manifold: Run a 1/16 in. bead.

Front Cover

A new front cover design houses the oil pump. The oil pump is driven by the distributor through an oil pump drive shaft and intermediate shaft (**Figure 10**). Since the distributor is mounted on the front cover instead of the block, it must be removed before the front cover is removed.

The intermediate shaft is held in place in the cover by a retaining clip. When the intermediate shaft is fully engaged in the oil pump drive shaft, the installed dimension to the top of the clip should be 1.18-1.29 in. (30-33 mm). See **Figure 11**.

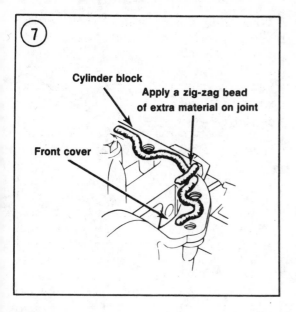

7

Cylinder block

Apply a zig-zag bead
of extra material on joint

Front cover

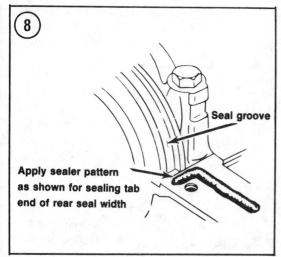

8

Seal groove

Apply sealer pattern
as shown for sealing tab
end of rear seal width

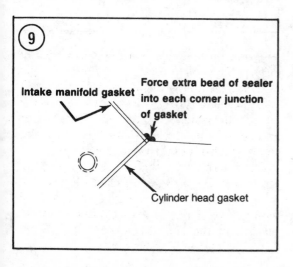

9

Intake manifold gasket

Force extra bead of sealer
into each corner junction
of gasket

Cylinder head gasket

A camshaft spring and button is used to maintain camshaft end play (**Figure 12**). This assembly is held in place by the front cover. Whenever the front cover is removed, the face of the camshaft button should be lubricated with Lubriplate or equivalent before reinstalling the cover.

Pistons and Connecting Rods

The shrouded intake valves used in 1984 and later 230 V6 engines reduce the size of the combustion chamber. To compensate for the reduced volume and maintain the compression ratio, a deeper dish is used on 1984 and later pistons. In addition, a higher piston dome increases quench. These pistons are not interchangeable with those used in 1983 models.

Aluminum pistons are connected to forged steel connecting rods in all models. Piston dome and rod button identification should be on the same side and facing the front of the engine when installed. Assemble the rod and cap with the cylinder bore number on the outside (when installed in the cylinder bore).

Piston and rod assemblies should be installed in the block in the following order: No. 1 and No. 5, No. 2 and No. 6, No. 3 and No. 4. Torque the rod nuts to 31-36 ft.-lb. (41-49 N•m). Back off the nuts 2-3 turns and retorque to 31-36 ft.-lb. (41-49 N•m).

Serpentine Drive Belt

A single serpentine drive belt is routed around all accessory drive pulleys and is driven by the crankshaft pulley (**Figure 13**). A spring-loaded idler pulley holds the belt tight against the accessory pulleys. Drive belt tension is adjusted by a vertical screw in the idler adjustment bracket located above the idler pulley.

Thermostat

The thermostat housing contains a locking recess to prevent incorrect thermostat

13

installation. The thermostat has locking tabs which engage this recess. To remove the thermostat, rotate it counterclockwise until the tabs disengage the housing recess. Thermostat installation requires a clockwise turn to engage the tabs in the recess.

REAR MAIN OIL SEAL

A one-piece, lip-type rear oil seal is used on 1984 and later 230 cid V6 and 302 cid V8 engines. The rear of the engine block and crankshaft rear main bearing cap are modified to accept the new seal. **Figure 14** shows the new seal and installation tools. The seal can be replaced with the engine in the vehicle by removing the oil pan. See Chapter Four of the main book for this procedure.

VALVE COVER GASKET

A "high-swell" cork gasket is used instead of RTV sealant on 1984 and later 260 cid V6 and 302 cid V8 engine rocker covers. See **Figure 15**. The rocker cover has been revised with a wider cover flange and raised attaching screw bosses for better gasket retention.

EXHAUST VALVES (302 CID V8)

Wear caps are not used on 1984 and later 302 cid V8 engine exhaust valve stems.

ROLLER TAPPET VALVE TRAIN

A roller tappet valve train (**Figure 16**) is used in 1985 302 cid HO V8 engines fitted with a manual transmission and all 1986 302 cid HO V8 engines.

The tappets have a small hardened roller at one end (**Figure 17**), making them longer than standard hydraulic tappets. Shorter pushrods are used with the tappets to maintain valve train geometry. The pushrods can be identified by a copper plating on the hardened ball end and a small bracket which indicates the "UP" position.

To maintain the tappet roller in alignment with the camshaft lobes, a tappet guide plate

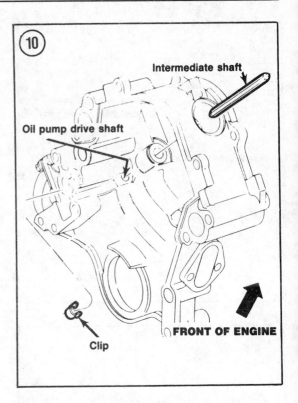

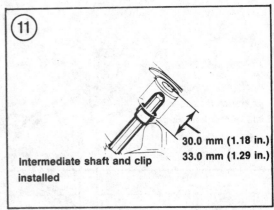

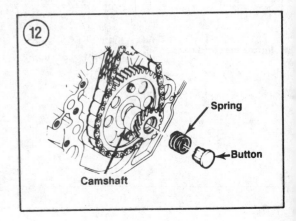

or tie-bar is used to retain alternate pairs of tappets (**Figure 18**). Each guide plate has a small round boss in the center of the plate which must face upwards when installed. The guide plate is also marked with the word "UP" to indicate proper positioning. A guide plate retainer of spring steel is installed in the valley cover area to keep the guide plates in position.

The camshaft is manufactured of billet steel and has specially ground and hardened lobes to withstand the loads of the roller tappets. The distributor drive gear is machined from hardened steel to match the new camshaft.

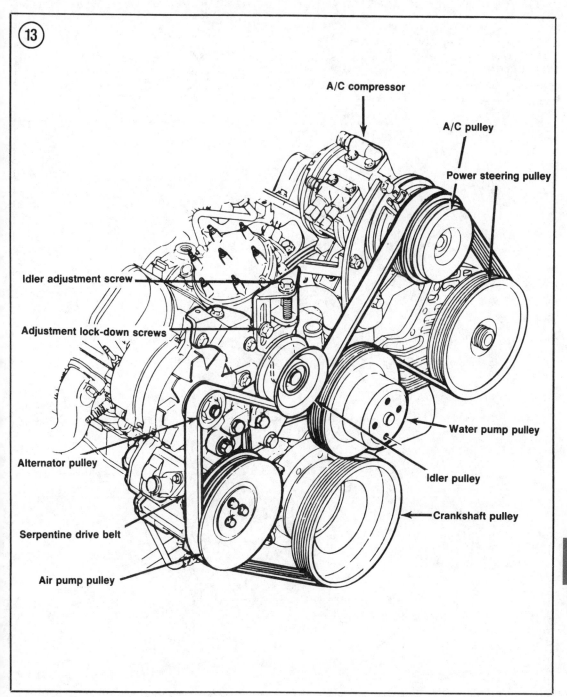

(13)

A/C compressor

A/C pulley

Power steering pulley

Idler adjustment screw

Adjustment lock-down screws

Alternator pulley

Water pump pulley

Idler pulley

Crankshaft pulley

Serpentine drive belt

Air pump pulley

13

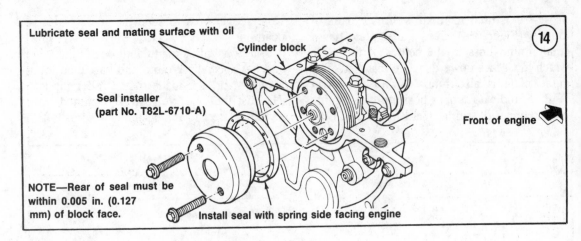

Lubricate seal and mating surface with oil

Cylinder block

⑭

Seal installer
(part No. T82L-6710-A)

Front of engine

NOTE—Rear of seal must be
within 0.005 in. (0.127
mm) of block face.

Install seal with spring side facing engine

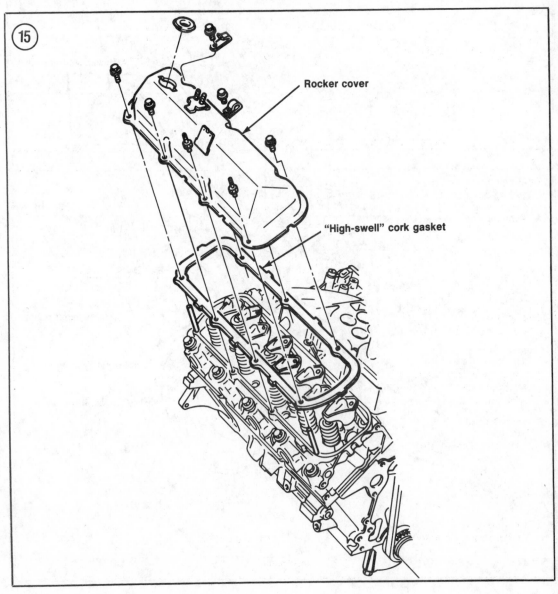

⑮

Rocker cover

"High-swell" cork gasket

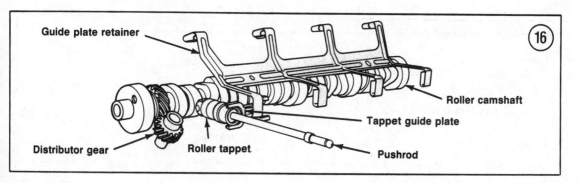

- Guide plate retainer
- Roller camshaft
- Tappet guide plate
- Pushrod
- Distributor gear
- Roller tappet

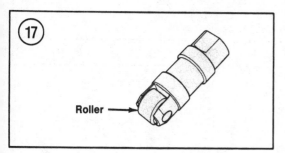

- Roller

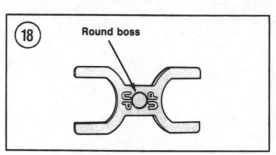

- Round boss

Table 4   ENGINE SPECIFICATIONS, 255/302 CID ENGINES

255 cid	
Valve Springs	
Pressure at length	
Intake	74-82 lb. @ 1.78 in.
	196-214 lb. @ 1.36 in.
Exhaust	71-79 lb. @ 1.60 in.
	195-215 lb. @ 115 in.
Valves	
Head diameter	
Exhaust	1.453-1.468 in.
Cylinder Block	
Bore diameter	3.6800-3.6845 in.
Crankshaft	
Main bearing journal taper	
(maximum)	0.0004 in. per in.
Connecting rod journal diameter	2.1228-2.1236 in.
Main Bearings	
Clearance to crankshaft	
Standard	
No. 1	0.0004-0.0025 in.
Permissible	
No. 1	0.0001-0.0030 in.
Connecting Rods	
Piston pin bore diameter	0.9096-0.9112 in.
(continued)	

13

Table 4   ENGINE SPECIFICATIONS, 255/302 CID ENGINES (continued)

Pistons	
Diameter, standard	
Coded yellow	3.6812-3.6818 in.
Clearance to bore	0.0014-0.0024 in.
Piston Pins	
Clearance to piston	0.0003-0.0005 in.

302 cid	
Valve Springs	
Pressure at length	
Intake	74-82 lb. @ 1.78 in.
	196-214 lb. @ 1.36 in.
Exhaust	71-79 lb. @ 1.60 in.
	195-215 lb. @ 1.15 in.
Valves	
Head diameter	
Exhaust	1.453-1.468 in.
Camshaft	
Journal runout (maximum)	0.005 in.
Crankshaft	
Main bearing journal taper	
(maximum)	0.0004 in. per in.
Main Bearings	
Clearance to crankshaft	
Standard	
No. 1	0.0004-0.0025 in.
Permissible	
No. 1	0.0001-0.0030 in.
Connecting Rod Bearings	
Clearance to crankshaft	
Permissible	0.0008-0.0024 in.
Connecting Rods	
Piston pin bore diameter	0.9096-0.0112 in.

Table 5   TIGHTENING TORQUES, 255/302 CID ENGINES

	302 cid
Intake manifold to cylinder head torque	18-20 ft.-lb.*
* Warm up engine, then retighten to specifications.	

Table 6 ENGINE SPECIFICATIONS (302 HO)

Firing order	1-3-7-2-6-5-4-8
Valve springs	
Pressure @ length	
Intake	74-82 lb. @ 1.78 in.
	196-214 lb. @ 1.33 in.
Exhaust	71-79 lb. @ 1.60 in.
	195-215 lb. @ 1.05 in.
Assembled height	
Intake	1 48/64-1 52/64 in.
Exhaust	1 37/64-1 41/64 in.
Camshaft	
Lobe lift	
Intake	0.2600 in.
Exhaust	0.1780 in.
Valve lift @ zero lash	
Intake	0.4130 in.
Exhaust	0.4420 in.

Table 7 ENGINE SPECIFICATIONS (230 CID V6)

General	
Bore	3.81 in.
Stroke	3.39 in.
Firing order	1-4-2-5-3-6 (No. 1 right front)
Cylinder bore	
Diameter	3.81 in.
Out-of-round (service limit)	0.0002 in.
Taper service (limit)	0.0002 in.
Piston	
Bore clearance	0.0014-0.0022 in.
Piston rings	
Ring width	
Top	0.0772-0.0783 in.
Bottom	0.0772-0.0783 in.
Oil	0.0006 in. (0.15 mm) maximum
Ring gap	
Top	0.001-0.002 in.
Bottom	0.001-0.002 in.
Oil	0.0015-0.0583 in.
Ring side clearance	
1st	0.0016-0.0037 in.
2nd	0.0016-0.0037 in.
Piston pin	
Diameter	0.9119-0.9124 in.
Clearance	
In rod	Press fit
In piston	0.0002-0.0005 in.
Crankshaft	
End play	0.004-0.008 in.
Main bearing journal	
Diameter	2.5190-2.5198 in.
Taper	0.0003 in. per one inch
Out-of-round (service limit)	0.0003 in.
Main bearing clearance	0.0005-0.0023 in.

(continued)

13

Table 7 ENGINE SPECIFICATIONS (230 CID V6) (continued)

Connecting rod	
Side clearance	0.0047-0.0114 in.
Bearing clearance	0.00086-0.0027 in.
Camshaft	
Journal diameter (all)	2.0515-2.0505 in.
Lobe lift	
Intake	0.240 in.
Exhaust	0.241 in.
Runout	0.02 in.
End play	None
Valve system	
Lifter type	Hydraulic
Rocker arm ratio	1.73:1
Intake valve	
Face angle	44°
Seat angle	45°
Stem-to-guide clearance	0.001-0.0027 in.
Seat runout	0.003 in.
Exhaust valve	
Face angle	44°
Seat angle	45°
Stem-to-guide clearance	0.0015-0.0032 in.
Seat runout	0.003 in.
Valve springs	
Free length (intake and exhaust)	1.70-1.78 in.
Load @ length (lb. @ in.)	
Closed (intake and exhaust)	75 @ 1.70
Open (intake and exhaust)	215 @ 1.79
Collapsed tappet gap	
(intake and exhaust)	0.088-0.189 in.

Table 8 TIGHTENING TORQUES, 230 CID V-6

Fastener	ft.-lb.	N•m
Camshaft sprocket bolt	15-22	20-30
Carburetor		
Stud	6	8
Nut	9-11	16-20
Clutch plate-to-flywheel	15-19	20-27
Connecting rod nut	31-36	41-49
Crankshaft		
Pulley-to-damper	20-28	26-38
Damper-to-crankshaft	93-121	125-165
Cylinder head bolt		
Stage 1	47	65
Stage 2	55	75
Stage 3	63	85
Stage 4	74	101
Stage 5	Back all bolts off 2-3 turns, then repeat Stages 1-4	
Distributor hold-down bolt	20-29	27-40
Exhaust manifold	15-22	20-30
Fuel pump	15-22	20-30

(continued)

Table 8 TIGHTENING TORQUES, 230 CID V-6 (continued)

Flywheel	54-64	73-87
Heater tube-to-intake manifold bolt	15-22	20-30
Intake manifold		
Stage 1	5.1	7
Stage 2	10.3	14
Stage 3	18.4	25
Main bearing cap bolt	65-81	88-110
Oil filter adapter	18-22	25-30
Oil inlet tube		
Nut	30-40	40-55
Bolt	15-22	20-30
Oil pan bolts	7-9	9-12
Rocker arm		
Cover	3-5	4-7
Fulcrum-to-head		
Stage 1	5.1-11	7-15
Stage 2	18.4-25.8	25-35
Spark knock sensor		
To adapter	14-17	18-24
Adapter-to-manifold	26-33	35-45
Spark plug	17-22	23-31
Thermostat housing	15-22	20-30
Thermactor check valve	8-11	11-15
Vacuum tree-to-manifold	6-10	8-14
Vacuum fitting-to-manifold	26-33	35-45
Water pump bolt	15-22	20-30

CHAPTER FIVE

FUEL, EXHAUST AND EMISSION CONTROL SYSTEMS

AIR CLEANER

New air cleaner assemblies are necessary to accommodate the YFA 1-V and Holley 4180-C 4-V carburetors on 1983 models. Removal procedures are similar to those given in Chapter Five of the main book except for bracket fastener locations. Refer to **Figure 19** (YFA 1-V) or **Figure 20** (Holley 4180-C 4-V) as required.

CARBURETORS

Holley Model 5200 2-V

The Holley model 5200 2-V carburetor used on 1981 and 1982 models is similar to the model discussed in Chapter Five of the basic book. However, changes have been made to the carburetor that will affect both carburetor operation and service. Refer to **Figure 21**. The changes are:

13

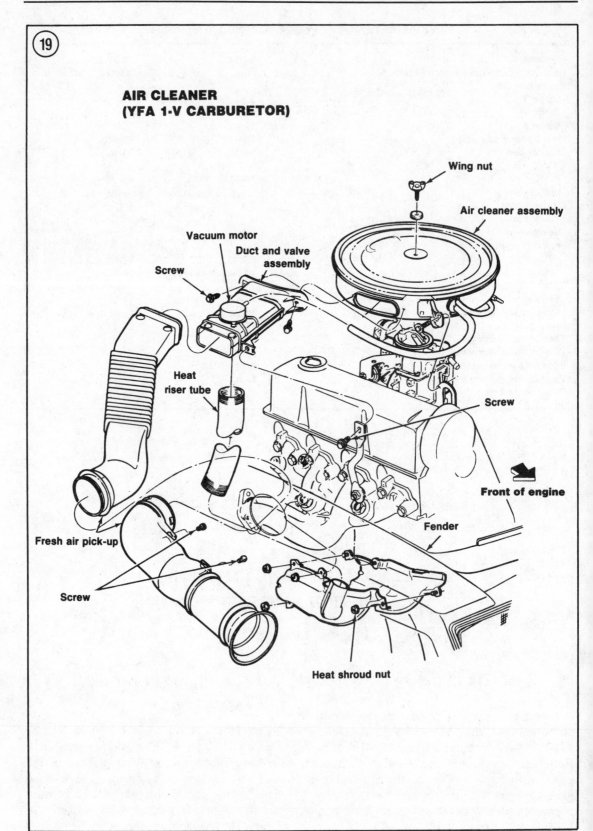

⑲

**AIR CLEANER
(YFA 1-V CARBURETOR)**

Wing nut

Air cleaner assembly

Vacuum motor

Duct and valve
assembly

Screw

Heat
riser tube

Screw

Front of engine

Fresh air pick-up

Fender

Screw

Heat shroud nut

20

AIR CLEANER
(HOLLEY 4180-C CARBURETOR)

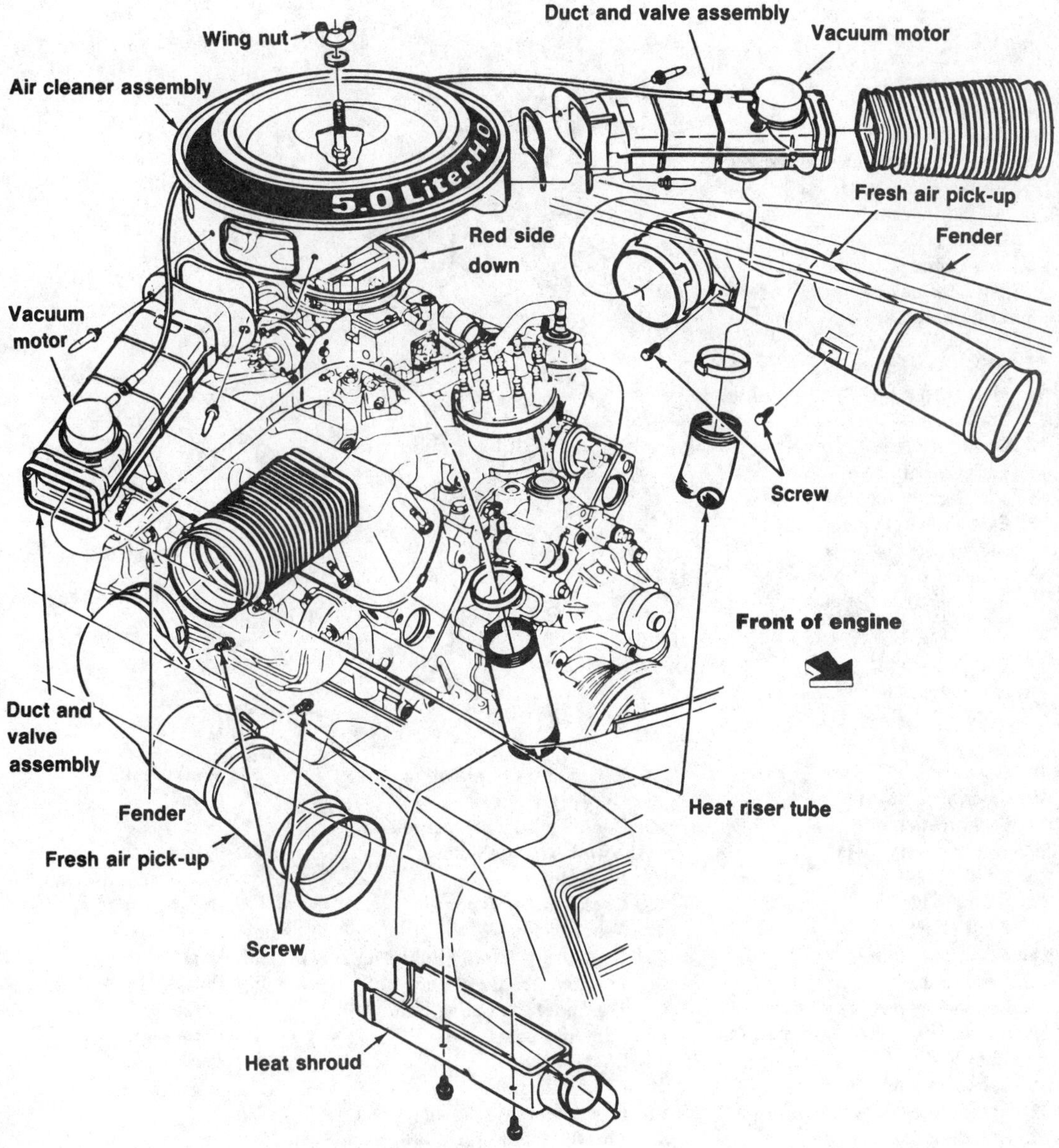

Wing nut

Duct and valve assembly

Vacuum motor

Air cleaner assembly

5.0 Liter H.O.

Red side down

Fresh air pick-up

Fender

Vacuum motor

Screw

Front of engine

Duct and valve assembly

Fender

Fresh air pick-up

Heat riser tube

Screw

Heat shroud

13

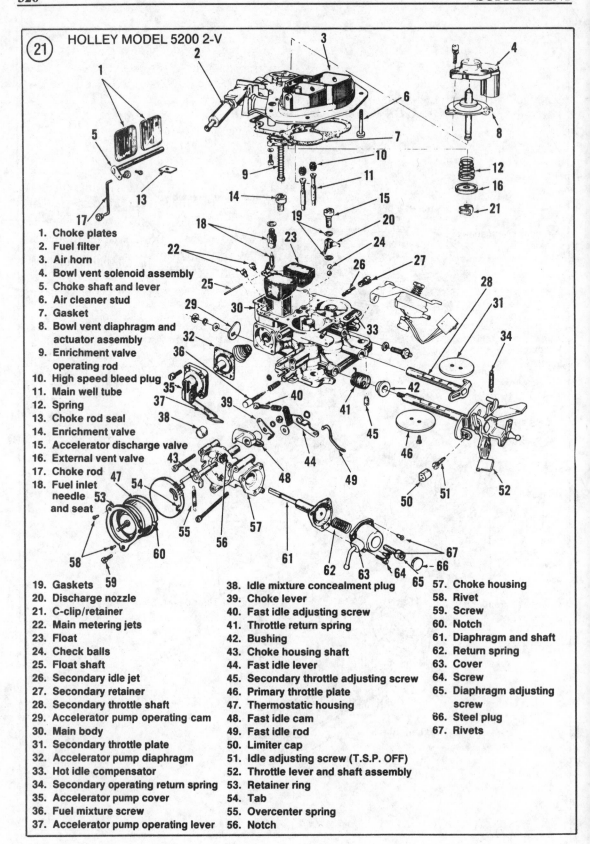

HOLLEY MODEL 5200 2-V (21)

1. Choke plates
2. Fuel filter
3. Air horn
4. Bowl vent solenoid assembly
5. Choke shaft and lever
6. Air cleaner stud
7. Gasket
8. Bowl vent diaphragm and actuator assembly
9. Enrichment valve operating rod
10. High speed bleed plug
11. Main well tube
12. Spring
13. Choke rod seal
14. Enrichment valve
15. Accelerator discharge valve
16. External vent valve
17. Choke rod
18. Fuel inlet needle and seat

19. Gaskets
20. Discharge nozzle
21. C-clip/retainer
22. Main metering jets
23. Float
24. Check balls
25. Float shaft
26. Secondary idle jet
27. Secondary retainer
28. Secondary throttle shaft
29. Accelerator pump operating cam
30. Main body
31. Secondary throttle plate
32. Accelerator pump diaphragm
33. Hot idle compensator
34. Secondary operating return spring
35. Accelerator pump cover
36. Fuel mixture screw
37. Accelerator pump operating lever

38. Idle mixture concealment plug
39. Choke lever
40. Fast idle adjusting screw
41. Throttle return spring
42. Bushing
43. Choke housing shaft
44. Fast idle lever
45. Secondary throttle adjusting screw
46. Primary throttle plate
47. Thermostatic housing
48. Fast idle cam
49. Fast idle rod
50. Limiter cap
51. Idle adjusting screw (T.S.P. OFF)
52. Throttle lever and shaft assembly
53. Retainer ring
54. Tab
55. Overcenter spring
56. Notch

57. Choke housing
58. Rivet
59. Screw
60. Notch
61. Diaphragm and shaft
62. Return spring
63. Cover
64. Screw
65. Diaphragm adjusting screw
66. Steel plug
67. Rivets

1. *Hot idle compensator:* This is a thermostatically controlled carburetor valve that opens when air inlet temperatures are high. At engine idle, additional air is allowed to discharge below the throttle plates. Idle stability is improved by preventing rich fuel mixtures when engine temperatures increase.

2. *Idle adjusting screw:* The idle adjusting screw is fitted with a limiter cap (**Figure 21**). The idle limiter is a cap placed on the head of the idle adjusting screw which prevents unauthorized persons from making incorrect idle adjustments.

3. *Idle mixture screw:* The idle mixture screw has been secured with a concealment plug which replaces the limiter cap on 1979 and 1980 models. The concealment plug prevents any adjustment of the idle mixture screw.

4. *Choke housing:* The choke housing diaphragm adjusting screw has been secured with a steel plug to prevent unauthorized adjustment of the diaphragm/shaft assembly. The thermostatic choke cap retainer is also riveted to the choke housing.

Holley Model 6500 2-V

The Holley Model 6500 2-V is basically a Model 5200 carburetor which substitutes an externally-variable auxiliary fuel metering system for the enrichment valve of the 5200.

The auxiliary system consists of a metering valve assembly, a metering valve operating piston and a diaphragm.

The auxiliary metering system provides a more precise fuel metering range which is required for those vehicles equipped with the feedback electronic engine control system. See **Figure 22**.

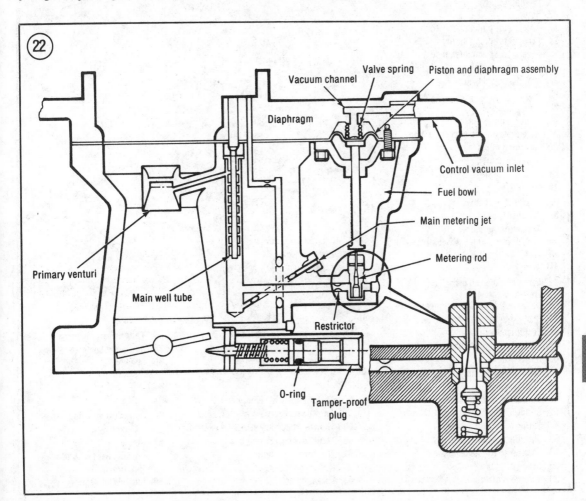

(22)

Vacuum channel — Valve spring — Piston and diaphragm assembly

Diaphragm

Control vacuum inlet

Fuel bowl

Main metering jet

Metering rod

Primary venturi

Main well tube

Restrictor

O-ring

Tamper-proof plug

13

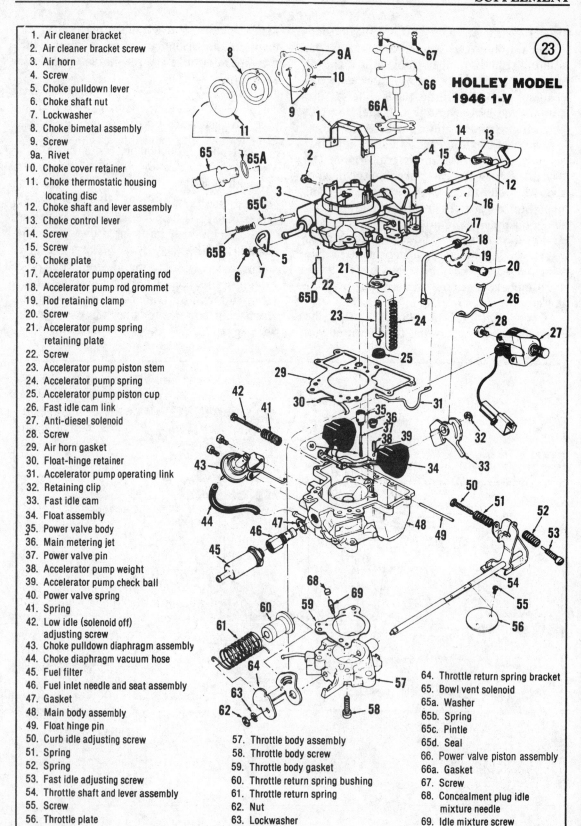

1. Air cleaner bracket
2. Air cleaner bracket screw
3. Air horn
4. Screw
5. Choke pulldown lever
6. Choke shaft nut
7. Lockwasher
8. Choke bimetal assembly
9. Screw
9a. Rivet
10. Choke cover retainer
11. Choke thermostatic housing
    locating disc
12. Choke shaft and lever assembly
13. Choke control lever
14. Screw
15. Screw
16. Choke plate
17. Accelerator pump operating rod
18. Accelerator pump rod grommet
19. Rod retaining clamp
20. Screw
21. Accelerator pump spring
    retaining plate
22. Screw
23. Accelerator pump piston stem
24. Accelerator pump spring
25. Accelerator pump piston cup
26. Fast idle cam link
27. Anti-diesel solenoid
28. Screw
29. Air horn gasket
30. Float-hinge retainer
31. Accelerator pump operating link
32. Retaining clip
33. Fast idle cam
34. Float assembly
35. Power valve body
36. Main metering jet
37. Power valve pin
38. Accelerator pump weight
39. Accelerator pump check ball
40. Power valve spring
41. Spring
42. Low idle (solenoid off)
    adjusting screw
43. Choke pulldown diaphragm assembly
44. Choke diaphragm vacuum hose
45. Fuel filter
46. Fuel inlet needle and seat assembly
47. Gasket
48. Main body assembly
49. Float hinge pin
50. Curb idle adjusting screw
51. Spring
52. Spring
53. Fast idle adjusting screw
54. Throttle shaft and lever assembly
55. Screw
56. Throttle plate

**HOLLEY MODEL
1946 1-V**

57. Throttle body assembly
58. Throttle body screw
59. Throttle body gasket
60. Throttle return spring bushing
61. Throttle return spring
62. Nut
63. Lockwasher
64. Throttle return spring bracket
65. Bowl vent solenoid
65a. Washer
65b. Spring
65c. Pintle
65d. Seal
66. Power valve piston assembly
66a. Gasket
67. Screw
68. Concealment plug idle
    mixture needle
69. Idle mixture screw

If the feedback fuel valve piston and diaphragm assembly is removed from the 6500 carburetor, perform the following to reinstall it.

1. Apply Motorcraft threadlock and sealer (Ford part No. EOAZ-19554-A) in each of the 3 metering system cover retaining screw holes.
2. Place the feedback fuel diaphragm and piston assembly over the spring while aligning the attaching screw holes with the tapped holes in the air horn (upper body). The diaphragm spring is installed correctly when one end of the spring is positioned over the end of the adjustment screw and the other is centered within the diaphragm and piston assembly cupped washer.
3. Install the retaining screws and tighten snugly.

Motorcraft Model 2150 2-V

The Motorcraft model 2150 2-V carburetor used on 1981 and later models is similar to the model 2150 discussed in Chapter Five of the basic book. However, some changes have been made to the carburetor that will affect both carburetor operation and service. The changes are:

1. *Idle adjusting screw:* The idle adjusting screw is fitted with a limiter cap. The idle limi-

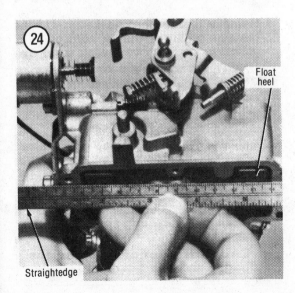

Float heel

Straightedge

ter is a cap placed on the head of the idle adjusting screw which prevents unauthorized persons from making incorrect idle adjustments.
2. *Idle mixture screw:* The idle mixture screw has been secured with a concealment plug which replaces the limiter cap on 1979 and 1980 models. The concealment plug prevents any adjustment of the idle mixture screw.

Holley Model 1946 1-V

The Holley model 1946 1-V (**Figure 23**) carburetor replaces the Holley 1946-C previously used on 200 cid engines with automatic transmissions. While both the carburetors are similar, changes have been made that will affect both carburetor operation and service. The changes are:

1. *Idle adjusting screw:* The idle adjusting screw is fitted with a limiter cap. The idle limiter is a cap placed on the head of the idle adjusting screw which prevents unauthorized persons from making incorrect idle adjustments.
2. *Idle mixture screw:* The idle mixture screw has been secured with a concealment plug which replaces the limiter cap on 1979 and 1980 models. The concealment plug prevents any adjustment of the idle mixture screw.
3. *Power valve piston assembly:* This is a vacuum-operated enrichment system used to provide fuel mixture enrichment for part throttle and wide open throttle operation. The system consists of an enrichment valve assembly containing a needle and a vacuum piston. See 66, **Figure 23**. To remove the power valve piston assembly, simply remove the 2 retaining screws (67, **Figure 23**).
4. *Choke retainer cover:* Rivets are now used to secure the choke retainer cover (10, **Figure 23**). This prevents unauthorized disassembly of the choke assembly and eliminates the possibility of incorrect choke adjustment.

Float Adjustment (Model 1946 1-V)

Refer to **Figure 24** for this procedure.

13

1. Remove the carburetor (see Chapter Five).
2. Remove the carburetor air horn. See *Carburetor Disassembly (Model 1946-C)* in Chapter Five of the basic book.

NOTE
A 2-piece plastic fuel bowl filler is used with 1982-on model 1946 carburetors to eliminate engine stall during hard braking. Remove the filler before proceeding to Step 3. Be sure to reinstall it after Step 7.

3. Place a finger over the float hinge pin retainer and turn the carburetor main body over so the float hangs down. Catch the accelerator and pump check ball and weight (**Figure 25**).
4. Lay a straightedge across the lower body surface and check to see that the float heel just touches the straightedge. If necessary, adjust by bending the float tabs contacting the needle seat.
5. If adjustment was required in Step 4, turn the main body over so that the floats are facing upward. Check the float alignment by making sure the float moves freely throughout its range without touching the fuel bowl walls. If the floats are misaligned, correct by bending the float arms. Recheck the float level (Step 4).
6. Insert the accelerator pump check ball and weight into the channel indicated in **Figure 26**.

Carter YFA 1-V

The Carter YFA 1-V carburetor is used in place of the Holley 5200 on 1983 2300 cc engines. Although similar to other YFA 1-V carburetors used on other Ford Motor Co. engines, it has been internally modified to increase durability and prevent wear caused by engine vibration.

Removal/Installation (Carter YFA 1-V)

1. Remove the air cleaner housing. See **Figure 19**.
2. Disconnect the throttle cable/rod from the throttle lever.
3. Label and disconnect all electrical connections and vacuum lines.
4. Disconnect the fuel inlet line. Plug the line to prevent leakage.
5. Remove the carburetor retaining nuts. Remove the carburetor, mounting gasket, spacer (if so equipped) and lower gasket from the intake manifold.

Accelerator pump check ball

Weight

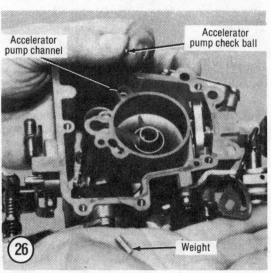

Accelerator pump channel

Accelerator pump check ball

Weight

27 CARTER MODEL YFA-IV

Screws

Air cleaner bail

Vent rod and spring

Screw

Choke plate

Air horn

Solevac and bracket

Fast idle choke lever

Locking and indexing plate

Indexing notch

Choke cup

Choke piston lever and shaft assembly

Gasket

Gasket

Clip

Rivets

Flapper valve

Air horn assembly

Air horn gasket

Choke pulldown diaphragm

Upper pump spring retainer

Metering rod adjusting screw

Spring cup

Upper pump spring

Needle pin spring, seat and gasket assembly

Metering rod arm assembly

Metering rod arm spring

Retainer

Screw

Metering rod

Anti-rock plate

Float pin

Pump check weight

Pump and wot enrichment lifter link

Float and lever assembly

Metering rod jet

Lifter link seal

Pump diaphragm spring retainer

Actuating lever with A/C

Low speed jet

Pump diaphragm spring

Retainer screw

Actuating lever

Main body casting

Pump check ball

Diaphragm housing attaching screw

Washer

Temperature compensated pump

Transfer tube

Pump diaphragm housing assembly

Operating lever

Clip

Fast idle cam

Wot cutout switch

Throttle shaft arm

Body flange gasket

Pump connector link

Pump diaphragm assembly

Screw

Washer

Anti-diesel throttle screw

Body flange attaching screw

Bushing

Spring

Cap

Throttle plate

Cup

Fast idle cam link

Idle fuel mixture adjusting screw and spring

Tamper proof cup

Fast idle adjusting screw

Throttle shaft and lever assembly

Spark port

Aluminum throttle body flange assembly

13

6. Installation is the reverse of removal. Tighten retaining nuts snugly, then torque in crisscross pattern to 13-14 ft.-lb. (20-21 N•m).

Disassembly (Carter YFA 1-V)

Refer to **Figure 27** for this procedure.

1. Remove the air cleaner bracket from the air horn.

2. Remove the solenoid or Solevac from the air horn.

3. Remove the air horn attaching screws.

4. Remove the retaining clip at the fast idle cam. Disconnect fast idle cam link from the fast idle cam.

5. Remove air horn from main body assembly.

6. Invert air horn and remove float pin. Remove float and lever assembly.

7. Turn air horn over and catch inlet needle valve assembly in your hand. Place in a small cup on the workbench.

8. Remove the inlet needle seat with a wide-blade screwdriver. Remove and discard gasket.

9. Remove hairpin retainer at the fuel bowl vent valve. Remove vent shaft rod, spring and valve. Note positioning of spring on vent rod for reinstallation. This completes air horn disassembly.

10. Invert main body and catch the accelerating pump check ball and weight (**Figure 28**) in your hand. Place in a small cup on the workbench.

11. Remove the screw holding the operating lever on the end of the throttle shaft. Remove the spring washer, vent rod, actuating lever and E-clip.

12. Loosen the throttle shaft arm set screw with a 3/32 in. Allen wrench. Remove arm and pump connector link. See **Figure 29**.

13. Remove shoulder screw holding fast idle cam. Remove fast idle cam.

14. Remove screws from accelerating pump diaphragm housing. Remove pump diaphragm assembly, lifter link and metering rod as an assembly. Remove and discard lifter link seal.

15. Remove main metering rod jet and lower speed jet with a jet remover tool or wide-blade screwdriver.

16. Remove throttle body screws. Separate throttle body from main body. Discard main body gasket.

17. Remove the wide-open throttle cut-out switch, if so equipped.

Inspection and Cleaning (Carter YFA 1-V)

Inspection and cleaning procedures are essentially the same as those provided in Chapter Five of the main book. However, the air horn should be suspended to prevent immersion of the tamper-proof choke housing in cleaner.

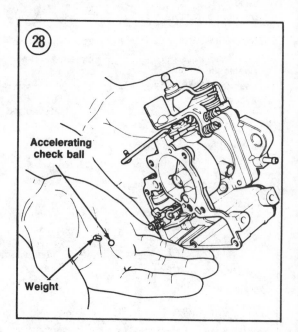

Accelerating check ball

Weight

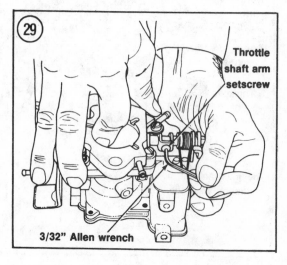

Throttle shaft arm setscrew

3/32" Allen wrench

Assembly (Carter YFA 1-V)

Refer to **Figure 27**. Assembly is the reverse of disassembly, plus the following:

1. Install new gaskets, O-rings and diaphragms as included in the overhaul kit.
2. Be sure the proper jets are installed in their respective positions.
3. Adjust float level and drop as described in this section of the supplement.
4. Adjust curb idle speed according to the instructions provided on the Vehicle Emission Control Information (VECI) label in the engine compartment.

Float Level Adjustment (Carter YFA 1-V)

Refer to **Figure 30** for this procedure.
1. Invert the air horn on a clean level surface.

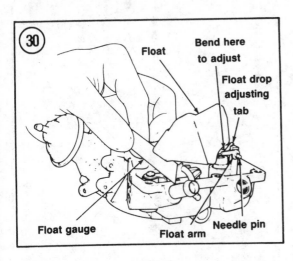

2. Position float level gauge from overhaul kit to check clearance between the indentation on the top of the float to the bottom of the air horn.
3. Hold air horn at eye level and check clearance in Step 2 with the float level gauge. The float arm lever should rest on the inlet needle pin.

NOTE
Do not bend the tab at the end of the float arm to make adjustments in Step 4. This tab prevents the float from resting in the bottom of an empty fuel bowl; it is not an adjustment point.

4. If adjustment is necessary, bend the float arm at the point shown in **Figure 30**.

Float Drop Adjustment (Carter YFA 1-V)

Refer to **Figure 31** for this procedure.
1. After checking float level, hold the air horn upright and let the float hang free.
2. Hold the air horn at eye level and measure the clearance between the casting and toe end of the float with the float drop gauge provided in the overhaul kit.
3. If adjustment is required, bend the tab at the end of the float arm until the specified drop is obtained. See **Figure 30**.

Holley 4180-C 4-V

A downdraft, 2-stage Holley 4180-C 4-V carburetor is used with 1983 302 cid V8 engine/manual transmission applications and 1984-on 302 cid HO V8/manual transmission applications.

Removal/Installation (Holley 4180-C 4-V)

1. Remove the air cleaner assembly. If equipped with the 302 cid HO engine, refer to Figure 20 for air cleaner components.
2. Disconnect the throttle rod at the throttle lever.
3. Label and disconnect all electrical connectors and vacuum lines at the carburetor.
4. Disconnect the choke heat tube.
5. Disconnect the fuel inlet line. Plug line to prevent leakage.

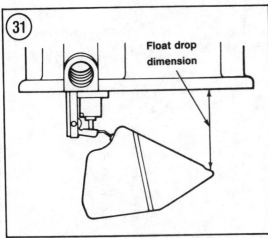

13

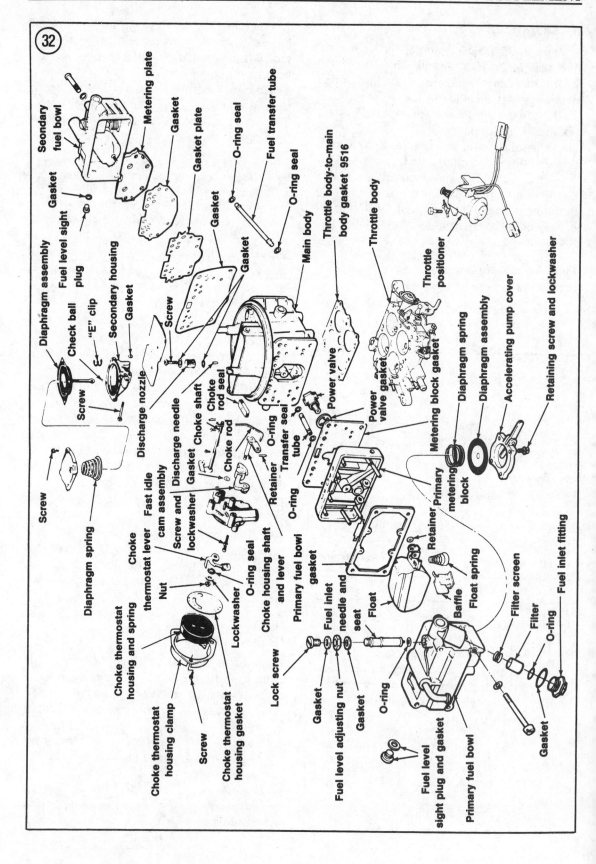

32

Seondary fuel bowl

Metering plate

Gasket

Gasket plate

Gasket

O-ring seal

Fuel transfer tube

O-ring seal

Throttle body-to-main body gasket 9516

Throttle body

Diaphragm assembly

Fuel level sight plug

Gasket

Secondary housing

Gasket

Gasket

Main body

Power valve

Throttle positioner

Check ball

"E" clip

Screw

Power valve gasket

Diaphragm spring

Diaphragm assembly

Accelerating pump cover

Retaining screw and lockwasher

Screw

Discharge nozzle

Choke rod seal

O-ring

Transfer seal tube

Metering block gasket

Screw

Discharge needle

Gasket

Choke shaft

Retainer

O-ring

Primary metering block

Screw and lockwasher

Choke rod

Fast idle cam assembly

Choke thermostat housing and spring

Choke thermostat lever

Nut

O-ring seal

Choke housing shaft and lever

Primary fuel bowl gasket

Retainer

Filter screen

Choke

Lockwasher

Baffle

Filter

Diaphragm spring

Lock screw

Fuel inlet needle and seat

Float spring

O-ring

Choke thermostat housing clamp

Gasket

Float

Fuel inlet fitting

Screw

Gasket

O-ring

Fuel level adjusting nut

Gasket

Fuel inlet fitting

Choke thermostat housing gasket

Fuel level sight plug and gasket

Primary fuel bowl

O-ring

Primary fuel bowl

Gasket

6. Remove the carburetor flange retaining nuts and lockwashers. Remove the carburetor and spacer from the manifold. Remove and discard the gasket.

7. Installation is the reverse of removal. Use a new gasket and tighten retaining nuts in crisscross pattern to 14-20 ft.-lb. (19-27 N•m).

Disassembly (Holley 4180-C 4-V)

Refer to **Figure 32** for this procedure.

1. Remove the primary fuel bowl and gasket. Remove metering block and gasket. Discard the gaskets.

2. Remove the pump transfer tube from the main housing/metering block. Discard the O-ring seals.

3. Remove the fuel line tube. Discard the O-ring seal.

4. Remove the main jets with a jet removal tool.

5. Remove the power valve with an appropriate size socket wrench. Discard the gasket.

6. Remove the fuel lever adjustment lockscrew. Discard the gasket.

7. Turn the adjusting nut counterclockwise. Remove the adjusting nut. Discard the gasket.

8. Remove the fuel inlet needle/seat assembly.

9. Remove the float shaft retainer clip with needlenose pliers. Slide float and spring from shaft.

10. Remove the baffle plate, fuel level sight plug, fuel inlet fitting and filter from the fuel bowl. Discard all gaskets.

11. Invert the fuel bowl and remove the accelerating pump cover, diaphragm and spring. This completes disassembly of the primary fuel bowl/metering block.

12. Remove the secondary fuel bowl. Remove the metering body and plate from the fuel bowl with a clutch-type screwdriver. Discard the gaskets.

13. Repeat Steps 7-9. Remove the baffle plate. This completes disassembly of the secondary fuel bowl/metering plate.

14. Remove the air cleaner stud from the main body.

15. Remove the secondary diaphragm link E-clip.

16. Invert the main body. Remove the throttle body screws and lockwashers. Separate the main and throttle bodies. Discard the gasket.

17. Remove the secondary diaphragm housing and gasket from the main body. Discard the gasket.

18. Remove the diaphragm housing cover, spring, diaphragm and check ball from the housing.

19. Remove the staked accelerator pump discharge nozzle screw. Lift the nozzle and gaskets from the main body. Discard the gaskets.

20. Invert main body and catch the pump discharge needle in your hand. This completes main body disassembly.

NOTE
The throttle body should not be disassembled. Its components are matched to meet emission standards. The throttle body is serviced as a complete assembly.

Inspection and Cleaning (Holley 4180-C 4-V)

Inspection and cleaning procedures are essentially the same as provided in Chapter Five of the main book. However, the tamper-proof choke housing on the main body should not be immersed in cleaner.

Assembly (Holley 4180-C 4-V)

Refer to **Figure 32**. Assembly is the reverse of disassembly, plus the following:

1. Install new gaskets, seals and O-rings provided in the overhaul kit.

2. Make sure the secondary operating and accelerating pump diaphragms are not ripped, torn or otherwise damaged.

3. Make sure the projection on the choke rod is located under the fast idle cam so the cam will be lifted when the choke is closed.

4. Stake nozzle screw in place with a flat punch.

5. Adjust fuel level as described in this section of the supplement.

13

**Fuel Level Adjustment
(Holley 4180-C 4-V)**

1. Assemble carburetor and reinstall on engine without air cleaner.

2. Start engine and run at 1,000 rpm for approximately 30 seconds to stabilize fuel level.

3. Stop engine. Remove sight plug on side of primary fuel bowl. Fuel level should be at the bottom of the sight plug hole. If fuel is below hole, raise fuel level. If fuel spills out of the hole, lower the level.

4. To adjust fuel level, stop the engine and loosen the lockscrew on the primary fuel bowl. Turn adjusting screw clockwise to lower or counterclockwise to raise the fuel level. Tighten lockscrew and install sight plug with old gasket.

5. Repeat Steps 2-4 until fuel level is correct, then install sight plug with a *new* gasket.

6. When primary fuel level is correct, repeat procedure with secondary fuel bowl, using the secondary throttle lever to stabilize fuel level.

FUEL INJECTION SYSTEM

The 1984-on 2.3L EFI Turbo engine uses a multi-point fuel injection (EFI) system. A tuned intake manifold contains 4 fuel injectors which are all fired simultaneously. See **Figure 33** (typical).

All the 1984-1985 302 cid V8 engines (except the HO/manual transmission application) and 230 cid V6 engines use a central fuel injection (CFI) system. A fuel charging assembly mounted on the intake manifold in place of a carburetor contains 2 solenoid injection valves which are fired simulatneously. See **Figure 34** (typical).

The 1986 302 cid V8 HO engine uses a sequentially fired multi-point (EFI) system. A fuel supply manifold consists of a tubular fuel rail, 8 injectors/connectors and mounting flanges. The injectors are fired in engine firing order. See **Figure 35** (typical).

2.3L EFI Turbo System Operation

The 2.3L EFI system is controlled by the EEC-IV microprocessor (see Chapter Seven

of this supplement). A high-pressure chassis-mounted electric fuel pump feeds filtered fuel to the fuel charging manifold assembly.

When the ignition switch is turned to the crank position, the EEC microprocessor activates the fuel pump through a relay mounted in the left rear kick panel. The microprocessor senses engine speed and will shut the pump down if the engine stops or cranking speed is less than 120 rpm.

Fuel flow is controlled by varying the duration of injection according to signals from the EEC-IV microprocessor. A pressure regulator mounted on the fuel supply manifold downstream of the injectors reduces pump pressure to 39-40 psi. Under idle or high manifold vacuum conditions, pressure is

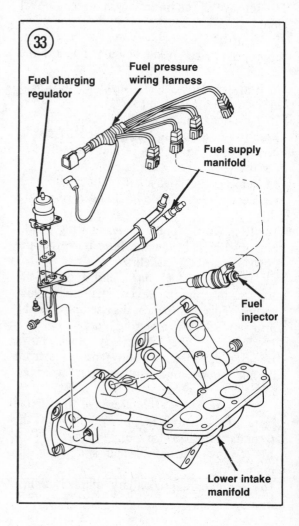

(33)

Fuel charging regulator

Fuel pressure wiring harness

Fuel supply manifold

Fuel injector

Lower intake manifold

reduced to 30 psi, while with 10 lb. turbo boost, it increases to 50 psi. Fuel supplied in excess of that required by the engine is returned to the fuel tank. A throttle position sensor (TPS) mounted on the air throttle body informs the microprocessor of throttle position. A throttle air bypass valve controls idle and fast idle speeds relative to engine coolant temperature.

An inertia switch mounted in the trunk shuts off the fuel pump on sudden impact. This is designed as a safety measure in case of a collision, but may also be triggered when the vehicle is "bumped" by another car

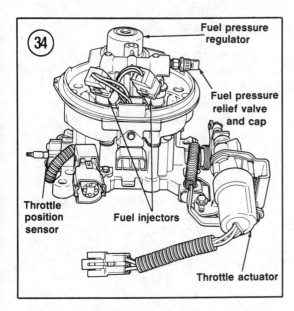

34

Fuel pressure regulator

Fuel pressure relief valve and cap

Throttle position sensor

Fuel injectors

Throttle actuator

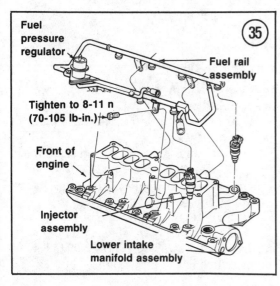

35

Fuel pressure regulator

Fuel rail assembly

Tighten to 8-11 n (70-105 lb-in.)

Front of engine

Injector assembly

Lower intake manifold assembly

during a parking maneuver. If a 2.3L EFI Turbo vehicle will not start when cranked, try resetting the inertia switch by depressing the button on the switch.

Since this EFI system is electronically controlled and functions in conjunction with the turbocharger system, owner service to the system is not recommended. If the EFI system does not seem to be working properly, take the car to a Ford or Mercury dealer for diagnosis and adjustment.

CFI System Operation

The CFI system is controlled by the EEC-IV microprocessor (see Chapter Seven of this supplement). A low-pressure electric fuel pump mounted inside the fuel tank feeds fuel to an external high-pressure pump mounted near the tank. The high-pressure pump supplies filtered fuel to the CFI fuel charging assembly.

When the ignition switch is turned to the crank position, the EEC microprocessor activates the fuel pump through a relay. The microprocessor senses engine speed and will shut the pump down if the engine stops or cranking speed is less than 120 rpm.

Fuel flow is controlled by varying the duration of injection according to signals from the EEC-IV microprocessor. A pressure regulator mounted on the fuel charging assembly maintains fuel pressure at 39 psi. Fuel supplied in excess of that required by the engine is returned to the fuel tank. A throttle position sensor (TPS) informs the microprocessor of throttle valve position. An idle speed control (ISC) DC motor actuator maintains a pre-programmed idle speed according to directions from the microprocessor.

An inertia switch mounted near the left hand taillamp in the trunk shuts off the fuel pump on sudden impact. This is designed as a safety measure in case of a collision, but may also be triggered when a CFI vehicle is "bumped" by another car during a parking maneuver. If a CFI vehicle will not start when cranked, try resetting the inertia switch by depressing the button on the switch.

Since the CFI system is electronically controlled, no attempt should be made to

13

adjust the idle speed. Owner service should be limited to replacement only. If the CFI system is not working properly, take the car to a Ford or Mercury dealer for diagnosis and adjustment.

302 V8 EFI System Operation

The 302 V8 EFI system is controlled by the EEC-IV microprocessor (see Chapter Seven of this supplement). A low-pressure electric fuel pump mounted inside the fuel tank feds fuel to an external high-pressure pump mounted near the tank. The high-pressure pump supplies filtered fuel to the fuel rail.

When the ignition switch is turned to the crank position, the EEC microprocessor activates the fuel pump through a relay. The microprocessor senses engine speed and will shut the pump down if the engine stops or cranking speed is less than 120 rpm.

Each injector is energized once per crankshaft revolution. Fuel flow is controlled by varying the duration of injection according to signals from the EEC-IV microprocessor. A pressure regulator mounted on the fuel rail downstream of the injectors reduces pump pressure to 39-40 psi. Fuel supplied in excess of that required by the engine is returned to the fuel tank. A throttle position sensor (TPS) mounted on the air throttle body informs the microprocessor of throttle position. A throttle air bypass valve controls idle and fast idle speeds relative to engine coolant temperature.

The air intake manifold is a 2-piece (upper and lower) intake manifold. The air throttle body, fuel rail, throttle cable bracket and EGR valve are mounted on the air intake manifold. Vacuum taps are provided to operate various engine sub-systems and accessories. The lower manifold is machined to accept the injectors.

An inertia switch mounted in the trunk shuts off the fuel pump on sudden impact. This is designed as a safety measure in case of a collision, but may also be triggered when the vehicle is "bumped" by another car during a parking maneuver. If a 302 V8 EFI vehicle will not start when cranked, try resetting the inertia switch by depressing the button on the switch.

Since this EFI system is electronically controlled, owner service to the system is not recommended. If the EFI system does not seem to be working properly, take the car to a Ford or Mercury dealer for diagnosis and adjustment.

Relieving System Pressure

Before opening any fuel connection on a fuel injection system, the fuel pressure must be relieved.
1. CFI vehicles—Remove the air cleaner.
2. Remove the fuel tank cap.
3. Remove the pressure relief valve cap. Release fuel system pressure at the valve with special tool T80L-9974-A or equivalent. **Figure 34** shows the location of the CFI relief valve on the throttle body. The 2.3L EFI Turbo valve is located on the fuel supply manifold at the upper right hand corner of the engine compartment. The 302 V8 EFI valve is located on the fuel rail at the lower left hand corner of the engine compartment.
4. When service is completed, install the relief valve cap, fuel tank cap and air cleaner (CFI vehicles only).

Fuel Filter Replacement

1. Relieve system pressure as described in this supplement.
2. Raise the vehicle with a jack and place it on jackstands.
3. Remove and discard the push-connect fitting retainer clips.
4. Remove the fuel filter from the pump mounting bracket.
5. Installation is the reverse of removal. Install the new filter with the arrow pointing in the direction of fuel flow. Install new retainer clips in the push-connect fittings.

CHAPTER SIX

COOLING SYSTEM AND HEATER

COOLANT

Coolant capacities for some models differ. These are listed in **Table 9**.

The 230 cid V6 engine requires a coolant containing a corrosion inhibitor. Prestone II is one of the recommended coolants which meets Ford specification ESE-M97B43-A.

DRIVE BELTS

Drive belt installation and adjustment remain the same as for 1980 and earlier models; drive belt tension specifications have changed. See **Table 10**.

THERMOSTAT (230 V6)

The thermostat housing on the 230 V6 engine contains a locking recess to prevent incorrect thermostat installation. The thermostat has locking tabs which engage this recess. To remove the thermostat, rotate it counterclockwise until the tabs disengage the housing recess. Thermostat installation requires a clockwise turn to engage the tabs in the recess.

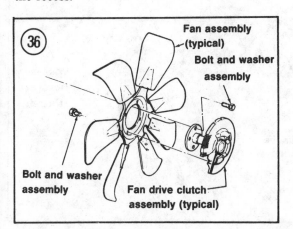

(36)

Fan assembly (typical)

Bolt and washer assembly

Bolt and washer assembly

Fan drive clutch assembly (typical)

FAN DRIVE CLUTCH

A fan drive clutch is used on 1981 and later 6-cylinder and V8 engines. This permits the use of a powerful fan without power loss or excessive fan noise. See **Figure 36**.

Removal/Installation

Refer to **Figure 36** for this procedure.
1. Remove the upper radiator support and/or fan guard.
2. Remove the fan belt.
3. Remove the fan drive clutch-to-water pump hub attaching bolts from behind the fan blade assembly. Remove the fan blade and drive clutch as an assembly.
4. Remove the fan blade-to-fan drive clutch attaching bolts and separate the clutch from the fan.
5. To install, align the fan blade-to-fan drive clutch attaching bolt holes. Install the attaching bolts and tighten to 12-18 ft.-lb.
6. Position the fan drive clutch and fan blade assembly in the engine compartment. Install the attaching bolts and tighten to 12-18 ft.-lb.
7. Check to see that the fan drive clutch is tightened squarely to the water pump hub.
8. Install the fan belt and tighten to specifications. See **Table 10**.
9. Install the upper radiator support and/or fan guard.

ELECTRIC COOLING FAN

An electric cooling fan is used on 1982 and later 2300 cc engines equipped with air conditioning and on all 1983 230 cid V6 engines. See **Figure 37** for typical installation.

The fan is attached to the motor shaft by a screw on 1982 models and by a spring clip on

13

1983 models. Air conditioned models use a 4-blade fan; non-air conditioned models use a 2-blade fan.

The electric fan operates whenever the air conditioning is on or when engine coolant temperature reaches 216-226° F (105° C). A temperature switch in the heater hose tube closes at this temperature to complete the fan relay ground circuit. The fan relay is located in a controller located near the steering column under the instrument panel. The fan will operate until the coolant temperature drops to about 201° F (87° C).

WARNING
Fan operation is automatic; it may come on during a heat soak condition after the engine has been shut off. Always disconnect the negative battery cable when working near the fan, unless the test procedure involved requires cable connection. In such cases,

exercise extreme caution to avoid possible serious personal injury.

Removal/Installation

Refer to **Figure 37** for this procedure.
1. Disconnect the negative battery cable.
2. Disconnect the fan wiring harness at the routing clip.
3. Depress the 2 locking tabs on the fan motor connector and separate it from the wiring harness.
4. Remove the mounting bracket screws. Remove the bracket and fan motor assembly.
5. Remove the screw or retaining clip from the motor shaft. Remove the fan.
6. Remove the nuts holding the fan motor to the mounting bracket.
7. Installation is the reverse of removal. Tighten fan motor-to-mounting bracket nuts to 70-95 in.-lb. (8-10.5 N•m).

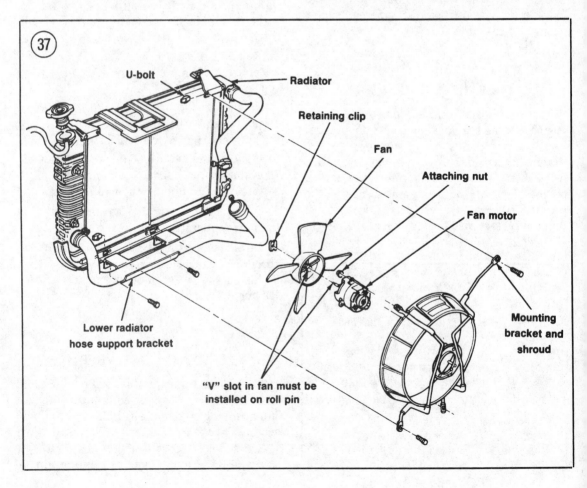

(37)

U-bolt — Radiator

Retaining clip

Fan

Attaching nut

Fan motor

Mounting bracket and shroud

Lower radiator hose support bracket

"V" slot in fan must be installed on roll pin

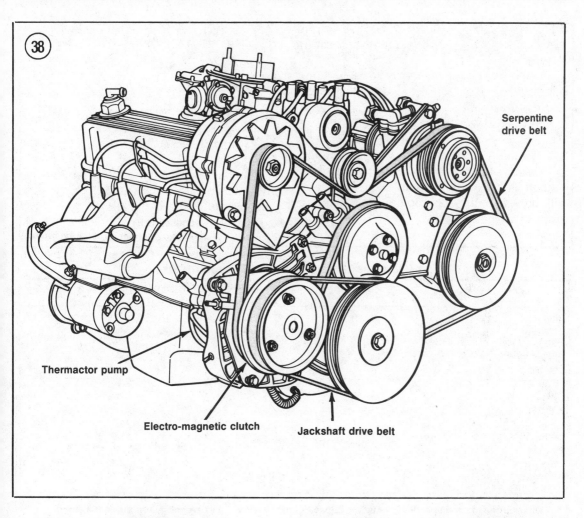

(38)

Serpentine
drive belt

Thermactor pump

Electro-magnetic clutch

Jackshaft drive belt

TWO-SPEED
ACCESSORY DRIVE
(TSAD) SYSTEM

A computer-controlled serpentine drive belt system (**Figure 38**) is used on 1985 302 cid HO V8 engine/manual transmission applications to reduce engine load. A separate microprocessor monitors accessory drive requirements, reducing belt speed by approximately 50 percent through a bracket-mounted electro-mechanical clutch (similar to that used with air conditioning compressors) when full speed operation is not required. A separate "jackshaft" drive belt operates the Thermactor pump at full speed under all driving conditions to maintain emission control.

Located in the right side passenger compartment kick panel, the TSAD microprocessor receives sensor input concerning engine rpm, coolant temperature, throttle position, blower voltage, fan switch position and clutch engagement. After comparing this data to its internal program, the microprocessor signals the electro-mechanical clutch to engage or disengage. In addition, the TSAD microprocessor can bypass Thermactor pump air or prevent cycling of the air conditioning compressor under certain conditions.

TSAD drive belt adjustment is automatically maintained by the belt tensioner. The Thermactor pump belt is adjusted by loosening the 3 bolts holding the jackshaft bracket and turning the adjustment stud nut to obtain a tension of 140-160 lbs. See **Figure 39**.

13

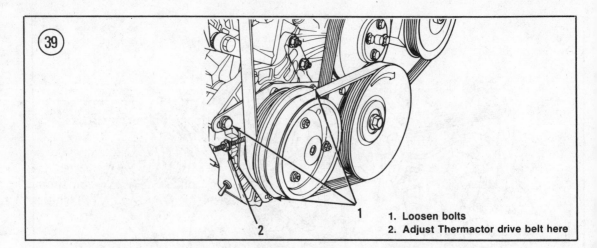

1. Loosen bolts
2. Adjust Thermactor drive belt here

Table 9 APPROXIMATE COOLANT CAPACITY *

	1981	1982-1983
2300 cc		
Non-AC	8.6	8.6
With AC	9.0	9.4
2300 cc turbo	9.2	9.4
200 cid		
Non-AC	8.1	8.4
With AC	8.4	8.4
230/255 cid		
Non-AC	14.7	14.7
With AC	15.0	15.0
302 cid		
Non-AC	—	13.1
With AC	—	13.4

* All measurements are specified in quarts. Capacity may vary by ±15 percent. AC = air conditioning.

Table 10 DRIVE BELT TENSION

Belt Type or Size	New Belt (lb.)[1]	Used Belt (lb.)	Allowable Minimum
All except 1/4 in. and air pump belt	120-160	90-120	65
Air pump belt	90-130	90-120	60
1/4 in. belt	50-80	40-60	40
V-ribbed			
4 grooves	90-120	90-110	60
5 grooves—fixed[2]	110-140	110-130	75
5 grooves—with absorber	75-140	75-140	75
6 grooves—fixed[2]	140-170	140-160	90
6 grooves—with tensioner	85-140	85-140	85

1. Tension is measured after belt is installed (engine has not been started).
2. Fixed systems are equipped with manually adjusted centers which are bolted in place.

CHAPTER SEVEN

ELECTRICAL SYSTEM

Service procedures are the same as for earlier models. Refer to Chapter Seven in the basic book. New alternators with different output ratings are used on some models. These are listed in **Table 11**.

EEC-IV SYSTEM

All 1984 and later engines (except the 1984-1985 302 cid HO/V8 manual transmission application) use the EEC-IV system to control emissions while providing maximum fuel economy, driveability and performance. A microprocessor reads inputs from a variety of sensors, compares the data against an internal program and sends controlling outputs to various components to maintain a proper air-fuel ratio and ignition timing.

The EEC-IV microprocessor contains a memory to store trouble codes when one or more EEC-IV system components malfunctions. Any malfunction of the EEC-IV system should be diagnosed and serviced by a dealer or qualified garage with the necessary special tools and test equipment.

All EEC-IV systems use a universal distributor with an attached TFI ignition module. The universal distributor contains a Hall-effect vane switch stator or armature assembly with one window in the vane or segment in the armature for each engine cylinder.

Due to a change in fuel injector firing order, the armature assembly used on the 1986 302 V8 EFI engine contains one segment that has been narrowed to signal the EEC-IV microprocessor when the No. 1 piston is approaching TDC. The microprocessor uses the slightly different signal received from the narrow segment to properly time and fire the fuel injectors in a sequential pattern. The new armature assembly is not interchangeable with earlier models.

The solid-state TFI module mounted on the side of the distributor turns the ignition current on and off. Periodic ignition timing adjustment is *not* required with a TFI ignition system.

IAR CHARGING SYSTEM

The IAR (integral alternator/regulator) system is used with some 1985 and later engines. The older charging system is now referred to as the EVR (external voltage regulator) system. The IAR system consists of the battery, alternator with integral voltage regulator, charge indicator light (or ammeter), fuse link and connecting wiring.

Charging System Test

A voltmeter with a 0-30 volt scale, an ohmmeter, a jumper wire, 2 blade terminals and an engine tachometer are required for an accurate charging system test.

1. Check alternator belt tension. See *Drive Belts*, Chapter Three.
2. Check the fusible link located between the alternator and starter relay. See *Fusible Links*, Chapter Eight.
3. Check the battery terminals and cables for corrosion or loose connections. Clean and tighten as necessary.
4. Check all wiring connections between the alternator, regulator and engine to make sure they are clean and tight.
5. Carburetted engine—Disconnect the electric choke lead at the alternator stator terminal. Check the lead for a ground condition. Do not reconnect until charging system testing has been completed.
6. Connect the positive voltmeter lead to the positive battery cable clamp. Connect the negative voltmeter lead to the negative battery cable clamp. Make sure the ignition and all accessories are off.

13

7. Record the voltage displayed on the voltmeter scale. This is the battery or base voltage.

8. Connect a tachometer to the engine according to manufacturer's instructions.

9. Start the engine and bring its speed up to about 1,500 rpm. The voltmeter reading should increase from that recorded in Step 7, but not by more than 2 volts.

10. If the voltage increase is within specifications in Step 9, perform the *Load Test*. If the increase is greater than 2 volts, perform the *Over-voltage Test*. If the voltage does not increase, perform the *Under-voltage Test*.

Load Test

1. With the engine running, turn the headlights on high beam and the heater or air conditioner blower on HIGH speed.

2. Increase the engine speed to about 2,000 rpm. If the voltmeter does not read a minimum of 0.5 volt more than the base voltage, perform the *Under-voltage Test*.

Over-voltage Test

Refer to **Figure 40** for this procedure.

1. With the ignition ON (engine OFF), connect the negative voltmeter lead to the rear housing of the alternator. Connect the positive voltmeter lead first to the alternator output connection at the starter relay, then to the A screw head on the regulator. If the difference in readings exceeds 0.5 volt, there is excessive resistance in the A wire circuit. Locate and correct as required.

2. Check for loose regulator-to-alternator ground screws. Tighten regulator ground screws to 15-26 in.-lb. (1.7-2.8 N•m).

3. If the voltage increase still exceeds 2 volts, connect the negative voltmeter lead to the alternator rear housing. With the ignition OFF, connect the positive voltmeter lead first to the regulator A screw head, then to the F screw head.

4. If the voltage reading is the same at both screw heads in Step 3, replace the regulator. If the reading differs, remove the alternator and

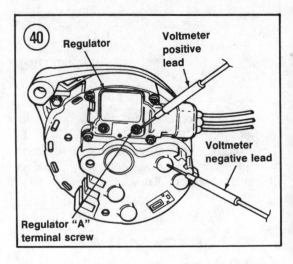

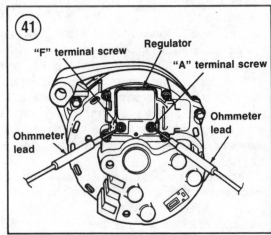

take it to a dealer for further testing and service.

Under-voltage Test

1. With the engine off, disconnect the regulator wiring plug and connect an ohmmeter between the regulator A and F terminal screws (**Figure 41**). The meter should read more than 2.4 ohms. If it reads less than 2.4 ohms, remove the alternator and have a dealer check for a shorted rotor or field service.

2. If the meter reads more than 2.4 ohms, reconnect the regulator wiring plug. Connect the negative voltmeter lead to the alternator rear housing. Touch the positive voltmeter lead to the regulator A terminal screw. If the meter does not read battery voltage, there is an open (break or bad connection) in the A

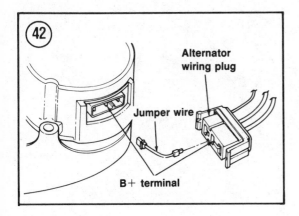

Alternator
wiring plug

Jumper wire

B+ terminal

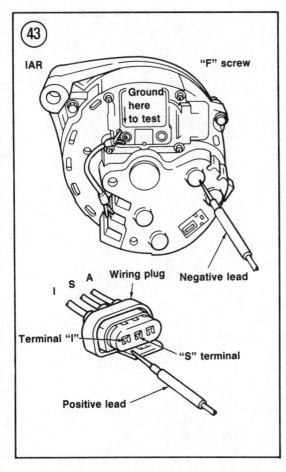

IAR

"F" screw

Ground
here
to test

Wiring plug   Negative lead

I   S   A

Terminal "I"

"S" terminal

Positive lead

in the field circuit. Locate and correct as required, then perform the *Load Test*.

4. If the voltmeter reads battery voltage in Step 3, connect the negative voltmeter lead to the alternator rear housing. Turn the ignition switch ON (engine OFF) and touch the positive voltmeter lead to the regulator F terminal screw. If the meter reading is 1.5 volts or less, proceed to Step 6.

5. If the meter reading in Step 4 exceeds 1.5 volts, perform the *I Circuit Test*. If this test is satisfactory, replace the regulator and perform the *Load Test*.

6. Disconnect the alternator wiring plug. Connect 12 gauge jumper wires between the alternator BAT (+) terminal blades and the corresponding wiring connector terminals. See **Figure 42**. Perform the *Load Test* but with the positive voltmeter lead connected to one of the jumper wire terminals. If the reading exceeds battery voltage by 0.5 volt, repair or replace the alternator-to-starter relay wiring.

7. If the reading in Step 6 does not increase more than 0.5 volt above battery voltage, connect a third jumper wire between the alternator rear housing and the regulator F terminal screw. Perform the *Load Test* with the positive voltmeter lead connected to one of the BAT (+) jumper wire terminals as in Step 6. If the voltage now increases more than 0.5 above battery voltage, replace the regulator.

8. If the reading in Step 7 does not increase more than 0.5 volt, remove the alternator and take it to a dealer for further testing and service.

I Circuit Test

1. Disconnect the regulator wiring plug. Connect a jumper lead between the regulator "A" terminal and the wiring plug "A" terminal. Connect another jumper lead between the regulator "F" screw and the rear of the alternator housing. See **Figure 43**.

2. Start the engine and let it idle. Connect the negative voltmeter lead to the negative battery terminal and the positive voltmeter lead first to the wiring plug "S" terminal, then the "I" terminal while noting the meter

13

wire circuit. Locate and correct as required, then perform the *Load Test*.

3. If the voltmeter reads battery voltage in Step 2, connect the negative voltmeter lead to the alternator rear housing. With the ignition switch OFF, touch the positive voltmeter lead to the regulator F terminal screw. If the meter does not read battery voltage, there is an open

readings. The voltage at the "S" terminal
should be about one-half that shown at the
"I" terminal.

3. If there is no voltage shown in Step 2,
remove the alternator and take it to a dealer
for further testing.

Internal Regulator Replacement

1. Remove the alternator as described in this
chapter.

2. Remove the 4 Torx-head regulator
attaching screws with a T-20 driver. Remove
the regulator/brush holder assembly. See
Figure 44.

3. Remove the A terminal insulator and 2
Torx-head screws holding the regulator to the
brush holder. When the regulator is separated
from the brush assembly, the brushes and
springs will come out of the holder. See
Figure 45.

4. Reinstall the springs and brushes in the
brush holder, then insert a 1 3/8 in. length of
stiff insulated wire into the brush holder pin
hole to retain the brushes in place. See **Figure
46**.

5. Insert the nut/washer assemblies in their
brush holder retaining slots. Fit each brush
terminal into its slot between the holder and
washer.

6. Fit the new regulator to the brush holder
(**Figure 47**). Install and tighten screws to
20-30 in.-lb. (2.3-3.4 N•m).

7. Loop the brush leads toward the brush end
of the holder and install the adhesive-backed
insulator on the A terminal screw head.

8. Clean the alternator and regulator/brush
holder mounting surfaces of all
contamination.

9. Fit the regulator/brush holder to the
alternator and tighten the screws to 25-35
in.-lb. (2.8-4.0 N•m).

> *CAUTION*
> *Do not omit Step 10. If the wire is not*
> *removed, it will cause a short circuit,*
> *destroying the regulator.*

10. Remove the wire inserted in Step 4 to
retain the brushes, then apply a dab of
waterproof (not silicone) sealer over the pin
hole in the brush holder.

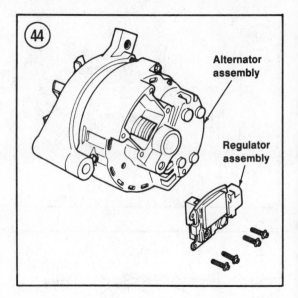

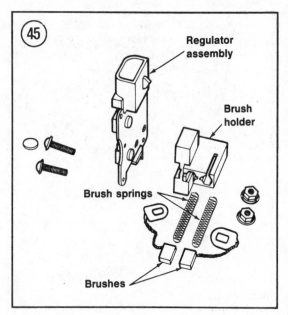

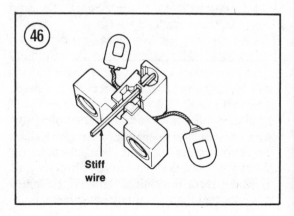

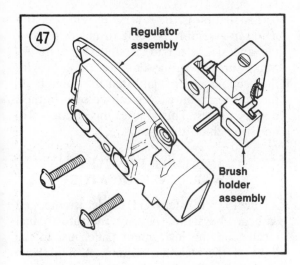

Regulator assembly

Brush holder assembly

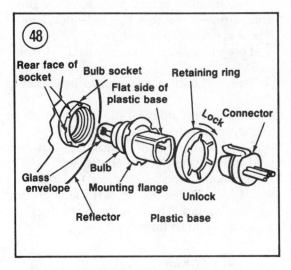

Rear face of socket

Bulb socket

Retaining ring

Flat side of plastic base

Connector

Lock

Glass envelope

Bulb

Mounting flange

Unlock

Reflector

Plastic base

LIGHTING SYSTEM

Aero headlamps replace the sealed beam headlamps on 1987 Mustang models. Aero headlamps consist of a replaceable halogen bulb mounted in a composite headlamp assembly that is designed as a part of the car's overall styling. A replacement halogen bulb should *not* be plugged into the headlamp connector to see if it is good unless the bulb has been properly installed in the headlamp assembly. Bulb replacement does not alter headlamp alignment, thus it should not be necessary to reaim the headlamp. To replace the bulb, refer to **Figure 48** and use the following procedure:

1. Make sure the headlamp switch is off or disconnect the negative battery cable.

2. Reach inside the engine compartment and unplug the electrical connector at the bulb.

3. Rotate the plastic retaining ring on the bulb assembly about 1/8 turn counterclockwise. Slide ring off the plastic base.

4. Carefully pull the bulb assembly straight back and remove it from the reflector socket. Do not rotate the bulb during removal.

WARNING
A halogen bulb contains gas under pressure and can shatter if scratched or dropped. Handle new bulbs only by their plastic base, as skin oils contacting the bulb envelope can cause staining and premature failure.

5. Hold the new bulb with the flat on its base facing up and align the grooves in the bulb base with the socket locating tabs. Insert the bulb straight into the reflector socket until its mounting flanges mate with the socket face.

6. Slide the plastic retaining ring removed in Step 3 into position against the mounting flange and rotate it clockwise until it stops.

7. Reconnect the bulb connector. Turn on the headlamp switch or reconnect the negative battery cable and check the lamp operation.

GAUGES

The base instrument panel on 1987 models contains magnetic gauges instead of the bimetal gauges previously used. A magnetic gauge indicator remains in its operating position when the ignition key is turned OFF. With the exception of the combination voltmeter/temperature gauge, all magnetic gauges are designed as sub-assemblies and can be removed from the front of the instrument cluster individually.

NOTE
*The voltmeter indicates voltage at the cluster, **not at the battery**. The voltmeter may read as much as 1 volt **less** than battery voltage due to resistance in the wiring.*

Gauge Replacement

1. Remove the 6 screws holding the cluster lens in place. Remove the lens.

13

2. Remove the 2 additional screws holding the mask. Remove the mask and retrieve the rubber bumpers for reuse.

3. Remove the thin metal mask.

NOTE
Always start sub-assembly removal from one end of the cluster, not from the center.

4. Gauges can be snapped out of place and removed. They should be removed in the following order:

    a. Fuel/Oil gauge sub-assembly.

    b. Speedometer/Odometer/Trip Odometer sub-assembly.

    c. Volt/Temp gauge sub-assembly.

    d. Tachometer sub-assembly.

5. If the volt/temp gauge sub-assembly requires replacement, it is necessary to pull the cluster out enough to disconnect the speedometer cable and unplug the 2 electrical connectors. Remove the 2 spring nuts holding the volt/temp sub-assembly in place and snap gauge out of cluster.

CAUTION
Do not remove the gauge pointers. They cannot be recalibrated when reinstalled.

6. Installation is the reverse of removal. If a new sub-assembly is being installed, remove the adhesive strip to produce a secure fit. Make sure the sub-assemblies are flush with the back plate edges and that the pointers on the volt/temp/oil gauges can be seen in their display ranges. This assures the pointers will not slip behind their stops.

MULTIPLE FUNCTION WARNING INDICATOR

The 1987 Mustang GT model is equipped with a 4-system warning indicator panel located on the instrument panel just to the right of the steering column. A fluid level module installed behind and above the glove compartment controls the indicator lamps. The 4 systems monitored are:

1. Low oil indicator (sensor installed in oil pan).

2. Low fuel indicator (sensor in fuel sending unit).

3. Low coolant indicator (float-type switch in coolant reservoir).

4. Low washer fluid indicator (float-type switch in washer fluid reservoir).

The coolant, washer fluid and fuel indicator lamps may flash when the vehicle is driving up steep grades. This is normal and does not indicate the need for service.

Table 11 ALTERNATOR OUTPUT RATINGS

Stamp Color (Side Terminal)	Rated Output (Amperes)
Red	100
Black	70

CHAPTER EIGHT

CLUTCH AND TRANSMISSION

Clutch Adjustment

All manual transmission models are now equipped with a self-adjusting clutch control mechanism which automatically adjusts the clutch. Clutch adjustment procedures described in Chapter Eight of the basic book are no longer required.

SELF-ADJUSTING CLUTCH ASSEMBLY

Refer to **Figure 49** for this procedure.

Removal

1. Disconnect the negative battery cable.

2. Remove the steering wheel as described in Chapter Nine of the basic book.

3. Remove the lower dash panel to the left of the steering column.

4. Remove the steering column shrouds.

5. Disconnect the brake lamp switch and the master cylinder pushrod at the brake pedal. See Chapter Twelve of the basic book.

6. Rotate the clutch quadrant forward by hand (**Figure 50**). Unhook the clutch cable at the quadrant and allow the quadrant to slowly rotate rearward.

7. Remove the bolt which secures the brake pedal support bracket lateral brace to the left side of the vehicle.

8. Disconnect all electrical connectors at the steering column.

9. Remove the steering column-to-brake pedal support bracket bolts. Slowly lower the steering column downward.

10. Remove the brake pedal support bracket-to-dash panel booster nuts.

11. Remove the brake pedal support bracket-to-underside instrument panel attaching bolts. Remove the brake pedal support bracket assembly.

12. Remove the clutch pedal attaching nut.

13. Pull the clutch pedal off the clutch pedal shaft.

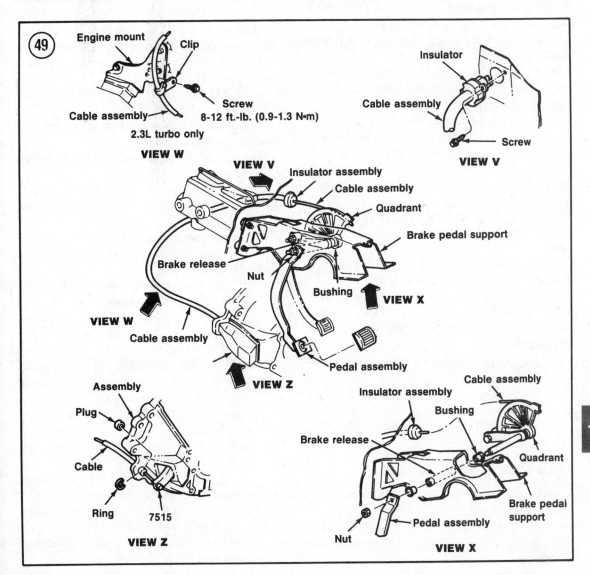

13

14. Slide the self-adjusting assembly out of the brake pedal support bracket.

15. Remove the bushings from either side of the brake pedal support bracket. Inspect the bushings for wear and replace if necessary.

Installation

1. Lubricate the self-adjusting mechanism shaft with engine oil.

2. Insert the self-adjusting mechanism into the brake pedal support bracket.

3. Turn the quadrant so that its top faces upward.

4. Install the clutch pedal onto the self-adjusting mechanism shaft by aligning both sets of flats. Secure the retaining nut.

5. Align the brake pedal support bracket with the dash panel studs. Install the attaching nuts loosely. Then install the bolts through the support bracket into the instrument panel and tighten securely.

6. Tighten the booster nuts that hold the brake pedal support bracket to the dash panel.

7. Attach the clutch cable to the quadrant.

8. Raise the steering column to align the studs in the support bracket. Start but do not tighten the nuts.

9. Connect all steering column electrical connectors. See Chapter Seven of the basic book.

10. Install the steering column shrouds and the brake pedal support lateral brace.

11. Tighten the steering column attaching nuts.

12. Install the lower dash panel section and the steering wheel.

13. Check the steering column for proper operation.

14. Depress the clutch pedal. This will adjust it properly.

15. Reconnect the negative battery cable.

Clutch Cable Removal/Installation

Refer to **Figure 49** for this procedure.

1. Disconnect the negative battery cable.

2. Push the clutch pedal upward and disconnect the pawl from the quadrant. See **Figure 50.**

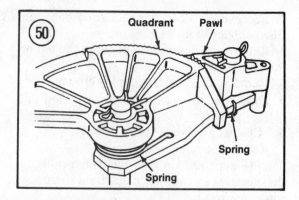

3. Push the quadrant forward and release the clutch cable at the quadrant. Let the quadrant return slowly.

4. Open the hood.

5. Remove the screw holding the cable assembly isolator to the dash panel. Pull the clutch cable through the dash panel and into the engine compartment.

6. Raise the vehicle and secure with jackstands.

7. Remove the release lever cover at the bell housing.

8. Disconnect the clutch cable clip retainer at the bell housing.

9. Slide the end of the clutch cable through the hole in the clutch release lever and remove the cable.

10. Remove the dash panel isolator from the old clutch cable and install it on the new cable.

11. Slide the end of the new clutch cable through the hole in the bell housing and through the clutch release lever.

12. Slide the ball on the end of the cable away from the hole in the clutch release lever. Install the rubber plug.

13. Secure the clutch cable to the bell housing with the clip retainer. Then install the release lever cover onto the bell housing.

14. Slide the clutch cable into the engine compartment.

15. Remove the jackstands and lower the vehicle.

16. Slide the clutch cable into the dash panel. Secure the isolator with a screw.

17. Push the clutch pedal upward to disengage the pawl and quadrant. Push the quadrant forward and hook the clutch cable over the quadrant.

18. Depress the clutch pedal to adjust the cable properly.

Self-adjusting Clutch Diagnosis

With the addition of the self-adjusting clutch, diagnosis may prove difficult because of the additional parts required with the adjusting mechanism. If clutch problems develop, refer to the general clutch troubleshooting procedures in Chapter Two of the basic book. Troubleshooting procedures unique to the self-adjusting clutch are found in **Figure 51**.

MANUAL TRANSMISSION

Some 1982 and later models are equipped with a manual 5-speed overdrive transmission. This transmission is designated as an "RAP" and is identified by the code number "5" on the vehicle certification label attached to the driver's door post.

The RAP 5-speed is essentially the RUG transmission modified to provide one extra gear range. The overdrive gear is relocated to the extension housing at the rear of the transmission case.

When fitted to a turbocharged engine, the RAP uses a 10-tooth spline input instead of

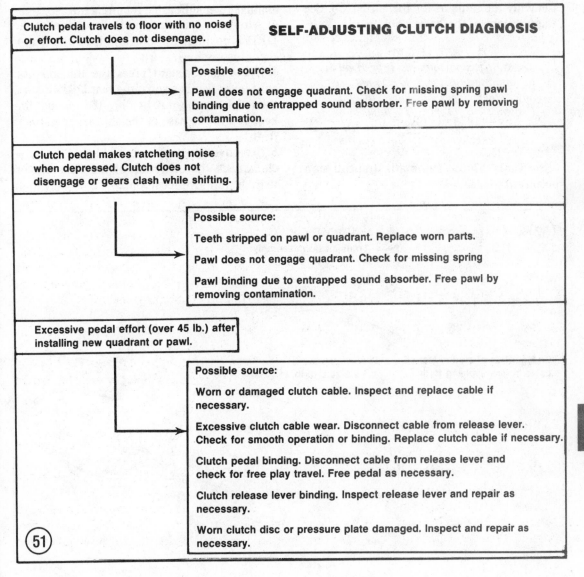

SELF-ADJUSTING CLUTCH DIAGNOSIS

Clutch pedal travels to floor with no noise or effort. Clutch does not disengage.

Possible source:

Pawl does not engage quadrant. Check for missing spring pawl binding due to entrapped sound absorber. Free pawl by removing contamination.

Clutch pedal makes ratcheting noise when depressed. Clutch does not disengage or gears clash while shifting.

Possible source:

Teeth stripped on pawl or quadrant. Replace worn parts.

Pawl does not engage quadrant. Check for missing spring

Pawl binding due to entrapped sound absorber. Free pawl by removing contamination.

Excessive pedal effort (over 45 lb.) after installing new quadrant or pawl.

Possible source:

Worn or damaged clutch cable. Inspect and replace cable if necessary.

Excessive clutch cable wear. Disconnect cable from release lever. Check for smooth operation or binding. Replace clutch cable if necessary.

Clutch pedal binding. Disconnect cable from release lever and check for free play travel. Free pedal as necessary.

Clutch release lever binding. Inspect release lever and repair as necessary.

Worn clutch disc or pressure plate damaged. Inspect and repair as necessary.

(51)

13

the 23-tooth spline used with normally aspirated engines. First and third gears have also been strengthened to absorb the greater torque of the turbocharged engine.

Removal and installation instructions for this manual transmission are the same as those provided in Chapter Eight of the basic book.

AUTOMATIC TRANSMISSION

The C5 automatic transmission with lock-up torque converter replaces the C4 application in 1982-on models. Adjustment, service, removal and installation procedures for the C5 automatic transmission are essentially the same as for the earlier C4. See Chapter Eight of the basic book.

NOTE
The C5 transmission uses Type H automatic transmission fluid. Do not use any other type of fluid in this transmission. Type H fluid was especially formulated for use with the C5 transmission and lock-up converter.

See **Table 12** for automatic transmission specifications.

Manual Linkage Adjustment
(200 cid)

See *Manual Linkage Adjustment* in Chapter Eight of the basic book.

Manual Floor Shift
Linkage Adjustment (255 cid)

Refer to **Figure 52** for this procedure.

1. Shift the selector lever into DRIVE.
2. Raise the vehicle and secure with jackstands.
3. Working beneath the car, loosen the manual lever shift cable retaining nut.
4. Move the transmission manual lever to the DRIVE position (third detent from the rear of the transmission).
5. Have an assistant press the transmission shift lever firmly against the rear DRIVE stop, then tighten the nut holding the manual linkage rod to the base of the shift lever to 10-15 ft.-lb.
6. Remove the jackstands and lower the vehicle. Check the operation of the transmission in each shift lever position.

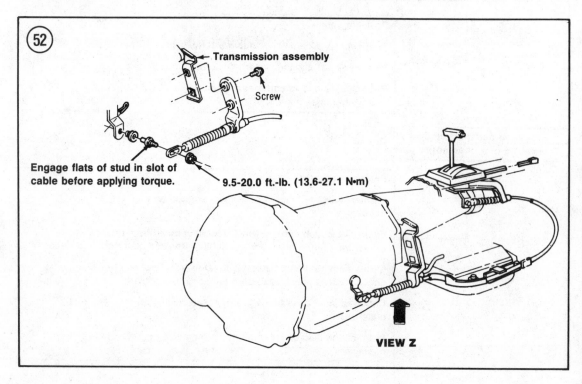

52

Transmission assembly

Screw

Engage flats of stud in slot of cable before applying torque.

9.5-20.0 ft.-lb. (13.6-27.1 N•m)

VIEW Z

Table 12 AUTOMATIC TRANSMISSION TORQUE SPECIFICATIONS

Item	C3 (Ft.-Lb.)	C4/C5 (Ft.-Lb.)
Flywheel-to-converter housing	27-49	20-30
Oil pan-to-transmission case	12-17	12-16
Converter housing-to-engine	28-38	40-50
Filler tube-to-oil pan	28-38	32-42
Neutral start switch-to-oil pan	7-10	4-6
Cooler line-to-transmission case	7-10	12-18

Table 13 STEERING SPECIFICATIONS

	FORD	TRW
Gear ratio (manual)		
At straight-ahead position	24.9:1	
At full turn	21.7:1	
Gear ratio (power)		
At straight-ahead position	20:1	20.1
At full turn	16:1	16:1
Number of turns		
Manual	4.08	
Power	3.05	3.50
Lubricant capacity		
Manual	5 oz.	
Power	2.5 pints	2.44 pints

CHAPTER NINE

FRONT SUSPENSION AND STEERING

Service procedures are the same as for earlier models. Refer to Chapter Nine in the basic book. Specifications for some components differ. These are found in **Table 13** (steering), **Table 14** (manual steering gear), **Table 15** (power steering gear) and **Table 16** (tightening torques).

Steering Wheel and Column

The steering wheel is no longer retained by an external nut on the steering shaft of 1986 and later models. The end of the upper shaft is now drilled and threaded internally to accept a bolt with integral head washer.

Steering wheel removal requires a slightly different procedure on this type shaft. After removing the steering wheel hub cover and disconnecting the horn wires, loosen the retaining bolt 4-6 turns. Install a wheel puller on top of the bolt and loosen the steering wheel. If the bolt is removed before the steering wheel is loosened, the internal shaft threads may be damaged. Once the steering wheel is loosened, remove the bolt and then the wheel.

Table 14 MANUAL STEERING TIGHTENING TORQUES

Item	Ft.-Lb.
Support yoke cover bolts	12-22[1]
Pinion cover bolts	12-22[1]
Steering gear to crossmember	90-100
Tie rod end to inner tie rod	41-50
Tie rod end to spindle arm	41-47[2]

1. 1982 models, 15-22 ft.-lb.
2. After tightening to specification, tighten additionally to nearest cotter pin slot.

Table 15 POWER STEERING TIGHTENING TORQUES

Item	Ford (Ft.-Lb.)	TRW (Ft.-Lb.)
Return line fitting	15-20	10-15
Pressure line fittings at valve	22-18	10-15
Pressure line fittings at power cylinder (gear housing)	22-28	10-15
Pinion bearing locknut	30-40	23-34
Tie rod socket locknut	55-65	55-65

13

Table 16 FRONT SUSPENSION TIGHTENING TORQUES (FT.-LB.)

Item	1981	1982	1983-on
Lower arm-to-No. 2 crossmember	200-220	215-260	150-180
Stabilizer bar mounting clamp-to-bracket	25-30	20-25	20-25
Stabilizer bar-to-lower arm	8-12	6-12	9-12
Shock strut-to-upper mount (nut)	60-75	100-120	55-92

CHAPTER TEN

REAR SUSPENSION

SPECIFICATIONS

Specifications for some components differ. These are found in **Table 17**.

SHOCK ABSORBER

Removal of shock absorbers remains the same as for 1980 and earlier models. However, installation procedures have changed due to the use of new lower shock mounting brackets and fasteners. When installing shock absorbers, perform the following.

> *NOTE*
> *Ford tool part No. D80P-2100-T55 is required to remove the new design shock absorber lower attaching bolt.*

1. Compress the shock absorber and install the shock mounting eye in the axle bracket mounting hole.
2. Place a new load bearing washer between the axle bracket and the shock eye. See **Figure 53**.

3. Insert a new Torx drive belt through the shock eye, washer and axle bracket. Start a new self-wrenching nut by hand onto the Torx bolt (**Figure 53**).

4. Place the inner washer and bushing onto the upper shock absorber stud. Then extend the shock absorber as necessary and direct the upper end through the upper shock tower mounting hole.

5. Tighten the lower Torx bolt to 70 ft.-lb. When tightening the bolt, do not hold the self-wrenching nut. Let the nut rotate freely (when tightening the bolt) so that it can seat into the axle bracket outboard leg.

6. Remove the jackstands and lower the vehicle.

7. Install the bushing, washer and nut on the upper shock absorber stud. Tighten the nut to 24-26 ft.-lb. On all except 3-door models, install the rubber cap on the shock stud. Install the inside trim covers as required.

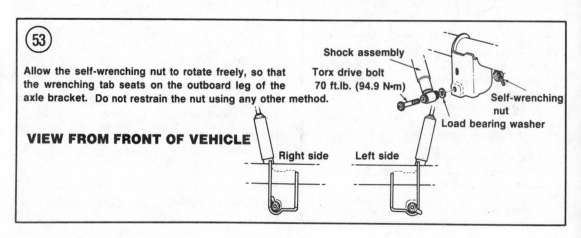

(53) Allow the self-wrenching nut to rotate freely, so that the wrenching tab seats on the outboard leg of the axle bracket. Do not restrain the nut using any other method.

Shock assembly
Torx drive bolt
70 ft.lb. (94.9 N•m)
Self-wrenching nut
Load bearing washer

VIEW FROM FRONT OF VEHICLE

Right side   Left side

Table 17 REAR SUSPENSION TIGHTENING TORQUES (FT.-LB.)

Item	1981	1982	1983-on
Oil filler plug			
WGG	15-30	15-30	15-30
WGX	15-30	15-30	15-30
Shock absorber nuts			
Upper	24-26	24-26	17-27
Lower	65-70	60-65	55-70
Upper arm-to-frame	100-110	100-110	100-105
Upper arm-to-axle	90-100	90-100	90-100
Lower arm-to-axle	90-100	90-100	90-100
Lower arm-to-frame	100-110	100-110	100-105
Stabilizer bar-to-lower arm	18-20	45-50	45-50

CHAPTER ELEVEN

BRAKES

BRAKE ADJUSTMENT

Drum Brakes

The rear drum brakes are self-adjusting. Manual adjustment is unnecessary unless the brakes have been repaired. Starting with 1981 models, Ford specifies that the rear brake adjustment must be performed using Ford tool part No. 11-0001 or equivalent while performing the following procedure.

1. Remove the rear brake drum as described in Chapter Eleven of the basic book.

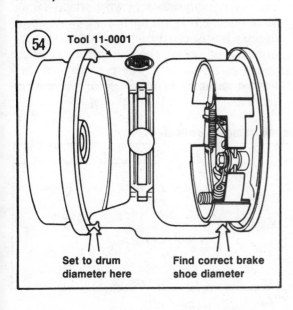

Set to drum diameter here   Find correct brake shoe diameter

NOTE
Before continuing, inspect the brake drum for cracks, distortion, scoring or excessive glaze or smoothness. Drums which are cracked or distorted should be replaced. Deep scores as well as roughness can be corrected by turning or grinding the drum as long as the finished dimension is less than the service limit (see Chapter Eleven of the basic book).

2. Set tool part No. 11-0001 or equivalent to the brake drum inside diameter as shown in **Figure 54**. (This determines the correct brake lining diameter.) The brake lining diameter can then be checked by placing the opposite tool jaws over the brake lining as shown in **Figure 54**. If the tool jaws do not fit over the brake linings or if the gap is too large, adjust by performing Steps 3-7. If brake adjustment is correct, proceed to Step 8. Repeat this procedure for the opposite wheel.

3. Pry the rubber cover from the rear brake backing plate.

4. Insert a narrow-blade screwdriver through the backing plate and push the self-adjuster lever away from the adjusting wheel (**Figure 55**).

5. Turn the adjusting wheel as required to bring the brake shoes into slight contact with tool part No. 11-0001.

13

6. Remove the screwdriver and allow the self- adjuster lever to return to its position on the adjusting wheel.

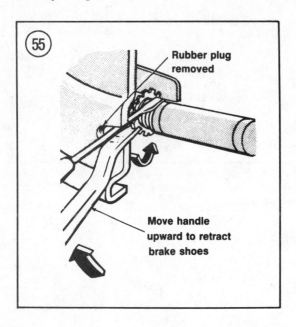

⑤⑤

Rubber plug removed

Move handle upward to retract brake shoes

7. Recheck the brake adjustment with tool part No. 11-0001.
8. Install the brake drums as described in Chapter Eleven of the basic book.
9. Start and back up the vehicle while applying the brakes to complete adjustment. After each stop, the vehicle must be driven forward.

BRAKE DRUMS

Installation

If it was necessary to loosen the rear brake adjustment to remove the brake drums or if new brake drums are being installed, perform the *Brake Adjustment, Drum Brakes* procedure in this supplement.

DISC BRAKE CALIPER

A new caliper locating pin (part No. E6SZ-2B296-A) is available for 1983-1986 models. The locating pin has a Torx T50 head instead of the previously used T45.

CHAPTER TWELVE

TURBOCHARGER

Service procedures for the turbocharger used on 1981-1982 2.3L engines are the same as for earlier models. Some additional tightening torques are provided in **Table 18**.

The turbocharger used on 1984 and later 2.3L engines differs from the 1979-1982 model. The earlier turbo is a "draw-through" unit in which fuel is introduced upstream of the compressor and is mounted on the left side of the engine. The current turbo is a "blow-through" unit in which fuel is introduced downstream of the compressor

(provides a much faster response) and is mounted on the right side of the engine.

Since the 1984 and later turbocharger is electronically linked with the fuel injection system and both are controlled by the EEC-IV microprocessor, owner service is not recommended. If the turbocharger on these engines is suspected of contributing to poor driveability, see a Ford or Mercury dealer who has the necessary test equipment and trained technicians to diagnose the system properly.

Table 18 TURBOCHARGING TIGHTENING TORQUES

Item	Ft.-Lb.
Turbocharger support brace bolts	13-19
Turbocharger-to-intake manifold bolts	
Vertical	13-19
Horizontal	9-13
Heat shield retaining nuts	70-90 in.-lb.
Accelerator cable bracket bolts	13-19
Turbocharger oil supply line fitting	10-13
Actuator diaphragm-to-compressor housing bolts	145-165 in.-lb.

INDEX

NOTES